Introduction
to
Christianity

Of related interest . . .

THE WADSWORTH SERIES IN RELIGIOUS STUDIES

America: Religions and Religion, Catherine L. Albanese

Ways to the Center: An Introduction to World Religions, second edition, Denise L. and John T. Carmody

Between Time and Eternity: Essentials of Judaism, Jacob Neusner

Exploring Religion, Roger Schmidt

THE RELIGIOUS LIFE OF MAN SERIES   Frederick Streng, editor

Understanding Religious Life, second edition, Frederick Streng

The House of Islam, second edition, Kenneth Cragg

The Way of Torah, third edition, Jacob Neusner

The Hindu Religious Tradition, Thomas J. Hopkins

The Christian Religious Tradition, Stephen Reynolds

Chinese Religion, third edition, Laurence G. Thompson

Japanese Religion, third edition, H. Byron Earhart

The Buddhist Religion, third edition, Richard H. Robinson and Willard L. Johnson

Native American Religions, Sam Gill

Islam From Within, Kenneth Cragg and R. Marston Speight

Life of Torah, Jacob Neusner

Chinese Way in Religion, Laurence G. Thompson

Religion in the Japanese Experience, H. Byron Earhart

The Buddhist Experience, Stephan Beyer

Native American Traditions, Sam Gill

Introduction
to
Christianity

Mary Jo Weaver

Indiana University

Wadsworth Publishing Company
Belmont, California
A Division of Wadsworth, Inc.

Religion Editor: Sheryl Fullerton
Production Editors: Sally Schuman, Leland Moss
Managing Designer: Detta Penna
Designer: Wendy Calmenson
Copy Editor: Lorraine Anderson
Cover: Wendy Calmenson

Printed in the United States of America

1 2 3 4 5 6 7 8 9 10—88 87 86 85 84

ISBN 0-534-02899-3

Weaver, Mary Jo.
 Introduction to Christianity.

 Bibliography: p.
 Includes index.
 1. Christianity. I. Title.
BR121.2.W35 1984   200   83-5907
ISBN 0-534-02899-3

Dedicated to
my colleagues in the Religious Studies Department
Indiana University
with thanks

CONTENTS

INTRODUCTION FOR TEACHERS

Those who teach introductory courses know that it is often harder to maintain teacher interest than student interest over the long haul. This textbook, an intentionally general introduction to Christianity, is meant to relieve teachers from the frustration of having to lay a large foundation and having too little time to build on it. My experience with students suggests that many of them come to religion classes knowing very little about Christianity. Years ago we could assume students had a general knowledge of the subject and we could launch out into our own bailiwicks of interest or speculation; the task of constantly rehashing the basics was left to colleagues teaching exotic, non-Christian religions. Perhaps I misremember or romanticize the past; I do not know. I do know that the high-minded ideas I had when I first began teaching have been increasingly displaced by the necessity of giving students a very basic introduction; those who come knowing something about Christianity often come from a narrow confessional background that needs to be expanded, and those who come knowing nothing need to begin simply.

Repeating the same "nuts and bolts" introduction every semester can be wearying. For years I searched for a book to do this for me so that I could do something else, something more interesting or perhaps just more my own. I wanted a small, inexpensive book that gave general information in a straightforward style, something the students could read easily with little or no help from me. For a while I thought I could rely on histories of Christianity, but I found two drawbacks to this approach: students got bored with too much historical material (unable to see its relevance to their lives), and they were unwilling or unable to read so many books each semester. I envy those who can solve their problems by assigning several books each semester in a beginning-level course; in a large state university setting, where all religion courses are electives, one tries to keep the reading list small.

The introductory textbook of my dreams began to take on specific characteristics gleaned from my own teaching experience. It had to be historical, but not just historical; I wanted to use the material to raise contemporary questions and to challenge the assumptions many of my students brought with them to the course. It had to situate Christianity clearly within its Israelite-Judaic context so that students could see what it had in common with Judaism and where it differed from the Jewish tradition. I was particularly eager for my students to see the integrity of Judaism, and I wanted to make it impossible for them to think of Jews as "too stubborn" or "too blind" to recognize Jesus as the Messiah. At the contemporary level, I was more interested in having my students know the practical difference than the doctrinal difference between a Mennonite and a Methodist. And I wanted them to have some sense of the complexity of Christianity in terms of the many different groups or denominations it inspired: they might never get into an argument about Christology, but they were likely (in the Midwest, at least) to encounter someone whose perspective is rarely mentioned in textbooks—a Dispensationalist, for example. I wanted the book to be clear on the major divisions within Christianity: Christians read Scripture differently, and may have antagonistic church polities and points of emphasis; but I also wanted to show the points of unity and agreement, especially within a context of worship. Finally, I wanted to give them some indication of how different groups of Christians could come to exactly opposite conclusions on contemporary issues.

Obviously, the more specific this textbook became in my head, the more impossible it became for me to find it. Had I been a little wiser, perhaps I would not have chosen to write it, but the approach I have taken in this book has worked for me and I thought it might be helpful for others. My intention, above all, is for the book to be *useful*. I have not aimed at innovative scholarship, nor do I have a single, dominating focus. I have tried to pose correctly, without pretending to solve, the major issues in Christianity. I hope my approach lends *flexibility* to the text, and that it places minimum restrictions on faculty subjectivity. Issues are not stated, resolved, boxed, and tied neatly with a ribbon; rather, they are presented from a number of different perspectives so that students can wrestle with them and come to some kind of personal understanding of them. I have aimed at *readability*—I want students to be able to read this text easily—at jargon-free, lucid prose. I have put notes, bibliography, and appendixes at the ends of chapters or the end of the book so that they do not interfere with the fluidity of the text itself.

In my mind, the strength of the book lies in its flexibility. It has no single dominating approach; it is *purposely* neither theology, nor history, nor sociology, nor philosophy, but dips into all of these perspectives in order to focus on a question or a practice from a variety of angles. It is intentionally brief and asks rhetorical questions in order to encourage instructor supplementation. I wrote it to be a basic framework on which one could build a variety of different structures: professors who want to be predominantly theological, or historical, or contemporary, can be, all using the same structural framework. It is, therefore, rather like the frame for a prefabricated house: it may not contain all the features one wants, may have some things in it one does not want, and may not be quite the house one would have designed, but it is useful, it can be modified, it serves its purpose. I hope instructors will develop material to go along with the book, and so I have not included graphics, cartoons, readings from primary sources, or summaries of current scholarly arguments. Each teacher will have his or her own such materials and I hope the book encourages personal accents and modifications.

The book is meant to be used in a semester, with room for supplementary material. The appendixes have packed together material that teachers may or may not want to pursue; they are meant to be helpful summaries of some of the points mentioned in the text. The glossary is made up of terms used in the book but not explained there, and is meant to be a handy reference aid for students. One could take the regular chapters, followed in some cases by the appropriate appendix, and come up with a fifteen-week, semester course; but I want to reemphasize my framework analogy rather than suggest that this book can be or should be the only text used in a course.

THE BOOK'S ORGANIZATION AND CONTENT

I have divided the book into three parts: two contain background material and the third is an introduction to contemporary issues with a summary of Christian commonality by way of worship. The first part contains three chapters, on God, Jesus, and the emergence of the early Christian church.

The first chapter's purpose is to introduce the concept of a revealed religion and to discuss simply (insofar as that is possible) what revelation means; it is *not* meant to be an introduction to Israelite history or to the Old Testament. I chose two aspects of God as background for Christianity: creation and providence. Other authors might have featured covenant or prophecy, the monarchy, or Israel's cultic life. Indeed, given the many aspects of the Jewish tradition, one could have chosen many other issues. I wanted to be brief and to highlight the divine word and deed in the history of a people. Those who want to know more about Jewish experience of divine self-disclosure should consult introductory textbooks on the Old Testament. It was not my purpose in the first chapter to come to grips with major scholarly issues of biblical criticism. I have tried to indicate where a question is complex and needs more explanation than I am giving it, and I hope some teachers will expand this chapter with their own material. Keeping the students in mind and my "nuts and bolts" approach as a guide, I tried to be simple and to provide a large context for the understanding of Jesus within his Jewish context.

The second chapter situates Jesus within his historical and religious context. Like the first, it is meant to be general and not to raise major issues; I was more concerned here to tell the Jesus story and to highlight Jewish expectation about the Messiah and understandable differences of opinion about Jesus. The third chapter concerns itself with the emergence of the Christian church. I was tempted to call it the emergence of the Christian church*es*. Again, I chose what I thought were the major controversies within early Christianity and then tried to move the early community out into the larger world without becoming too complex or confusing. My main purpose was to show the early community as divided over important questions. Students too often think about Christian antiquity as a time of unity, total charity, and blissful contentment when no one needed to argue because they all knew what they were supposed to do. Some students want to get back to such a "golden age," and I was constrained in this chapter to show it as an exciting time, but not at all an age of unanimity. In all three chapters one could be much more complex; any of the issues I have raised—revelation, exegesis, the Jewish context for Jesus, the development of the early church—admit of more than one interpretation, and my choices and explanation will please some and not others.

The second part of the book, containing four chapters, is meant to give a wide-ranging and relatively brief historical overview. I have tried to recapitulate the central core of Christianity, but no book can cover it all. I decided to include some groups not usually included in such texts and to give what looks like short shrift to others. Why? My intention here was to explain the historical roots of Christian *diversity*. I did *not* intend to write a history of Christianity and have thus omitted what some people think of as major figures. I do not, for example, discuss Aquinas and Augustine, nor do I talk about the development of some major religious orders, nor of specific popes in the Middle Ages; I do not feature personalities in the development of American Protestantism or American Catholicism. Anyone coming to this textbook with a list of major historical figures, therefore, will be disappointed or surprised not to find them. Let me repeat, this part is *not* intended to be a history of Christianity, but is meant to be a history of Christian diversity. I wanted the students to see the major and minor divisions within Christianity in order to better understand both Christian complexity and their own times when new groups and sects spring up like grass.

Chapter 4 is meant to show the differences and similarities between the two oldest forms of Christianity, Orthodox Christianity and Roman Catholicism. It focuses on power and politics because that is where the practical issues were and are. At the same time, it introduces students to ancient concepts like monasticism and the value of tradition as a religious authority with which Protestants later took great issue. The chapter is not meant to be a conclusive or comprehensive history of Christianity in the first several hundred years. Chapter 5 is also about similarity and difference and is meant to further the explanation of Christian *diversity*. It, therefore, tries to pull in the major aspects of the Reformation and to show the roots of the many different Christian groups that emerged from that controversy; it is *not* a history of medieval and Renaissance Christianity and so simply does not discuss the many other aspects of Christianity or Christian history in that time. For that, we need to refer students to good histories of Christianity that are meant to be inclusive.

Chapter 6 continues the story of diversity in its European and American contexts. Here, too, one will find major omissions if one is looking for a history of Christianity. The purpose of this chapter is to bring the European divisions up to date and then to a new geographical and religious context, America. In so doing, I also try to explore the general context in order to explain the emergence of new Christian groups. By the end of Chapter 6 students should have some idea of how and why many different Christian groups were formed during the sixteenth, seventeenth, and eighteenth centuries; but the proliferation in those times is mild compared to the explosive nineteenth century, so Chapter 7 is meant to continue the story of diversity through an incredibly prolific era. By the time I got to the twentieth century I was more interested in gathering groups together around a major controversy than I was in delineating further divisions, and I wanted to lay the foundations for the next section of the book. I made the section on the twentieth century general and centered it around fundamentalism versus liberalism because that battle continues to resonate in the contemporary religious atmosphere. As in the previous part, any of the material in Part Two can and should be supplemented, expanded, and deepened according to the interests and proclivities of the teacher.

Part Three contains four chapters and is meant to do a number of things: to gather together the many different groups and redivide them according to practical or ethical positions; to explain why Christian churches are structured differently; and to emphasize the points of commonality and unity Christians have in their worship. The diagram I use to introduce these chapters is something I have worked out teaching and have refined in conversation with colleagues over the years. It is not derived from H. R. Niebuhr's *Christ and Culture*, at least not in a firsthand way. It ought not to be judged, therefore, according to how well it reflects Niebuhr's intentions (which is not its purpose) but according to how well it works to interpret some of the varieties of Christian behavior and, in the process, to raise the kinds of questions students face today.

The first two chapters of this last part, Chapters 8 and 9, take the different Christian groups that we have just understood historically and look at them from a different perspective. Historically, Catholic monks and Pentecostal Christians have little in common and share no great love for one another, but in terms of their relationship to the lure of the world they *do* have some common beliefs or reactions. Doctrinally, a group like evangelicals might look monolithic, but in response to issues of social justice we find many different kinds of belief and behavior. These chapters, then, are meant to flesh out the picture and to make the story of Christian diversity both more complex and more contemporary, to make the historical sections relevant, and finally, to raise some large issues within Christianity in a way that will engage students and provoke thought and discussion.

Chapter 10 delineates some of the varieties in Christian polity, a topic I have not seen treated in other textbooks. It responds to questions from my students about why some churches operate in one way and other churches in quite a different way. The last chapter, Chapter 11, is an attempt to draw all the groups (or most of them) back together again in terms of worship. No matter what historical differences, doctrinal feuds, or ethical arguments Christians have had, they *do* agree about the importance of worship and they basically agree on a remarkable number of things about worship. The chapter is meant to bring the story to a unified conclusion so that at the end of the book students know about the great variety of Christian belief and practice—or at least know it exists—and also that there are important points of correspondence across the whole Christian spectrum.

The appendixes provide near-at-hand information about some of the themes mentioned in the book but not elaborated on. Appendix 1 simply shows the different ordering of books in the Hebrew Bible and the Christian Bible. Appendix 2 provides a simple, story-line synopsis of books in the Old and New Testaments and is meant to be used like a reference table. Appendix 3 is an outline of early Christian literature, an area not really covered in the book, but alluded to in the discussion of tradition (Chapter 4). Appendix 4, also meant to be used as a reference table, pulls together the various ecumenical councils in the history of the Christian church and shows which groups follow which councils; here the Romanness of the Roman Catholic church is perhaps more visible than it is in the text itself. Appendix 5, another reference table, simply delineates some of the creeds (or confessions) within Christianity in an attempt to show some of the doctrinal developments that were not treated within the text. Appendix 6, a historical time line, is a study aid for students, as is the glossary, made up of terms from the text itself that are not fully explained there. All of these are meant to provide useful information without intruding into the text itself. The bibliography is selective and provides some additional sources of information.

I have found it helpful in the course to build on the parts of this book by assigning four short papers on a specific Christian group chosen by the student. The first paper deals with the background of the group and its relation to Jesus, the second with the historical experience of the group, especially in America, the third with its place on the diagram for Part Three, and the fourth with its polity and worship. By investigating one Christian group from all these angles, students get a deeper understanding of one group and of the broader phenomenon. The bonus for them is the ease with which they are able to tackle two- to three-page papers and their amazement at the end of the semester that they have a ten- to twelve-page term paper and a good grasp of either their own religious background or one completely new to them.

ACKNOWLEDGMENTS

In his classic text, *American Renaissance,* F. O. Mathiessen said this:

> During the course of this long volume I have undoubtedly plagiarized from many sources—to use the ugly term that did not bother Shakespeare's age. I doubt whether any criticism or cultural history has ever been written without such plagiary, which inevitably results from assimilating the contributions of your countless fellow-workers, past and present. The true function of scholarship as of society is not to stake out claims on which others must not trespass, but to provide a community of knowledge in which others may share.[1]

Without elevating myself and my task to the stature of Mathiessen, I must acknowledge that I share his general feeling. This book was produced from my research and teaching experience, anecdotes told to me by friends, and informative arguments with colleagues. Students have helped me by confronting my assumptions and descriptions with their own experience. I am not always able to say where I have found a particular definition or distinction, nor do I always know whether my ways of organizing the material are original or suggested to me from elsewhere. Two standard reference books have been invaluable to me over the years and in the production of this volume: *The Oxford Dictionary of the Christian Church,* edited by F. L. Cross, and the *Corpus Dictionary of Western Churches,* edited by T. C. O'Brien. I have not, to the best of my knowledge, quoted from them directly, but I have surely relied on them heavily. Both of these books give pithy and accurate definitions as well as manageable explanations of complex historical and theological debates. Because I have tried to insinuate some theological questions as well as historical material, I have sometimes relied on important or memorable works that were especially helpful. My discussion of the nature of tradition in Chapter 4 is indebted to Gershom Scholem's essay, "Revelation and Tradition as Religious Categories in Judaism";[2] my summary of the conservative/liberal debate in twentieth century Protestantism (at the end of Chapter 7) owes much of its organizational style and information to William E. Hordern's fine little book, *A Layman's Guide to Protestant Theology.* Some of this material appeared in an earlier version in an Indiana University Independent Study Division text, and I thank the trustees of the University for allowing me to use it again here. Most of the refinements, however, have been suggested to me by colleagues in conversations over the years. Where they got the information originally I do not know, but I am grateful to them for sharing it with me so generously.

I have noticed that all books that thank friends end with the author taking responsibility for all mistakes. I take that responsibility but I am also aware that my friends and advisors share in the liabilities of the book as well as in its strengths. I would not have made certain decisions to include or excise material without an argument from one or more of my readers, nor would I have been as sensitive to certain issues or phrasings without their different kinds of insight. When I began this book I thought I should get friends representing as many different perspectives as possible to read it: ministers, atheists, fundamentalist Christians, sectarians, humanists, historians, and skeptics. I thought this would protect me and help me to stretch the book as widely as possible to

---

[1] (Oxford: Oxford University Press, 1968), paperback, p. xx.
[2] In *The Messianic Idea in Judaism and Other Essays on Jewish Spirituality* (New York: Schocken Books, 1971), pp. 282–303.

include many different viewpoints. I did not anticipate that I would have to argue for so many points or work so hard to make myself clear. I hope the result is felicitous. Whether it is a success or failure, however, I am deeply grateful to those people who helped me. James Ackerman, Howard Berkowitz, Anne Carr, John Gillman, Anne Hauerwas, Luke Johnson, Jack Kinnard, A. E. Lacy, Lauree Meyer, Sam Preus, David Smith, and Bill Storey all read parts of it carefully, and offered me valuable suggestions and new perspectives. Bob Epps, Stan Hauerwas, David Felter, Jim McDonald, Jan Shipps, and Stephen Stein helped me when I could not figure out a fine point of history or polity. My secretary, Star Kelley, relieved many burdens with her superlative skills; she suggested ways in which I could improve consistency and kept me from unfortunate turns of phrase more than once. Paula Jentgens typed the final version with speed and accuracy. I owe a special debt of thanks to Barbara Nelson. She argued and supported me through a first rewriting with steadiness, persuasion, and editorial savvy.

Working with the people at Wadsworth Publishing has been a revivifying experience for me. The religion editor, Sheryl Fullerton, is a dream come true: she supported me, helped me to interpret criticism, and guided me through a major manuscript revision with skill, insight, and (always) good humor. Sally Schuman and Leland Moss, my production editors, have been clear, trustworthy, and supportive. I have felt wafted through this process with ease, due, in good measure, to their talent. My copy editor, Lorraine Anderson, is smart and skillful and has in many ways made the rough way smooth. I am deeply grateful to them all.

None of this would have been possible for me outside the atmosphere of Indiana University. My colleagues in the Department of Religious Studies have led me to see other viewpoints and to think fairly about them. I owe them many thanks and make a small gesture of gratitude by dedicating this book to them.

Mary Jo Weaver

NOTE TO STUDENTS

All religions can be looked at from either the inside or the outside. When Christianity is viewed from the inside, one gets a believer's perspective and sees Christianity as *the* religion, the only possible truth. If Christianity is viewed from the outside, one gets a nonbeliever's perspective and sees Christianity as *a* religion, one perception of the truth among many. A clear and determined choice between these two approaches leads to considerable distortion from the very outset. To avoid this distortion, this book attempts to incorporate both perspectives, though within limits. This book takes an outsider's perspective insofar as it does not attempt to proclaim Christianity or prove it to be true. At the same time, it is faithful to an insider's viewpoint as it tries to read and understand the doctrines and practices of Christians as they are understood within the believing community.

Christianity has a doctrine about God that includes a belief in the life, death, and resurrection of Jesus; and it offers a method for getting in touch with God that involves a relationship with Jesus. Christians agree that it is important to know, or to believe in, or to experience Jesus, but they disagree about how that is done. There are, accordingly, many varieties of Christian belief and practice, most of which reflect differences in biblical interpretation, historical experience, and Christian self-understanding.

An introduction to Christianity can do many things, some of them more ambitious than others. This book is modest in intention and general in scope: it intends to *introduce* Christianity from a number of perspectives so that students can have some appreciation of its richness and diversity without being overwhelmed by its differences of opinion and practice. Christians are extraordinarily diverse in their beliefs and behavior, but they also share common understandings. This book delineates the historical differences and commonalities in order to introduce the dynamism and diversity of one of the world's largest religions.

A book like this is bound to be controversial however hard the author tries to be fair-minded and judicious in choosing material, examples, and topics. I can only hope that those who see significant gaps in interpretation and historical awareness will fill those gaps with supplementary reading. Though I wrote this book with a definite audience in mind—the college freshman who has little knowledge about Christianity and perhaps a minimal understanding of religion—I have been conscious throughout that it will be read by teachers and reviewers. It has been tempting, therefore, to insert complex digressions in order to preserve a professional image. I have nonetheless tried to keep the needs of the student uppermost in mind while writing.

Accordingly, though I usually allude to the fact that most issues are more complex than they may appear to be in this general introduction, I do not raise difficult questions of scriptural exegesis (critical explanation) or sophisticated historical argumentation in the body of the text itself. The notes and suggestions at the ends of the chapters and the appendixes at the back of the book give more nuances and further explain controversial issues. My approach to the Bible is informed by historical and critical scholarship and grounded in a deep appreciation of the ways Scripture is used by believing communities of Christians. Different groups of Christians read certain texts differently and I have tried to recognize that fact without attempting to solve the issues. I have tried to raise some questions about scriptural interpretation without urging one interpretation over another. I have not taken time to explain some historical material or to identify certain personalities, but I have added a glossary of terms and names to elaborate upon areas not covered in depth in the text. Use the glossary like a dictionary: when you find a word or the name of a person in the text that you want to know more about, turn to the glossary for a further explanation.

Finally, I have accepted the statements from each group about itself and have made no speculations about the possible truth or falsehood of certain claims. My intention is to give each group an impartial reading and to present its history and its positions straightforwardly. I have been more interested in practical issues than in theological ones, and more interested in presenting an explanation for Christian diversity and unity than I have been in writing a comprehensive history of Christianity. My hope is that you will find the text clear, accurate, and challenging.

Introduction
to
Christianity

PART ONE

Biblical and Historical Background for Christianity

T HE FIRST PART of this book introduces the background against which the varieties of Christianity have emerged. Christianity is a revealed religion; Christians believe that God has communicated with them and has been manifested in words and in a history of saving actions. For Christians, the most important self-communication of God is Jesus Christ, whose life, death, and resurrection form the foundation of the Christian religion.

The first three chapters focus on the work of God, the life of Jesus, and the presence of the Holy Spirit in the church. Most Christians believe that God is the creator and savior of people, that Jesus Christ is God's most important self-disclosure, and that the Holy Spirit is God's power at work in the Christian community. Christians trace their roots back through Judaism to the Creation. So we will begin with some general perceptions about God as creator, as providentially interested in the world and in the history of a special people, the Jews. The second chapter situates Jesus within his historical context: the apocalyptic mood and messianic hopes of the Jews provided Christians with a way to understand Jesus and to interpret his mission. The third chapter outlines the emergence of the Christian church and the importance of the Holy Spirit within the church.

Christianity did not develop easily or smoothly. There were serious arguments among Christians and between Christians and Jews about the person and mission of Jesus. Christianity is a complex religion that has been growing and changing from its beginning. The first part of this book explains the basis of the dynamic growth within Christianity, and introduces the foundations of the Christian experience.

CHAPTER 1

God as Revealed in the Bible

W estern religions aim to help believers follow the will of God. And how do believers know the will of God? If you ask that question of followers in any revealed religion (Judaism, Christianity, Islam) they will tell you that God has spoken, has been made manifest, has communicated with people. That is the claim of *revelation,* a word that comes from the Latin *revelare,* which means to unveil or to disclose. When people criticize a dress or a bathing suit for being too *revealing* they mean it unveils or uncovers too much. When the word is applied to God, it means that God unveils—not by disrobing but by disclosing the divine will and personality through words and actions. Believers, therefore, know the will of God because it has been revealed to them.

DIRECT REVELATION: BASIS OF CHRISTIANITY

Revelation is an article of faith for believers and a complex problem for theologians.[1] There is no single way to explain it. One simple classification distinguishes two types of revelation: *direct* and *indirect*. In *indirect* revelation, a person or group of people has a sense or feeling that "something" is up there or out there. People have a conviction that what they see in the natural world must reflect an unseen reality, and they may speculate that there is a God of some sort. Indirect revelation is often associated with experiences of something wonderful or impressive in nature: the stars, the seasons, cycles of growth. Indirect revelation often leads to a sense of creatureliness: one may have a peaceful sense of order in the universe or an eerie, uncanny feeling about the powers in the cosmos.

In *direct* revelation, a person or group has a direct communication from God. It is not so much rooted in the natural world as it is in a conviction that God has actually appeared in some fashion, or done something—that a vision of God has been seen or God's voice has been heard. Often people cannot arrive at the contents of direct revelation by following logical or rational processes (as in indirect revelation). An experience of direct revelation is often awe-ful and gives people a strong sense that they have been called and must respond. Direct revelation is more confrontational and demanding.

Convictions held by people on the basis of direct revelation are not necessarily more firm than those based on indirect revelation. The difference lies in the root of the conviction. Those who experience indirect revelation may have a strong sense of an orderly universe and a creator who is a highly intelligent artist. Those who experience direct revelation (especially those whose stories form the basis of Judaism and Christianity) usually believe they have understood the will of a *personal* God. Someone who sees the beauty of the sunset and is convinced there is a God, or a scientist who reasons from perceptions of the natural universe that there must be a God both experience *indirect* revelation. Moses's experience of revelation was *direct*. He believed that God spoke and empowered him to lead the Hebrews out of bondage in Egypt.

Christianity is based on *direct* revelation. In this book when the word *revelation* is used it means direct revelation, people's experience of God as a person who has entered into a conversation or relationship with them. Revelation is not a one-way street, but the beginning of a partnership. God reveals, but people must choose whether or not to live in accordance with that revelation, a choice that often involves whether to believe that a revelation has occurred. If people choose to accept the revelation, they usually reflect on it, write it down, refine it, and apply it to new situations. They may even receive new revelations and come to deeper understandings of God. Revelation is God's self-communication and can apparently occur in a number of ways. Each time, however, the pattern recurs: direct communication from God on the one hand, the response of people on the other.

Revelation may be either public or private. Some individuals claim to have received private communications from God in mystical experience. Christianity, however, is based upon *public* revelation. The experiences of mystics may or may not be interesting to the Christian community,[2] but they are surely not necessary for an understanding of Christianity. Public revelation is a direct communication from God *intended for a group of people*. It may have been originally delivered to an individual, but the content applies to a whole people, and invites response and belief from a group.

Revelation, once it is accepted, is interpreted. An incident of God's action may be interpreted differently by groups of believers. Jews, Christians, and Muslims agree that Abraham is extraordinarily important as a partner of God's self-communication, but they interpret Abraham's life and history differently. Muslims trace their connections with Abraham through Ishmael (see Genesis 16, 17, and 21), Jews through Isaac (Genesis 17–22), and Christians have taken the story of the sacrifice of Isaac (Genesis 22) as a typology for the sacrifice of Jesus on the cross. Christianity is based on an interpretation of God's self-disclosure that the Bible traces back to creation. Jews and Christians believe that God has established a relationship with people; in that relationship they believe they have discerned God's intentions for their lives. Christianity grew out of Judaism and the Israelites' experience of revelation. For Christians and Jews the Bible is the primary account of God's revelation, the primary way to learn God's will.

THE BIBLE

For Jews, the Bible is divided into three parts: the Torah, the Prophets, and the Writings (see Appendix 1). Christians rearranged the Jewish Bible and renamed it the Old Testament. For Christians, the Bible is made up of two parts: the Old Testament and the New Testament. Because they used different versions of the Hebrew Bible, Catholics and Protestants disagreed about how many books should be in the Old Testament (see Appendix 1). In the Revised Standard Version, used by most Christians today, there are thirty-nine books in the Old Testament and twenty-seven in the New Testament (see Appendix 2).

The word *Bible* means "book". To Jews and Christians it is a holy book, set apart from others because of its sacred content and origin. The Bible has a central place in Jewish and Christian worship all over the world. Worshippers believe that the use of biblical texts in liturgy puts them in touch with God's actions in history. Since those actions are regarded as saving ones, liturgical use of Scripture enables believers to be touched by God's saving acts. The Bible has been translated into more languages than any other book; it exists in a variety of versions, and is constantly studied, read, quoted from, and treasured. For all that, however, it is rare to find many people who can understand the whole book, especially the Old Testament. Parts of it seem obscure or peculiar, some of it is hard to read, and some of it (for example, lists of ancient genealogies) appears to be irrelevant to life in the present.

Jews and Christians agree that the Old Testament is inspired,[3] though they disagree about which parts are and which are not. Whether there is inspiration and how it occurred or functions is a matter of theological dispute. Some believers are content with the idea that God dictated every word of the Bible to chosen authors; others prefer to understand inspiration as a more subtle psychological process. For the most part, however, all these people believe that God somehow directed the writing of the book; that is what inspiration means. We need not belabor the way inspiration is explained by various religious groups and theologians. A broad, working definition might see inspiration as God acting and revealing through a particular community. Within that community authors reflect on their collective experience, treasure it, and write it down. What the author writes and the way it is written is inspired, has divine influence behind it. The issue is not simple; the debate about it and refinement of its definition continues.

Even though Jews and Christians agree that the Old Testament is inspired, that God is revealed in it, that does not mean that biblical content and meaning will be immediately evident to the reader. Any reader of the Bible needs to understand the enormous range of history and literature it contains. One help in understanding a particular book or passage is discovering the intention of the author. Not all books were written to respond to the same circumstances. They may all deal with God's relationship with people, but they have been written in a number of different styles, in different contexts, with probable differences of purpose.

There is considerable disagreement among Christians about how to read the Bible. There are some who believe that the Bible, as God's word, need only be read and understood simply and literally; that every word and explanation is absolutely true. Others believe the Bible was written for and by a particular people and that one needs to understand this historical context before the real message can be understood. Still others approach the Bible with tools of scholarship—ancient languages, archaeology, history—in order to understand different strands of the stories and the levels of intention behind those stories. From whatever direction one approaches the Bible there is both agreement and disagreement with other Christians. For example, the first book, Genesis, begins by telling the story of the creation of the world and gives an explanation for the frustration all people feel sometimes. One form of sin referred to in the Bible is alienation (from God and from other people); Genesis 1–3 takes such alienation seriously and describes its devastating consequences. Whether the author intended to describe the actual events leading to that sin in historical and scientific terms is a matter of dispute among Christians, but Christians do not dispute the profound way the story explains the presence of sin in the world.

When one turns to the Bible, therefore, one finds a great variety of literature. The Bible contains straightforward historical information as well as poetry and prose. Law and lore are included along with prophetic and devotional books; there are books that deal with serious human problems (like suffering) and books that describe ancient battles and dynasties. But for all the differences of style and literary types, one finds some central themes. Throughout the Bible God is revealed in history as generous, eager to save people from bondage and draw them into a relationship. God makes agreements (covenants) with human beings and wants them to respond with trust and obedience, to be a faithful people.

We will look at two major aspects of divine purpose as revealed in the Bible as groundwork for our understanding of Christianity. These two are creation and providence: God is the powerful, transcendent creator of the world and is, at the same time, interested in its history and willing to enter into its story in partnership with people.

GOD AS CREATOR

The first three chapters of Genesis give us a complex picture of God as creator. We notice that

1. *God masters chaos or creates out of nothing.* Scholars read the creation account in two ways, depending on how they translate Gen. 1:1. In one, God masters primal chaos; in the other, God creates out of nothing. God is the one who can assert creative mastery over the universe.
2. *God creates in both word and deed.* In the first chapter of Genesis, God does not conjure up a spell, but simply says the word and what is spoken happens; in the second chapter of Genesis God fashions a man from the earth, makes a person from already-existing material.
3. *God says that creation is good.* The world is not an evil place, and the material universe is not to be disparaged. One need not have a dreary attitude toward the world or think of it as a prison; it is seen by God as a good place.
4. *Man and woman are created in God's own image.* People have been made to have dominion over creation, to act as God's representatives in this world.

All these testify to the power and goodness of God. The power of God's word recurs in the Old Testament. "By the word of the Lord the heavens were made," says the psalmist (Ps. 33:6). God's word is connected with revelation and with the law: Psalm 119 is a long meditation on the law replete with references to God's word. Psalm 19 compares the brightness of the sun to the enlightenment brought by God's word in the Torah. God's word is also bound up with prophecy: all the prophets speak God's word and are prophets precisely because "the word of the Lord" came to them and empowered them. In the New Testament, Jesus is described as the preexistent "word of God" and said to be "the word made flesh." Christians believe that Jesus is the Son of God, that he incarnates the creative power of God's word.

The biblical authors tell us about God's goodness, power, and generosity but also explain that the creative act of God was disrupted. The Christian term usually used to describe this disruption is *the Fall,* a falling away from the original intention of creation. The world began as a good thing, but it is not as good as it once was. Something must have happened to account for the fact that God created a paradise, yet people experience the world as a nonparadise. The biblical authors knew from their own experience that something happened because they did not live in a paradise. They knew that life is hard work; that people can be wicked, aggressive, and selfish; and that no matter how much people have, they want more. Biblical writers were able to incorporate these human experiences into their descriptions of the dim beginnings of world history. The experience of the community and their understanding of God shaped the way they explained the beginnings of the world. The story of the Creation and the Fall belong to a period usually designated as prehistory, the time for which we have no written records. All ancient people had some explanation for the creation of the world and the status of people within that world. When the story of creation was finally written down by the biblical authors, it reflected the experience and beliefs of their own community.

Let's look at some of the ways the Israelites might have seen creation and the presence of evil in the world. Like other peoples of the ancient Near East they could have reasoned that the gods are like people, both good and bad, which accounts for evil in the world. They could have said, "Life is hard and people are wicked, and that must be God's fault." Neither of these explanations is bad so far as logic goes, and both of them appear in ancient literature written around the same time as the biblical story of creation. They could have said, "Oh, life is not all that bad if you look on the sunny side," and that explanation, flawed as it might be by experience, appeals to some people. They knew from their experience as a community and from God's self-communication that God was good and the created order was good; they could not, therefore, blame God for the mess of the world. They knew just as well, from experience, that the world was a mess. How could it be explained? The Genesis story accounts for both kinds of experience. In the story in Genesis, God remains good and powerful, and creates people as an act of generosity; evil gets into the world, but not through God's fault. The story tells us three things:

1. People were made in the image of God (they are like God in some way, and God longs for a relationship with them).
2. People, freely, as an act of curiosity and willfulness, chose their own will over God's will and disrupted creation.
3. God promised to restore good relations among them.

To retell the story briefly: God created a man and a woman, gave them everything they could possibly want in terms of comfort and power, and added one more gift, freedom. God wanted them to respond freely, not by force. Now, the biblical authors tell us, this gift of freedom was put to a test in a very direct way. God told them they could eat the fruit of every tree in the garden except one. It is the doctrine of conditional joy, rather like a fairy tale: "You can have the beautiful princess *if* you bring her a magic radish," or "You can have three wishes *if* you bring me the little blue light." According to the Bible, the people failed the test, and in failing it, they acted as we all act. We all know what it is to have someone say, "You can do anything but. . . ." In *The Magician's Nephew* by C. S. Lewis, two children are exploring an underground world where everyone is asleep and the whole atmosphere is mysterious. In the middle of a courtyard they find a little silver bell and a hammer and an inscription that reads:

> *Make your choice, adventurous Stranger;*
> *Strike the bell and bide the danger,*
> *Or wonder till, it drives you mad,*
> *What would have followed if you had.*[4]

Lewis's ditty clarifies the dilemma the biblical author was trying to convey, exquisitely evoking the first problem of human freedom. In religious language we say that the first man and woman were tempted, egged on to do something they were not supposed to do. In the biblical story the man and woman weakened and gave in, and the biblical author says it was because they were tempted by a clever serpent. How can we interpret this story, then? Were the man and woman outsmarted? Were they just weak and curious? Did they sin? Some believers interpret the action of the first man and woman as one of pride and self-deception, others as an expression of the desire of people to set their own limits, be their own God. Whatever the interpretation, their action, their disobedience, changed things—life was no longer lived in a beautiful garden. Painful realities entered into human life: work now included frustration and might be fruitless as well as difficult, birth occurred within a context of pain, and sickness and death became part of human existence. In Christian religious language this moment of separation and alienation is called Original Sin; it is the religious explanation for the facts of life as the biblical authors and the community experienced them.

The story says something about God as creator, that God is powerful and good, and wants people to have good relationships with each other and with the deity. We also learn about the reality of sin: people are capable of it through weakness and willfulness, and it does damage and pulls people in a direction away from God.

Many times in the Bible sin is explained in terms of direction: people turn away from God or go astray, or follow the wrong leaders or false gods. Repentance and conversion imply a change of direction, a move back towards God. Repentance is an important concept throughout the Old Testament. The prophets especially call upon people to remember the covenant and turn back to God. In the New Testament Jesus calls people to repentance and conversion, which is precisely a change of direction and a turning away from sin.

GOD AS PROVIDENT

In the creation account we learned that things began well but, because of sin, people found themselves in a muddle. God's response to this situation discloses another divine attribute. When people ruined a good situation, God (as all powerful) could have let them die and then could have started over, or could have left them to their own devices. Some explanations about God's relationship with the world argue that God created the world and then left it to itself; some explanations of human life rely on concepts of fate or determinism. The biblical account, however, says something different and extraordinary: God is willing to enter into the muddle and bring the divine creative energy to bear on it without interfering with human freedom. God recreated their good options; when people moved away from God, God was willing to help them find the road back. God moved into the history of these people. God created a world, watched people make a mess of it, and then entered into that mess creatively, fashioning out of it a people, a law, and a way. Christians call God's involvement in the world *providence,* the divine provision for humanity.

Some people have wondered how an all-powerful God relates to people without violating their freedom. God's actions in history come as calls, not demands. The Bible does not usually picture God as manipulative or overbearing, but as interested and compassionate. People are invited to be in partnership with God. The pattern of providence and continuing revelation in the Bible, therefore, can be interpreted as a pattern of call and response. God still initiates the conversation and relationship; but human freedom is intact because people may choose to reject the invitation or to accept it.

The fifth book of the Old Testament, Deuteronomy, contains a summary statement about what God has done for a particular people (26:5–10). It begins by saying, "A wandering Aramean was my father" and goes on to explain what happened to him. He became the father of a great nation. That nation or people was in the course of time welcomed into the land of Egypt, but later made slaves. The passage goes on to say, "And the Egyptians treated us harshly, and afflicted us, and laid upon us hard bondage. . . . Then we cried to the Lord the God of our ancestors, and the Lord heard our voice, saw our affliction, our toil and our oppression and the Lord brought us out of Egypt with a mighty hand and an outstretched arm, with great terror, with signs and wonders . . . and he brought us into this place and gave us this land, a land flowing with milk and honey." Something has happened in the lives of this particular people which reveals how God's providence works. The creation story was about all people, the first people of the human race; it offered an explanation for universal destiny. The summary of God's works in Deuteronomy is about a specific people, a people called by God to be special and to be the bearers of God's self-communication, and to begin the work of restoring what was lost in the Fall.

The Story of Abraham

If we look in Genesis 9 we see that God promised to do something about the havoc people brought upon themselves through disobedience. What God would do is not clear, but there are grounds for anticipation of some action in the future. The first specific idea we get about the divine plan occurs in Genesis 12 when God called Abraham.

The Abraham story has five important elements. First of all, God's intervention into Abraham's life came with no explanation—it was pure gift, *gratuitous*. Second, Abraham was an old man with an old, childless wife when God told him that he would be the father of a great nation. The story tells us that Abraham found God's promise confusing, funny, and awesome, but that in spite of misgivings, he responded. In religious terms we can say that he responded *in faith*. We might note here that many of the biblical heroes respond to God in faith. Although they initially have many doubts, they finally accept the assurance of God's presence and help in what they are called to do. Third, Abraham did have a son (two of them, in fact, though the first, Ishmael, drops out of this story)[5] and named him Isaac. This child was born when Abraham's wife, Sarah, was old and barren, so a *miraculous element* was involved: God acts with power and demonstrates divine lordship. Fourth, God made a pact with Abraham, a *covenant*. Finally, God *tested* Abraham's faith and obedience by asking him to sacrifice Isaac. Faith and trust in God is not a one-time event, but part of an ongoing relationship.

The word *covenant* occurs repeatedly in the Bible. Covenants spell out the terms of God's relationship with people; they are partnership agreements, contracts. In the modern world, contracts are written down with the terms specified and penalties explained for breaking the agreement. In the ancient world there *were* written contracts, but there were also spoken agreements, which were solemn and sacred. In contracts and covenants there are witnesses to the signing and to the terms. Often covenants were enacted before the gods (who acted as witnesses); all parties bound themselves rigorously to the terms. A covenant, therefore, is a solemn form of the spoken word, a binding and sacred agreement.

The terms of God's covenant with Abraham were clear: God would see that Abraham was the father of a great nation, which God would then bless and protect, and Abraham in turn was to honor God and see that every male member of his family was circumcised as a sign that he belonged to God. A further divine promise was that through Abraham and his descendants the nations of the world would be blessed; the promise was universal as well as particular. When Abraham agreed to the terms, responded to God's specific step toward partnership with a people, he made it possible for God to do something about the muddle.

The Story of Moses

The Moses story (Exodus) has some parallels to the Abraham story and clear links with it. Abraham was the father of Isaac and grandfather of Jacob. The biblical tradition maintains that Jacob had twelve sons who were the fathers of the twelve tribes of Israel (God changed Jacob's name to Israel). They continued to honor God and to follow the terms of the covenant and so, through them, the covenant between God and Abraham passed down through history and the God of the Hebrews came to be known as the God of Abraham, Isaac, and Jacob. One of Jacob's sons, Joseph (see Genesis 37–50) is the main character in the story of the Hebrews in Egypt, which is where we must go for the Moses story.

The covenant with Abraham occurred some time between 1850 and 1600 B.C.E. (Before the Common Era), and the flight from Egypt under the direction of Moses probably took place between 1250 and 1200 B.C.E. The Hebrews had lived in Egypt, first as welcomed guests and finally as slaves, for many generations. Moses enters the story as God's chosen liberator, sent to free the Hebrews and bring them to a new land and a new covenant. We can find some of the same elements in the Moses story that we found in the Abraham story. First of all, according to the biblical authors, God's intervention into Moses's life is *gratuitous*. His birth was no different from any other Hebrew boy's and nothing explains why a hidden providence protected him and eventually selected him as the mediator for the covenant. Second, when Moses first heard God's voice (Exodus 3) he was awestruck and impressed, but also confused and afraid. His decision to return to Egypt to lead people out was his response *in faith* and trust, made in spite of his hesitation about what God wanted him to do. Third, the great events in Egypt—the plagues, the Passover, the Red Sea event (see Exodus 7–15)—were *miraculous*. God acted with power, and the Hebrews and Egyptians saw God's power in those events. Fourth, God made a *covenant* with the whole people at Mount Sinai. Finally, these people were *tested* in the wilderness.[6]

Besides these parallels with the Abraham story, other features of the Moses story stand out. The Hebrew people in bondage in Egypt "cried out" and God "heard them" and determined to help them. Because of the covenant with Abraham, because God promised to protect this people, they had a claim on God and could cry out with reminders of the divine obligation to them. When God responded to the people and sent Moses to liberate them, God said, "I am the God of Abraham, Isaac, and Jacob," thereby showing a continuity between the Mosaic and the Abrahamic covenants.

Three months after they left Egypt, God brought the people to the wilderness at Sinai, and the high point of the Moses story is the covenant made at Sinai. God not only delivered the Israelites, but called them into a partnership agreement. At Sinai, through the giving of covenant law (including the Ten Commandments), the relationship between God and Israel took on a new dimension of particularity. While the people camped below, Moses went up the mountain, "up to God." There God told Moses to say this to the Hebrews: "You have seen what I did to the Egyptians and how I bore you on eagles' wings and brought you to myself. Now therefore, if you will obey my voice and keep my covenant you shall be my own possession among all peoples; for all the earth is mine, and you shall be to me a kingdom of priests and a holy nation" (Exod. 19:4–5). Moses went down the mountain and gave that message to the people and they responded, "All that the Lord has spoken, we will do" (see Exod. 19 and 24:3). It is clear that the people responded on the basis of their experience of God's liberation. They heard thunder and understood it as the divine voice; they demanded a mediator to interpret God's words for them, and Moses brought them the terms of the contract; they agreed to the terms of the covenant and willingly bound themselves in a relationship with God that required that they keep the commandments.

The People of the Covenant

God entered into history to make these former slaves into a special people, and did so through the covenant. Biblical tradition sees the Law as an act of divine providence enabling Israel to maintain the covenant relationship with God. They had been set free in Egypt by an act of divine justice; the Law was given to help them maintain that freedom and justice within their new society.

The history of Israel from the covenant at Sinai onwards is one of keeping and violating the covenant and of God's continued intervention to restore a proper relationship. People read the Bible for many reasons, one of which is because it discloses parts of the divine personality; but the Bible also shows a deep understanding of human nature and conveys the two-steps-forward-one-step-backward kind of progress most people experience in life. Even with God as their protector and guide, the people of Israel continually went astray. Why? The story in Genesis about the first man and woman help to explain the tension people find themselves in: people are attracted to good (because they were made in the image of God, who is good) and to evil (because of their sinfulness). Israel's experience demonstrates that those attractions can be equally strong, that human beings are easily confused. Is good more attractive than wickedness? The Bible is not clear on this question, and the history of Israel bears out the ambivalence. Israel's history is not unique. All human history reveals similar patterns of fidelity and betrayal.

The rest of the history of Israel builds on the same themes. During the first two centuries in the Promised Land, the people of Israel led a varied existence, both politically and religiously. When they were in trouble and cried out, the Lord sent help by way of heroes and heroines (see Judges). As the small band of nomadic slaves brought out of Egypt grew into a larger people and settled into the land, they were torn between wanting to maintain their uniqueness (as

God's people) and their desire to be like their neighbors. The story of Israel's move towards kingship is ambivalent. For a number of reasons, and with mixed results, Israel solidified into a kingdom that reached its zenith of organization and power under David and Solomon around the year 1000 B.C.E. David's son, Solomon, was the last king to rule over a united Israel. For political reasons (that had theological significance for Israel) the twelve tribes split into two separate kingdoms—ten tribes in the north (called Israel) and two in the south (called Judah). Although early Israel felt deep ambivalence about the kingship of David (as a dethroning of the divine king), the later biblical tradition generally sees it as an important part of God's plan.

The two kingdoms did not last. Why not? The prophets had claimed that unfaithfulness to the covenant would lead to destruction, and later biblical writers saw that they had been correct. Prophets were those who spoke for God in some way, especially in terms of the covenant. The word *prophet* comes from the Hebrew word *nabi,* which, perhaps, means "called by God." As people neglected their contractual obligations and ignored their God, the prophets tried, often poetically and with a sense of desperate urgency, to get people to remember their relationship with God. The kingdom of Israel lasted from 922 to 722 B.C.E., when it fell to the Assyrians. Prophets—Amos, for example, and Hosea—had warned people in the northern kingdom that God would punish them for their infidelity, but, according to the Bible, they paid no heed and were destroyed. The kingdom of Judah lasted from 922 to 587 B.C.E., when they were destroyed by the Babylonians and carried off into exile. Again, prophets—like Jeremiah and Isaiah—had warned them, urged them to return to the covenant obligations, but with no success.

The People in Exile

What is the relationship between God and an exiled people? During and after the exile, many Jews looking at the grim events of history tended to see their hardships as punishment for their sins. The exile was not, for them, a sign that God had forgotten the covenant, but a sign of God's care. The exile was a punishment for disobedience, a purification. The word of the prophets—before, during and after the exile—helped the Jews to understand their experience. We can see clearly here the interrelationship between historical experience and ways in which a group understood God's role in their lives. In all of Israel's history and in the Bible there is a connection between their historical experience, their self-understanding, and their perceptions about God. Even when things were at their worst—when the people were in exile in Babylon—prophets continued to speak God's word. When the people wondered what would happen to them after the exile, the prophets had visions of a renewed Israel where the original purposes of the Abrahamic covenant would be fulfilled and where Israel would become a universal blessing to all nations. Thus, in 538 B.C.E., when a small group was returned to Palestine, many Jews felt that they were being brought back and given another chance, a fresh start. They would never again have a kingdom, or much political power, but they still had the covenant. Their history from their return onwards is one of domination by foreign powers—Persians, Greeks, and Romans. During one brief period (from 143–63 B.C.E.; see next chapter) the Jews were in control of their political lives, but in 63 B.C.E., Pompey, a Roman general, captured Jerusalem and the Romans were in control of the country when Jesus was born.

When we look at the Hebrew Bible we can find books that tell these stories in much more elaborate detail (see Appendix 2). The books of the Torah and the Prophets tell us about Israel's history and prophetic experience. The Writings fill in another dimension of Israel's experience of God. The Psalms, a magnificent, poetic prayerbook containing hymns for almost every occasion and feeling; the so-called Wisdom literature with its philosophical reflections (for example, Job), moral maxims (for example, Proverbs); the erotic poetry of the Song of Songs (or Song of Solomon); the apocalyptic visions of Daniel—all indicate an extraordinarily rich experience of God's action and presence in their lives. All of these books and most of this experience were used later by Christians to explain Jesus. For the time being, however, it is enough to know the main outline of the story, to realize that it is inexhaustibly rich and amenable to a wide variety of interpretation, and to remember that, according to the Bible, God did not abandon the Jewish people.

CONCLUSION

This chapter has set forth the ancient context and foundation of Christianity, along with some basic concepts. We have seen what revelation means and noted that the Bible is a record of God's revelation. Since both Christians and Jews look to the Bible as the record of God's revelation, we looked there to find out some of its basic perceptions of God. We found that the God of Jews and Christians is the powerful, transcendent creator of the world. More importantly, however, we found that God did not leave people to their own devices but remained interested in them even when they made a mess of God's good creative work. We have focused on the Abraham and Moses stories in the history of Israel as a demonstration of divine providence: the initial promise, the covenant with Abraham, the rescue of Abraham's descendants, and the covenant at Sinai all disclose God's personality. We have seen that being in a covenant relationship with God did not mean that all went smoothly or that people were never tempted to do anything wrong. On the contrary, people, even though they were in a relationship with God, continued to go astray and follow the wrong paths. An important insight from the Bible is that God continues to be interested in a people, even when they fail to keep the covenant. God judges them and redeems them; God's self-communication is revealed in an ongoing history of invitation and response.

CHAPTER 1 NOTES

1. Revelation is an enormous problem, one that is never solved. For a clear and brief history of the issues see Avery Dulles, *Revelation Theology—A History* (New York: Herder & Herder, 1969). The complexity of the problem is exemplified right now by some of the questions that the women's movement raises about biblical language. The Bible consistently speaks about God as "He," generally contains stories about men, and is addressed to "men" or to "brothers" and "sons." Some women have no problems with this language because they believe "man" to be a generic term, used to denote both men and women. Other women have argued that the language of the Bible is sexist and its biases patriarchal. See, for example, Rosemary Ruether, "Male Chauvinist Theology and the Anger of Women," in *Cross Currents* 21 (1971), 173–85; see also Phyllis Trible, *God and the Rhetoric of Sexuality* (Philadelphia: Fortress Press, 1978). Here's the question: Is male God-language *revealed*? Must one understand God as masculine? Or can one change the language? Or add new insights from extrabiblical literature? As feminist theologians pose the questions, the whole theology of revelation becomes a lively and practical issue.

2. William James, in *The Varieties of Religious Experience* (New York: New American Library, 1958), pp. 292–328, makes a case for mystical experience, but argues that the community does *not* have to accept it. Still, he says, it is hard to ignore completely. Private revelations take many forms: some are mystical experiences of God's loving-kindness, some are deep awarenesses of divine pain, and some are angry messages of impending doom. Whatever their content or circumstances, private revelations usually do not bind a Christian community.

3. Inspiration, like revelation, is a very complex problem both theologically and practically. Almost every Christian group has its own history of understanding and explaining it. Care should be exercised in talking about it, and the student is urged to consult standard reference works like *The Interpreter's Dictionary of the Bible* or *The Jerome Biblical Commentary* just to get some idea of the range of the problem.

4. (New York: Macmillan, 1955), p. 51.

5. See p. 5 of this chapter. Muslims believe themselves to be descendants of Ishmael, the son born to Abraham and his wife's maidservant, Hagar. One of the ritual actions of the Islamic pilgrimage to Mecca (undertaken once in a Muslim's lifetime) is to visit the place in the desert where God promised to make Ishmael a great nation (Genesis 21).

6. Almost immediately after accepting the covenant, the people who agreed to keep it broke it. Furthermore (as reported in stories in Numbers), their lack of faith finally resulted in their not being permitted to enter the promised land; instead, they were forced to wander in the desert for forty years.

SUGGESTIONS FOR FURTHER READING

1. For a simplified and accessible explanation about prehistory see Joseph Blenkinsopp, *From Adam to Abraham: Introduction to Sacred History* (Glen Rock, N.J.: Paulist Press, 1965).

2. Form criticism, understanding of scriptural passages through an analysis of their structural forms, is a relatively new and important interpretive skill, one that cannot be ignored as we try to understand the Bible. For a clear and well-illustrated introduction to

form criticism, one that has easy-to-understand examples, cartoon illustrations (by Bill Woodman), and straight language, see Gerhard Lohfink, *The Bible, Now I Get It: A Form Criticism Handbook* (Garden City, N.Y.: Doubleday, 1979). The author argues that form criticism is not just for experts but is for everyone and that a basic understanding of it is not a luxury but a fundamental tool for understanding Scripture.

3. For some sense of the geography of the Bible see The National Geographic Book Service, *Everyday Life in Bible Times* (Washington, D.C.: National Geographic Society, 1967).

4. For a clear, readable treatment of the whole of the Old Testament see Bernhard W. Anderson, *Understanding the Old Testament,* 3rd ed. (Englewood Cliffs, N.J.: Prentice-Hall, 1975).

CHAPTER 2

The Context for and Life of Jesus

Jesus was born into a volatile political situation and a complex religious milieu. The Jews had been exiled to Babylon in 587 B.C.E. after the Babylonians destroyed the southern kingdom (Judah); they remained in exile until 538 B.C.E. When the Jews returned from Babylon to Palestine, they were faced with problems of survival and of interpreting the meaning of the exile. Their attempts to resolve those problems had a bearing on how they perceived Jesus's life and teaching. Their interpretations of the exile and their reactions to hellenization were bound up with renewed seriousness about the Law, so Jesus's relationship to the Law was also very important to them. Jewish ideas about the kingdom of God along with the divided political situation within Judaism itself made gaining acceptance difficult for any powerful preacher: no matter what the preacher said, there was always a different but equally valid interpretation. Jesus's life and teaching, therefore, must be understood against this complicated background. Similarly, writings about Jesus (and early Christians) have to be read in light of the religious and political situation of the times. One of the important questions for early Christian interpreters was where Jesus fit with regard to Jewish expectations. In this chapter we will see what those expectations were, where they came from, and how they were reinterpreted by early Christian writers to fit the life and message of Jesus.

JEWISH INTERPRETATION OF THE EXILE

The covenant at Sinai was the major event that shaped the lives and understanding of the Jewish people. It not only provided them with their specific identity as God's people, but gave them a perspective from which to interpret their history. Whatever happened to them, they could look back to the covenant, to the basis of their relationship with God, and find a way to explain it. What did the Jews think about the exile? And what do you think their captors thought of the Jews and their religion? How do you think the belief that they worshipped the one true God and were God's people looked in the face of the defeat and exile of the Jews? It is not hard to imagine that many people wondered just what had happened: Had God deserted them? Was God no longer interested in the Jews? Psalm 137 tells us how the Jews themselves felt: "By the waters of Babylon, there we sat down and wept when we remembered Zion" (137:1).

It must have been tempting, even for the Jews, to think that God had lost interest in them. Because of the covenant, however, and because of their long experience of God's faithfulness and mercy, the Jews did *not* interpret the exile as a sign of divine abandonment. In fact, they interpreted it in just the opposite way. When they reflected on their dislocation and their return to Palestine, they saw a sign of God's continuing interest in the covenant relationship. God was, indeed, bound up with them, repeatedly warning them and reminding them of the terms of the covenant. God continually sent messengers, the prophets, to call the people back to observance of the Law and to a better relationship. Only because they would not listen and because there was no other way, God was constrained to punish them, to uproot and replant them. Their sinfulness, their "going astray," meant that they had to be redirected. The exile was seen as the means God used to cleanse the people, forcing them to develop a clearer vision of the relationship between God and Israel. When they were brought back from Babylon (in 538 B.C.E.) it was with a renewed sense of obligation to be loyal and obedient to the commandments.

How did they intend to be God's faithful people in the future? How would they be true to the one God in their belief, worship, and everyday life? The answer—present in the terms of the covenant—lay in keeping the Law. Since they were no longer one people in one land with one ruler, the Law provided internal coherence for them. They had learned that keeping the Law was sometimes difficult when they were surrounded and tempted by a foreign culture. Their renewed efforts to keep the Law, therefore, were coupled with an intense effort to keep themselves apart from influences that might seduce them or force them away from the Law. This meant, in effect, that the Jews had a strong interest in keeping themselves separate from other people. They might be forced to live under foreign political domination, but they could resist any attempts at religious domination; by obedience to the Law they could refuse to intermarry and become part of another culture.

When the Jews were restored to Palestine in 538 B.C.E. they were subject to a number of different foreign powers. The most serious threat to their resolution to remain faithful observers of the Law, however, occurred during the Hellenistic period.[1]

HELLENIZATION AND THE JEWS

The conquests of Alexander the Great spread Greek ideas and culture to the Near East and well into Asia. Greek influence continued to spread after Alexander's death (in 323 B.C.E.) and the Hellenistic era is usually thought to have ended politically with the conquest of Alexandria by the Romans in the first century B.C.E. During the Hellenistic era the descendants of Alexander's generals hoped to consolidate their empire, unifying it in language, customs, law, and philosophy. They hoped to do this by insinuating their culture and practices into the lands they conquered, and by pursuing a policy of intermarriage with the peoples they ruled. Their policies were thus in direct conflict with the Jewish resolve to keep themselves separate.

One can imagine that some of the Greek ideas and philosophy must have seemed tempting to some of the Jews. The impulse of Hellenism was felt in Israel as everywhere else. The Jews continued to keep themselves apart from some of its demands, but at the same time they began to disagree about how far they *could* go in accommodating themselves to this new cultural influence. Could a Jew be true to the Law and study Greek philosophy? Could a young Jewish boy participate in the athletic games at the local Greek-styled gymnasium? Could Jews allow *some* statues of Greek gods in their towns? Issues like these divided the Jews not only in theory but in practice. Some Jews felt that they could enter into the spirit of the Greek culture (some even had operations to "uncircumcize" themselves) and maintain their Jewish identity; others believed that any participation in Hellenistic civilization violated the covenant and displeased God. A strong opposition party, the predecessors of the Pharisees, arose against hellenization and those Jews who favored it. The party argued that Greek customs were foreign and idolatrous and that no Jew could legitimately participate in them.

Once aversion to hellenization took the form of a party, the arguments against Greek ways had a more political character. The opposition to hellenization grew stronger and more vocal; in the minds of Greek officials at least, it began to appear that things could not be resolved without a test of power. In 168 B.C.E., Antiochus IV, whose rule extended over Jerusalem, from Palestine to Syria and eastward to the Euphrates, and who had already offended the Jews by selling the office of high priest (in direct violation of Jewish practice and law), began a campaign to destroy the religion of the Jews. He issued an edict that forbade Jews to practice circumcision, to celebrate any festivals, or to keep the Sabbath. All copies of the Torah were to be destroyed and the Jewish temple turned into a Greek temple. A statue of the Greek god Zeus was put up in the Jerusalem temple and Jews were forced to worship the pagan gods.

Even the Jews who had favored hellenization found the policies of Antiochus IV abominable. Opposition to Antiochus solidified behind the leadership of Judas Maccabeas and his four brothers, who revolted against Syrian domination. The revolt, which is recorded in the first book of Maccabees, and their victory is celebrated each year in the Jewish feast of Hanukkah. The struggle for religious freedom turned into a battle for political freedom. From 143–63 B.C.E. the Jews retained political control of Israel. But in 63 B.C.E., the Roman general Pompey captured Jerusalem and began Roman domination of the Jews.

At the time of Jesus, Herod was the regional governor of the Jews, picked by the Romans. He collaborated with the Romans and was despised by the Jews. The Romans had always allowed the Jews religious freedom, but were beginning to find them a political nuisance. It was possible, the Romans thought, that the Jews might be secret political allies of the Syrians, an alliance that would constitute a serious threat to the Romans, while either the Syrians or the Jews alone would not. Remember that the Jews had a stake in maintaining their own identity, in refusing to intermarry and to take on customs of the conquering power. Since they had maintained their own identity, they had not been absorbed into the empire. Such political autonomy, therefore, made them appear dangerous to the Romans. It was into this Jewish world ruled by Romans that Jesus was born.

JEWISH HOPES FOR A KINGDOM OF GOD

To fully understand the religious context into which Jesus was born, you must understand that faithfulness to the Law was bound up with popular Jewish expectation that God would somehow and some time act decisively in their behalf.[2] God had rescued them from the land of Egypt and had restored them to Israel after the exile. Thus they had reason to expect that God would continue to act for them. Whereas most Jews searched the Law for guidance about everyday behavior, there were others who searched in other parts of Scripture for what God might do in the future. A strong vocal minority centered their hopes on the concept of a *kingdom of God,* perhaps because it recaptured the old ideal of a chosen people in a promised land under a divinely sanctioned king. However it was understood, the kingdom of God became a slogan for what would happen in a new age. The coming of the kingdom would mark the establishment of God's rule forever, everywhere. Within this general understanding of divine victory, however, there were differences of opinion. Some Jews believed the Messiah would be a wise and ideal king who would establish justice all over the world. Some thought a Messiah-king would surely be of the Davidic line since David had been the greatest of the ancient kings. Some believed that the establishment of the kingdom of God would mean Jewish political prestige throughout the world: Israel would be the most powerful nation on earth, ruling over everyone.

As the Jews became more threatened by events, especially in the second and first centuries before the Common Era, popular beliefs about the kingdom of God began to take on more militant aspects. During this time a literature and outlook called apocalyptic began to flourish. Since Jews were involved in crucial political and military struggles, their ideas about the Messiah and the kingdom of God incorporated more political and military expectations. Some people began to see the kingdom of God not so much as an ideal kingdom of righteousness, but as some kind of powerful event. The kingdom of God began to be tied up with the expectation that God would perform some great act. Since the world was in such a mess, God would have to bring about a complete transformation of people and of the world.

The second and first centuries before the Common Era were times in which the influence of religious dualism began to be felt and an apocalyptic tone heard: people began to look at the world as a place under the influence of evil powers that could not be defeated by human powers alone. To defeat these evil powers, God would have to intervene and conquer them with divine power. People saw the world as a battleground between the forces of good and evil; they believed the universe was divided between the kingdom of God (which they hoped was coming to the rescue) and the kingdom of Satan (which they believed was now in power). The day was surely coming, they thought, when God would destroy the power of Satan and master the evil that abounded.

During the two centuries before the birth of Jesus, an enormous body of literature developed about the coming of the kingdom and the overthrow of the demonic powers. There was a popular concept of what would happen. The world, dominated by evil powers, would be a place of great suffering and hardship until God rose up and overthrew the kingdom of Satan. In this mood, many ideas about the Messiah focused on military conquest. The Messiah might be wise, but most of all he would be a powerful warrior-king who could conquer evil and begin the age of bliss.

THE JEWS DIVIDED

Judaism at the time of Jesus's birth was not monolithic, but varied, especially in attitudes toward Roman domination and in expectations about the Messiah. There were probably many different groups of Jews at the time of Jesus. Descriptions of four of them will give you some idea of the situation.[3]

The Sadducees

The *Sadducees* were the wealthy aristocratic ruling class. In modern terms they might be called the Establishment. They were conservatives who kept the

Torah strictly, allowed no doctrinal innovations, and were strongly associated with the temple. They controlled the office of high priest and held a dominant position in the Jewish governing body, the Sanhedrin. Because of their political power over the Jewish community, they were the Jews the Roman politicians dealt with. Because the Sadducees were wealthy and established, they tended to deal with the Romans in a polite way. They were political collaborationists who were willing to adapt to Roman rule because the status quo worked in their favor. In terms of their religious beliefs, the Sadducees thought the Torah (the Law, the first five books of the Bible) the single most important religious text and were not, therefore, interested in apocalyptic literature or Jewish tradition. It is not altogether clear what they expected in a Messiah, but it is safe to assume that they did *not* expect a Palestinian peasant from Nazareth.

The Pharisees

The *Pharisees* were made up of artisans and merchants, descended from the party that opposed Greek ideas at the time of Antiochus. In order to keep the Jews faithful to the Law and away from any foreign influence, they were inclined to extend the Law to every phase of life and insist on perfect observance. They were liberal in that they constantly applied the Torah to new situations and built up a whole new tradition of interpretation. The Pharisees associated not so much with priests, but with lay people, with scholars and teachers. They believed that every decision in life could be governed by the Torah, and they developed a system of elaborate interpretation (which later became the Mishnah and Talmud). They did not approve of political collaboration with the Romans and desired separatism. They accepted as authoritative the prophetic and other writings of the Bible, which the Sadducees did not accept, and incorporated some of the apocalyptic notions of the time into their religious understanding. Since they were not interested in political matters and were not established economically like the Sadducees, they had different expectations of a Messiah. The Pharisees were more religious than political, and their opinion of the future of Israel was a religious one. The Messiah, for them, would probably be a religious leader and teacher who perfectly observed the Law and who could lead people to repentance and the power of the Torah.

The Essenes

The *Essenes* were disenchanted ascetics and apocalyptic visionaries who withdrew from general society to form communes in the desert where they waited for the Messiah and the destruction of the Romans. We know something about this group because of the discovery of the Dead Sea Scrolls, documents of the ancient Essene desert community of Qumran. Like the Pharisees, the Essenes had been part of the revolt against Greek customs, and their protest finally took the form of complete withdrawal from society. They lived by themselves in the wilderness, preparing for the coming of the kingdom of God. Their expectation was apocalyptic. They believed that the end of the world was near and that their lives should be lived in perfect obedience to God in the short time remaining. They believed that God was about to begin the messianic kingdom on earth and would form a new covenant with them. The new covenant and the Messiah would be bound up with the defeat of the Romans and with the promise of eternal life. They believed they had been called by God into the desert to be recipients of the new covenant. Thus, they called themselves the community of the new covenant and thought they were the true Israel.

The Zealots

The *Zealots* were underground activists who expected another armed uprising against the Romans in Israel. In modern terms they were potential guerrilla warriors, collecting arms and soldiers for an impending struggle. They looked on the Romans as enemies to be overthrown and expected the Messiah to be a warrior-king who would lead them into battle against the Romans.

The common people were variously influenced by these and other groups and by apocalyptic literature; they probably had a number of different ideas about what a Messiah should be. One interpreter claims that the "majority of Jews were the ordinary peasants of Israel, who were in general lukewarm about religion."[4]

SUMMARY OF THE CONTEXT

The Jews saw the covenant as the central event of their lives; it provided the central motif for their interpretation of history. The most important part of the covenant was the keeping of the commandments. In order to keep themselves from foreign corruption of their practices and beliefs, the Jews kept themselves apart and maintained religious and ethnic purity. The Jews were looking for God to enter into history in a radical and transforming way, for a Messiah who would defeat the powers of evil, and for the establishment of a new kingdom. Finally, the Jews had differing expectations about the Messiah. Some thought he should be a warrior-king, others a strict observer of the Torah, others that he should be a man of the temple, and still others expected a revolutionary or the one who would usher in the end of the age. When Jesus came, Christians perceived that he was none of these, that he did not at all fit into the expectations of the time, but they claimed that he was the Messiah nevertheless.

THE LIFE OF JESUS

Jesus was born into the situation described above. Scholars generally agree that he was born in 4 B.C.E., but they disagree about the date of his death; some say he died in 30 C.E. and others in 33 C.E. He is not mentioned in non-Christian literature until the end of the first century C.E.,[5] and when he is mentioned, references to him are vague. Most of what we know about Jesus was written down by Christians, and most of the New Testament material was not written until at least thirty-five years after his death. The earliest Gospel, Mark, was probably not written until about 70 C.E.; Matthew and Luke were both composed about 85 C.E.; and John was probably not written until sometime between 80 and 100 C.E.

There is no one story of Jesus; each of the Gospels has a different idea about him. We could, however, draw out a story based on reading all four Gospels. Jesus was born in Bethlehem during the reign of Herod the Great, probably around 4 B.C.E. He was born into obscurity and some traditions assert that he was conceived by the Holy Spirit (that his mother's pregnancy was a direct act of God and a miracle), and that he was born of a virgin named Mary (who had not had intercourse with her husband Joseph before her pregnancy).

Jesus grew up in a small town, Nazareth, where he was the son of a carpenter. Whether or not he had any education or was ever part of a particular religious group within Judaism, we do not know. A few years before his death, perhaps somewhere between 27 and 29 C.E., Jesus was drawn to the preaching of John the Baptist, a Jewish preacher calling people to repent and believe that the kingdom of God was at hand. John the Baptist embodied some of the apocalyptic and messianic hopes of the time and was, according to Luke, a cousin of Jesus. The writers of the Gospels understood John as one sent to prepare the way for Jesus, to attract those with messianic hopes and then point them to Jesus.

John baptized Jesus in the Jordan River, an event of great significance for the gospel writers. They interpreted Jesus's baptism as the time when Jesus was anointed as Messiah: the Holy Spirit descended on Jesus and God said, "This is my beloved Son." In the Old Testament, the Spirit's presence indicated a special calling or mission. What is clear from the Gospels is that Jesus spent some time in a special ministry around Galilee and northern Palestine. He was renowned for his teaching and powers of healing. Pharisees and Sadducees sought him out to ask questions and were astonished at the depth of his answers. He was, apparently, a threat to both groups and a disappointment to the Zealots. We know nothing about his relationship to the Essenes. Like John, he preached the coming of the kingdom of God and called people to repent. The significance of his words and actions was not always clear. Even his close friends and disciples did not always understand his mission. Still, he attracted crowds and had many followers.

For reasons clear only to himself, he was determined to go up to Jerusalem and preach there. His friends warned him against this because he was not in favor with the authorities there, but he believed that his mission called him to Jerusalem. The people of Jerusalem welcomed him and some of them may even have been drawn to him as the Messiah, but within a week he was arrested, accused of blasphemy and sedition, tried, and killed. He celebrated the Passover with his disciples one night and the next day was flogged, mocked, and sent back and forth between Pontius Pilate and Herod as a strange and interesting prisoner; he was then crucified by the Roman officers stationed in Jerusalem.

After he died his body was sealed in a tomb with a great stone in front of it. His followers were stunned and afraid. The Gospels affirm that three days after his death, however, the tomb was empty. Some people said that his disciples stole the body and were going to claim that Jesus had risen from the dead. His followers, however, said that they did not steal the body, but that Jesus in fact rose from the dead and appeared to some of them. The resurrection of Jesus was the sign to his followers that he was the chosen one of God, the Messiah. The early preaching about Jesus was simple: Jesus, who was crucified, has been raised from the dead; repent and believe that he is Lord and Messiah.

THE ACCOUNT OF JESUS IN THE NEW TESTAMENT

The New Testament is the Christian holy book. It contains twenty-seven books, some about the life of Jesus, others about practical problems within the young Christian community; it ends with an apocalyptic vision, a Christian version of the end of the world. Taken together, these books are the canonical literature of Christianity: they are considered to be inspired by God. Most of what we know about Jesus comes to us from the Gospels; much of what we know about the early Christians comes to us from the Epistles. The Book of Revelation is in a class by itself; it is representative of an apocalyptic consciousness and was probably written during a severe persecution of the Christian churches.

The Gospels

The Gospels (the first four books of the New Testament) are not biographical materials in any sense of the word. They are, rather, specific reflections on the life, death, and resurrection of Jesus written by people who were mainly interested in the last few years (or even months) of his life. They all reflect the perspective of faith: the gospel writers believed that Jesus was the Messiah, and that he had been crucified in Jerusalem and had risen from the dead. They based their perspective of Jesus on their belief in his resurrection, and they shaped the material available to them about his life according to that belief and to the needs of their audience.

No one gospel contains a complete, objective account of the life, death, and resurrection of Jesus. Each gospel was written from a specific perspective and used the material about Jesus to emphasize particular things about him. The first three gospels—Mark, Matthew, and Luke—are similar in content and tell many of the same stories about Jesus. If you put these gospels in parallel columns you can see how similar they are. Because they can be seen together, they are called synoptic (from the Greek for *seeing together*). The style and content of the synoptic Gospels is different from that of the fourth gospel, John.

The Gospel of Mark is the shortest and probably the earliest gospel. It presents Jesus as the Son of God tragically misunderstood by his followers, and its picture of Jesus has an apocalyptic edge: he expects the end of the age to come soon. In the Gospel of Mark, Jesus is pictured as *a Messiah who must suffer*. Jesus is clearly the Messiah, but he does not conform to any of the expectations of some groups; he is not a warrior-king or a revolutionary, but a man with power to work miracles, the Son of God, who must suffer and die. The Resurrection is a sign of his power over death. In Mark the powers of evil (demons being exorcised) recognize Jesus before people do. People expected God to establish his kingdom by overthrowing the powers of evil. Jesus, in Mark, has the power to do that and the demons see that their reign is about to end.

The Gospel of Matthew sees Jesus as *the new Moses,* the giver of the new law. Jesus, for Matthew, is the fulfillment of the biblical prophecies; for many of Jesus's sayings and actions Matthew finds a parallel in the Old Testament. All the expectations about where the Messiah would be born, how he would enter Jerusalem, and what he would do are used by Matthew to explain Jesus. The parallels between Jesus and Moses are strong in this Gospel: Moses gave the people the old law from Mount Sinai, Jesus delivers the new law in the Sermon on the Mount. The main stress in Matthew is on God's generosity to people manifested in Jesus and the kingdom. Human beings are to respond to that generosity by loving one another joyfully.

The Gospel of Luke and the Book of Acts should be read together as the first conscious history of the Christian movement. Scholars agree that the same author wrote both books. Jesus, for Luke, is a merciful savior who grants forgiveness to those who repent. There is a special focus on Jesus's compassion and tenderness. Luke emphasizes *universality*—Jesus came for everyone, not just for the Jews—in his account of Jesus's work and message; Luke traces the geneaology of Jesus back to Adam (the father of the human race) rather than back to Abraham (the father of the Jewish people) as Matthew does. Luke has many stories about the poor and downcast; in his view Jesus relates positively to the Samaritans (a despised people) and gives women a place of importance.[6] The great parable of forgiveness—the parable of the prodigal son—is found only in Luke. In the Resurrection, God reveals Jesus as the one who brings mercy for all. The message of Jesus is to be taken to the ends of the earth. The Book of Acts takes up the theme of the universal mission of the Christians and will be discussed in the next chapter.

The Gospel of John differs from the synoptics in organization, style, and content. John presents the *mystery* of Jesus, who is like other people but above them in some way. John focuses on the eternal origin and divine nature of Jesus. The gospel begins with Jesus as the preexistent Word of God—an important concept when you remember that the world was created through God's *word*. John says the Word through whom the world was made had now been made flesh. Jesus was more powerful than death even before his resurrection: the story about Jesus raising Lazarus from the dead is found only in John. Remember that many Jews believed that in order to establish the kingdom, God would have to enter the world in some radical, transforming way. The Gospel of John says that Jesus is God become a man, God entering the world in a radical, transforming way. John also structures his gospel differently. Some interpreters say the Gospel of John contains two books—a book of *signs* (John 1–12; see, for example, the miracle at Cana, 2:1–12), and a book of *glory* (John 12–21; see, for example, the farewell discourse, 17:1–26).

The Epistles

The other literature found in the New Testament is in the form of a series of letters. There are twenty-one letters in the New Testament; at least nine of the major ones were written by the apostle Paul. The Epistles are not about the life of Jesus as the Gospels are. They reflect the life, questions, and conflicts of the early community, and they show a developing theology or reflection about Jesus and his mission. The Resurrection is central to them as it is to the Christian message as a whole, as a sign of God's action and a vindication of Jesus's life and work. It was the Resurrection that enabled Jesus's followers to understand him as the Messiah and Lord, and the Resurrection provided the key to his author-ity—his teachings and his miracles all pointed to his power over death and his divinity. Death and the Resurrection make Jesus the Savior. His power to forgive sins and to restore the created order are tied up with his victory over death. And the Resurrection shows people that God does not mean for death to be the end of things, but indicates that God calls people to fellowship even beyond death. Paul said that nothing can separate the believer from the love of God, not even death.

The Book of Revelation

Revelation is the last book of the New Testament. It pictures the end of the world and is written in highly symbolic language. Its author had visions of God's merciful government of all Creation, and wrote this book to sustain Christian hope during severe persecution. It has functioned to sustain Christian hope ever since. It is not an easy book to read because it is full of symbols, numerical calculations, strange beasts, and other apocalyptic figures. Many con-temporary Christians use it to predict the end of the world, to speculate about what Jesus will do when he comes back to judge people, though its probable purpose, like the rest of the New Testament, is to reveal the gospel and to inspire Christians to check their lives and see if they are living according to the gospel.[7]

JESUS AND JEWISH EXPECTATION

Some Christians think that Jesus was so clearly the Messiah that no one could fail to recognize him as such. People who believe this often see Jews as stubborn, blind, or deprived of their chance for salvation. This hostile interpretation of Judaism, which has been present in Christianity from the beginning, has led to a long and painful history of atrocities against the Jewish people. Jews who did not accept Jesus as the Messiah had good reasons for not doing so. Not everyone, after all, was expecting a Messiah. Jesus's life and teaching, therefore, was of no interest to some, and unconvincing to others. Insofar as Jewish history was full of God's action on their behalf and also full of hope for a *decisive act of God,* there were, in some quarters, hopes for a Messiah. Whether Jesus lived up to those hopes is precisely the dividing issue.

When Jesus lived and died, some people were expecting a Messiah. Christians believed that Jesus had been raised from the dead and was the promised Messiah. Belief in the Resurrection was not a matter of evidence, it was a matter of faith—recall the faith perspective needed to interpret some of the events in Jewish history. The earliest Christians were also rooted in Jewish history. Jesus was a Jew. His apostles were Jewish—they knew the biblical stories about Abraham, Isaac, and Jacob; they understood deeply the meaning of the covenant and the experience of the exile. Their belief in the resurrection of Jesus enabled them to believe that he was the Messiah. When they preached about Jesus they said that with Jesus a *new history*—built upon the old, but also different from it—began.

It is important to see what this means. The Jews believe that history has a purpose, that God has acted and will continue to act in it. Christians claim that history has a purpose, that God has acted in it so decisively in Jesus that a *new* history has begun. Jews are still waiting for the messianic age to begin because they do not accept the Christian claim that Jesus was the promised one of God. For Jews, many of the messianic promises were *not* fulfilled in Jesus: in Isaiah (11:6–7), for example, it says that people will live together in peace when the Messiah comes, that the lion will lie down with the lamb; those events did not happen with Jesus. Christians and Jews interpret the Bible differently. For Christians, Jesus shakes up the old order of things and makes it possible to see everything that went before him as pointing essentially toward *him.* For Jews the events of the Bible do not point toward Jesus at all, but beyond him to a future Messiah. The differences in interpretation are profound: for the Jews the Hebrew Bible points toward something still to come, but for Christians it sets the stage and provides an explanation for someone who has already arrived.

Look, for example, at Jeremiah 31:31–33: " 'Behold the days are coming,' says the Lord, 'when I will make a new covenant with Israel . . . not like the covenant which I made with their ancestors when I took them by the hand to bring them out of the land of Egypt . . . but I will put my law within them, and

I will write it upon their hearts; and I will be their God, and they shall be my people.' " For Jews, this new covenant is yet to come, but Christians have, from earliest times, applied these words to Jesus. In the early eucharistic formulas (in 1 Corinthians, for example) it relates that Jesus, on the night before he died, blessed the cup and said, "This cup is the new covenant in my blood" (11:25). Later, in Hebrews (8:8–12), the author quotes from Jeremiah explicitly to draw theological conclusions from it: if there is a new covenant found in the New Testament it is based on an experience of Jesus and is not understandable apart from that experience. One cannot expect non-Christians, therefore, to read those texts in the same way.

Early Christian authors used the Hebrew Bible as a typological gold mine—events in Israelite history were interpreted as "types" or symbols for what would happen to Jesus. The Hebrews passed through the Red Sea during the Exodus. This event was taken as a symbol that Jesus would pass through death. Similarly, the sacrifice of Isaac might symbolize the Crucifixion. Again, these events only become types in a specifically Christian interpretation.

The new perspective of the Christians is most evident in what they did to the Hebrew Bible (see Appendix 1). They adopted it as their own book, but renamed it the Old Testament (old covenant), a name that implies the existence of a new one. And they changed the order of the books. The Jewish Bible ends with the exile, with the expectation that God will act in the future. The Christian Old Testament ends with the books of the minor prophets, which are full of references Christians apply to Jesus. Micah, for example, says, "But you, O Bethelehem . . . who are little . . . from you shall come forth for me one who is to be ruler in Israel" (5:2). Where does the New Testament say Jesus was born? In Bethlehem. The Book of Habakkuk is about the sovereignty of God and contains the phrase that appears later in the Epistle to the Romans: "The righteous shall live by faith" (Hab. 2:4; Rom. 1:17). The Book of Haggai records God's promise, "I am about to shake the heavens and the earth" (2:21), interpreted in Hebrews (12:26) as accomplished in Jesus. All of these books have an edge of expectation. The Book of Zechariah pictures the Messiah as prince of peace and a good shepherd and contains the quotation: "Lo, your king comes to you; triumphant and victorious is he, humble and riding on an ass, on a colt the foal of an ass" (9:9). The New Testament authors used that quotation to describe Jesus's entry into Jerusalem. The Book of Malachi is about the impending coming of the Lord and about a forerunner. All these books were written in the sixth or fifth centuries B.C.E., and were therefore full of meaning for the Jews quite apart from any link with messianic hopes, but Christians saw them as an immediate foreshadowing of the coming of Jesus. It is a big step from the end of the Jewish Bible to the New Testament, from the exile to Jesus, but when one reads the Old Testament minor prophets one expects something to happen. Jesus appears as the proper and natural end of these prophecies. That was the Christian intention in reordering the books. But one can see how both the Jewish and the Christian interpretation of the life of Jesus could have grown out of the same Scripture.

CONCLUSION

I have outlined the life of Jesus and set it within its Jewish context. That context was, of course, a great deal more complex than I have indicated here: Judaism at the time of Jesus was enormously varied—politically, religiously, and sociologically. The groups I have described, for example, were comprised of relatively few Jews and my purpose in choosing and presenting them was to give you some indication of the variety within Judaism at the time. It is tempting to think that there was a normative Judaism, very neat and tidy, and that Jesus offered a clear alternative to it. Such thinking indulges in fantasy, though. There was no single Judaism at the time of Jesus, people were incredibly divided on all sorts of issues, and whatever alternative Jesus offered, it was probably no more clear than anything else at the time.

In major matters, Jewish opinion was divided. Most Jews were moved by Israel's institutions and were loyal to the temple, the Law, feasts, Jerusalem itself, and the idea of a holy land, but differed over theological concepts and methods of interpretation. It is not clear, for example, how many Jews were waiting for a Messiah. Christian interpretation is most congenial to a view that many were, but it is likely that very many Jews scarcely gave it a thought. You might compare it to a contemporary Christian interest in the end of the world. Do most Christians think often about the end of the world? Would you say that most of them are eagerly or even consciously waiting for it? Some are, of course, but are most of them? Probably not, even though, as a concept, it is part of their tradition. I suspect the same thing was true of the Jews and messianic expectation. At the same time, since I was trying to situate Jesus in a clear and relatively simple context, I placed an emphasis on messianic expectations here.

There were certainly major differences of opinion within Judaism about the appropriateness of an apocalyptic edge in scriptural interpretation, just as there are major differences within Christianity on the same issue. I focused on the apocalyptic vision because the intertestamental period (one hundred years before Jesus to one hundred years after) *was* a time when hundreds of apocalyptic books were written and when it did seem to be "in the air."

Finally, a word about the Torah. The Torah as such—the first five books of the Bible—was being edited, refined, and written down about the same time the Jews were returning to Palestine from the exile. When I talk about their hope to be more faithful to the Torah, therefore, I am speaking in a general way about fidelity to the covenant and the commandments. Even on this crucial issue of the Law, Jews were of different minds—Sadducees (conservatives) kept to the letter of the Torah *as it was written* and did not allow for refinements or interpretations or extensions, while Pharisees (liberals) extended applications of the Torah to every phase of life and generated a body of interpretation that, in time, became as binding as the Torah itself.

I have simplified the life of Jesus in order to present a fairly coherent view of him and his work. On the level of pure story this is quite possible—I have woven strands together to come up with a composite picture which is, itself, an interpretation. I think it is appropriate at this level to look at the life of Jesus in this way, but one should also do so with certain cautions. Scholars argue about almost everything—which gospel was earliest, where the gospel writers got their material, how accurate they were, who their audiences were—and I have tried to spare you those arguments here. At the same time, I have to say that it is very hard to really reconstruct the life of Jesus. The Gospels are not biographies; they are theological interpretations that tell us more about what Jesus meant than what he actually did. How many of the words attributed to Jesus are actually his is disputed not only by scholars, but by Christians in general. Even the *geographical* details cannot be taken without further investigation—did Jesus have a mission in Galilee and then "go up to Jerusalem"? Most scholars are not quite sure about this. Luke's journey motif is brilliant and rich, but that does not make it historically precise.

This chapter, therefore, has given you a simplified version of the context for and life of Jesus, what I hope is a good beginning for your understanding. As you read more widely you will discover some of the nuances I have tried to allude to here.

CHAPTER 2 NOTES

1. The Hellenistic period began with the death of Alexander the Great (323 B.C.E.) and was a time when Greek ideas, culture, philosophy, manners, language, and art were extremely influential in the ancient world. The Jews were touched by Hellenistic civilization, as evidenced in the Bible by the so-called Wisdom literature.

2. Some groups of Jews did not believe this since it was not written in the Torah itself, and it is not altogether clear just how many Jews *did* believe that God would act in this way.

3. David Rhoads, *Israel in Revolution, 6–74 C.E.: A Political History Based on the Writings of Josephus* (Philadelphia: Fortress Press, 1976), pp. 32–46 discusses these groups within their political context.

4. Rhoads, p. 33.

5. See Cornelius Tacitus, *The Annals of Tacitus, Books One to Six*, edited with a commentary by R. R. D. Goodyear (Cambridge: Cambridge University Press, 1972), 15.44. For a look at "Jesus in Extrabiblical Sources," see Howard Kee, *Jesus in History: An Approach to the Study of the Gospels*, 2nd ed. (New York: Harcourt Brace Jovanovich, 1977), pp. 40–75.

6. Jesus's conduct towards women was simply extraordinary, especially when read against the background of Jewish practice and the place of women at the time. See

Joachim Jeremias, *Jerusalem in the Time of Jesus* (Philadelphia: Fortress Press, 1969), pp. 359–76.

7. One statement of this view can be found in Vernard Eller, *The Most Revealing Book of the Bible: Making Sense Out of Revelation* (Grand Rapids: Eerdmans, 1974).

SUGGESTIONS FOR FURTHER READING

1. For more on the context and Jewish background of Jesus consult Joachim Jeremias, *Jerusalem in the Time of Jesus* (Philadelphia: Fortress Press, 1969), and Marcel Simon, *Jewish Sects at the Time of Jesus* (Philadelphia: Fortress Press, 1967). Simon provides a good bibliography as well, pp. 163–68.

2. It is hard to choose any one book as a New Testament introduction, but Norman Perrin, *The New Testament, An Introduction: Proclamation and Parenesis, Myth and History,* 2nd ed. (New York: Harcourt Brace Jovanovich, 1982) is a good beginning. It is a textbook and therefore geared for students, clearly written and illustrated. See also Howard Kee et al., *Understanding the New Testament,* 3rd ed. (Englewood Cliffs, N.J.: Prentice-Hall, 1973).

3. Jesus has been interpreted in many ways over the last two thousand years. For an introduction to some of the different pictures of Jesus we can find in history see Hugh Anderson, editor, *Jesus* (Englewood Cliffs, N.J.: Prentice-Hall, 1967). It contains essays on Jesus, nineteenth century liberal views, existential understandings, scholarly reconstructions, and other essays.

4. For a condensed introduction to New Testament writings, one which provides a good introduction without oversimplifying things, see Günther Bornkamm, *The New Testament: A Guide to Its Writings* (Philadelphia: Fortress Press, 1973).

CHAPTER 3

The Emergence of the
Christian Church

C hristians interpreted the Bible as they did because they believed that Jesus
was the Messiah, a belief supported by their experience of Jesus as risen
from the dead. Christians today sometimes think the apostles saw the risen
Jesus, obtained a blueprint from him, and proceeded in happy agreement to
construct the Christian church. The truth is that members of the early Christian
community disagreed and misunderstood each other. They were no more compatible than any other group, no less immune to argument, no more peaceful.

The early Christian community began with the energizing belief that God's
spirit had been sent to them in Jesus, and the first believers were enthusiastic,
eager to share their good news. While they were unified in their belief in Jesus,
they were divided over other issues. This chapter discusses some of those issues
and also introduces some of the complex questions Christians had to face as they
encountered other religions, incredulous reactions, and persecution.

THE EXPERIENCE OF THE APOSTLES

According to the Acts of the Apostles, Jesus, after he was raised from the
dead, stayed on earth for forty days and then ascended into the heavens (1:1–
12). We can speculate that the apostles were overjoyed about the Resurrection
but, at the same time, were mystified about what it really meant. They were

convinced that Jesus had risen from the dead—they had heard about it, seen him, eaten with him, touched him—but they were not sure what the implications of that experience were. What did the Resurrection mean, for example, for their behavior? What were they now to *do*? Relate this for a minute to some biblical stories. Abraham believed that God had spoken to him, but he wasn't initially sure what that meant; God led him to understand it step by step. Moses believed he had had an encounter with the "God of Abraham, Isaac, and Jacob," but was appalled to find out that God wanted him to go back to Egypt and confront the powerful pharaoh there. The prophets, too, were sure about their encounter with God, but mystified or reluctant about what that meant for their mission. So, too, with the experience of the risen Lord. The apostles believed it, experienced it as a miracle of prodigious proportions, but were also stunned by it. Even after the Resurrection, there was not such clarity that there were no questions, and not such charity that there were no arguments.

The experience of the Resurrection empowered human beings by God's spirit (life) so that their lives were changed. Not all New Testament writings agree on exactly what that meant. The Acts of the Apostles talks about the role of the Holy Spirit a great deal, by means of a narrative recounting of the church's beginnings. It is clear that things are idealized considerably. We suspect, for example, that the first believers were not so completely united as Luke suggests (see Acts 5:1–5). But the story does help us to see how the history of the Christian movement was seen as a continuation of the story of Israel, precisely because the same Holy Spirit was at work in both.

The Old Testament tells us that the Spirit was sent to people who had a special mission (prophets and judges for example), but was to be poured out on all people in the final age. The prophet Joel states an especially clear prophecy about the Spirit: "And it shall come to pass, afterward, that I will pour out my spirit on all flesh; your sons and your daughters shall prophesy, your old men shall dream dreams, and your young men shall see visions" (Joel 2:28). The coming of the Spirit to the apostles, therefore, is set within the context of God's promises about the last days. Throughout Acts one can see how the power of the Spirit is interpreted. The Spirit is the driving force behind the proclamation of the gospel, the agent who brings about conversion and faith in Jesus as the Christ; the Spirit strengthens people and helps them endure persecution, guides the early missionary efforts—especially those of Paul—and inspires the Gentile mission. Through the Spirit's work the loose group of early believers begins to form the Christian church.

The story of the coming of the Spirit to the apostles is found in Acts 2. Just looking at the story, we are struck by certain things. Notice that the Spirit came to the apostles on the Jewish festival of Weeks, Shebu'ot, also known as *Pentecost*. This feast commemorates and celebrates the giving of the Law at Sinai. The New Testament account is written to stress this parallel. It has the sense of something new happening, something that can replace or go beyond the old way (the old covenant).

The outline of the story is this: the apostles were gathered together in one place and were confused and frightened. All of a sudden they heard a sound like a mighty wind (in Greek the word *pneuma* means both spirit and wind) which filled the house, and tongues of fire hovered over the head of each of them. God's appearances in the Bible are often accompanied by wind and fire; the New Testament account, therefore, is surely meant to convey that the apostles experienced the presence of God in wind and fire. The apostles were filled with the Holy Spirit and began to speak not according to their own designs, but as the Spirit directed them. They spoke in languages they did not know, and visitors to Jerusalem from all over the Middle East heard them speaking about the mighty works of God.

After they received the Spirit, the apostles spoke to the crowd. The most famous speech was delivered by Peter, who quoted Joel's words about the pouring out of the Spirit and ended by saying, "And it shall be that whoever calls on the name of the Lord shall be saved" (Acts 2:21). Notice the word *whoever:* not just Jews, but all who call upon the name of the Lord will be saved. This is a radically new idea and one, the author suggests, that the Spirit gave to Peter. The apostles are supposed to go beyond the terms of the covenant at Sinai and extend the saving message of Jesus to everyone. The Acts of the Apostles is a partisan record of this extension.

After that startling statement, Peter told his audience the story of Jesus, especially how he was crucified but had been raised up from the dead. Imagine the impact of a statement like this! Some listeners thought the apostles were drunk or crazy; others were moved and asked what they should do. Peter told them to repent (to change their direction, to turn toward God by following Jesus) and to be baptized. According to the Pentecost story in Acts, three thousand people were baptized that day.

Acts 2 summarizes the enthusiasm characteristic of the early Christian community, but it also gives the impression that it was united in mind and heart from the beginning. The account in Acts implies that the coming of the Holy Spirit clarified the meaning of Jesus's words and life. It is historically naive to think this was the case. The New Testament says the apostles were enlightened, had an experience of the risen Lord, received the Holy Spirit, and were filled with a desire to carry the saving message of Jesus to others. Acts presents Pentecost as the inauguration of a truly universal preaching about Jesus that ultimately transcended all boundaries of nationality, speech, and religion. That universalist understanding about Jesus, however, was not something clearly evident at the outset. The argument about who should hear the gospel was the most serious controversy in the young community.

CONFLICTS IN THE EARLY CHURCH

A popular picture of earliest Christianity is that it began in perfect uniformity and split into groups. A better picture is that it began with *variety,* and only in the course of generations came to an explicit sense of *unity*. Some deep issues caused conflict among the first believers, and only time and the accidents of history brought them to a shared view.

Four general questions arose within the early community:

1. Who can hear the gospel? (universality)
2. Who is in charge? (authority and doctrine)
3. What does it mean to be free? (law and freedom)
4. Where can the words of and stories about Jesus be found? (formation of the New Testament)

Because these questions caused conflicts, a principle emerged that came to be used as a norm against which to measure everything. That principle was *apostolicity:* when people wanted to know if a writing was reliable, if the right person was in authority, and so on, they asked whether it was apostolic, clearly connected with the work and intentions of the apostles. Understanding the conflicts is essential to understanding the principle, which developed along with the community.

Universality of the Gospel

For whom was the gospel intended? Did Jesus offer his message for everyone or just for Jews? There is no single answer to this question in the Gospels themselves because the Gospels reflect, in part, the life of the early community, which was divided on this question. So in the Gospels sometimes it seems as if Jesus has come only to preach to the Jews (Matt. 10:5–7), and other times his words seem intended for all who believe (Matt. 28:19). Jesus, remember, was Jewish and so were his apostles; his life and mission were interpreted in the light of Jewish prophecies and expectations. It was logical to assume—as some did—that the message of Jesus was intended only for the Jews. Yet the account of Penetecost in Acts includes "all who call upon the name of the Lord." That statement represents a position adopted by the early community only after a severe struggle.

A particularly vivid account of this argument is found in the Epistle to the Galatians (chapters 1 and 2) where Paul recounts his own growth in understanding. He began, he tells his readers, hating Christians and persecuting them precisely because he was "so extremely zealous for the traditions of my fathers" (1:14). God called him, converted him and made it clear that he was to "preach among the Gentiles" (1:16). He was asked by God to do an extremely difficult task, namely to abandon his background, training, and beliefs to set out on a daring new path. He did not do so without approval from the rest of the community, and Galatians tells the story of his approval by the Jerusalem community, especially by Peter (who was preaching to the Jews). Peter himself, however, was not free from ambivalent feelings on this issue. He welcomed Paul's approach in Jerusalem but on a visit to Antioch, he reverted to an anti-

Gentile position (Gal. 2:11–17) and was confronted by Paul. The early community made no attempt to hide the fact that they argued over this issue, and we should remember the arguments as we read those stories that make the concept of a universal mission seem much more smooth.

In Acts, for example, one finds the story of Philip going to Samaria and bringing about a remarkable conversion there (chapter 6). Most Jews regarded the Samaritans as heretics and enemies,[1] yet, according to the story, the Samaritans received the word of the Lord eagerly and were converted. The author's point is that the power of God's word and the Spirit are not put off by heresy— this Spirit can work in any situation. Later in Acts there is an even more dramatic story. Peter was preaching, for the most part, to Jews, but one day received a message from a Roman soldier, Cornelius, inviting him to dinner. It is hard for us, perhaps, to grasp the impact of the invitation. Jewish dietary regulations were considered to be part of God's will. The terms of the covenant forbade Jews to eat certain foods and to eat with non-Jews, a Jew could not eat dinner in a Roman house, therefore, without being in serious violation of divine law. What was Peter to do? In Acts (chapter 10) the author takes the question out of Peter's hands and says that the Spirit instructed Peter to go, that he did go, ate, preached to Cornelius, and saw that "God shows no partiality . . . the Spirit has been poured out even on the Gentiles" (11:34 and 11:44).

The stories in Acts make the decision to pursue a universal mission look much easier than it was because Acts was written after the fact and from a perspective that favored universality. The climax to this question occurs in Acts 15 when some members of the Jerusalem community said, "Unless you are circumcised according to Moses, you cannot be saved" (15:1). In other words, the message of Jesus could be extended, but only through Judaism. In order for one to be a Christian, one had first to be Jewish, to be circumcised, and to follow the Law of Moses. This position of the so-called Judaizers precipitated a clash, and an important meeting was held in Jerusalem to resolve the issue. When all sides had been heard, they deliberated and decided that the gospel was to be extended freely to all and that one did not have to become Jewish in order to become a Christian. In the letter written to different Christian communities about this meeting, the leaders assembled in Jerusalem used a very telling phrase. Describing the process of decision making they said, "It seemed good to the Holy Spirit and to us. . . ." The implications of that statement are large: the young community considered itself to be in *partnership* with the Spirit. They decided this important matter together and would decide future matters together.

This assertion about the presence and guidance of the Holy Spirit is a fundamental principle within Christianity. God is continually present to Christians by way of the Holy Spirit, who resides in the church. The continual presence of the Spirit keeps the church alive and faithful to God's commands and leads it to deeper understandings. Christians agree about the importance of the Spirit in the church but, as we shall see, they disagree intensely about where the Spirit resides, how it is experienced, and what its powers are. For now, it is enough to see that the early church resolved the issue of a universal mission and, in the process, established the principle of the abiding and guiding presence of the Spirit in the church.

Authority and Doctrine

The Christian church, as you can imagine, grew increasingly complex as it grew in numbers and extended itself to a wide range of cultures and peoples. All religions are, to some extent, shaped by the cultural milieu in which they thrive; Christianity in Syria was different from Christianity in Rome and from Christianity in Egypt or Palestine. Questions arose about behavior and practice. How should the Lord's Supper be practiced? Who may participate? Must one practice perpetual virginity after baptism? How is the forgiveness of sins to be practiced? How is discipline to be maintained? What prayer forms are appropriate? Which stories about Jesus are trustworthy? To complicate the situation, Christianity arose at a time when many different religions were practiced and in an environment where interchange and cross-fertilization were inevitable.[2]

Should the Christian community be seen as an organization needing officers, or as a community of believers trusting the guidance of the Spirit and willing to attempt consensual decision making? Both views were present in the early church and continue to be present in the modern Christian church. Some think Christians should form themselves into small, manageable groups of believers who are "of one heart and soul" (Acts 4:32). Others believe that the church needs an organizational model with certain people in charge and streamlined, hierarchical methods of decision making.

Structures of authority grew along with the church: they were not there from the beginning, nor was it immediately clear that such structures were needed.[3] In Paul's first letter to the Thessalonians, there is no mention of church leaders. Yet, in the Acts of the Apostles, we find not only leaders, but several kinds with different functions—elders and deacons, for example. Paul's farewell address to the elders at Ephesus (as reported in Acts) is a handing on of his authority, and pictures Paul as an authority figure. By the time the pastoral Epistles were written (two letters to Timothy and one to Titus) we find a strong, directive interest in church administration. These letters were not written by Paul—scholars are nearly unanimous in their agreement about this point—and so do not show a development in Paul himself; but they do show a development within the early community. The first letter to Timothy not only mentions bishops, but also lays down qualifications for them (3:1–7) and suggests some regulations for worship (2:1–15); the letter to Titus also specifies qualifications for bishops and elders. Christian literature not included in the New Testament—the Didache, for example, or the Apostolic Constitutions—is primarily devoted to administrative matters and questions of true teaching and practice.

As the church developed, a certain organizational model eventually emerged as the dominant one. Officers (bishops) were elected by congregations to teach and to supervise. You can imagine that as long as a particular community remained fairly homogeneous, few problems arose. Once the Christian church began to attract large numbers of new members from all classes and occupations, however, controversies and questions arose on every conceivable issue. We can see already in Paul's letter to the Corinthians that Christians had to *learn* how to celebrate the Lord's Supper properly (chapter 11), and that is an early letter. Imagine the complex problems that would arise in a church that had communities throughout the ancient world, and members who were from all social and economic classes, with different educational and religious backgrounds.

Questions arose at all levels. Within the structure of the church there were questions of discipline (what to do if someone violated a commandment), of jurisdiction (whether priests from one place could work in another without the permission of the local bishop), membership (whether a soldier could be a Christian without resigning from the army), and doctrine (whether Jesus was truly the son of God), to name a few. Sometimes questions were handled locally within the church or within the district, but as time went on and as questions grew more complex, church leaders from a large region met to discuss them. In later centuries (beginning at 325 C.E. at Nicaea) worldwide meetings (or councils) were held to decide important matters of doctrine and practice.[4]

Little by little the ancient equivalent of a corporate flow chart emerged within the Christian church. In terms of regional organization, the church owed some debts to Roman imperial structures which, after all, had enhanced the smooth administration of a massive empire. In terms of teaching and moral authority, the bishops, individually or collectively, came to decide things. In matters that involved the entire Christian world—especially matters of doctrine—all the bishops of the world gathered to debate, reflect, and decide. In their decision-making process they were conscious of the partnership they had with the Spirit, so their decisions were considered to be extensions and refinements of divine will.

Law and Freedom in the Spirit

The apostle Paul preached a gospel of freedom and believed that God had given him the authority to do so. "It is no longer I who live," he said, "but Christ who lives in me" (Gal. 2:20). As a serious young Jew, Paul knew the Law and upheld it; as a Christian, converted by God to preach to the Gentiles (Acts 9) he was constrained to explain, from many different perspectives, the relation between the Law and the gospel. One gets some sense of the brilliance with which he held these two concepts together in his Epistle to the Romans: in chapter 7 he discusses the Law and its place in Christian life, and in chapter 8 he discusses life in the Spirit.

Paul's claim that his authority was God-given rested on two things: his vision of the risen Christ and his style of servant leadership (following Jesus's model). On his missionary journeys he founded churches and he thought of himself as a nurturing parent (1 Thess. 2:7, "like a nurse"; 2:11, "like a father") to those congregations. He was loath to build a superstructure of rules or legal authority but not at all afraid to give his opinions about specific questions. Some groups in Christian history point to their reading of the early Pauline model precisely to argue for Christian freedom. Some Christians see Pauline congregations as congregations in which the chief presiding officer was Christ and his Spirit, not priests or bishops or even Paul. He told communities they were called to freedom (Gal. 5:13), but a freedom that did not lie in doing whatever one pleases. The freedom of the gospel is the freedom to love one another, to be servants, to be solicitous for each other's needs. Care for one another does not mean slavery; rather people are called to "freedom in the Spirit," freedom from the old law, freedom from attempts to domineer over other people's faith, freedom to support one another.[5]

Paul did not create a new norm, but saw Christ as a new standard. He exhorted people to live in communities of freedom and to be faithful, to "be imitators of me as I am of Christ" (1 Cor. 11:1). The ancient moral commandments are not up for discussion—they hold; yet, in Romans 10:4 he says that Christ is the end of the Law. The new law of Christ is Paul's gospel of freedom.

Formation of the New Testament

One problem the early community faced, especially as it expanded into the Hellenistic world, concerned the place of the writings that were later to be known as the New Testament. During the first two centuries of the Christian movement, the preaching of Jesus and stories about him were recorded and circulated to Christian congregations, accepted in these congregations in some forms and not in others, regarded first as an interpretive key to the Hebrew Bible, regarded later as a book with religious authority of its own, and eventually regarded as inspired and as the word of God.

The New Testament was written down and its form fixed because people had serious questions about doctrine, practice, and worship and needed a consistent, universal guidance. The books of the New Testament came to be regarded as norms in these matters. The problem was complex because many books were written about Jesus within the Christian movement:[6] there were stories of what Jesus was like as a little boy, what his mother was like, how he grew up, what Joseph thought about Jesus. Some books demanded rigorous asceticism for all Christians, arguing that all should abstain from sex, alcohol, and dancing; some writers claimed that because Christians were free, they could not sin and could therefore live licentiously. There were treatises on the Second Coming of the Lord with all the signs of the times; some books dealt with points of doctrine, arguing that Jesus was or was not God, was or was not a man, did or did not die, rise, ascend to heaven, and so forth. How was it possible to make a selection from all this literature? By what criterion could some books be selected as inspired and some rejected? Why does the New Testament contain the Gospel of Matthew and not the Gospel of Thomas?

In the early church the norm that developed and prevailed from the selection of New Testament books was *apostolicity,* as mentioned earlier. Had a particular book been handed down from the apostolic church, and was it attributed to an apostle or a disciple? Did it reflect the mind and practice of the apostolic church and did it have the capacity for continuing this mind and practice? This last question is an interpretive one: What *was* the "mind and practice of the apostlic church"? Was there just one? Who determined whether a book was a reflection of the apostolic church? These questions are not only ancient ones. Scholars today ask the same questions from contemporary perspectives and use developments like the formation of the New Testament to argue that the so-called apostolic tradition (as it has come down to Christians today) is *not* the authentic tradition of Jesus.[7]

These four conflicts were, by no means, the only ones to trouble early Christians, but they reflect some of the major arguments not only within the young Christian community but within Christian churches yet today. Christians do not wonder whether or not to extend the gospel to the Gentiles, but they do wonder how much they can adopt from non-Christian religions; they continue to differ about authority and doctrine, about the meaning and function of apostolicity,[8] and about the limits of Christian freedom. No one wants to add or subtract books from the New Testament canon—it took nearly four centuries to fix it—but there is some argument about the books that *were* left out at the time and an increasing interest in the variety of literature written during the early Christian period.[9]

THE CONTEXT OF THE EARLY COMMUNITY

The church in its first three centuries, from New Testament times to the reign of the first Christian emperor, Constantine (d. 337), grew from a small group of dedicated believers with no uniform structure to a worldwide movement with organized structures of management and established norms of behavior. As we have seen, early believers differed, sometimes radically, about practice and doctrine, and one can understand their differences from two perspectives: from looking at some of the early conflicts (as we have just done) or from looking at the context in which these and other conflicts were worked out.

The world of early Christianity was geographically large, religiously diverse, and culturally heterogeneous. In a variety of ways Christians had to learn to answer for themselves. How were they different from Jews? What did Christianity have in common with Judaism? How could their beliefs be reconciled with

Hellenistic philosophy: how could they explain Jesus to someone who read and loved Plato? How were they going to define their beliefs? And what relationship was there between doctrinal and practical matters: what kind of structure or teaching authority would work best? Why were Christians rigidly monotheistic? Why did they refuse to worship any other gods? How would they adapt to the rich and enticing variety of Roman religions?

No matter what cultural context they found themselves in, they had to address these and other questions. In this section I will discuss three different cultural contexts and three specific facets of Christian identity. Like all simplifying generalizations, this one is imperfect since much more was going on in each of these contexts than I can discuss here; but it is also useful to give a general sense of developing Christian identity. Christians developed their religious, philosophical, and political identity as they grew and interacted in the complex ancient world. Let us focus on their *religious* identity within the Jewish context, their *philosophical* identity within the Greek context, and their *political* identity within the Roman context.

The Jewish Context and Religious Identity

Christianity was born into a Jewish context and emerged from it with a separate religious identity. Early Christians did not think of themselves as separable from Judaism, but as a Jewish sect distinguished by their belief that Jesus was the Messiah. Their worship was modeled on Jewish services and their understanding of the mission of Jesus was derived from the Hebrew Bible. Christians believed Jesus had come to gather the Jews together in preparation for the final days; they voted to extend his saving act beyond the Jewish community.

What do you think a universalist position meant to Jewish Christians? Their position was determined to some extent by the political and religious situation, especially growing Roman antipathy and their own apocalyptic expectations. Because of political and religious tensions, Christianity's relationship to Judaism was precarious from the outset. The early Christian community in Jerusalem perceived itself as a temporary community living in the interim between the coming of the Messiah and the final coming of the kingdom of God, the end of the age. It is not clear that Jewish Christians welcomed the mission to the Gentiles, or saw much reason to set up enduring structures or policies.

The Jews were in a precarious political situation punctuated by periodic outbreaks of insurrection. Any rebellion could give the Romans the excuse they wanted for crushing the Jews, and from 66–70 c.e. there was an unprecedented revolt of the Jews against the Romans. It was one of the most savage wars in history: more than a million Jews were killed or sold into slavery. Since a large part of the early Christian community was Jewish, this war of national liberation presented a serious problem to the early church. Jewish Christians were caught between the demands of national identity and the words of the gospel. Full of apocalyptic expectation and reminded of the words of Jesus about the last days (Matt. 24:15–21), Jewish Christians felt obliged to flee the city, an action that made them traitors in the eyes of the Jews.

The fall of Jerusalem in 70 C.E. marked the end of any Jewish Christian hope to convert the Jews. In the minds of Gentile Christians it vindicated the decision for universality. Gentile Christians pointed to the fall of Jerusalem to argue that Jewish Christian apocalyptic hopes were false; later they claimed that the Jewish aspects of Christianity were unnecessary. Jewish Christians were homeless: they were not welcome in Judaism and not comfortable with a universalist Christianity. Accordingly, the Jewish Christian discussion of early Christianity diminished and the way was paved for a separate Christian church.

When the Sanhedrin was restored in Jerusalem (90 C.E.) many Jews wanted to condemn any Jew who had accepted Jesus and to rid Judaism of any trace of Christianity. Liturgical practices that had been in any way contaminated by Christian usage were changed; a formal curse against Christians was added to Jewish morning prayer. Christians were no longer able to associate with Jews.

The de facto and de jure segregation of the Jews from Christians gave the Christians a profound cultural shock. Christians regarded their faith as the extension of the covenant between God and Abraham; they believed they were part of the Jewish heritage even if they did not agree with Jewish cultural exclusivity. When the Jews severed connection with *them,* Christians were forced to rethink their position.

Christians made a variety of responses to their dilemma, as reflected in early Christian writings (see Appendix 3). In the heat of the controversy, some writers disparaged Judaism, arguing that it was worthless and unnecessary to Christianity. Christians made changes in the practical order to complete the severance: they celebrated the Lord's Day (the Sabbath) on Sunday instead of Saturday, and celebrated the Lord's Supper (Eucharist) every week instead of once a year (at Passover).

Christianity therefore developed an identity separate from Judaism; but it could never leave Judaism totally behind. Christians were indebted to Jews for liturgical consciousness and forms of worship, for a sense of roots, and for the Bible. Like Jews, Christians believe in one God, the Creator and Judge of the universe; like Jews, Christians accept providence, free will, and a history of salvation. Without the Hebrew Bible, Christians would have been unable to make sense of the life, death, and resurrection of Jesus.

The Greek Context and Philosophical Identity

Christianity matured in the Hellenistic world, the world of pagan philosophy and ideas. Since the Greek world respected philosophical sophistication, members of the early Christian community began to adapt themselves to the task of making Christian faith philosophically respectable.[10] In their encounters with Greek philosophy early Christian writers and scholars laid the philosophical foundations for what would later become an elaborate Christian theology.

The task was a difficult one because of internal and external opposition. Externally, Christian philosophers had to learn to talk to people who had just freed their understanding of the divine from a mythological tradition: when Christians arrived on the scene talking about the Son of God, Greek philosophers thought they were dealing with a backward people. Internally, there were problems of definition and interpretation: What did it mean to be free from the Law, or to be free in the Lord? Some people thought they were bound by no laws and could, in effect, be a law unto themselves; others felt free to pick and choose parts of the Bible or parts of Jesus's teaching to suit their own particular philosophical interpretation. Some people thought they were saved by faith; Gnostics thought they were saved by *knowledge* (Greek, *gnosis* = knowledge) and developed elaborate systems of secret knowledge, passwords, and esoteric doctrine.

In an effort to define orthodox Christian views *and* to make their beliefs understandable to a philosophically sophisticated audience, early Christian writers borrowed some of the philosophical ideas of the time and attempted to present a systematic Christianity. Justin Martyr (100–165 C.E.) arranged the sayings of the gospel under the headings of "self-control," "universal love," and "being blameless." Theophilus of Antioch (late second century), did much the same thing, adding insights from the Ten Commandments. Once they had a set of Christian maxims, writers could combine them with Greek philosophical ideas about spiritual perfection through the cultivation of the soul. Clement of Alexandria (d. 215 C.E.) and Origen (185–254 C.E.) interpreted the Christian life as one beginning in faith and ending with a real likeness to God; they tried to synthesize philosophical Christianity and Neoplatonic philosophy.[11]

Christian philosophers were relating to the outside world effectively, but there were other pressing matters; internal problems plagued the Christian church. Early Christian writers wrote philosophical works; they also wrote treatises on behavior, decorum, and Christian practice. Originally, members of a local church handled problems of belief and discipline in that congregation. In the second and third centuries, however, bishops began to exercise their power and authority more strongly. The Christian church became larger and more complex; the bishops believed that the church needed centralized authority, which rested in the office and administrative power of the bishop. With authority to judge doctrinal matters, bishops believed they could protect people from dangerous doctrines and practices. Accordingly, the early church moved slowly but surely toward a monarchical episcopacy; the bishop was like a king, a man with high authority who could decide (by himself or in consultation with other bishops) whether a certain position was right or wrong.

In the context of the Hellenistic world, then, Christianity developed a structure for handling problems. The office of the bishop and the authority of the bishops culminated in a series of meetings called councils (see Appendix 4) where Christian doctrine was defined and Christian practice regulated. Philosophically, the church adopted new vocabulary and ideas. Christian philosophy and apologetics (explaining Christianity to a potentially hostile audience) was the work of theologians and was central to the church's development in both East and West.

The Roman Context and Political Identity

Christianity was born into a Jewish religious context and learned how to negotiate in a Hellenistic philosophical environment, but the real rulers of the world into which Christianity emerged were the Romans. At the beginning of the second century, the Roman Empire stretched from Mesopotamia to Scotland, from the Danube to the Sahara Desert. Within this area lived many peoples with different cultures and world views. The Roman Empire was one of the most highly organized, well-ruled, sophisticated civilizations the world has ever seen. Two languages dominated: Latin in the West and Greek in the East. The emperor, an absolute ruler with pretensions to divinity, stood at the top of this large edifice.

The ideals of human decency (called *philanthropeia* in Greek, *humanitas* in Latin) and universal brotherhood were supported by the power and uniformity of Roman law. The empire was not without problems: huge slave populations, horrible slums, and terrible poverty existed side by side with Roman elegance. In addition to social ills there were serious political problems. Lack of a peaceful way to choose a successor to the emperor caused periodic anarchy and instability; a nonindustrial base caused gold drainage and severe inflation; a farm crisis and decimating plagues undermined the empire; and the army was mercenary rather than comprised of Roman citizens. The political reforms of Diocletian (in the third century) helped to ease some of these situations, but the real reform came in the fourth century with the emperor Constantine, who chose to favor Christianity over all the other religions in the empire.

Roman religion, an amalgam of various cults throughout the empire, was often more concerned with form and rite than with spiritual teaching; in some ways their religion focused more on devotional practices than on inner experience. As the empire expanded, the mystery religions of the Mediterranean people gained influence precisely because they emphasized internal aspects of religion: a savior-God, mysterious rites (sacraments—*sacramentum* is the Latin translation of the Greek word *mysterion*), intimacy, and emotional response. The spiritual side of Roman religion was shaped by outside influences, by the beliefs and practices of conquered peoples. The most important outside influences were Stoicism, Epicureanism, Mithraism, the mystery religions, and Christianity.

Stoicism and Epicureanism, philosophical systems developed in the Greek world, both rested on a theory of human perfectibility. Epicureans thought that everything hung on *fate,* and since there was no given order in the universe, they advocated the freedom to pick and choose the very best things in life. Stoics, on the other hand, believed in an ordered universe, a cosmic intelligence or world soul that permeated the universe and made it possible for people to attain perfect freedom by living in total harmony with reason. Stoics are sometimes pictured in our minds as withstanding pain and refusing to admit their feelings or fears. They *did* attempt to control their passions by living fully in accord with reason, but a more accurate picture of them would show them trying to get in touch with the universe, feel its vibrations, resonate with its harmonies. Both these attitudes continue to appeal to people today (though not, perhaps, in their pure philosophical form) and you can imagine that they appealed to the Romans as well.

The mystery cults were an entirely different matter and appealed on a more experiential level. Through their mysterious rites they not only offered a way to an emotional religious experience, they offered immortality: if one believed in the savior-God and followed the mysteries, one could live forever. The fertility cult of Cybele celebrated its feasts orgiastically; the Egyptian cult of Isis had magical initial rites including a ceremony of death and rebirth. The most important mystery religion for the Romans was probably Mithraism, a dualistic system that may have developed in Persia. Dualism divides the world into two parts, good and evil, and the followers of Mithraism believed that there were powers of light and powers of darkness at work in the universe. What one hoped to do, through religious rites, was to get in touch with the powers of light and withstand the powers of darkness.

Christianity developed in the Roman Empire on the heels of these other religions and philosophical systems and learned to adapt some of the best parts of them to its own belief system. In some ways of looking at it, Christianity did not have to prepare its own ground, but was able to grow in the soil prepared by others. Hellenized Judaism in Alexandria brought a consciousness of monotheism to the empire and provided it with a Greek translation of the Bible. Stoicism, with its concept of universal brotherhood, prepared the Romans for a universalism unknown in other religious circles. Neoplatonism, with its quest for ultimate perfection and mystical awareness of the divine, introduced an aspect of spiritual exaltation. The mystery religions were especially important: they had emotional appeal, a concept that everyone could be saved, a savior-God who died and was reborn, and a sacramental rite that brought believers immortality by association with the sufferings and eventual triumph of God.

Christianity knew how to adapt itself, where to borrow and how to shape its message into the atmosphere of the times. It was universalist and aimed (in some quarters) at ultimate perfection through mystical union. Baptism and the Lord's Supper developed into sacramental rites, with ceremony and emotional appeal. Christianity was ancient because it was rooted in the Hebrew Bible: it could trace itself back to the creation of the world and the first inklings of a divine-human partnership. Most of all, however, Christians offered a savior-God who was historically concrete. According to Christians, Jesus was not a mythic savior but a real person, a man who had lived and died on earth and in history (*not* "once upon a time"), one who talked and suffered in the sight of others, who died publicly and rose again where people could see and touch him. Christianity endured longer than these other religions and was eventually declared the official religion of the empire. In the second and third centuries few people could have predicted the *survival* of the Christian religion, let alone its rise to a position of favoritism. In order to understand how phenomenal the rise of Christianity was, we must look back at the first three hundred years of its life when the Christian church was persecuted.

The Romans were essentially tolerant of different religions, yet their policy towards Christians in various parts of the empire was one of periodic but severe persecution. Christians were strict monotheists who refused to recognize the Roman gods; in times when *everyone* in the empire was supposed to make some sacrifice to the gods—to insure victory or forestall harm—Christians refused to offer sacrifice. Christians also refused to worship the emperor. Instead they held their own unauthorized gatherings on the Lord's Day, and were regarded with suspicion both by the Roman populace and the authorities. Christians were sometimes killed or tortured by officers of the state. Why? Some Romans believed that Christians subverted good order and that they ought to attempt to eliminate Christianity by killing its bishops and burning its books.

Christians responded in different ways to persecution. Some witnessed to the truth of their beliefs by suffering and dying and are remembered as martyrs (the Greek word *martus* means witness); others endured torture and were honored as confessors. (They confessed their Christian faith and were tortured but not killed for doing so.) Another group escaped persecution either by denying their beliefs or finding some loophole in the law that allowed them to avoid a confrontation. When these people are remembered at all—many people believe the persecutions only produced heroes—they are recalled as the *lapsi*, people who lapsed from their religion. Because of the martyrs the Christian church developed a cult and theology of martyrdom: their deaths were interpreted as heroic imitations of the passion and death of Jesus; the martyr was the true disciple who followed Jesus even into death at the hands of the state. Because of the *lapsi* the Christian church was challenged to a more systematic administration of the sacrament of reconciliation or penance.

In the Roman context, therefore, Christians had sufficient freedom to adapt a variety of religious ideas and practices to their own beliefs, but they also suffered persecution because their religious stance put them at odds with the empire. Their survival convinced them, even more, of their special mission to the world.

CONCLUSION

The early Christian community was small, adapted to new situations, was courageous in the face of death, and was agile in adopting new solutions to problems. Despite differences, a catholic consensus about doctrine and discipline was growing. Ancient ecclesiastical functions and early models of church structure—a bishop, a board of elders, and a college of deacons—eventually gave way to a monarchical episcopacy. By the beginning of the fourth century the small group of believers had become a large body with members in all parts of the Roman Empire and beyond its bounds; it was universal in outlook, well organized, and theologically complex. Christians developed methods of discipline, a growing philosophical literature, and political autonomy. Early in the fourth century Christians comprised probably less than 10 percent of the Latin-speaking population of the West and not more than 35 percent of the Greek-speaking East. But with the support of the state, its ascendency as the dominant religion of the Roman Empire was assured, and Christianity became the universal religion of the Mediterranean.

As Christianity moved into a more complex world and spread, the challenges and problems presented to it by new cultures and religions increased. Christians in New Testament times thought the world would end soon; after that many had a negative view of the world, regarding it as presenting a strong temptation to sin. By the end of the third century Christians had a more positive response to the world; they had learned to live with it, to adapt to it, and, to a great extent, were ready to conquer it.

CHAPTER 3 NOTES

1. According to Joachim Jeremias, *Jerusalem in the Time of Jesus* (Philadelphia: Fortress Press, 1969), p. 352, Samaritans were considered "the lowest degree of the scale" and a group with whom the Jews had a particularly embittered relationship during the time of Jesus.

2. For a readable and informative essay about the effect of a cultural milieu, read Stephen Benko and John J. O'Rourke, editors, *The Catacombs and the Colosseum: The Roman Empire as the Setting of Primitive Christianity* (Valley Forge, Pa.: Judson Press, 1971).

3. Roman Catholics argue that the structures were not only needed, but that Jesus instituted them by making Peter the first among the apostles. For an ecumenical and contemporary discussion of the place of Peter and the claims for a papal church, see Raymond Brown et al., *Peter in the New Testament: A Collaborative Assessment by Protestant and Roman Catholic Scholars* (Minneapolis: Augsburg Press, 1973). For a more dated but engagingly written and useful assessment, see Oscar Cullman, *Peter, Disciple, Apostle and Martyr: A Historical and Theological Essay* (New York: Meridian Books, 1958).

4. See Appendix 4 on councils, and look at Jaroslav Pelikan, *The Christian Tradition: A History of the Development of Doctrine—The Emergence of the Catholic Tradition (100-600)* (Chicago: University of Chicago Press, 1971). This book is hard to read, but you might leaf through it to get some sense of the complexities involved.

5. For a theological approach to Paul, see Joseph A. Fitzmyer, *Pauline Theology: A Brief Sketch* (Englewood Cliffs, N.J.: Prentice-Hall, 1967). This is a short, compact book

that you may need some introduction to, but that outlines an interpretation of Pauline theology in a fairly accessible way.

6. Look through some apocryphal books in Edgar Hennecke and Wilhelm Schneemelcher, editors, *New Testament Apocrypha,* two volumes (Philadelphia: Westminster Press, 1963).

7. See, for example, Elisabeth Schüssler-Fiorenza, "Sexism and Conversion," *Network* 9 (1981), pp. 15–22.

8. Roman Catholics use *apostolic* to describe something identified with the church of the apostles by succession and continuity of doctrine; Protestants use it to mean primitive in contrast with real or supposed corruptions from postapostolic times. For both groups the notion of apostolicity is a key concept in defining authority and in defining authentic ministry within the church. The phrase *apostolic succession* provides a foundation for Christian ministry and refers to the derivation of Christian ministry from the apostles by way of continuous succession. Bishops, in this perspective, are held to be the successors of the apostles; that is, they perform the function of the apostles and can trace their ministry back to that of the apostles. The fact of continuity has been disputed within Christianity and the necessity of physical continuity has been denied by most of Protestant Christianity. Roman Catholics believe they can trace the office of the bishop of Rome—the pope—back to Peter in an unbroken line, and that such a continuity of succession confirms their claim to be the true church. This understanding of Roman Catholicism has been modified somewhat since the Second Vatican Council (1962–65), but not so much in official documents. For a more subtle understanding of the Catholic position see Richard McBrien, *Catholicism* (Minneapolis: Winston Press, 1980), pp. 657–729.

9. See, for instance, Elaine Pagels, *The Gnostic Gospels* (New York: Random House, 1979), for a survey of some of the more interesting issues raised by Gnostic literature of the period.

10. We can see some attempts at this kind of adaptation already in the Acts of the Apostles, in Paul's speech to the Athenians (17:16–34).

11. It is worth looking Neoplatonism up in an encyclopedia and following some of the leads it gives you—the whole tradition of divinization (human beings becoming divine) has its roots there. For a modern interpretation of a medieval expression of this doctrine see Matthew Fox, *Breakthrough: Meister Eckhart's Creation Spirituality in a New Translation* (New York: Doubleday, 1980).

SUGGESTIONS FOR FURTHER READING

1. For more on the development of early Christian literature, see Henry Bettenson, editor, *The Early Christian Fathers* (Oxford: Oxford University Press, 1969) and *The Later Christian Fathers* (Oxford: Oxford University Press, 1970), which together contain textual excerpts from the earliest times (Clement of Rome) to the sixth century. For a sketchy introduction to the "Fathers" see Patrick J. Hammell, *Handbook of Patrology* (New York: Alba House, 1968). For a clear and readable introduction to major issues and figures see G. L. Prestige, *Fathers and Heretics: Six Studies in Dogmatic Faith with Prologue and Epilogue* (London: S.P.C.K., 1940).

2. For a deeper understanding of Christianity as it developed from earliest times see (for a *general* history) Henry Chadwick, *The Early Church* (London: Penguin Books,

1967); (for a *sociology* of early Christianity) Abraham J. Malherbe, *Social Aspects of Early Christianity* (Baton Rouge: Louisiana State University Press, 1977); and (for a critical evaluation arguing that there was never a golden age and that Jesus was a radical), Robert L. Wilken, *The Myth of Christian Beginnings: History's Impact on Belief* (New York: Doubleday, 1971).

3. For an introduction to Gnosticism see Hans Jonas, *The Gnostic Religion: The Message of the Alien God and the Beginnings of Christianity* (Boston: Beacon Press, 1963), a survey of literature and beliefs, not easy to read, but very good. Or, for an introduction, see Robert M. Grant, *Gnosticism and Early Christianity* (New York: Harper & Row, 1966).

4. For a clear and detailed analysis of martyrdom see W. H. C. Frend, *Martyrdom and Persecution in the Early Church: A Study of a Conflict from the Maccabees to Donatus* (New York: Doubleday, 1967).

5. For the intersection of Christianity and the classical tradition see Henry Chadwick, *Early Christian Thought and the Classical Tradition: Studies in Justin, Clement and Origen* (Oxford: Clarendon Press, 1966), which contains clear, witty lectures on Alexandrian Christianity. A classic that explains the impact and attraction of Christianity in the classical world is A. D. Nock, *Conversion: The Old and the New in Religion from Alexander the Great to Augustine of Hippo* (Oxford: Oxford University Press, 1969).

6. For more on the relationship between Christianity and the Roman world see Robert M. Grant, *Augustus to Constantine: The Thrust of the Christian Movement into the Roman World* (New York: Harper & Row, 1970), an extremely readable and clear history of the issue. For a discussion of Christianity as a small sect that eventually triumphed in the West, one that is straightforward and contains pictures and maps, see R. A. Markus, *Christianity in the Roman Empire* (London: Thames & Hudson Ltd., 1974).

7. Some recent works take seriously the *urban* character of many early Christian communities. See for example Wayne A. Meeks and Robert Wilken, *Jews and Christians in Antioch in the First Four Centuries of the Common Era* (Missoula, Mont.: Scholars Press, 1978) or Gerd Theissen, *The Sociology of Early Palestinian Christianity* (Philadelphia: Fortress Press, 1979).

Historical Roots of Christian Diversity

T HE SECOND PART of this book introduces the variety of Christian belief and expression by focusing on the roots of Christian diversity. It is not meant to be a history of Christianity, but a general explanation for the major divisions—between Eastern and Western Christianity, Roman Catholicism and Protestantism, and among the various expressions of Christian belief that have grown up in the last one hundred years. Christians differ substantially in doctrine, practice, and ecclesiastical structures, and those differences all arose within specific historical contexts. The more serious arguments among Christians led to major divisions within Christianity itself and the formation of separate churches and denominations. These chapters explain those differences.

The first major rift in Christianity occurred between what are now called the Roman Catholic church and the Eastern Orthodox church. These groups grew up in different parts of the vast Roman Empire and, from the early fourth century especially, confronted radically different problems: Western Christians battled to survive while Eastern Christianity, protected by the state, hammered out the foundations for Christian doctrine (see Appendix 4). They developed different liturgical practices and patterns of ecclesiastical authority, and eventually separated into two distinct forms of Christianity.

The second major division occurred in the West during the Reformation. Reform attempts within and outside of the church led to the formation of several new forms of Christianity distinguishable from one another in terms of polity, belief, and practice. We will follow the Reformation itself and then watch the reforming spirit of the sixteenth century move through the seventeenth and eighteenth centuries. By the beginning of the nineteenth century there were many new varieties of Christianity.

The proliferation of new Christian groups has occurred, for the most part, in the New World (America) and we will concentrate on the American religious experience from the eighteenth to the twentieth centuries in the last chapter in this section. These chapters—all of them—cover an enormous range of history and development and have been written specifically to explain how and why there are so many different kinds of Christianity. Part Two should therefore not be read as a history of Christianity, but as an attempt to look at Christian controversy over the centuries and to explain how some of those controversies led to the formation of separate denominations.

CHAPTER 4

Orthodox Christianity and Roman Catholicism

T wo distinct forms of Christianity grew up in the eastern and western parts of the Roman Empire: Roman Catholicism in the West and Orthodox Christianity in the East. Orthodox Christians and Roman Catholics are the largest and most ancient Christian groups. They share central assumptions, but because they developed in radically different religious and political climates, they also have differences. Roman Catholic Christianity tends to be more legalistic in the structures of church life and in its approach to the sacraments; Orthodox Christianity is more mystical in its liturgical preoccupations, more concerned with inner spiritual content. It may even appear, as I once heard a colleague suggest, that the Roman Catholic church stresses Truth, Orthodox Christians stress Beauty, and Protestants stress Goodness; but such generalizations have limitations. Differences in perspective have shaped the way each group articulates doctrine and celebrates liturgy. One general example may make this difference more clear. Western Christianity explains that the word of God became flesh in order to save people from their sins; thus, Western Christians stress justification. Eastern Christianity explains that the word of God became flesh so that people could become like God; thus, Eastern Orthodox Christians stress deification.

My approach to the material in this chapter is somewhat different from my approach in later chapters and, perhaps, deserves some word of explanation. Because we will not *specifically* follow later developments in Orthodox Christianity, especially in relation to Roman Catholicism, I have put more into this chapter than one would expect in a purely historical discussion. Roman Catholicism and Orthodoxy, in contrast to Protestantism, put a premium on the development and canonization of tradition; both groups also have very strong roots in the monastic tradition. My discussion of these two phenomena are meant to give you some idea of the deep unity of ancient Christianity. At the same time, because these two groups developed in very different geographical and political situations, they became, for all their shared heritage, two quite distinct expressions of Christianity. Those differences, then, get worked out even in terms of worship. This chapter, therefore, does not simply describe a profound historical breach; it attempts to show some of the consequences of that break in terms of different structural and liturgical expressions.

POINTS OF CORRESPONDENCE

Belief in the authority of tradition distinguishes Roman Catholics and Orthodox Christians from other Christian groups. Both Roman Catholics and Orthodox Christians posit the need for a religious authority alongside the Bible based on postbiblical experience and practice. They share an ancient doctrinal system and have liturgical preoccupations that are accepted only in part (if at all) by other Christian denominations. Both also place a high value on monasticism and avowed religious life, institutions that have not been important in other Christian groups. We explore these points of similarity between the two churches first.

Tradition as a Religious Authority

In some Christian groups the Bible is the most important source of religious authority, but not the only one. Why? The Old and New Testaments were written in a particular place and time and their messages respond to the spiritual and psychological needs of the people to whom they were addressed. Since the written sources of Christianity were intended for a people in a historical situation that no longer wholly obtains, some groups believe the written words need to be continually studied and applied to new problems. This reinterpretation then forms a parallel source of religious authority: tradition.

The Bible and tradition are not opposed to one another. Tradition is the way the Bible is read and applied in the church, and almost all Christians see the need for it. A debate arises, however, over how much authority different groups invest in tradition. Not all Christians accept the dogmatic decrees of the early councils (see Appendix 4) as authentic interpretations of the gospel; and none but Roman Catholics accept the councils after the ninth century as an authentic expression of Christian tradition. As we shall see, Protestant reformers were especially critical of the Roman Catholic acceptance of traditions (like the claims of the papacy, or innovative explanations about the Lord's Supper) that (as they perceived it) had no roots in the New Testament at all.

Tradition is a specific interpretation of Scripture as elaborated within the Christian community and affirmed by the church. It is meant to be fluid, not fixed, and tension can result when a group shows a tendency to absolutize or canonize tradition. Originally tradition was meant to allow for new interpretations, but at certain points tradition itself appeared to be fixed and unmovable. The development of tradition is not meant to lead to an ecclesiastical fundamentalism, but to recognize the dynamic interplay between the concrete, fixed authority of Scripture and the fluid, developing authority of daily practice.

Tradition adds something new: it enlarges upon and gradually builds up the written words. Human ingenuity is a factor in the development of tradition because people often expand a concrete communication beyond its original scope. Tradition is built up slowly, almost imperceptibly, until it becomes authoritative and sometimes even supercedes the authority of Scripture. In Judaism the original revelation was contained in the Torah; the Prophets and the Writings were considered "only tradition." Much later, however, when the canon of the Hebrew Bible was established, these traditions had come to be considered inspired, worthy to be called Scripture. In Christianity, the original message of Jesus was contained in the early preaching—Jesus who was crucified has risen from the dead—and then written down in the synoptic Gospels. The stories recounting the words and deeds of Jesus were considered superior to the writings of Paul (written before the synoptics) and John (written after the synoptics); their writings were regarded as interpretations or commentaries, only part of the tradition. Yet when the canon of the New Testament was finally drawn up, many of these writings were accepted as the word of God and were placed in the New Testament.

The tradition included in Scripture is not the same as the tradition that has developed since then, the postbiblical collection of opinions, practices, and dogmatic definitions. Roman Catholics and Orthodox Christians dispute about some parts of the tradition—especially the authority of the pope—but they do not dispute about the principle of tradition; both see a need for an extrabiblical religious authority. For them Scripture without tradition lacks vitality, tradition without Scripture lacks foundation, and either one of them without observance and practice lacks credibility.

Monasticism East and West

One model of the Christian life portrayed in the New Testament is life in common: people shared work, prayer, and food; lived simply; and grew in fellowship. Another New Testament concept is the life of perfection. Jesus once said, "You, therefore, must be perfect, as your heavenly Father is perfect" (Matt. 5:48). Christian monasticism derives from these two concepts as they developed in a world where an ascetic ideal already existed. Greek philosophers used the word *asceticism* to describe a system of discipline intended to combat vice and enhance virtue. The word comes from the Greek word for training or exercise; ascetics are people who train themselves for virtue. In Christianity the words of Jesus about denying oneself, taking up one's cross, and following him (Mark 8:34) provide inspiration for Christian ascetic life: negative self-denial on the one hand and positive following of Jesus on the other. But what does it mean to deny self and follow Jesus? For some early Christians it meant living in anticipation of martyrdom, to others it meant living an ascetic life: being alert and watchful, praying and fasting, giving up earthly possessions, and turning away from pleasures of the flesh (food, drink, and sex). Those who chose asceticism were monks.

The life of perfection sought by monks cannot be lived "in the world." They must retire to faraway places removed from the cares and stresses of worldly life. The first people to withdraw from the world went to the desert; the Greek word for desert is the root of the word *hermit*. By the middle of the third century many hermits lived in deserts and caves in remote areas of Egypt and Syria. Monks differ from hermits in that they live not in isolation but in community, and follow a common rule; the first monastic communities formed when groups of hermits came together for safety or fellowship and then built a fence or wall around all of their hermitages. Later communities lived in monastic houses where monks slept, ate, and prayed under the same roof. Monastic life was open to both men (monks) and women (nuns). They spent their days in prayer and work, and lived under vows (solemn promises) of *poverty* (without private possessions or money), *chastity* (no sex), and *obedience* (to the will of the local superior). These vows are sometimes called the counsels of perfection, a phrase that indicates that those who follow them desire to live a life of religious perfection, in line with the command of Jesus (Matt. 5:48).

As the ascetic life flourished, some of the early Christian writers undergirded it with theoretical and theological support. In the third century, Clement of Alexandria and Origen both extolled asceticism and encouraged Christians to live pure and perfect lives. Because Clement and Origen lived and wrote in a Neoplatonic environment, they combined their interest in asceticism with the Neoplatonic concept of contemplation. Monasticism combined a desire for perfection (the ascetic life) with mystical ascent (the contemplative life). In the Eastern church, contemplation and mysticism were always the central preoccupations of monastic life, and Eastern monasticism has remained contemplative. Monastic life in the West was similar, but also developed a more active concept of religious community life: Western Christianity supported religious congregations and orders of friars and canons who lived under a semimonastic rule (life in common and specific vows) but followed specific active vocations in the church like preaching or teaching.

The church both East and West contained some extremists in the monastic life. In the West were Irish monks who put themselves out to sea in open boats with few provisions and no oars so they could see where God would send them.

They manifested an ascetic ideal—an individual pilgrimage to God embodied in a life of wandering—that was not commonly practiced. In the East were extravagant ascetics who spent many years on top of high pillars in one position in order to discipline the flesh and draw closer to God in attitudes of eternal prayer. In both East and West were some who thought the ascetic life required extreme penances: long fasts, the wearing of spiked chains close to the flesh, and so on. For the most part, however, monastic life was not extreme; it was community life lived under a sensible rule.

The Eastern church has had essentially one monastic rule and one monastic order. The rule is that of St. Basil the Great (330–379 c.e.) written in the middle of the fourth century. Subsequent monastic rules are so thoroughly based on Basil's that all monks in the Eastern church are in some sense Basilian monks. Basil stressed communal life in which people practice manual labor and obedience, prayer and work. Orthodox monasteries have never become great centers of learning or scholarship; they are places where people can dedicate themselves totally to prayer and contemplation. Eastern monasticism is much the same today as in its origins: monks still conform to the Rule of St. Basil and wear the same clothing; their life combines asceticism, mysticism, and discipline in search of a direct experience of God. The chief mystical experience is the vision of divine light: the monk tries to achieve union with God.

In the Roman church the Rule of St. Benedict has been the common rule of monastic life. Introduced in the sixth century, the Benedictine Rule was the first piece of Western monastic legislation developed for monks living in the politically unstable European situation. Benedict of Nursia (480–550 c.e.) stressed work and prayer, and monks were to bind themselves to a single monastery for life. Later there was a proliferation of rules for friars, canons, and religious congregations. According to the Benedictine Rule, monks were to live a traditional monastic life, but in practice they were often involved in religious reform and politics. In contrast to the monks in the East, monks in the West were interested in and primarily responsible for the preservation of learning. Some friars devoted most of their energy to teaching or begging, to crusading or spiritual knighthood, to religious or political reform. According to some interpreters, the role of monks and religious communities in the civilization of the West after the fall of Rome was of utmost importance.[1,2]

POLITICAL ARRANGEMENTS AND ARGUMENTS

For all their shared heritage in tradition and monasticism, the two ancient churches grew into distinct branches of Christianity, mostly because of widely different political experiences. Two different systems of church-state relations developed in the East and West. The Orthodox church organized itself along the administrative lines of the Roman Empire wherein the chief administrative officer was the emperor, thought to be God's agent on earth. The patriarch of

Constantinople, the highest-ranking church official in the Eastern church, understood that his standing was tied to the emperor and that the emperor was, in a very real sense, the head of the church. The Roman church organized itself according to the claims of apostolicity, especially the claims that Peter was *the* most important apostle and that his territory (Rome) was *the* seat of religious authority. The patriarch of Rome, the highest-ranking church official in the Western church, understood that his standing was greater than the emperor's and that he (the bishop of Rome, later called the pope) was the head of the church. Both pope and patriarch thought of themselves as Roman and as heirs of the greatest political empire in the history of the world. We look next in greater detail at each of the two systems of church-state relations, as they developed in their historical contexts. We can see how this led to a great schism between the two churches that has endured until the present day.

Constantinople as the New Rome: The Greek Orthodox System

When Constantine reunited the fragments of the Roman Empire in the early part of the fourth century, he did so under the sign of the cross.[3] The claim made by Constantine's biographer Eusebius was that Constantine—like Paul in the New Testament—was called directly by God to embrace Christianity. The political results of this claim were momentous for the church: it meant that Constantine ruled by divine right, that he considered himself appointed by God, and that his government was a theocracy (that is, the people believed that God, through a mediator, the emperor, ruled Byzantium). Neither Constantine nor the emperors after him ever claimed to be divine, but they did see themselves as God's representatives on earth, ranking just below Christ in the administration of earthly justice. The office of the emperor was, in a sense, the visible manifestation of God on earth. The emperor was like God because God's business was to bring the heavens into a peaceful unity and harmony and the emperor's business was to create a state in which all people coexisted in unity and harmony. God ruled the cosmos and the emperor ruled the earth.

Through a series of victories and treaties, Constantine became the sole master of the western half of the empire by 313 C.E., and master of the entire Roman Empire—East and West—by 324 C.E. The decisive battle in which Constantine won control of the West was the Battle of the Milvian Bridge (outside Rome). Before this battle Constantine had a dream/vision which he later understood as a revelation: he saw a cross superimposed on the sun and heard the words, "In this sign conquer." Constantine took control of the West under the Christian sign of the cross, and from that time was more sympathetic to Christianity than to any other religion. It was Constantine who passed the Edict of Milan, which granted religious freedom to all and ended the persecution of Christians; it was Constantine who began the process of making the empire Christian. He began gradually to transfer all the religious revenues of the ancient world to the Christian church, and by 324 C.E. began a massive church-building program so the most impressive buildings in the empire were Christian places of worship.

Constantine called the first ecumenical council at Nicaea in 325 C.E. (see Appendix 4). Politically astute, he saw that the Roman Empire needed a unifying ideology, that a geographically massive empire with a variety of philosophical schools and cultures needed some common belief to unite people and bind them together. Constantine saw Christianity as the perfect unifying force. Universal in scope, it was beginning to take hold of people's religious imaginations. It combined some rituals and beliefs of the mystery religions with belief in a historically concrete savior-God, and it had developed a sophisticated philosophical and political framework that enabled discussion of issues and evaluation of positions. And, it was *organized*. Besides, Constantine believed he had been called by God, blessed with a revelation experience, appointed to build a Christian empire.

The religious symbols associated with the Christian empire solidified his claims. Constantine's mother, Helena, made a pilgrimage to Jerusalem and found there some of the implements of Jesus's death—the cross, the nails, and the sign of the cross that identified Jesus as king of the Jews—which became the great religious talismans of the empire and tokens of divine favor.[4] The people of Byzantium—renamed Constantinople when Constantine moved the capital of the empire there in 333 C.E.—considered themselves both Romans and the chosen people of God. Coins were stamped with pictures of Jesus and the motto Jesus Christ, King of Rulers. The actions of the emperor took on a sacred and symbolic character; military expeditions were sacred and the ceremonies of war were holy. People believed the real ruler of the empire was Christ: the cross was carried into battle as a standard and laws were passed in the name of The Lord Jesus Christ, Our Master.

Constantinople, the capital of the eastern part of the Roman Empire, was called the new Rome. All the weight and civilizing importance of Roman history was adopted by Byzantium. The new Rome differed from the old in that the new one was Christian; the task was no longer just to civilize, but to bring all people to salvation in Christ. Constantine perceived himself as an apostle sent by Christ to bring the gospel to the world; one of his titles, carved on his tomb when he died, was Equal of the Apostles. When Constantinople fell to the Turks in 1453 the title and the claims to be the new Rome—the third Rome—fell to Moscow and the Russian Orthodox church. In the fifteenth century Russia was the only politically independent power remaining in the Orthodox world. The czar called himself Beloved of Christ, as the emperor of Constantinople had done. The claims and tasks of the Orthodox system fell to the czar and the Russian Orthodox church, and in Russia religious and political destinies were intertwined as in old Byzantium. The idea of an Orthodox Christian state lasted until July 16, 1918, when the last Russian czar, Nicholas II, was killed.

Where was the church in this theocratic system? It was bound up with the state, supporting and reinforcing the state's power. The head of the church, the patriarch of Constantinople, seldom had occasion to exercise direct *political* power because the East always had a strong emperor. When Constantine moved the capital to the East, a political vacuum was created in the West. Rome and the West lacked a strong political system, and the result was political chaos. The head of the church in the West, the bishop of Rome, finally managed to rise to power, to make order of the political disorder. The patriarch of Constantinople seldom had that opportunity; as head of the church he had full spiritual power, but what political influence he had he exercised in support of the emperor in the East. No independent religious authority in conflict with the emperor's political authority emerged in the East.

In the Eastern system the church was protected and established by the state: it was supported by state-collected taxes, met with no persecutions, feared no attack from outside. But sometimes the state became overprotective, and the church had to deal with emperors who wanted to take on spiritual functions and make spiritual decisions. It was not the patriarch of Constantinople or the bishop of Rome who called the first ecumenical council; it was the emperor.[5] When Constantine entered the hall where the bishops were meeting in Nicaea to open the council, Eusebius described him as "an angel of God descended from heaven, radiant in the fiery glow of the purple and adorned with gold and precious gems—such was his outward appearance. But his soul was visibly ornamented with the fear and adoration of God."[6] This description is both political and spiritual, and emphasizes the enormous power of the emperor in both realms.

The patriarch of Constantinople was the chief celebrant of the sacraments and the one who presided over the synod of bishops; he was the leader of the church, but it was the emperor who bore the title Vicar of God on Earth. The power of the patriarch of Constantinople was to be exercized in the spiritual realm; he was not to interfere with political decisions. Even his spiritual functions were to be exercised in cooperation with the emperor, who was—by virtue of his titles and power—permitted to operate within the spiritual realm. At its best, the cooperation between patriarch and emperor on the spiritual front was what the Greeks called a *symphonia*, a harmony of spirits.

Things were not always at their best, however, and the patriarch often had to struggle against the emperor and to safeguard the spiritual freedom of the church. By definition the patriarch was to be spiritually free, but sometimes that freedom was encroached upon by the powers of the state. When the Orthodox system moved to Russia in the fifteenth century, the harmony between patriarch and emperor (czar) was destroyed; the czars took full control of the church. In the eighteenth century, Czar Peter the Great abolished the patriarchate and established the internal life of the church along lines he thought were better suited to it and to an enlightened view of church structure.

In summary, then, the Orthodox system conformed to the model of the Roman Empire; Constantinople was the new Rome and Constantine was appointed by and beloved of God. The old Roman emperors sometimes proclaimed themselves gods; Constantine and his successors did not need to make such a claim because even without it they held an enormous amount of power and prestige in an essentially theocratic state. As the Vicar of God on Earth the emperor also held a central position in the church. He protected and subsidized the church, called and presided over the ecumenical councils, and promulgated all the conciliar dogmas. In this situation the church could not compete for political power and sometimes had to fight even to maintain its own spiritual power. A much different situation obtained in the West.

The West as Roman Catholic: The Rise of the Papacy

Constantine sought to establish a new Rome in Constantinople and to be the earthly ruler of a theocratic state. He wanted to replace the old (pagan) Roman Empire with a new (Christian) one, and he succeeded in the eastern half of the empire. The situation in the West, however, did not support the same kind of result. Constantine left a politically chaotic situation in the West. In that situation the bishop of Rome tried desperately to bring the various barbarian chieftains[7] and their peoples into the Christian communion so that religious and political unity would flourish in the West as they had in the East. In order to establish his claim to moral authority in the Western world, the bishop of Rome began to interpret Jesus's words in Matthew 16—"You are Peter, and on this rock I will build my church"—to justify his attempt to control and supervise the Latin church and the peoples in the western part of the empire. Constantine claimed to rule by divine appointment, citing his revelation experience before the Battle of the Milvian Bridge; the bishops of Rome also claimed to rule by divine appointment, citing the words of Jesus about Peter. The principle of apostolic succession and the power of the keys given by Jesus to Peter provided the theoretical foundation for the power of the bishops of Rome.

In the East the emperor's political power was so strong that it sometimes spilled over into the spiritual realm; in the West the bishop of Rome's power inevitably embraced the political realm. In both parts of the empire spiritual and political power overlapped; at best there was a *symphonia,* a harmonious cooperation of interests, but at worst—in the chaotic Dark Ages—confusion and a battle for power resulted. The political situation in the West was precarious; the collapse of the Roman Empire, the devastating effect of the barbarian invasions, an unstable economy, and other serious problems created a need for a strong leader located in the West. The leader who emerged was the bishop of Rome, a spiritual leader who found it possible to become politically powerful as well. The first task in the West was not unity (as in the East) but survival; beyond that the church in the West set itself the task of making the gospel known to various tribes and unsophisticated peoples. The bishop of Rome began to insinuate himself into the political vacuum and to suggest that the most natural place to look for moral leadership was to the old capital of the empire, Rome. By the fourth century the bishop of Rome began to call himself the pope, the president of the whole Western Christian church.

From the Council of Nicaea on, Christians clearly recognized that the bishop of Rome had a *primacy of honor*. Rome had been the capital of the empire, it was renowned for its orthodoxy, and people believed its church was founded by Peter and Paul. Peter was believed to be the apostle of Rome. His bones and those of Paul were buried there and it was, after Jerusalem, the most popular place to go on pilgrimage. But the bishops of Rome said that Peter was the first bishop of Rome and that they were his successors. Peter, they reasoned, was first among the apostles and his successor should be first among the successors of the apostles, the bishops. The bishop of Rome did not want to be first among equals, but wanted simply to be first.

The hierarchical system of authority that developed in the Christian church and that was legislated at the Council of Chalcedon rested in the five patriarchs: the leaders of the church in Rome, Constantinople, Alexandria, Antioch, and Jerusalem. The bishop of Rome was the undisputed patriarch of the Western church and was accorded a primacy of *honor* among his fellow patriarchs; he wanted the other patriarchs to recognize that the bishop of Rome had a *juridical* primacy over them, but they never did. The *papal* claim is the assertion by the bishop of Rome of his authority over the entire universal church, a claim rejected by Orthodox Christians and Protestants. The *patriarchal* claim is the assertion that the bishop of Rome is the undisputed head of the Western church, a claim that was accepted by Orthodox Christians and rejected later by Protestants. Friction between East and West usually involved the papal claim.

The history of the papacy is primarily of attempts on the part of the bishops of Rome to exercise their authority over the church in the West. In establishing their authority in the West, however, they also asserted their authority over the entire church. The papal and patriarchal claims have, therefore, been confused in the minds of the popes themselves and in the minds of most Christians. Popes began to press their claims over the entire church in the fourth century. By the end of the sixth century the theological claims for papal power had been worked out and supported with the reforming and evangelistic initiatives of the popes.

The strongest papal assertion of political power did not come until the year 800, when the pope made a political alliance with a particular Frankish tribe and sealed that alliance by crowning the Frankish king, Charlemagne, emperor. This was a politically momentous move that proved disastrous for the papacy on some counts. An emperor (actually an empress, Irene) reigned in Constantinople when the pope conferred that title upon a barbarian king. Now there was a genuine political rival in the West who adopted many of the titles and functions of the emperor in the East: he protected and subsidized the church and also sometimes interfered in its life.

Once the pope introduced the idea that he had power to name and crown the emperor, the office of the papacy was elevated to a political importance it had never known before. With the collapse of the Carolingian Empire[8] and the onset of the so-called Dark Ages, the papacy became a pawn in a dirty game of Italian politics. The first reform attempts were made in the tenth century by Otto I, an emperor who wanted a holy papacy. The reformed papacy—culminating in the reign of Gregory VII (pope from 1073–85)—then wanted to establish autonomy and reform the empire. That desire led to the medieval church/state controversies. The history of church/state relations in the West up to and beyond the Reformation was a history of conflict: sometimes the pope was strong enough to control the emperor and sometimes the emperor was strong enough to control the pope. The controversies usually involved a clarification of roles.

The ever-present danger in the Eastern Orthodox system was that the emperor would use his power to interfere in spiritual matters; in the West, the danger was both that the pope would use his spiritual power to interfere unduly in politics *and* that the emperor (or king) would use political power to interfere with the life of the church. Neither the popes nor the kings would relinquish their powers in the name of peace, for roughly the same reasons that the powers of the modern world insist they cannot disarm unilaterally. In the West neither pope nor king ever had a total victory, just as in the East the patriarch never had an opportunity to develop political independence. Whether the popes should have been involved in the political order to the extent that they were is a matter of dispute among Christians. Some argue that the church had no business wielding political power, and some argue that without papal involvement the state would have controlled the church in the West as it had in the East. Whatever the merits of each side of the argument, the history of the papacy is an integral part of Western political *and* spiritual history.

The East/West Schism and Contemporary Relations

To review the preceding two sections, the types of church government in Eastern and Western Christianity were remarkably similar but were distinguished from one another by their relationship to the emperor. In the East the emperor was, in many ways, the head of the church while the patriarch functioned as its liturgical leader; in the West the pope was the head of the church, though he sometimes had to defend himself from imperial interference. Both churches tended to think of themselves as the kingdom of God on earth.

Given the role of the pope in the West and the claims he made for jurisdiction over the universal church, it is not surprising that a schism arose between East and West. Orthodox Christians never acknowledged the theological claims of the papacy, yet the church in the West grew up assuming those claims were true. The church in the West thus grew less recognizable to Christians in the East. The situation was exacerbated by a growing cultural division: Greeks ceased to speak Latin and Western Christians could not speak Greek. Thus, when they met they could not understand one another's language and did not recognize one another's system of church authority. They argued as heatedly about relatively peripheral matters—the kind of bread to use for the Eucharist, whether to allow priests to have beards—as they did about more substantial things—the *filioque*[9] clause in the Nicene Creed (see Appendix 5) and clerical celibacy.

When the old Roman Empire collapsed, the new Rome interpreted that fall as God's vengeance, as a sign that the Orthodox church was to carry forth God's plan in the world. When the popes, through a series of shrewd political moves and some luck, emerged from the ruins of the old empire as the leaders of the West, they interpreted their recovery as a sign that God intended the power of Peter to be passed down through the line of the bishops of Rome. Orthodox Christians developed a legend of St. Andrew to counter the claims about Peter: they argued that Andrew was called to be an apostle before Peter and that Andrew had come to Constantinople. The popes responded with a systematic exploitation of the texts of Matthew 16, which say that the church will be built upon Peter. Both were at pains to deny the claims of the other.

The addition to the Nicene Creed of the *filioque* clause was partly a doctrinal wedge between the two churches, but more than that it was a symbolic manifestation of the differences between them on the issue of spiritual authority. Orthodox Christians could simply not understand how anyone could add something to the doctrines or words of a council. There were jurisdictional disputes between East and West about new Christian territories, especially Bulgaria, Moravia, and Byzantine provinces in southern Italy; some old ethnic rivalries—between Serbians and Croatians, for example—date back to religious arguments. The frequent clashes between East and West over religious matters led to a formal schism between the two churches in 1054.

The final clash between them came with the Crusades. In 1204 Constantinople was captured by crusaders from the West; monasteries, churches, palaces, and libraries were robbed and fire destroyed many of the Byzantine art treasures. The crushing blow was the establishment of a Latin patriarch and emperor in the city. When the Turks threatened to capture Constantinople in the early part of the fifteenth century, an attempt was made to reunite the two churches, but it did not last. The rift between them was too old and too deep. The Turks captured Constantinople in 1453. Thus ended the Byzantine Empire, but the "third Rome," Moscow, took over the Byzantine tradition and the principles of the Orthodox church and gave them soil in which to survive and flourish.

The main stumbling block between Roman Catholic and Orthodox reunion today is church authority. The Orthodox churches do not accept the office and universal authority of the pope. Some Greek churches do accept the authority of the pope, but are otherwise quasi-autonomous. Roman Catholics call them *Uniate* churches. In discipline (clergy may marry) and liturgical practice they resemble the Orthodox church. A variety of Orthodox churches exist: Russian, Greek, Rumanian, and so forth, each with its own system of authority. These have been unable to unite; attempts to form an American Orthodox church have failed. They remain ethnically identified as Greek, Rumanian, and so on.

Roman Catholics have been more open to dialogue with all other religious bodies since the Second Vatican Council (1962–65). Members of the Orthodox church attended the council and (with the exception of the Greek church) agreed to begin dialogue with Rome on equal terms. Recent popes have been eager for reunion, and have visited Orthodox patriarchs and welcomed them to Rome.

LITURGY AND DOCTRINE IN THE TWO CHURCHES

Roman Catholicism and the Orthodox church both have distinctive patterns of worship and ancient systems of doctrine. They display some crucial differences in liturgical art and practice as well as in doctrinal issues. Some of these differences are culturally explainable, but many derive from orientations established in the early Christian church. We look at these differences next.

Icons and Doctrine: The Orthodox Perspective

One of the most beautiful manifestations of Orthodox piety is the icon.[10] The artistic style and the place of the icon in Orthodox life and worship sometimes seem strange to a Western Christian, especially to a Protestant Christian. There were not always icons. Christianity, growing as it did from Judaism, was very much against idolatry and the veneration of pictures of holy persons. For a number of reasons, however, pictures of Jesus and Mary began to be prevalent from the fifth century onward.

According to Orthodox belief, icons are not made by human hands. They are not products of an artistic imagination as much as they are manifestations of heavenly archetypes. They are always painted on a gold background (to represent a heavenly atmosphere) and they are recopied as they are, not embellished or made subject to new artistic styles. They are consecrated, sacred images, not objects of art. The original icons, it is said, just appeared by some miracle of divine presence in the world. In Orthodox belief, heaven comes down to earth, especially in the celebration of the Eucharist where the earthly congregation meets and eats with the heavenly congregation. The icons represent this coming to earth of God and the angels and saints.

Orthodox believers venerate icons (bowing in front of them, kissing them, lighting candles before them) both at home and in church. In an Orthodox home, in the eastern corner of the living room and/or bedroom there is the so-called beautiful corner, a series of icons and candles, often decorated with flowers. An Orthodox church has an *iconastasis,* originally a low barrier, presently a high wall completely separating the sanctuary from the rest of the church.

Icons are arranged on the iconastasis in a fixed order. On the center door of the iconastasis are icons of the angels Michael and Gabriel, to the right of the door is an icon of Christ, and to the right of that is an icon of John the Baptist. On the left side of the door is an icon of the Mother of God and to the left of that, an icon of the saint to whom the church is dedicated. Above these major icons are rows of smaller icons representing the story of redemption and presenting a visible image of eucharistic piety and belief.

Icons are an integral part of Orthodox dogma. Genesis records the words that people are made "in the image of God." The Orthodox interpretation of this is that people carry an image (or icon) of God within themselves. This idea has interesting doctrinal consequences: sin is understood as a distortion or tainting of the image of God within oneself. The doctrine of the Trinity and explanations of Christology and the role of the church are all defined in terms of images.

Though for political reasons Constantinople was considered the new Rome, for liturgical reasons it was more of a new Jerusalem, a holy city. There were many different churches, all of which were filled with tangible reminders of the saints (relics) and decorated with icons. Religion was a way of life for people: religious controversies were not so much abstract arguments as they were matters of great popular interest. The notion that the divine energy was present in everything fostered a piety that tended to revere the whole created order. The bond between the sacred meal celebrated in the Eucharist, and the Resurrection made the liturgy essentially a joyful event. The endless reenactment of the Christian mysteries in the liturgy was the way in which the corporate life of the people found its religious expression.

Orthodox liturgy is elaborate, rich in gestures, vestments, and hymns. Many forms developed in the context of certain historical prohibitions. A ban on instrumental music in Orthodox churches led to a highly developed tradition of choral singing and chanting that uses the human voice as an instrument of praise; a prohibition against sculpture led to an elaborate range of art in murals, mosaics, and icons. A ban against the theatre and drama encouraged people to use their dramatic energies and talents in the celebration of the liturgy. In both East and West came rich, dramatic developments of liturgical prayer and style, and a proliferation of different liturgies. In both cases the liturgy was finally standardized and celebrated in the same way everywhere. Both Orthodox and Roman Catholic liturgies are substantially different from most Protestant worship.

The doctrinal complexion of the Orthodox church is mystical: the great dogmatic preoccupations are deification, sanctification, rebirth, resurrection, and transfiguration. The emphasis is not so much on truth and justice as on beauty and love. The Orthodox believer's aim is to become a new creation, to be transfigured by grace. God did not become human in order to satisfy divine justice, but to enable people to become like God. Sin is not so much a violation of a law as a diminishment of the original image of God in a person; redemption is, therefore, bound up with renewal and transfiguration. Orthodox Christians lack a concept of predestination and do not emphasize eternal punishment of sinners. They expect the final judgment to be a time of grace and love more than separation and judgment. This doctrinal view is very much at odds with that of Roman Catholicism.

Legalism and Doctrine: The Roman Perspective

Recall that the circumstances in which Roman Catholic Christianity developed differed greatly from those of Orthodox Christianity. Where Orthodox Christianity interacted with Hellenistic philosophy and mystery religions, the Roman church faced barbarian tribes. Where Orthodox Christianity developed within a stable government system, the Roman church built upon the old Roman legal system to prevent the total collapse of civilization in the West. Where religious life in the East was confined to monasticism, it developed into monasticism plus a variety of functional religious orders in the West. The liturgical preoccupations of Orthodox Christianity were essentially mystical; the church in the West developed a fascination with legal understandings of doctrine and worship.

One can find both mystical and legal aspects in the New Testament; Roman Catholicism was more moved by the legalistic aspects though it was not without a mystical tradition. Roman pagan religion had been a very legalistic affair: the priest knew the correct forms of prayers and sacrifice, how to please the gods. Pagan piety was not concerned with dogma and ethics, but with proper cultic acts scrupulously performed, with precise rules and rigorous exactitude in religion. Roman Catholicism was preoccupied with sin and justification. In Orthodox Christianity, the church is the place where one can become transfigured by meeting with the heavenly community. In Roman Catholicism, the church is a place of justice; God has laws, people break them, and justice demands that people make reparation. The church is the place where reparation is made possible: the bishop—or his agent, the priest—determines the degree of sin and the kind of reparation necessary. Penance (which in Orthodox Christianity is more pedagogical than punitive) developed into a system very much like jurisprudence: sins, like crimes, were weighed, and punishments (penances) determined for them. The priest was the legitimate agent of divine law.

Western Christianity also rallied its resources to define doctrines as precisely as possible. In the Orthodox tradition after the great councils, the elements of the Nicene Creed have never been rigorously rationalized and defined; in Roman Catholicism, the need to explain doctrines to new and primitive peoples, and the fascination with logic and Scholasticism tended to foster doctrinal definitions and systems of theology. Doctrines of sin, grace, eschatology, and predestination, as well as explanations of sacramental power and papal primacy were all based, to some extent, on a legal interpretation of the relationship between God and people. Anselm of Canterbury (1033–1109) made the legal understanding of this relationship the key to his theological explanation of the Incarnation. For Anselm, the Word of God became flesh in order to satisfy the demands of divine justice: when people sinned and upset God's original plan (the Original Sin story in Genesis), they so offended divine justice that only a perfect sacrifice could satisfy its demands. Christ, therefore, is the perfect victim, the one who died in order to satisfy divine justice and save people from their sins.

The legalistic perspective is evident in Roman liturgy and in the more general life of the church. Whereas the observance of the Eucharist in the Orthodox church was a joyous celebration of Christ's presence and the Resurrection, in the Roman church it emphasized the sacrifice of Christ on the cross. Both the Orthodox and Roman churches hold that the bread and wine are transformed into the body and blood of Christ but only the Roman church developed a precise theory of how and when this transformation occurs, the doctrine of transubstantiation.[11] For various reasons, the Roman church set the number of sacraments at seven; the Orthodox church was not constrained to put a limit on the way God's power operates on people, though they did finally adopt the Roman system.

Up to the Reformation the Roman Catholic church was involved first in survival and then in consolidation of church authority. Its self-perceived mission was to dominate the political situation; it was that or be dominated by it and lose spiritual freedom. From the eleventh to the fourteenth centuries the Roman church was, for the most part, the dominant power in the West; it was a highly organized, legally defined, tightly governed organization with the pope at its head. The church dominated the culture, managing art, architecture, music, learning, politics, and law. The pope saw himself as the chief administrative officer of a grand, and divinely founded, international system of government. A system of ecclesiastical courts was developed in order to administer God's justice to everyone, supervised catechetical schools were established to teach the Christian religion to pagan people, fighting and violence were either minimized (through enforced days of peace) or channelled into holy causes (as in the Crusades), monastic life was reformed and regulated, and the religious life of the populace as a whole was specified by law. It is no wonder that the flavor of Roman Catholicism was legalistic.

CONCLUSION

The schism between the Greek Orthodox church and the Roman Catholic church in 1054 was the first major split in the Christian church, which continues down to the present day. One of the issues between them was their relation to the state. The church in the East developed under the protection of the emperor and had no chance to assert its independence from the empire; the church in the West was able to become more politically independent. In the course of its history, the Roman church asserted the primacy of the pope as the supreme leader of the entire Christian church, a claim that Orthodox Christians could not—and still cannot—accept. In addition to the issue of church authority, concepts and traditions crucial to both churches developed differently East and West: monasticism and liturgy are ancient and central in both churches, but they have become quite different in ethos and practice.

The difference in general perspective between East and West reflects the history and early environment of each church. The tasks of the Christian church were different for both groups, and they developed different outlooks. At the same time, however, they are remarkably similar: both are committed to certain doctrinal positions though they have different emphases; both observe an ancient, fixed liturgy; both recognize the importance of tradition; and both believe the church includes the communion of saints (dead and alive). The Christian groups that derived from the Reformation disagreed with the Roman church on nearly all of these issues. It is important, therefore, to see the points of correspondence between the Orthodox and the Roman Catholic churches as well as to know where their differences lie.

CHAPTER 4 NOTES

1. Christopher Dawson, *Religion and the Rise of Western Culture* (New York: Doubleday, 1958), pp. 44–67. From a different perspective, but one still laudatory about the role of monks in civilization, see Kenneth Clark, *Civilization* (New York: Harper & Row, 1969), pp. 1–60. Clark is an art historian and focuses on the emergence of civilization by way of its art.

2. For a discussion of monastic life in the modern world see Chapter 8.

3. One clear account of Constantine's life and rise to power can be found in Hermann Doerries, *Constantine the Great* (New York: Harper & Row, 1972).

4. According to Roman Catholic tradition, Helena is a saint. She made her famous pilgrimage to Jerusalem in 326 C.E. You can imagine the sense of power attached to Constantine's claim to be in possession of the very cross on which Jesus died.

5. Let me suggest a way to begin to understand the human side of the Council of Nicaea. Dorothy L. Sayers' *The Emperor Constantine* (Grand Rapids: Eerdmans, 1976) is fictional, but created from historical sources. Sayers (you may know her through Peter Wimsey mystery books) wrote this play for the Colchester Drama Festival in 1951. In it she shows you how Constantine understood his church-state arrangements, what his role in the council was, and how he made his own inner pilgrimage to Christianity. Sayers does an amazing (if imaginative) job of getting inside this man's mentality.

6. Eusebius of Caesarea, *The Life of Constantine.* See *A Select Library of Nicene and Post-Nicene Fathers of the Christian Church*, second series (Grand Rapids: Eerdmans, 1952), pp. 481–560, quotation from p. 522.

7. The Roman Empire in the West fell in the fifth century for a number of reasons, one of which was plunder by various barbarian tribes. The interaction between the leaders of some of these tribes and the leaders of the Roman Catholic church helped to

set the stage for a new kind of civilization. When we talked about the universal mission of Christianity (in Chapter 3) we talked about Christian adaptation to different, but fairly civilized societies (Hellenistic and Roman). In the West, however, the Christian message had to be made understandable to tribal peoples whose gods were understood not so much in terms of reason but in terms of power. For an unusual and striking interpretation of this interaction and the rise of "miracle cults" see Albert Mirgeler, *Mutations of Western Christianity* (Notre Dame, Ind.: University of Notre Dame Press, 1968), pp. 44–66.

8. Charlemagne began a movement to solidify, educate, and reform, and his empire was one of the high points of civilization before the eleventh century, but (for complicated reasons based on patterns of feudal succession) it did not last. For a readable and detailed account of the history of this period see Norman F. Cantor, *Medieval History: The Life and Death of a Civilization*, 2nd ed. (New York: Macmillan, 1969).

9. *Filioque* means "and the Son." In the creed adopted by the Council of Nicaea (325 C.E.) there is a statement about the Holy Spirit that says, "The Holy Spirit proceeds from the Father." This is a complicated bit of theology about the Trinity and you need not pursue it, just notice that it says "from the Father," period. Later, especially in the West (and to strengthen the arguments for the divinity of Jesus Christ) many people began to add the word *filioque*, so that the phrase now said, "The Holy Spirit proceeds from the Father *and the Son*." The theological point was never much in dispute since everyone believed in the divinity of the Son. The question at issue was whether or not one could add (or subtract) words from a sacred council document. The Eastern Christians said no, and when the West adopted the *filioque* as part of the creed, they invited a fierce and hostile argument. For a clear explanation of this complicated problem, see R. G. Heath, "The Western Schism of the Franks and the *Filioque*" in *Journal of Ecclesiastical History* 23 (1972), pp. 97–115.

10. For a short introduction to icons see Ernst Benz, *The Eastern Orthodox Church—Its Thought and Life* (New York: Doubleday, 1963), pp. 1–20. You cannot really appreciate icons until you see them in color, so check the subject catalog in your library and see what art books you can find with icons in them. In ancient churches where few could read, the stories about Jesus had to be told and pictured. Icons and the great mosaics of Orthodox churches give you a good indication of how beautiful the Christian story was for those people.

11. The doctrine of transubstantiation was based on a distinction between the substance of a thing (its essence) and its accidents (how it looks, feels, tastes, and so on). In trying to explain the unexplainable, philosophers argued that the accidents of the Eucharist remain the same (it still tastes like, looks like, smells like bread), but its substance changes (*trans* = change; *transubstantiation* = change in substance): its essence is the body and blood of Christ.

SUGGESTIONS FOR FURTHER READING

1. For a good general introduction to Eastern Orthodoxy see Ignace Dick, *What Is the Christian Orient* (Westminster, Md.: Newman Press, 1967). Dick explains the patriarchates, Orthodox doctrine, liturgical families, and languages, and shows how Orthodoxy developed in various parts of the world. One also gets a sense from this book about the linguistic complexity of Orthodoxy. Whereas Christianity in the West developed mostly in Latin for the first thousand years or so, Eastern Christianity took root in

cultures that spoke Greek, Syriac, Coptic, Armenian, Georgian, Arabic, and Slavonic (to name a few).

Another good introduction to Orthodox Christianity is John Meyendorff, *The Orthodox Church: Its Past and Its Role in the World Today,* 3rd rev. ed. (Crestwood, N.Y.: St. Vladimir's Seminary Press, 1981). This book originally appeared in 1960 and has been revised to be more informative about contemporary issues and present-day ecumenical relations. It contains a useful bibliography.

2. For a clear account of the differences between Eastern and Western patterns of religious authority, one that untangles things, see Francis Dvornik, *Byzantium and the Roman Primacy* (New York: Fordham University Press, 1966).

3. For a look at some primary sources chosen especially for students to give them an introduction to the events of this period, see Marianka S. Fousek, *The Church in a Changing World: Events and Trends from 250–600* (St. Louis: Concordia, 1971).

4. The following books are general introductions to a variety of areas that I have not tried to cover in the text. We talked about hermits in the desert: for an engaging account of their lives, mostly by way of quotation from them and their stories, see Helen Waddell, *The Desert Fathers* (Ann Arbor: University of Michigan Press, 1966). I mentioned people who believed God wanted them to wander, who set out with no goal: they were not a large group, but an unusual one. See Eleanor Duckett, *The Wandering Saints of the Early Middle Ages* (New York: W. W. Norton, 1964). Finally, I mentioned early Christian writers and referred to Appendix 3, which gives a very brief sketch of their tasks. In many ways there is no substitute for reading to get some idea of who they were and what they wrote about, and then reading what they said. One biography of (perhaps) *the* major writer in the Latin West is worth citing because of its sympathy, lucidity, and general excellence: Peter Brown, *Augustine of Hippo: A Biography* (London: Faber & Faber, 1967). Brown makes Augustine not just a major religious figure and philosophical/theological thinker, but a human being I think you can relate to; read pages 1–181 for the story of his search for himself and for God.

CHAPTER 5

Aspects of the Reformation

The Reformation was not so much an isolated incident of protest as a series of reform attempts and movements between the fourteenth and seventeenth centuries. During that time the political and cultural climate changed substantially; old connections between church and state broke down in the face of emerging nationalism. It was a time of great upheaval when the issue of religious authority finally divided Christianity into a variety of factions that persist to this day.

This chapter focuses on the historical context for these great reform movements, and on aspects of each of the reform movements themselves. The protests of Wycliffe and Hus, the reforming moves of the conciliar movement, and the atmosphere of the Renaissance all provided support for some creative reforms within Christianity. Unfortunately and inevitably, those reforms also led to a severe break within Christendom, and from the sixteenth century onwards there would no longer be two branches of Christianity (Roman Catholic and Eastern Orthodox) divided geographically; the Protestant Reformation resulted in the formation of new churches and distinct denominations. We will look briefly here at the four major strands of the Protestant Reformation, and at the reformation of the Catholic church from within.

THE HISTORICAL SITUATION

From the fourth to eleventh centuries, the church in the West had been challenged to survive, to withstand political pressure from outside, and to convert barbarian tribes to Christianity. To some ways of thinking, the church had been a remarkable success: most Europeans were Christians, there was a system of international church law that tried to insure justice and fairness, liturgical life and ecclesiastical discipline were being made uniform, religious life flourished in a variety of forms, and the church had managed to secure autonomy by becoming a powerful political entity as well as the highest spiritual authority in the West. To other ways of thinking, the church had assumed too much power, meddled in the wrong issues, and devoted insufficient attention to spiritual matters. This perception, prominent from the late eleventh century onwards, increased markedly throughout the Reformation.

From the eleventh to fourteenth centuries, the Western Catholic church was in a process of consolidating its power. Because the political world was changing so dramatically, the church found itself involved in intense political struggles.[1] The image of an international church presided over by a wise pope was being challenged by the emergence of a new kind of *national* ruler. Kings, in England and France particularly, resented what they considered papal intrusion in their own political affairs. There was no longer a political vacuum in the West for the pope to fill, as had been the case earlier; and there was no longer a predictable political struggle between the *one* secular ruler (the Holy Roman emperor) and the pope, as had been initiated with the crowning of Charlemagne. Some people believed that the pope ought to give up all political power, leave politics to kings, and become a strictly spiritual ruler.[2] They argued this position on both political and religious grounds. The response on the part of the official church was to exaggerate the papal claims: popes claimed to have power over the entire world (as vicars of Christ), or to be able to step into any situation in which sin had been committed—into any situation, in other words.[3]

At the beginning of the fourteenth century, a startling response to papal claims was made by Philip IV, king of France. Pope Boniface VIII and the king had been involved in a series of moves and countermoves against each other for some time, and animosity grew on both sides. The conflict was over power and money and had long since passed the point where polite conversation or arbitration could resolve it. The pope, counting on power that had worked in centuries past (power he no longer had), threatened to depose the king. In 1302 the pope issued a document, *Unam Sanctam,* which ended thus: "We therefore declare, say and affirm that submission on the part of every human creature to the bishop of Rome is altogether necessary for his salvation."[4] In earlier times the king might have capitulated; this time the king began a plan to depose the pope. Boniface VIII was arrested and died on his way to Paris to stand trial. The new pope was not Italian but French, and the papacy moved from Rome to Avignon, a small town in France. The papacy was now under the control of the French monarchy; the popes became in effect agents of the king.

The Avignon papacy lasted from 1304–1378, after which time the Great Western Schism occurred: through a series of complex moves and for a variety of reasons, from 1378–1415 *two* men claimed to be pope. There was a French pope at Avignon and a Roman pope in Rome. The schism divided Europe on religious/political grounds: England (the traditional enemy of France) backed the Roman pope, while Scotland (the traditional enemy of England) backed the French pope. In addition to experiencing political turmoil and religious confusion, Europe was recovering from the outbreak of bubonic plague that had occurred in the 1340s. The Black Death, as it was called, was quick and fatal; it killed one-fourth to one-half of the population of Europe.

The situation by the latter part of the fourteenth century was terrible: it was a time of division and death, religious uncertainty, and political chaos. The widespread dimensions of the upheaval caused some people to believe that what had happened was divine retribution for sins. Because of this belief, people took part in extreme rituals of repentance and self-torture. There were flagellants who moved from town to town, preached a message of doom, and then whipped themselves and each other, all the while calling on others to repent for their sins. People had a morbid fascination with death. At the same time, mystical religious experience increased, especially in England. Because the general society was off balance and things were not improving, there were also a series of peasant revolts and uprisings in various countries. More important for the religious situation and for our understanding of religious diversity, however, were a series of religious reform movements.

RELIGIOUS REFORM BEFORE LUTHER

The two most important reform movements that began in the fourteenth and extended into the fifteenth centuries were those associated with John Wycliffe and John Hus, on the one hand, and the conciliarist movement on the other. Wycliffe and Hus wished to free the church from control of the ecclesiastical officials, from specified forms of liturgy, and from complex creeds and dogmatic tests. The conciliarist movement aimed to reform the institutional church and to restructure it. One of the central questions concerned religious authority: Where did one turn for the truth? Some of the answers to that question included the pope, ecumenical councils, the Bible, classical antiquity, tradition, mystical experience, and one's own conscience. These answers are not unlike the options available in the modern Christian church, nor are they peculiar to the fourteenth century; some of them had been present within Christianity from the beginning. In the climate of the Reformation years, however, the variety of answers divided Christians from one another and split apart what had once been a united Christendom.

Reforms of Wycliffe and Hus

One of the most significant protest movements before Luther was that associated with John Wycliffe (c. 1330–84) in England and John Hus (c. 1372–1415) in Bohemia (present day Czechoslovakia). Wycliffe was a philosopher at Oxford who gained support and fame by arguing that religious authority ought to be reserved for the righteous and that unworthy, immoral people (like the Avignon pope and many priests) had no legitimate right to exercise religious authority over people. Since he believed that religion had become too much a matter of clerical authority and esoteric doctrines, he attacked the authority of the pope and extolled the authority of the Bible. He argued that the office and claims of the pope had no support from Scripture and that the only way one could judge holiness was by whether or not one's behavior accorded with the gospel, not by whether one possessed a certain ecclesiastical title.

One of Wycliffe's most daring reforms was a translation of the Bible into the language of the people (in this case, English). The Catholic church had for centuries used the Latin translation of the Bible, known as the *Vulgate,* and had for some time forbidden translations into the vernacular. They held that Scripture was to be read and interpreted by the church; that is, by designated authorities within the church. Wycliffe thought all Christians should be free to read and interpret the Bible for themselves, and that to do so they needed to read it in their own languages.

Wycliffe's followers were called Lollards; the Lollard movement is remembered as one of ecclesiastical reform. Their chief authority in religious matters was the Bible as they read and interpreted it. Based on their reading of the Bible they attacked unscriptural *doctrines* (like transubstantiation and clerical celibacy) and unscriptural *practices* (like indulgences and pilgrimages). They extolled evangelical poverty and contrasted the poverty of early Christians (and many contemporary Christians) with the wealth of church officials. The Lollard movement was at first one of academic criticism (which was denounced by the church and persecuted) and later a more popular religious reform movement. People from the poorer classes were drawn to it and, for a while, it looked as if it might lead to an active revolt against the institutional church. By the middle of the fifteenth century, however, the movement had dwindled and effectively ended. But not before it had influenced John Hus.

Hus was a reforming priest in Bohemia who had been deeply moved by the teachings of Wycliffe. His life coincided with the Great Western Schism and the political divisions caused by that schism, so his reform attempts were, to some extent, linked with political issues. He denounced the hierarchical organization of the church and preached against an immoral clergy. In the middle of a stormy religious controversy, he was invited to the Council of Constance (see Appendix 4) where his safety was guaranteed by the emperor. At Constance, however, he was brought to trial, condemned as a heretic, and burned at the stake in 1415.

His followers, the Hussites, continued the revolt after his death. They demanded communion under both species, bread and wine (at this time, priests received both bread and wine, but the laity received only bread), and reduction in the church's wealth and property. A series of battles—the Hussite wars— lasted through the Protestant Reformation and were the first consistent armed attack on feudal politics and the Roman Catholic church. As such, the Hussite movement helped to pave the way for the Protestant Reformation.

Conciliarism

Conciliarism was the most notable internal reform movement to arise out of the chaotic situation of the Great Western Schism. Wycliffe and Hus were not so much interested in reforming the existing church as in denouncing it as unreformable: their message, in general, encouraged people to leave the corrupt church, read the Scriptures, and live a decent Christian life. The conciliarist movement, on the other hand, believed that the institutional church was necessary but that it needed a basic constitutional reform, one that would limit papal power and restore a more ancient—collegial—type of church government.

Gregory VII (pope from 1073–85) had set the tone of the medieval papacy by arguing that the pope was the supreme authority within the church.[5] Gregory VII had said that no council could be called without papal permission, that papal decrees could be annulled by no one, and that the pope could be judged by no one. The conciliarists opposed this position. Armed with a growing body of reform literature and opinion, they set out to argue that an ecumenical council is superior to the pope as a source of religious authority.

The first council called to heal the schism and restore the church under the leadership of one pope was the Council of Pisa (1409). People loyal to both popes came to Pisa, deposed both popes, and elected a new one, who, unfortunately, died within months. Most people attending the council had already gone home, and those who were left at Pisa elected another man, a powerful leader who, they thought, could heal the schism by force if not by persuasion. He took the name John XXIII. His election and the Council of Pisa did not heal the schism but made it worse; after Pisa *three* men claimed to be the pope—John XXIII, the French pope, and the Roman pope. Pisa was, at best, a step toward the Council of Constance, called by John XXIII in 1414 at the urging of the emperor Sigismund.

The Council of Constance deposed all three popes and elected a new one, who ratified his election by pronouncing the council a valid ecumenical council. Two important conciliar documents were passed at the Council of Constance: the first, *Haec Sancta* (1415), asserted the supremacy of the council over the pope as a religious authority; the second, *Frequens* (1416), declared that ecumenical councils should be held at least every ten years. Finally, the council drew up a list of abuses and called for significant reform in the church. It looked, for a while, as if the Council of Constance would lead to a major reformation in church structure and policy. As it turned out, however, the council did *not* reform the church, a failure that some interpreters argue led directly to the Protestant Reformation.[6]

HUMANISM AND THE RENAISSANCE

In the nineteenth century Lord Acton, a famous historian, said, "Power tends to corrupt and absolute power corrupts absolutely." Perhaps that explains why popes did not reform the church along lines that limited their power. It may also explain why national leaders developed into national despots when they assumed broad political power. Whatever the reasons, the battles between church and state in the fifteenth and sixteenth centuries were mostly fought over political power. The old prerogatives from the medieval papacy were at odds with the spiritual and intellectual uneasiness of an awakening world. The agent of that awakening was a loosely defined movement known as humanism and, later, as the Renaissance. Humanists responded to the religious and political chaos around them by hearkening back to ancient conceptions of humanity, culture, ideals, and destiny. Their goal was to rediscover the sources of and to delight in the type of life portrayed in classical Greek and Roman documents. Their efforts led to a rebirth of classical learning, the Renaissance.[7]

The religious consequences of the Renaissance view were enormous. Popes began to feel they did not need to confine themselves to religion and politics, but that they should make the church the great patron of the arts. Rome should be the spiritual and cultural capital of the universe, the popes thought, and they set out to rebuild it, endow museums, and patronize artists. In order to do this, popes felt they had to oppose rising nationalism and conciliarism, both threats to their political power. They began by systematically building a competitive state in Italy; they became Renaissance princes, who wielded power and maintained an army. In this situation there were a series of popes whose interests were not so much spiritual as political and financial. The rationale behind their policies was the protection of the church; they wanted to keep the papacy (and, by extension, the church) free from secular control.

Recall that the Catholic church understood itself to be based on papal power; according to their position Jesus had given a mandate to Peter that needed to be carried out if the church was to remain free and able to pursue its spiritual functions. Popes believed—and rightly so—that the strength of the church had been the agent of unification and civilization in centuries past. Could it still be so? Reformers thought not and argued that the medieval conception of the papacy had simply outlived its usefulness; others believed it needed simply to be refortified. That disagreement, in some ways, was at the heart of the Protestant Reformation. And the humanist/Renaissance movement supported that reformation by providing an alternate reading of the sources of papal power. Luther's position was not fundamentally new—Wycliffe and Hus had said many of the same things before—but he backed up his protest with the fruit of humanist/Renaissance labor. He was able to supply some of the critical scholarship from which real reform and (to some ways of thinking) revolution would come.

THE PROTESTANT REFORMATION

The reform movements before Luther did not lead to separate and distinct groups within Christianity; Luther himself did not intend to found a different church, but hoped to reform the existing one. Since the reform movements of the sixteenth century led to a major break in Western Christianity, since they were protests with more severe consequences than earlier movements, we mark them with a distinctive title and call those who departed from prevailing Christian beliefs, Protestants.

The Protestant Reformation drew the arguments in the church back to *religious* issues, always with an impact on political arrangements. There were four main channels of the Reformation: Lutheran, Reformed (associated with Zwingli and then Calvin), Tudor (or Anglican), and Radical (or Anabaptist). All of these movements were interested in the same basic issues, but their approaches differed. They were united in their opposition to traditional Roman Catholic notions of the nature of salvation, the church, and religious authority. We look at each of these four movements in greater detail next.

The Lutheran Reformation

When they went back to original sources, the humanists rediscovered the Greek New Testament; they learned Greek and began to see what it meant to understand a text in its historical setting. As they studied, they found that the Vulgate was not just a translation from the Greek, but a Latinized interpretation of Scripture, and they began to consider what it might mean to the church to base doctrinal interpretations upon the original Greek rather than the Latin. One of the scholars influenced by the humanists was a young German monk and professor of Bible studies at the University of Wittenberg, Martin Luther (1483–1546). Luther was a reformer in an age of unreformed abuses within the church; his Scripture studies and humanist scholarship helped him to articulate a strong position. The specific target of Luther's protest was the practice of indulgences.

Over a long period of time and for a variety of philosophical and historical reasons, the Roman Catholic church had developed the doctrine of purgatory, a place where the punishment due for sins could be worked off after death.[8] The reasoning was that God's *justice* demands that sinners pay a penalty (in this life or the next) for sins, while God's *mercy* will not allow a repentant (but not fully paid up) sinner to spend eternity in hell. Therefore, it was speculated, there must be a state en route to heaven where sinners can stop for a while and pay their penalties in full. This speculation seemed logical at a time when the task of theology was rational inquiry about God and the divine relationship to humanity, and when scholars worked to formulate systematic, all-encompassing explanations. The idea of purgatory was one such logical speculation. When it was coordinated with ideas about the church's power, the rationale for indulgences was developed.

The church believed that the obedient sacrificial death of Jesus and the good works of Mary and the saints had built up a treasury of merit, like a bank account that the church could draw on to pay the debts of sinners. Indulgences were a "draft" on the "account." Sinners could earn indulgences by doing what the church suggested: good works, prayers, and devotions. People who went on pilgrimages received indulgences, as did those who did good works, bore their sufferings patiently, or said certain prayers. During the Avignon papacy the popes, in need of money for a variety of projects, began to *sell* indulgences; one wit noted that the popes had discovered the fiscal possibilities of purgatory. The practice of selling indulgences went from bad to worse and was in a scandalous state when Luther began his public protest against the church's corruption in 1517.

Luther was a young law student when he experienced a profound spiritual crisis. To fulfill a vow he made during a thunderstorm, he entered a monastery in 1505 and was ordained a priest in 1507. From 1513 until his death he was a professor of theology and Scripture at Wittenberg. Monastic life did not resolve Luther's religious uneasiness; he was not led to an experience of Christian perfection and peace. Scrupulous as he was in his performance of devotions and disciplines, he did not gain from those exercises any confidence about his relationship with God. Quite the contrary: he was in a mood of despair and pessimism about his own salvation.

In this melancholy context, somewhere between 1512 and 1515, Luther had what is referred to as the Tower experience, which convinced him that the essence of the gospel lay in faith alone. The context of his experience was significant. At the time it occurred Luther was working to understand Paul's Epistle to the Romans. Romans 1:17 says this: "For in it [the gospel] the righteousness of God is revealed through faith for faith; as it is written, 'He who through faith is righteous shall live.'" Luther's experience led him to believe that good works—including the whole theological foundation for the theory of indulgences—were absolutely useless for one's salvation. A person is saved, Luther said, *by faith alone*. The freedom and sense of release he felt in the wake of this insight was phenomenal.

Luther believed that Roman Catholic doctrine and practice put up walls around religion, that the church operated as a power structure that so controlled the means of religious experience that it was virtually impossible for people to have an assurance of God's love and their own salvation. The church, as he perceived it, controlled *Scripture* by insisting that it only be read in Latin and not translated into the vernacular, and that the church was the sole authorized interpreter; it controlled *doctrine* by means of theological complexity and clerical formulations; and it controlled *grace* by binding grace to reception of the sacraments and the practice of acts that would secure merit. All of this control was tied up with the power of the priesthood, a power that extended up and down a hierarchical ladder from pope to bishops and from bishops to priests.

Luther set out to free the gospel from the control exercised over it by the Roman church; he wanted to extend the freedom and assurance of faith-alone salvation to others. He translated the Bible into German and made it available to the people. For Luther, hearing Scripture was a kind of sacrament; he believed that if people could just hear the word of God in Scripture, in language they understood, it would have a powerful effect on them. Scripture, he argued, creates its own unity; people do not need to be confined to the official interpretations of the church, nor do they need to have their own interpretations of the gospel regulated in some way. He shared his own insights and told people what the best interpretations were; those interpretations, he believed, could be discovered and bear fruit in a more scriptural model of the church. He insisted that the church was not a hierarchy, but a "priesthood of all believers," and a fellowship. Finally, he insisted that salvation was granted to believers on the basis of faith alone. People did not need to rely on complex doctrines, or on a system of sacraments and indulgences dispensed by priests; they had only to trust that God would regard them as righteous.

Luther did not intend to form a new church, but to reform the existing one. By 1519, however, it was clear that his positions were radically at odds with Roman Catholic doctrines and a break from Rome seemed inevitable. In 1520 he wrote three famous treatises—*Address to the Christian Nobility of the German Nation, The Babylonian Captivity of the Church,* and *The Freedom of a Christian Man*—which spelled out his political and religious positions. Luther argued for German (*not* Roman) control of the German churches; he denied the power of the pope as the final interpreter of Scripture; he denied the power of priests to mediate between the believer and God; and he rejected all sacraments except baptism and the Eucharist. He was excommunicated from the Roman church in 1521.

Luther spent most of the rest of his life alternately supporting and curbing his reform movement, translating the Scriptures into German, and writing catechisms and hymns. His reading of Scripture and his experiences led him to support certain theological conclusions, and fortified his conviction of the uselessness of human effort and reason in matters of salvation. His religious experience convinced him that God is gracious and looks upon people as if they were righteous, if only they have faith and confidence in God's goodness and Christ's atonement. Righteousness was not demanded by God; it was granted to people freely through the grace of Christ. Luther drew religion away from its political entanglements in the Roman church and insisted that it was based on Scripture and faith alone; religion, therefore, was a personal matter between God and the individual believer. At the same time, however, he did not free it from political involvement: he allowed the church to be subordinate to the political power of the state and appealed to the political power of the German princes to suppress quasi-religious revolts like the Peasants' Revolt (1524).

Luther's reform movement led to the formation of a separate church and inspired similar revolutions by other reformers. Lutheranism was systematically defined in various Lutheran creeds (see Appendix 5), all of which were combined in the Book of Concord (1580). Justification by faith alone and the primacy of Scripture as a religious authority are major tenets of Lutheranism. Luther was essentially conservative within his own movement; he did not support those who argued for extreme spiritualization. He was also cautious in relation to other reform movements; he did not support what he considered to be the extreme reforms of Zwingli, our next topic.

The Reformed Tradition

The man who initiated the movement that later became associated with the Reformed church was a contemporary of Luther's, Ulrich Zwingli (1484–1531), a Swiss reformer. Zwingli had been influenced by the humanists, especially by Erasmus, and was drawn to the reform movement through his studies of Scripture. Based on these studies, he argued against clerical celibacy, monasticism, and indulgences. In 1519 he gave a series of lectures on Scripture using Erasmus's edition of the Greek New Testament. Zwingli's position was simple: the word alone is enough, and one does not need the accumulated interpretations of the church and the commentaries of scholars. Zwingli, like Luther, argued that churches should be freed from Roman control. In 1523 the city council of Zurich approved Zwingli's positions about restoring the practice of the primitive church and ordered all priests to comply with them: organs were destroyed and images and statues removed from churches, priests were encouraged to marry, the liturgy was simplified, and monasticism abolished.

One of Zwingli's central positions concerned the Eucharist (or Communion). Roman Catholics believed the actual body and blood of Christ were present in the bread and wine consecrated in the Divine Liturgy. Catholics even had a philosophical explanation for *how* that happened. Luther rejected the metaphysical explanation but not the belief; he accepted the notion that Christ is really present in the bread and wine. Zwingli rejected the belief as well, emphasizing that the Communion was a *memorial*,[9] that it had nothing to do with Christ's actual presence in bread and wine. Luther felt that Zwingli had gone too far with his denial of real presence and there was a break between them from that point. Those who would later be called Anabaptists felt that Zwingli had not gone far enough; they, too, broke away from his movement. When Zwingli was killed in a religious war in 1531, his ideas were taken up by a second generation reformer, John Calvin.

Calvin (1509–64) was a French Protestant theologian and the person most closely associated with the Reformed tradition. He originally intended to be a

Roman Catholic priest, but apparently had some doubts about his vocation and about the Roman Catholic church. He studied to be a lawyer even though he was more attracted to Hebrew and classical studies; as a student he was influenced by the humanists. His active role in the Reformation was precipitated by a religious experience in 1533 in which he felt himself called to join the movement to restore the Christian church to its original purity. When he turned his energies to the Reformation he used them to systematize Protestant theology—his *Institutes of the Christian Religion,* 1536–59, were revised several times during his lifetime—and to develop his doctrinal system in the context of a theocratic state, the Geneva experiment, 1541–64.

Calvin continued the disagreement with Luther about the Eucharist. That argument led to the separation of the Protestant church in Germany into the Lutheran church on the one hand and the Reformed church (Calvinist) on the other. A more serious disagreement between Luther and Calvin, however, involved politics and the relation of the state to the church. Calvin restored the political power of the church and organized a church-dominated society. For Calvin it was not enough to define the church as a "priesthood of all believers"; the church, he believed, needed power as well as fellowship.

Calvin was invited to Geneva, Switzerland as a reformer; there he hoped to create a refuge for French Protestants (who were being persecuted by the Catholic government of France) and to design a city government based on early Christian polity. An initial attempt (1536–38) failed, but from 1541 until his death, Calvin governed Geneva and was able to develop a theocratic government there: God was the supreme authority and God's laws were clear, but Calvin interpreted them and utilized the secular powers to enforce them. He organized a constitutional government based on New Testament offices and hoped that the state would be subordinated to the church. Calvin had far-reaching powers not only in religious matters, but over the private lives of all the citizens of Geneva. He established disciplines for everything, religious and secular; his laws were based on the Bible and enforced by civil magistrates. Any deviation from the law was punished, and opposition was punished severely. Geneva was a haven for religious refugees, a place for a new beginning. In a chaotic time full of injustice, persecution, and religious confusion, it promised a visible and godly order and a chance for a well-regulated Christian life under the providence and sovereignty of God.

In Calvin's theology, God's providence governs everything and the fate of everything and everyone in the world is in God's hands; the believer should strive to have his or her own will taken up into the sovereign will of God. But how does one know God's will? Calvin proceeded from the premise that the Bible contained God's will and divine laws for every facet of human life: everything necessary for salvation has been revealed in Scripture in a clear and certain way. The Bible is read and understood in the church, which is a community under the sovereignty and grace of God. The church, therefore, is essential for salvation: it is the locus of God's covenant of grace because it is supported by the person and work of Christ. People are freed from anxiety about their salvation because it lies in God's hands.

To people who look at it from the outside, one of the striking features of Calvin's theology—a logical extension of his beliefs about the absolute sovereignty of God—is the theory of divine election and predestination. Since God knows everything and is absolutely powerful, it follows that God knows who will be saved and who will be damned. In fact, Calvin argued, God elected those to be saved and predestined those to be damned, and then God saw to it that those on the road to damnation were sinners and those on the road to salvation were saints. God's people—the elect—have been put on earth to work out the divine plan; election, therefore, is a calling and the Christian life a serious vocation.

Both Luther and Calvin had a gloomy view of human nature: both of them believed that people were sinful by nature and unable to do any good of their own accord; both perceived the Roman Catholic doctrine of intrinsic justification[10] as unbiblical and hopelessly wrong. According to Luther, salvation was accomplished by Christ and was granted freely to people on the basis of faith. Calvin agreed, but emphasized that faith and salvation depended upon election. The teaching about predestination has borne most of the anti-Calvinist criticism, but ought not to be taken out of context or given disproportionate attention: it was meant to release people from anxiety about their salvation, to give them a sense of sinfulness and a profound sense of God's forgiveness, an experience that resulted in feelings of thankfulness and joy. The doctrine was also meant to divert their attention from worries about personal worthiness, and to focus it on Christian life as a calling and on God's sovereign role in the salvation of a person.

One of the followers of Calvin, Jacob Arminius (1560–1609), changed his mind about the doctrine of predestination even while he was trying to defend it. He and his followers in the Dutch Reformed church argued for conditional predestination and a more liberal theology. Arminianism is usually associated with honoring the role of free will (as opposed to Calvinistic determinism) and the concept of unlimited atonement. Arminius's followers were condemned at the Synod of Dort (1618–19) in Holland.

From this Reformed synod one can find a clear expression, in brief form, of Calvinist doctrine. There are five major points:

1. *Unconditional election:* Once a person is saved (by faith) that person is always saved.
2. *Limited atonement:* Christ died to save the elect, not to save everyone.
3. *Total depravity of humankind:* Since the Fall people can only sin; they are incapable of sinless acts.
4. *Irresistible grace:* There is no freedom to resist God's grace.

5. *Final perseverance of the saints:* The elect must lead saintly lives and persevere to the end; they cannot assume they are saved, nor can they rest in an assurance of salvation.[11]

Once one accepts the sovereignty of God and the certainty that Scripture is the supreme rule of faith, one is to accept the world as created by God and is challenged to maintain its order. If the Bible is normative for every facet of human life, following the Bible allows one to uphold and glory in God's sovereignty and world order. The Calvinist system blended well with the demands of emerging capitalism: Calvin extolled thrift, hard work, sobriety, responsibility, and self-reliance, the very virtues that were crucial for those who wished to make substantial progress in modern mercantile society.

Calvin wrote a systematic theology of major Reformation positions and laid the groundwork for a theocratic society. Calvinism has been defined in various creeds (see Appendix 5), the most famous of which is probably the Westminster Confession. The form of church government Calvin proposed—Presbyterianism—and his religious ideas had a major impact on the religious future of English Protestants in the sixteenth and seventeenth centuries. The principles of the Synod of Dort and some of the ideas associated with the Geneva experiment—new beginnings, a refuge from religious persecution, and a visible, godly society under divine sovereignty—were the predominant influence in the minds and intentions of the Puritan founders of the American colonies.

The Tudor Reformation

The reformations of Luther and Calvin were doctrinal, liturgical, and disciplinary as well as structural, and they were pursued for predominantly religious reasons. Both Luther and Calvin set out to change the situation in the church. Luther hoped to reform the Catholic church by calling it back to its religious roles and informing it with more scriptural understanding; Calvin set out to purify Christianity and to organize Protestant Christianity into a theocratic system. The Tudor (Anglican) Reformation was not like either of its European cousins. It took place in England, and when it was over, much of what was Roman remained in liturgy, doctrine, and practice, despite its break with the papacy. Like Catholics, Anglicans continued to accept the episcopal structure of the church whereby authority moved from the top down; the liturgy was not substantially altered and there were, at first, no great doctrinal changes as in Lutheranism and the Reformed tradition.

The Roman Catholic church in England had been a rich and powerful institution dating back to the sixth century. One of the first missions of Pope Gregory I had been to organize the English church on the model of papal primacy.[12] At the same time, England was the first country to have a strong monarchy (able to oppose the pope on some issues) and a strong parliamentary government (able to oppose the king on some issues). England was a religiously vibrant country: the first significant reform movements occurred there (with Wycliffe and the Lollards), and an impressive array of mystics flourished in fourteenth century England (Julian of Norwich, Richard Rolle, Walter Hilton, and the author of *The Cloud of Unknowing*).

The precipitating cause of the Tudor Reformation was a conflict between King Henry VIII (1491–1547) and the pope about divorce. Henry wanted to divorce his wife, Catherine of Aragon, to marry another woman, Anne Boleyn. The breakdown in negotiations between the king and the pope led to an administrative and judicial change in the structure of church government in England. Henry asserted the royal primacy over the church, declaring that the king (or queen), *not* the pope, was to be head of the church in England. Theologically, Anglicans attempted to find a middle way between Roman Catholicism and continental Protestantism. Accordingly, they kept much of the Roman Catholic doctrine and liturgical celebration, adopted a significant structural change, and allowed changes in some disciplinary matters like clerical celibacy.

When Henry VIII died, his son Edward VI (only a child) was king, and England was ruled by regents. The regents were substantially more sympathetic to European Protestants—especially to the Reformed tradition—than Henry VIII had been. At this time some changes were introduced into the Anglican Book of Common Prayer and it looked as if the Anglican church might become more thoroughly reformed. Edward VI died in 1553 and Mary Tudor, Henry's oldest daughter, granddaughter of the King of Catholic Spain, and a strong Roman Catholic supporter, became queen. With her ascension to the throne the stage was set for a confrontation between Anglicans (who had accepted the Reformation and the changes in the Church of England) and Roman Catholics (who had not accepted Henry's changes but had remained loyal to Rome). Mary at first simply forbade the practice of the Protestant religion, but within a year she established ecclesiastical courts to find and sentence heretics. She is remembered as Bloody Mary because of the severe persecutions during her reign. John Foxe's Book of Martyrs (1563) was written to chronicle the stories of many Protestants who were cruelly tortured and executed for their religious beliefs.

Mary was succeeded by her half-sister Elizabeth I, daughter of Anne Boleyn. Elizabeth (queen from 1558–1603) was suspicious of Catholics (who judged that she was not the legitimate monarch) and of Protestants (who would have destroyed some of the protection offered by the episcopal polity of the Anglican church). In 1570 Pope Pius V issued a formal condemnation and excommunication of Elizabeth and released all English people from allegiance to her. If Catholics had had some problems before this condemnation, the problems more than doubled afterward. Up to this time English Protestantism and Roman Catholicism existed side by side; after the condemnation, Roman liturgy (the Mass) was forbidden and Catholics met increased persecution. By the end of Elizabeth's reign, England was the foremost Protestant country in Europe.

The Radical Reformation

The word *radical* comes from a Latin word meaning root. Radical reformers separated from other reform movements because they did not believe those reform movements really returned to the root of primitive Christian faith. Some radical reformers were called Anabaptists, a derogatory name from a Greek word meaning to *re*baptize. Anabaptists did not believe that it was scriptural to baptize babies and so *re*baptized one another and from then on baptized only adults. They wanted more than a structural and doctrinal reform: they wanted to restore apostolic Christianity, to live in conformity with Scripture and the faith of the first Christians. In order to do this, they saw the New Testament as the sole norm for Christian life and understood their relationship to Jesus as one of discipleship. For the Anabaptists, the life, death, and resurrection of Jesus were not important merely as elements in a doctrine of justification, but as norms for Christian behavior: the Christian was one who lived as Jesus had lived.

There were several disparate groups of Anabaptists in the early part of the sixteenth century, some of which were not typical of later Anabaptist practice. The Zwickau Prophets, for example, joined the Peasants' Revolt, and a group of Münster Anabaptists under the leadership of John Leyden established a theocracy and practiced polygamy. Two important early groups were the Mennonites and the Hutterites. Mennonites were named for Menno Simons (c. 1496–1561), a Dutch reformer. Their views were similar to those of the Swiss Brethren, a group that split from the state church in Zurich (Zwingli's church) because the Reformation there hadn't been radical enough and because they regarded the whole notion of having church affairs subordinate to state control as unscriptural. The Hutterites took their name from Jacob Hutter (d. 1536) and were distinguished from other Anabaptist groups by their adoption of common ownership of property.

Anabaptists differed radically from other reform groups in practice and behavior. Their reading of the New Testament led them to some ethical conclusions about their life as and in the church that were at odds with the practices of both Catholics and Protestants. Thus the Anabaptist vision was threatening to other Christians, and Anabaptists were persecuted by both Catholics and Protestants. Five Anabaptist beliefs were particularly radical:

1. *Separation from the world:* The world was perceived as a place controlled by evil and Anabaptists believed they should separate themselves from it; that is, be disinterested in politics or the affairs of the state.
2. *Refusal to swear oaths:* Taking Jesus's words, "Do not swear at all. . . . Let what you say be simply 'Yes' or 'No' " (Matt. 5:34, 37) literally, they refused to swear oaths; since the oath was the basis of the juridical feudal system, it looked as if they stood against the basic organization of society.

3. *Nonresistance:* Doing as Jesus did and refusing to fight evil with evil, they refused to do anything violent; that is, they refused to fight in wars for any reason.
4. *Adult baptism:* They regarded baptism and responsible faith as matters of adult conviction, not the province of children, who were regarded as innocent until they reached an age of accountability.
5. *Community of goods:* They believed in sharing one's goods with everyone, friend and foe alike; in its extreme form, everything was owned in common, as with the Hutterites.

Anabaptists were a small but important strand of the Reformation. Their beliefs and their radical discipleship distinguished them from other groups and had the effect of keeping their numbers small. As we shall see in later chapters, Mennonites and Amish (a later Anabaptist group) continue the traditions of the Radical Reformation not only in terms of belief and religious practice, but sometimes in the (very old-fashioned) way they live in the contemporary world.

These four major strands of the Protestant Reformation all grew into separate denominations which, as we shall see, inspired the growth of other churches. The creative protests of Wycliffe and Hus, the reforming decisions of the conciliar movement, and the supportive atmosphere of the Renaissance all worked together to energize the reforming impulses of Christianity. The Protestant Reformation was the beginning of a rich period of religious growth which, for Protestant denominations, was especially vibrant in nineteenth century America. Catholicism was also urged to reform during this time, and it is to that group that we now turn.

THE CATHOLIC REFORMATION

The Catholic Reformation is sometimes called the Counter-Reformation, a term that implies little more than a reaction to Protestant reform movements. It would be more accurate to say that reform movements had been going on within and outside Catholicism for some time, and that some of the early Protestant reform movements were originally attempts to reform the Catholic church. Still, there *was* a significant Roman Catholic response to the Protestant Reformation.

The charter of the Roman response was contained in the decrees of the Council of Trent (1545–63), a reforming council that met on and off for nearly twenty years. Roman Catholics refused to meet Protestant reformers halfway on any issue and used Trent instead to reassert church authority, to clarify traditional doctrine, and to establish a solid basis for the renewal of discipline and spiritual life within Catholicism. After Trent, the Roman Catholic church emerged with a clear system of doctrine and discipline, and some significant moral and administrative reforms. Among the doctrines and practices affirmed by the Council of Trent were the following (notice that they respond to Protestant questions or positions by denying them):

1. A creed is important and the official creed is the Nicene Creed.
2. Scripture is *not* the only source of divine revelation; *tradition* is on an equal footing with Scripture as a source of religious authority.
3. Individuals may *not* interpret the Bible for themselves: the church is the sole interpreter of the Bible and the official Bible is the Vulgate.
4. The Protestant doctrine of sin and justification is false; people have free will, and justification is intrinsic and related to grace.
5. There are *seven* sacraments instituted by Jesus Christ, and sacraments are necessary for salvation.
6. The doctrine of transubstantiation is the official explanation for the real presence of Christ in the Eucharist.
7. The eucharistic doctrines of Luther, Calvin, and Zwingli were condemned.
8. The chalice (wine) was denied to the laity.
9. The value and importance of the Liturgy (the Mass) was reaffirmed.
10. Reforming moves aimed at bishops, seminaries, and diocesan synods were established.
11. The doctrines that supported purgatory and the use of relics and indulgences, all of which were severely criticized by Protestant reformers, were upheld.

To insure the success of the Catholic Reformation two offices were established (or reestablished under different rules): the *Inquisition* (a final court of appeals for heresy cases, not to be confused with the Spanish Inquisition, which was established in the late fifteenth century by the Spanish crown as a means of using state power against Muslims and Jews); and the *Index* (an official list of books that members of the Roman church were forbidden to read).

Protestant reformers had protested that religious orders and monastic institutions in Catholicism were corrupt. In the sixteenth century a number of new reformed religious orders were established; a particular one, the Jesuits, was established for the militant support of the church.[13] In all of these religious groups, members had a reputation for piety and austerity as well as great preaching and teaching ability. On a popular level, as a tangible example of reform in the church, they were effective.

The Catholic church made no significant overtures to Protestants or to members of the Orthodox church until the Second Vatican Council (1962–1965). At that council efforts were made to talk with and understand Protestants, and much of what has been characterized as the "seige mentality" of Trent began to disappear. The primary importance of Scripture was affirmed, the importance and role of lay people in the church was stated, Protestants were recognized as true Christians, it was declared permissible to celebrate the Liturgy in the vernacular, more congregational participation in worship was encouraged, and the Index was abolished. The Second Vatican Council was sweeping in its changes, and the effects of those changes as well as the development of some of them into significantly different practices and attitudes continue to be felt.

CONCLUSION

Throughout his public life, people asked Jesus, "By whose *authority* do you do these things?" Questions of religious authority have marked the Christian church from the beginning and have contributed to the variety in its life. During the Reformation, questions of religious authority were bound up with questions of doctrine and practice and led to a full-scale division of the Christian church into Protestant and Catholic in the West. Orthodox Christians were interested in the reformers' protests against papal power, but not much inspired to make doctrinal and liturgical changes; the Reformation, therefore, did not significantly influence them.

By the middle of the sixteenth century Protestants and Catholics had begun wars against one another; each group understood itself as the instrument of God's will and wrath, commissioned to bring the other group to its knees. Both Catholics and Protestants persecuted Anabaptists whenever they could, and otherwise killed and tortured each other in the name of religion. The wars of religion (involved with political issues as well) formally ended with the Peace of Westphalia in 1648. The wars ended, but not the controversy, and not the proliferation of Christian churches.

CHAPTER 5 NOTES

1. See Brian Tierney, *The Crisis of Church and State 1050–1300* (Englewood Cliffs, N.J.: Prentice-Hall, 1964), or Bennett D. Hill, editor, *Church and State in the Middle Ages* (New York: John Wiley & Sons, 1970). Political struggles were not the whole story at this time. There were struggles, changes, and growth in every sector of life and in religion; but the political emphasis I give helps to more clearly focus the beginnings of protest.

2. The spiritual road for the pope was suggested periodically throughout history, but never willingly taken. The first pope to rule without power over the so-called papal states (a large and significant slice of present-day Italy, right across the middle) was Pius IX (pope from 1846–78), and then only because they were taken away by force. Why didn't the popes give up their political power? No one can answer for sure, but read what a Renaissance pope himself had to say about the matter: "These are not times in which virtue is regarded. It is of all importance whether it resides in the strong or in the weak. A helpless virtue is despised by the princes. I have often felt inclined to agree with those who think that the temporal power ought to be separated from the spiritual; for I thought that the priests would be better enabled to perform their functions and that the

princes would be more obedient to them. But now I have learned that virtue without power is scorned, and that the Pope without the patrimony of Peter [the papal states] is but a servant of Kings." These are the words of Pope Pius II, from *De Concilio Basil.*

3. These positions can be found in the writings of Pope Innocent III (pope from 1198–1216) who, perhaps more than any other pope, embodied the extremes of ecclesiastical-political doctrine.

4. For a translation of excerpts from this document see Anne Freemantle, editor, *The Papal Encyclicals in Their Historical Context* (New York: New American Library, 1963), pp. 71–77.

5. There are, as you can imagine, countless books on the rise of the papacy, and few of them are as objective as one would like. One clear introduction to the issues and personalities from the beginning to the fifteenth century is Geoffrey Barraclough, *The Medieval Papacy* (New York: Harcourt, Brace & World, 1972). The book is beautifully illustrated and Barraclough gives you a sense of the controversy and flavor of the times.

6. The conciliarist movement has an interesting historical footnote. In 1516 the pope issued a decree that condemned conciliarism. The first words of that decree—the words that should have set it apart from all other papal documents, past and future, because no two papal documents ever begin with the same words—were *Pastor aeternus.* Yet in 1871, when papal infallibility was declared by the First Vatican Council, the first words of their decree were *Pastor aeternus.* Coincidence, or symbol of a return to papal absolutism? Let me add something to it. The great conciliarist council (Constance— which held, among other things, that councils were superior to popes) was called by Pope John XXIII. Since he was deposed right after the council, his name and number were forgotten until 1958 when Angelo Roncalli was elected pope and took the name of John XXIII. Coincidence, or symbol of a return to conciliarism? The modern John XXIII called the Second Vatican Council (1962–65), the most sweeping reform council in modern Roman Catholic history and one which again extolled a collegial kind of church government.

7. For some sense of the scope of the Renaissance see Donald Weinstein, editor, *The Renaissance and the Reformation 1300–1600* (New York: The Free Press, 1965). Weinstein's introduction to this collection of documents is brief and clear.

8. Purgatory is one of those doctrines that makes sense to believers and appears utterly incomprehensible to nonbelievers. One way to get to the medieval understanding of salvation (including concepts of heaven, hell, and purgatory) is through Dante's *Divine Comedy.* It was written at the beginning of the fourteenth century and gathers the doctrines, corruptions, personalities, and questions of the times into a cosmic vision, and, as one of the first and most important pieces of Italian national literature, is a pleasure to read. For a clear explanation of purgatory see the introduction to the second part of the *Divine Comedy,* the *Purgatory,* in the translation by Dorothy L. Sayers (London: Penguin, 1955), pp. 1–71.

9. The word *memorial* is a tricky one. Zwingli meant that at the Lord's Supper one simply shared bread and wine with the community and remembered what Jesus did. For an analysis of the word with its Jewish roots and Christian understandings through history see Louis Bouyer, *The Eucharist* (Notre Dame, Ind.: University of Notre Dame Press, 1968), pp. 103–6.

10. A general way to distinguish between Roman Catholic and early Protestant doctrines of justification is through the terms *intrinsic* (Roman Catholic) and *extrinsic* (Protestant). The key question is whether or not something really happens to human

nature through grace. Let's start with the premise that human nature is sinful to begin with (a dungheap): extrinsic justification says that if you have faith, then even though you remain a dungheap, you smell like a bed of roses to God; nothing really happens, but by virtue of the grace of Christ, God treats you like a garden. Intrinsic justification says that if you do those things that give grace (say your prayers, live virtuously, and so on), you will be changed into a rose garden; something really happens, or, to put it in the religious language of the times, "grace transforms nature." Luther did not believe this.

11. One way to remember these five points is with the word *tulip: t*otal depravity, *u*nconditional election, *l*imited atonement, *i*rresistible grace, and final *p*erseverance.

12. See for example Bede, *A History of the English Church and People* (London: Penguin, 1955). This book was written in the eighth century by Bede, a Benedictine monk. In it one can see how the English church was set up along the lines of Roman primacy, and one can see how power was passed along.

13. The Jesuits (the Society of Jesus) were founded by Ignatius Loyola (1491–1556) to be a missionary order, but they became the great religious force of the Catholic Reformation.

SUGGESTIONS FOR FURTHER READING

1. For two general background books see R. W. Southern, *Western Society and the Church in the Middle Ages* (London: Penguin Books, 1970), and Roland H. Bainton, *Early and Medieval Christianity* (Boston: Beacon Press, 1962). Southern is more dense with information and gives an excellent general introduction to the divisions in the religious world in the Middle Ages, the proliferation of religious orders, the various fringe groups, and the papacy. Bainton is straightforward and eminently readable and deals with the patristic period, medieval theology, and its transformation before and during the Renaissance.

2. For a documentary introduction to the Reformation see Hans J. Hillenbrand, editor, *The Reformation: A Narrative History Related by Contemporary Observers and Participants* (Grand Rapids: Baker Book House, 1964). This is full of pictures and documents linked together by a simple narrative style.

3. For good histories that were written for students and are full of pictures and illustrations, see A. G. Dickens, *Reformation and Society in Sixteenth-Century Europe,* and *The Counter Reformation* (New York: Harcourt, Brace & World, 1966 and 1969).

4. For an insider's history of the Radical Reformation see Donald F. Durnbaugh, *The Believers' Church—The History and Character of Radical Protestantism* (New York: Macmillan, 1968).

CHAPTER 6

The Reformation Continues

T he Reformation responded to and proliferated religious ferment. The main groups of the Reformation were relatively clear-cut and confined to a small geographical area, new offshoots of a unified Christianity within a fairly uniform cultural context. As Christianity moved into the seventeenth and eighteenth centuries, the social and religious situation became much more complex. Religious reform continued, but not in such a way that it could easily be classified as Lutheran or Calvinist. New religious groups formed, sometimes within a particular Reformation church and sometimes as a more generalized response to some secular attitude. In the eighteenth century especially—when the Enlightenment and new scientific discoveries threatened all religions—new Christian groups were formed on the basis of widespread religious response to a particular cultural development.[1]

This chapter summarizes some significant developments within Christianity in the sixteenth, seventeenth, and eighteenth centuries. We review the European situation in the first two of these centuries briefly and then focus on Christian diversity in England. The English situation merits closer attention for two reasons: it was extraordinarily rich in new forms of Christianity, and it is the parent of the American religious experience. After some discussion of the struggle between science and religion in the eighteenth century (which provides a context for the birth of Deism and Pietism and the growth of Methodism), we move to the American context where we will concentrate throughout the rest of this book.

SIXTEENTH AND SEVENTEENTH CENTURY CHRISTIANITY: INCREASING DIVERSITY

The Reformation raised issues of polity, doctrine, and practice so profound that its reverberations continued for centuries. In the sixteenth and seventeenth centuries we can often identify and define issues as one specifically religious view in competition with another. It is even possible, with only slight modifications, to continue to differentiate religious groups as further divisions of the major strands of the Reformation. For our purposes, the developments within Lutheranism, Catholicism, and the Radical Reformation can be described simply and briefly. I will discuss the Reformed tradition within the context of English Puritanism at some length so that you can begin to understand the roots of the American religious experience. It is within the English context that I will mention—only briefly—developments within the Tudor Reformation.

Roman Catholicism

The reverberations of reform were felt in the Roman Catholic church in a proliferation of new religious orders but not in new liturgical or doctrinal forms. Church/state issues—the political power of the pope, the role of the church in the conquest of the New World, and relations between European nations and the Vatican—continued to play an important role in the history of Roman Catholicism. The Council of Trent strengthened the Roman Catholic church against the demands of the reformers and inspired a real reformation within the church. Roman Catholicism was defined by the teachings of the Council of Trent up until the middle of the twentieth century. Because of its strong centralized model of ecclesiastical authority, Roman Catholicism did not foster or accept divisions within itself: one was either a loyal Roman Catholic or one left the church (by choice or through excommunication). By definition, a loyal Roman Catholic was one who followed the teachings of the church, accepted the hierarchical structure with the pope at its head, and participated in the specified liturgical and sacramental life of the church.

Lutheranism

Lutheranism spread throughout Germany and the Scandinavian countries without division. The Lutheran church was strongly congregational; issues of polity and practice were left up to the local congregation.[2] Accordingly, Lutheranism developed in different but not divisive ways: in some places one could find a liturgy that looked vaguely Roman Catholic—structured, formal celebration of the Eucharist—and in other places services which were more clearly

Protestant—worship consisting mainly of hymns and Bible study. The primacy of the gospel was the most important Lutheran principle; it was solidified in creeds like the Augsburg Confession, part of the Book of Concord (see Appendix 5).

Radical Reformation

The polity of Radical Reformation groups was strongly congregational and was therefore able to support a variety of practical forms within the general framework of Anabaptist vision. Anabaptists were often victims of brutal persecution by both Catholics and Protestants and by both religious and secular authorities. Their strategy during this time was one of survival. The two main groups—Mennonites and Hutterites—continued to exist and to move from place to place to be free from harassment. One new Anabaptist group emerged at this time, the Amish. They were the conservative followers of Jacob Amman, about whom little is known. The Amish split from the Mennonites because they wished to see a strict enforcement of *Meidung,* the practice of shunning the excommunicated. They became a separate group at the end of the seventeenth century and migrated to America in the eighteenth century.

The Reformed Tradition in the Context of the Puritan Reformation

The most fertile soil for religious proliferation was England, and the most productive Protestantism to flourish there was the Reformed tradition. The specific nature of the Tudor Reformation made England a place where some of the fundamental arguments of the Reformation could continue. The religious situation on the Continent stabilized with the Peace of Westphalia (1648):[3] France and much of southern Europe were Catholic, northern Europe was Protestant (either Lutheran or Reformed and not at war with one another), and Germany was a patchwork quilt of Catholicism and Protestantism depending upon the religion of the regional ruler. England was a Protestant country, but not in the sense that some of the European countries were. The rationale for the Tudor Reformation had been *political;* the key document, the Act of Supremacy (1534), stated that the monarch was the legitimate head of the church in England. The argument focused on the rights of the monarch versus the rights of the pope in religious matters. The issues of the continental Reformation—polity, liturgical practice, and doctrine—were not as important in England as the question of supremacy. Thus the Church of England continued to operate within a hierarchical structure (versus the congregationalism of Luther or the presbyterianism of Calvin), continued to celebrate the eucharistic liturgy (versus the more simplified worship services found in many Protestant churches), and continued to support ancient doctrinal formulations (not the new doctrinal positions of the continental reformers). In some senses, therefore, the Church of

England under Henry VIII had not been reformed; it had simply been cut loose from Roman supremacy.

Let's review the English situation briefly. After Henry's death England was ruled by regents and the Church of England grew a little more Protestant, but when Mary I (Henry's daughter) came to the throne, Protestant measures were reversed, Roman Catholicism restored, and severe anti-Protestant persecution began. During these persecutions many religious reformers fled to the continent where they imbibed a pure Calvinism and nurtured a strong desire to reform the Church of England. Their chance would come, they hoped, with Mary's death.

Mary's successor, her half-sister, Elizabeth I (1533–1603) wanted religious and political stability. She tried to find a middle ground between Roman Catholicism (still practiced by many of her subjects and favored under Mary) and the Calvinism urged by some of her colleagues. She held fast to the episcopal structure of the church, but restored the autonomy of the English church by asserting its independence from Rome. Under her supervision the church adopted the 1552 version of the Book of Common Prayer and revised and reduced the Forty-two Articles to the Thirty-nine Articles, which were adopted as the standard expression of the beliefs of the Church of England (see Appendix 5). During Elizabeth's reign a movement for religious reform began that stressed a purification of the church, purging it of anything Roman in practice, liturgy, or doctrine. The followers of this movement were called Puritans.

There were two main groups of Puritan reformers: Presbyterians and Congregationalists. One of the fundamental issues of the continental Reformation was church polity; the reformers protested against the unscriptural basis of a hierarchical church. The Puritans were united in their protest against the hierarchical structure of the Anglican church, but they were divided about which continental model to adopt. Both Luther's congregationalism and Calvin's presbyterianism derived from the New Testament. Since both models had a biblical base there was no agreement about which one to choose, and no authoritative way to decide between them.

Congregationalists. Congregationalism is a form of church government that rests upon the autonomy and freedom of the local congregation, and defines a church as a group of believers bound together under the headship of Jesus Christ. In Congregationalism, each local church is truly and fully the church. Those people holding congregational views who found themselves unable to remain within the Church of England separated from it and are sometimes referred to as Separatists.

Presbyterians. Presbyterianism is a form of church government that combines some congregational insights (the importance of the local church) with some advantages of the hierarchical model (more centralized authority). This model was adopted by two major groups: the Reformed church (in Europe) and the Presbyterian church (in England and Scotland). The Presbyterian church is the English and Scottish branch of the Reformed church founded by John Knox (c. 1513–72).

Presbyterians were the dominant Puritan group in England in the sixteenth and seventeenth centuries. Elizabeth had not cooperated with them and neither did her immediate successors, because there had been an old and mutually advantageous relationship between the monarchy and the episcopal form of church government. When the cry for religious reform (from the Puritans) was combined with the cry for political reform (from the Parliamentarians) the result was the English Civil War (1642–48). The monarchy was defeated, and this also meant the defeat of episcopacy—at least for a while. In 1646 Presbyterianism was substituted for the episcopal polity of the Church of England. During the interregnum (the period in which there was no monarch: 1649–60) it was a crime to use the Book of Common Prayer. When the monarchy was restored in 1660, it was not merely a political victory; it was a victory for the Church of England over the Puritans. In 1662 the Act of Uniformity required episcopal ordination of all ministers (restoring power and control to the bishops) and decreed that the Book of Common Prayer was the only legal worship book in England. In reaction to the Act of Uniformity more than two thousand clergymen resigned from the Church of England to celebrate their own worship in Nonconformist *chapels*.[4]

Thus by the end of the seventeenth century the Reformation in England had resulted in the establishment of the Anglican church as the official Church of England. It had an episcopal structure, was protected by the monarchy, affirmed the Thirty-nine Articles, and used the Book of Common Prayer as its sole liturgical source. Not all Christians in England belonged to the Anglican church. Roman Catholics, still suspected of disloyalty to the crown, maintained a low profile and did not take a prominent place in English life until the end of the nineteenth century (when they were again permitted to attend English universities). Nonconformist groups—both presbyterian and congregational— existed along with Anglicanism and continued to attract new members. Two new religious groups were formed within this Nonconformist context: Baptists and Quakers.

Baptists. The Baptist church was a new denomination that had Congregationalist roots. It shared the church polity views of the English Congregationalists, but developed a distinctive teaching about baptism. Since 1644 the name Baptist has been applied to those who believe two things about baptism: that it must be done by immersion (not by pouring water over the head or sprinkling), and that it can only be administered to convinced believers; that is, to adults and not to babies. The first group of Baptists formed in Holland at the beginning of the seventeenth century. A group of Separatist Congregationalists led by John Smyth (1554–1612) migrated to Holland to live in an atmosphere of religious freedom; there, influenced by some Mennonites, they repudiated infant baptism and formed the first English Baptist congregation.

Quakers. The Religious Society of Friends, or Quakers, was a new religious group founded by George Fox (1624–91) that attracted many unattached Nonconformists.[5] Fox, disillusioned with the ferocious wars fought for Christian truth and frustrated with the disparate claims of the churches, sought a new religious understanding. In 1646 he had a religious experience that caused him to find peace within himself, an experience that led him to the doctrine of the Inner Light. According to Fox, all people have the inner voice of God within them; the Inner Light is the fundamental source of religious certainty and deep spiritual assurance. The Quakers presented a new religious alternative for people by opposing traditional Calvinist doctrines of human depravity and the preeminence of biblical revelation. A person with the Inner Light is not depraved, but possesses the voice of God within; if God speaks directly to the heart, biblical revelation is less central. Since the Inner Light is so important, Fox believed that all outward forms of religion should be rejected: church institutions, sacraments, ritual, ministers, hymn singing, all signs of outward established institutional church life were dropped. Like the Anabaptists, Quakers refused to swear oaths or to participate in wars and were persecuted physically and legally.

Summary of Sixteenth and Seventeenth Century Christianity

By the end of the seventeenth century there were many more religious groups than there had been at the beginning of the Reformation.[6] Roman Catholics did not divide into separate churches, but did continue to be touched by the reforming spirit of the times. Lutherans moved into Germany and Scandinavia, forming new congregations without any significant division, though the Pietist movement (see next section) was very important in Lutheranism at this time and beyond. The Anabaptists struggled to survive and the main groups—Mennonites and Hutterites—continued to baptize members into their fellowship. The only significant division was the formation of the Amish church at the end of the seventeenth century. In England, the Reformed tradition inspired the Puritan movement, which eventually split into and inspired several different groups: Congregationalists, Presbyterians, Baptists, and Quakers. Ultimately, the Anglicans were the established Church of England, though non-Anglican chapels were permitted to exist in England and continued to attract new members throughout the country. Representatives from all these different religious groups immigrated to America and played an important role in American religious history.

THE EIGHTEENTH CENTURY: THE STRUGGLE BETWEEN SCIENCE AND RELIGION

In the eighteenth century, religious arguments did not occur as frequently between one church and another, but most churches had members who began to challenge some of the fundamental assumptions of Christianity. New religious alternatives such as Deism and Pietism were generated in response to some of these challenges. To understand eighteenth century Christianity we must understand the beginnings of science and the general context of the Enlightenment. We look at these topics next.

The Scientific Revolution

The church in the Middle Ages was the single most powerful institution in the West and claimed (as we have seen) to have jurisdiction over virtually everything. Conflicts arose when someone challenged that claim (as, for example, when political leaders challenged the church's political power). As scientists began to learn more about the world and its wonders, they began to challenge some long-held and religiously supported views. The Protestant Reformation gave an implicit impetus to the scientific revolution by questioning religious authority and thereby making it easier for scientists to question established patterns.

The discoveries of Copernicus (1473–1543) and Galileo (1564–1642) upset old notions of the order of the universe and undermined what some people believed to be an immutable view of the cosmos and our centrality therein. One of the most famous cases in which the church condemned a scientific view (one we all know today to be true) was the condemnation of Galileo. His support for the Copernican view that the sun is the central body in the universe and that the earth moves around *it* was not the officially sanctioned view. In 1633 he was called to Rome by the Inquisition and forced to retract his (scientific) views.

René Descartes (1596–1650) and Francis Bacon (1561–1626) established the importance of the scientific method based on empirical observation and systematic doubt; Isaac Newton (1642–1727) brought the world to the threshold of modernity with his physical and mathematical discoveries. Very few people believed that science could really endanger religious beliefs; yet as the world was changed by new discoveries, a great change came over the way educated people looked at the heavens and the earth. The discoveries of the scientific revolution suggested that the whole universe might be subject to the control and domination of human ingenuity.

The Enlightenment and the Beginnings of Deism

The Enlightenment followed on the heels of the scientific revolution. People were called out of the darkness of religion (perceived as mystery or superstition) and into the "enlightened" world of reason: they were given light to see the world around them and encouraged to believe in a reasonable universe. "Dare to know," the Enlightenment philosophers challenged, and their followers stretched toward a new individualism and a theory of human perfectibility. Immanuel Kant (1724–1804), perhaps the greatest of the Enlightenment philosophers, wrote *Religion within the Limits of Reason Alone* to argue for the need for moral consciousness without miracles. Old Christian doctrines like divine providence were seen as needless interference in the orderly lives of people.

The combination of scientific discoveries about the universe and Enlightenment philosophy challenged old and cherished Christian assumptions. During the next hundred years, Christians reacted in various ways to this challenge, as they still do today. Some grew defensive, spending their energy denying the legitimacy of the challenge; others tried to defend Christianity by using the skills and tools of post-Enlightenment scholarship. Still others, in the eighteenth century at least, tried to combine Enlightenment insights with religious impulses and so developed a new religion, Deism.

The old religion was criticized for being ponderous and superstitious, for crippling rather than enhancing human freedom. Deism was extolled for its simplicity and reasonableness and for its insistence on religious toleration and freedom. Deism is a religion of logic and reason that believes that God is sufficiently revealed in the natural world. There is, accordingly, no need for supernatural revelation. According to Deist belief, God created the world and filled it with reasonable people and discernible natural laws; one's task is to discover the laws of nature and to live according to one's reason. John Locke (1632–1704) wrote his essay "The Reasonableness of Christianity" to prove that the ethical injunctions of Christianity were in conformity with the dictates of reason: the excellence of Christianity lay precisely in its reasonableness.[7]

The rationalism of the Enlightenment and Deism was a philosophical response to some of the confusion and distress present in Christianity in the sixteenth and seventeenth centuries. Wars fought in the name of Christianity and the systematic use of torture by one group against another caused many people to abandon organized religion altogether or to be less than enthusiastic in their religious devotion. A religious response to the rationalism of the Enlightenment and Deism and to a growing sense of moral laxity and confusion was evangelical Pietism. It not only regenerated some churches, but also inspired new ones.

Pietism and the Emergence of New Christian Churches

The original impetus for Pietism arose during the seventeenth century in a new reformation within German Lutheranism. Associated with the teachings of Philipp Jakob Spener (1635–1705) and August Hermann Francke (1663–1727), this movement was a reaction to moral laxity, formalism, secularism, and religious indifference. Spener longed for a rebirth of religious seriousness within the Lutheran church. He organized Bible study groups in his home, which were known as the *collegia pietatis,* later the Pietists. Spener was more interested in a right feeling in the heart than he was in pure doctrinal formulation and his teachings were ultimately condemned by the Lutherans, though they continued to have an effect on the Lutheran church. Francke, a professor at the University of Halle, built Pietism into the ministerial curriculum of the university. More than two hundred Lutheran ministers graduated from the university every year, each with some exposure to Pietistic doctrines. Pietism has some dominant characteristics: a Bible-centered faith, a keen sense of guilt and forgiveness felt in the heart, personal conversion, practical holiness in simple Christian living, and a concern for the needs of other people. All of these characteristics were thought to be manifested and supported by an emotional outpouring of one's feelings and aspirations. Pietism influenced members of many different churches and inspired the formation of new religious groups, including the Brethren and the Methodists.

Brethren churches. The Brethren were an Anabaptist group formed in Germany by Alexander Mack (1679–1735). Mack had been a member of the Reformed church, but separated from it—along with some others—in order to find a more biblical expression of Christianity. His group was composed mostly of Pietists and Anabaptists; in 1708 they formed a new fellowship and elected Mack as their leader. Because of persecution, they migrated first to the Netherlands and then to Germantown, Pennsylvania; they had all come to America by 1735. They were sometimes called Dunkers or Dunkards though their official name was the Fraternity of German Baptists. Brethren are distinguished in practice by a threefold immersion at baptism and a threefold Holy Communion service: footwashing, the Lord's Supper, and an *agape* or fellowship meal, sometimes called a love feast.

Methodists. Methodism was a revivalist movement within the Anglican church influenced by Moravian Pietists.[8] John Wesley (1703–91), his brother Charles (1707–88), and their friend, George Whitefield (1714–70) were at Oxford University together when they experienced a religious awakening. They and a few other students were interested in a more heartfelt religious experience than they found among people in the Church of England, and they spent much time in prayer and spiritual discipline in search of it. Other students ridiculed them for trying to devise a method for religious experience and the name Methodist stuck to Wesley and his work. John Wesley was influenced by Moravians in the American colony of Georgia (where he went as a missionary in 1735) and in England (where he returned dejected a year later). On a visit to a Moravian settlement at Aldersgate in 1738, Wesley had a conversion experience in which he felt his heart "strangely warmed," when he knew that God took away all his sins. From that warm assurance, his acquaintance with Pietist doctrine through the Moravians, and his own early preoccupations with religious experience, Wesley built a significant religious movement.

Wesley called the world his parish: he rode more than 250,000 miles on horseback and delivered in excess of forty thousand outdoor sermons: he preached in slums and prisons, anywhere people would listen to his message of religious regeneration. The stress on personal conversion, warm fellowship, and fervent preaching made Methodism attractive to thousands of people inside and outside the Anglican church. One important factor in the spread of Methodism was the hymnody; the Methodist hymnal, said Wesley, was a "distinct and full account of scriptural Christianity." The hymns were comforting and easy to sing; they reassured people about God's love for them.

Methodism, as a revivalist movement within the Church of England, was never intended to become a separate religious group; Methodists were members of the Anglican church and Methodism was their style of fellowship and religious revival. Because of its emphasis on an emotional religious conversion, it attracted many followers and was a means of regeneration within the church as Methodists desired inner holiness and wanted to live lives of prayer, discipline, and fellowship. In order to maintain a disciplined prayer life for converts Wesley established Methodist societies and classes, and specified weekly prayer meetings and other means of communication and fellowship. All these disciplinary innovations made Methodists *feel* separate from the Church of England. They were not separate, however, so long as they were dependent upon the Anglican church for sacraments and ordination. The English Methodists did not become a separate body until 1897.

While the scientific revolution and the Enlightenment inspired Deism and a reaction to it, the migration of various religious groups to America caused further religious changes in the seventeenth and eighteenth centuries. We look next at the American context and the changes it engendered.

THE AMERICAN CONTEXT

We have to step back for a moment to the seventeenth century in order to understand the American experience in the eighteenth century. Puritan Congregationalists and Presbyterians who did not stay in England fled to America in the early part of the seventeenth century; the Pilgrim colony at Plymouth was founded in 1620 by the first of such groups. In 1648 representatives of the Congregational churches of New England met in Cambridge, Massachusetts; there they adopted *A Platform of Church Discipline,* which quickly became known as the Cambridge Platform. The statement was not a creed, but a plan of action based upon Congregational principles. One of the points stressed in the Cambridge Platform was *covenant theology.* Puritan New England was not founded upon principles of religious toleration, but upon federal or covenant theology. The Puritans believed that God operated in history through covenants and was now forming a new covenant with them in this new land; interpretations of covenant theology had an important influence on the political and religious order in New England. Because the community was a covenanted one, each member of the community was to follow God's law as it was found in the Bible and enforced by local religious and civil magistrates.

By the middle of the seventeenth century the Puritan ideal was crumbling; preachers accused people of infidelity and called them to return to the principles of the covenant. People did not respond to the challenges of the Puritan ideal, however, perhaps because they were occupied with settling the new land. Puritanism lost much of its persuasive power. By the middle of the seventeenth century survival was no longer the primary issue in people's lives; Puritan exhortations about fear of the Lord did not strike responsive chords in them. Ideas from the Enlightenment—a reasonable God and the advantages of religious toleration—undermined the Puritan system, which was built upon a sovereign (not always reasonable or understandable) God and intolerance of other forms of religious expression. The lures of the modern world—mercantilism and commercialism—affected Americans as it had Europeans: they were often more interested in the fun of making money than they were in the drama of salvation. Within this context, two different movements are worthy of attention: the revivalist impulse of the Great Awakening and the rationalist religion of Deism in its American form.

The Great Awakening

The eighteenth century began with a total religious decline. It is not clear how many of the American colonists were church members: probably only a few. Religious indifference was as much a part of the American scene as it was in Europe. One of the revivifying factors for European Christianity was Pietism; American Christianity was regenerated by revivalism in a movement known as the Great Awakening, a series of revivals that spread throughout the American colonies from 1725 until the 1760s. The Great Awakening cut across denominational lines and engendered a spirit of religious cooperation based on shared religious feeling.

The revivalist movement began in specific churches. Theodorus Frelinghuysen (1692–1747) was a member of the German Reformed church who was influenced by Pietism; he came to America in 1720 to preach personal repentance and a more emotional expression of religion to people of several Dutch Reformed churches. Gilbert Tennent (1703–64), a Presbyterian minister influenced by Frelinghuysen, brought the revivalist message to Presbyterians and to Christians of the middle colonies. The most famous figure of the period was Jonathan Edwards (1703–58), a Congregationalist theologian and preacher responsible for the New England phase of the Great Awakening. By the 1740s, these evangelical preachers had high hopes for a religious revival in America; there was, after all, a religious revival occurring in England under the impulse of Methodism. About this time George Whitefield, Wesley's friend and a phenomenally successful preacher, came to America. Whitefield was a strong Calvinist-Methodist and he took America by storm; he set the pattern for roving revivalist preaching in the colonies.

American Evangelicalism was born in the Great Awakening; it emerged from the Reformed tradition and the Puritan experience, but it also stressed new forms and some new content in the Christian message. The religious strategy of Evangelicalism is designed to elicit a response: it stresses *new birth*, which is sudden and which determines whether one is or is not a Christian; the importance of the *emotions* to demonstrate that the conversion is of the heart and not just of the head; and the *sufficiency of God*, underlining the Calvinist preoccupations of the message. This last point underwent some rather profound changes in subsequent revivalist movements, but during the Great Awakening God's sovereignty was a fundamental tenet; evangelists recognized that God glories in a person's absolute dependence, that God alone grants the conversion experience.

The Great Awakening regenerated American Christianity, but also caused further divisions within it. Tennent's preaching about the dangers of an unconverted ministry caused a division within the Presbyterian church: New Side Presbyterians welcomed the revivalist message, Old Side Presbyterians repudiated it. The Congregational church split into New Lights and Old Lights. Charles Chauncy (1705–87) was the outspoken opponent of revivalism within the Congregational church and the leader of the Old Lights. He was a spokesman for the rationalism of the Enlightenment and a forerunner of the Unitarian schism in the Congregational church in the nineteenth century. Even those who favored the message and tactics of the Great Awakening argued about the place of the emotions: radicals said that the heart alone accounted for conversion, moderates recognized the importance of the heart but did not want to deny the importance of an intellectual understanding of Christianity as well.

Deism in America

Many of the founding fathers of America were Deists: Benjamin Franklin (1706–90) and Thomas Jefferson (1743–1826) were both deeply touched by the rationalism of the Enlightenment; both believed that religion could be reduced to ethical consciousness and good moral conduct. Deism, remember, was a reasonable religion; doctrines not understandable through reason—miracles or the doctrine of the Trinity—were denied. Many of the accents of Deism are echoed in the American Constitution: reason, religious toleration, optimism about the pursuit of happiness, and a trust in a reasonable God. Deism was able to attract people because it stood in judgment on many of the troublesome religious trends of the time: it was against dogmatism, sectarian infighting, enthusiasm, and clericalism. On those grounds it appealed to many people who were formally connected with churches.

Growing Denominationalism

By the end of the eighteenth century, America was an independent nation with a highly diverse religious population. During the early years of settlement there was reason to predict regional churches in America—different religious groups tended to settle together in different regions—but by the end of the eighteenth century *denominationalism*[9] was a fact of American religious life. Many different churches were allowed to coexist peacefully within the same region. As a consequence of the Enlightenment, the Constitution of the United States supported the "great experiment" of religious freedom and toleration. No church was supported by the state, nor did the state interfere with the internal life of the churches. The separation of church and state supported a relatively new religious idea—voluntarism—whereby church membership was understood to be purely a matter of personal choice.

The census of 1790 showed the following numbers of Protestant churches in America: Congregational, 749; Presbyterian, 495; Baptist, 457; Anglican, 406; Lutheran, 240; German Reformed (Calvinist), 201; Quaker, 200; and Dutch Reformed, 127. There were no figures in that census for Roman Catholics because Catholics were still not welcome in the English colonies: they were not allowed to live in some places, not permitted to hold public office or own land in others. In 1785 there were fewer than twenty-five thousand Roman Catholics in a population of four million; there were 56 churches.

Roman Catholics. Though scarce in the English colonies, Roman Catholics were the dominant religious group in the Mississippi basin by the end of the century. Catholics had come to the New World with the Spanish and French explorers and settled peacefully into French and Spanish territories. The city of New Orleans and the southern Louisiana territory were predominantly Catholic.

Quakers, Mennonites, and Amish. The religious climate of Pennsylvania was unique in the American colonies and made it a haven for a variety of religious groups that were unwelcome or actively persecuted in other colonies. William Penn (1644–1718) was a convinced Quaker whose interest in founding an American colony was motivated by principles of religious freedom and liberty of conscience. The federal theology of the Puritan colonies did not allow religious toleration, and many of the other colonies had legislated restrictions against one religious group or another (usually Roman Catholics, Quakers, and Anabaptists). Penn founded his colony as a "holy experiment," and established it upon a constitution that permitted all forms of worship compatible with monotheism. Mennonites and Amish settled there and moved west from there in the nineteenth and twentieth centuries. The Quakers also settled in Pennsylvania. Their positions, especially their pacifism, made them victims of persecution. Their history in eighteenth century America is a relatively quiet one; they separated themselves from the rest of the society by their plain dress, their obscure biblical forms of speech, and their avoidance of worldly ways.

Brethren. The Brethren originally settled in Germantown, Pennsylvania. But they were persecuted during the Revolutionary War for their refusal to participate in it, and the geographical scattering of the Brethren occurred during this time. They experienced one minor schism, but not over pacifist principles:

the Ephrata Community advocated celibacy and mystical religious experience and formed as a separate group in 1728, but lasted as a society less than one hundred years.

Lutherans. The Lutherans settled into the colonies with no major divisions.

Puritans (Presbyterians and Congregationalists). The Puritans divided denominationally into Congregationalists and Presbyterians, the major religious groups within the colonies. Both groups were regenerated during the Great Awakening, and both groups experienced some division because of the revivalist nature of that regeneration, as we have noted earlier.

Baptists. The Baptists, led by Roger Williams (1603–83), had originally grown out of the Congregational church in England, and continued to grow and to attract members of that church. During the Great Awakening hundreds of people separated from the Congregational church in order to become Baptists. The decline of the Baptist religion during the first half of the eighteenth century was totally reversed during the Great Awakening; by the end of the eighteenth century the Baptists were the largest single Christian denomination in the United States with their greatest strength in the South.

Anglicans. The Anglican church in America was supported by the British crown and suffered many of the vicissitudes of seventeenth-century English history. The early Anglican communities reflected the variety of opinion within the Church of England. The most pressing problem for the American Anglican church was the lack of native bishops; for complex political reasons bishops were not sent to the American colonies. With the support of the English government, Anglicans established missionary societies, colleges, and influential churches. These gains, however, were outweighed by their liabilities: Anglicans were politically suspect during the Revolution, their ministers were forced to go back to England for ordination (by a bishop), they tended to attract mostly aristocratic people and had little common appeal, and they refused to participate in the Great Awakening. In 1789 the Anglican church in America reformed itself as a separate entity within the Church of England: they were in communion with the Church of England, but established their own episcopacy and called themselves by a new name, the Protestant Episcopal church.

Methodists. The situation for Methodist societies in America changed the course of Methodist history. Once Anglican priests (who could administer the sacraments) began to return to England (during the Revolution), American Methodists were left without access to the sacraments. In response to this situation John Wesley ordained two lay leaders as deacons and elders, and appointed a superintendent for the American group. Wesley was a minister in the Church of England and knew that ordinations could only be valid when performed by a bishop. By the end of the eighteenth century, however, he had become convinced that bishops and priests differed from each other in terms of function but not in terms of power. His ordination of the two lay leaders, therefore, was done in good faith and with no intention of forming a separate denomination. Thomas Coke (1747–1814) was the man appointed by Wesley to be the superintendent of American Methodists; he in turn ordained Francis Asbury (1745–1816) as a general superintendent at the Christmas conference of Methodist preachers held in Baltimore in 1784. At that conference the American Methodists established themselves as a separate denominational group with the name Methodist Episcopal church. Asbury assumed the title of bishop and, despite severe remonstrances from Wesley, would not relinquish it. When Asbury first came to America in 1771 there were 1200 Methodists in various Methodist societies and prayer groups; when he died, there were more than 214,000 members of the Methodist Episcopal church.

Summary. By the end of the eighteenth century, a wonderful and somewhat surprising arrangement had taken root in America: almost every conceivable variety of Christianity practiced in relatively peaceful coexistence with other groups and even with professed Deists. This is not to say that some groups did not continue to feel the sting of religious persecution; sectarians and Roman Catholics continued to encounter prejudicial laws and bigoted behavior from some of their neighbors. For the most part, however, Christians in America were free to practice their religion without interference from the government and without hostility from other groups.

CONCLUSION

The Reformation continued in Europe, stimulated in part by a growing antagonism between science and religion. Although significant religious growth occurred throughout Europe, we have focused mainly on England where the arguments between Anglicans and Puritans (and later, the influence of Pietism) produced a rich variety of religious responses. Representatives of nearly all Christian groups moved to America in the seventeenth and eighteenth centuries and settled in specific regions of the country. The Great Awakening regenerated much of Protestant Christianity in America and stimulated new growth in many churches. The American experience stimulated the formation of two new denominations that had formerly been part of the Church of England: the Protestant Episcopal church remained in communion with the Church of England, but acquired its own separate hierarchy; the Methodist Episcopal church separated from the Church of England—against Wesley's intentions and desires—to form a new religious body. By the end of the eighteenth century the American religious climate was ready to foster the phenomenal growth that characterized nineteenth-century Christianity.

CHAPTER 6 NOTES

1. For a clear introduction to these issues see Gerald R. Cragg, *The Church and the Age of Reason 1648–1789* (London: Penguin Books, 1960).

2. I do not mean to suggest here that one cannot also find episcopal polities in some Lutheran churches—in fact, there are Lutheran bishops. For a more complete discussion of church structures and differences see Chapter 10.

3. This was the general treaty that ended the Thirty Years' War (1618–48—a complicated struggle involving many political and religious issues) and also ended religious warfare.

4. The word *chapel* here does not denote a small church (as in a little country chapel) nor does it mean an alcove or secondary place of worship within a big church. The distinction between *church* and *chapel* in England is based on establishment: the *Church* of England is supported by the state and is the official religion of the English people. Those who do not worship in the Church of England do not, therefore, belong to the church (so designated) but are said to worship in *chapels*. That distinction is not so alive today as it was in the seventeenth century, but one still finds it in literature sometimes.

5. Not everyone who was disenchanted with the Church of England was attracted to one of the new groups that developed into a major denomination. In England at this time there were many small religious sects: Familists (the Family of Love), for example, or Ranters, or Seekers (waiting for the emergence of the true church, convinced that it did not exist in any group). Many of these people were attracted to the Society of Friends (Quakers).

6. I have not covered here all the religious groups that sprang up because I thought it would be more confusing than helpful. There was, for example, a minor schism within Roman Catholicism in the Jansenist movement. It was mostly a movement of French intellectuals and did not lead to a separate religious group, but it did leave an attitude of moral pessimism and religious rigorism in parts of the Roman Catholic church. There was a minor schism within the Lutheran church as well, a kind of sixteenth-century version of born-again Christianity—the Schwenkfelders. They were named for their founder, Kaspar Schwenkfeld (1489–1561), whose doctrines were condemned by the Lutheran church. He preached a spiritualized Christianity where justification was not merely external but a continuous inner experience, and where one's worship focused on hearing the inner word of Jesus spoken in the heart. The Schwenkfelders moved to America in 1734 with about 2500 members.

7. The distinction I made in Chapter 1 between direct and indirect revelation is important to recall here. Revelation, as I said earlier, is a complex question for religious thinkers, and it is virtually impossible to separate direct revelation from experiences of indirect revelation. Knowledge of God as the creator of the universe may result from a direct experience, and the belief that the earth is good may result from an indirect experience, and the balance between them is delicate. So when we come to the Enlightenment thinkers and Deists we should remember the distinction and the complexity of the problem.

8. Moravians trace their heritage back to the reforms of John Hus in the fourteenth century, a movement re-formed under the impetus of Pietism. Through the help of a wealthy Pietist, Count Zinzendorf (1700–60), the Moravian church was able to solidify and become ongoing. They settled in Pennsylvania—both Nazareth and Bethlehem are

Moravian colonies—and were pioneers as missionaries and leaders in American Christian education.

9. For more on the emergence of denominationalism see Sidney Mead, *The Lively Experiment: The Shaping of Christianity in America* (New York: Harper & Row, 1963), pp. 16–38 and 103–34.

SUGGESTIONS FOR FURTHER READING

1. For further reading on specific denominations, consult the bibliography at the end of the book.

2. For an excellent introduction to the Puritan ethic and a feel for Puritanism in the young American colonies, read Edmund S. Morgan, *The Puritan Dilemma: The Story of John Winthrop* (New York: Little, Brown, 1958).

3. For a documentary introduction to the Catholic experience in America see John Tracy Ellis, editor, *Documents of American Catholic History* (Milwaukee: Bruce Publishing, 1956). Ellis begins with the document "dividing the new world between Spain and Portugal" (a line drawn by Pope Alexander VI) and goes up to the 1950s. Just looking at the table of contents of this book will give you some indication of where Catholics were in America at this time and what their main issues were.

4. For an engaging and informative history of Protestantism in America see Martin E. Marty, *Righteous Empire: The Protestant Experience in America* (New York: The Dial Press, 1970). Marty draws from a vast number of stories and documents.

5. For an extremely useful and clear look at American religious history through documents and commentary see George Bedell, Leo C. Sandon Jr., and Charles T. Wellborn, editors, *Religion in America* (New York: Macmillan, 1975). This book was written as an introductory text and tries to deal equitably with Protestants, Jews, and Catholics. The documents they include are interesting and their introductions good. See especially pp. 131–88 on revivalism in America.

CHAPTER 7

Modern American Christianity

The American atmosphere in the nineteenth and early twentieth centuries was exuberant and expansive; American Christianity reflected that atmosphere. The nineteenth century was one of extraordinary religious diversity that continued into the twentieth century. Many of the more complex issues of worship, interfaith cooperation, varieties in church structure, and Christian attitudes toward the world versus American cultural values will be explored in subsequent chapters. In this chapter we explore the proliferation of religious groups in America. A section on the twentieth century at the end of this chapter is a general summary of the results of some of the religious hopes stirred in the nineteenth century, and the continuation of some of the arguments begun after the Civil War.

THE NINETEENTH CENTURY: AMERICAN
RELIGIOUS DIVERSITY

The nineteenth century, like the eighteenth, began with a general religious decline in America. The enthusiasm of the Great Awakening had subsided, religion had become a purely voluntary matter, and people were moving away from the cities to settle the new frontier. A new wave of revivalism, sometimes called the Second Great Awakening, began in the nineteenth century and added new accents to American Evangelicalism. Enlightenment philosophy continued to be felt in what came to be known as Liberal Protestantism. In the climate of religious freedom and the turn of the new century several communitarian groups and some new churches were founded in expectation of the Second Coming of Christ. Two new American religions were founded in the nineteenth century: Mormonism and Christian Science. Churches that had settled in America still faced problems: those from non-English-speaking countries sometimes disagreed about adopting the customs and language of the new country; those with more conservative intellectual traditions were pressed to respond to the enthusiasm of revivalism in the churches. The Civil War divided almost every church over the issue of slavery and spawned specifically black churches within the established denominations. Not surprisingly, divisions continued within the churches over internal matters; some new groups formed because of disagreements about church discipline and doctrine.

For purposes of convenience and internal unity this section on the nineteenth century covers some new religious movements and denominations up to the outbreak of the First World War in 1914. Many churches that were divided over a number of issues in the nineteenth century then attempted to reunite or to join with other churches to form a new denomination. We cover the continuation of these efforts into the twentieth century so that we can have a coherent idea of the general history of the group.

American Evangelicalism

The nineteenth century began with a new wave of revivalism that differed significantly from the Great Awakening. The central figure of this new wave was Charles Grandison Finney (1792–1875), a lawyer whose religious experience transformed him into a preacher. Finney understood revival as the controlled manipulation of religious phenomena. During the First Great Awakening preachers tried to elicit a response and commended emotional conversions, but they did not pretend to understand the mysterious inner working of conversion itself; the work of conversion was God's. Nineteenth-century revivalism, conducted in camp meetings[1] and on the frontier, proceeded from the notion that holiness is voluntary and conversion a matter of personal choice more than divine action. This idea is most clearly associated with Finney.

After the Civil War, Dwight L. Moody (1837–99) applied business and advertising techniques to religious revivalism and developed large interdenominational urban meetings similar to the large camp meetings of the first part of the century. He founded Moody Bible College to train evangelical ministers. The revivalist message was simple and often antiintellectual; it centered on the redemptive love of God in Jesus Christ and contained a strong call to repentance. Revivalism was designed to be an emotional experience leading the sinner to rebirth and to a healing experience of God's love. Evangelicals expected conversion to be accompanied by a manifestation they themselves called exercises, which might include crying, running, or some kind of physical tremors.

American Evangelicalism often promised and produced social as well as moral improvement, readying people for a life of action. The Evangelical Alliance was formed in 1846 to concentrate evangelical energy in the service of scriptural Christianity and against what were considered to be unscriptural religions (for example, Roman Catholicism). Societies were formed throughout the nineteenth century to spread the evangelical message—the American Bible Society and the American Tract Society—and to inspire moral improvement—the American Temperance Union.

Evangelicalism has often been used to describe an emotional approach to religion: Methodist revivals in England, ridiculed by some as too emotional, were known as evangelical. For the most part, however, it describes those who stress religious experience and the importance of making a clear, definite decision for Jesus Christ. Evangelicals stress biblical authority and human sinfulness; they insist on the need for a new birth and a life of holiness and personal witness.

In addition to specifically evangelical denominations,[2] evangelical groups exist within mainline Protestant denominations: one can find Evangelical Mennonites, Evangelical Presbyterians, Evangelical Methodists, Evangelical Lutherans, and so on. It cannot be assumed that these churches are always characterized by American evangelical beliefs or practices. The word *evangelical* is sometimes used (in Europe especially) to distinguish Protestants from Roman Catholics; it sometimes refers to Christians influenced by Methodist revivalism; in American religious history, it has often meant personal religious experience and new birth in Christ combined with Christian fundamentalism.[3]

Liberal Protestantism

Inspired by the rationalist philosophy of the Enlightenment and Deism, and often in reaction to the emotionalism of revivalism, some groups of Christians became more liberal in their interpretation of Scripture. The clearest example of a new denomination with these characteristics is Unitarianism. Formed within American Congregationalism and associated with the work of William Ellery Channing (1780–1842), Unitarianism rejects the mysterious doctrine of the Trinity in favor of a belief in the unity of God. Unitarians base their positions on the Bible and refuse to accept some theological tenets of the Reformation, especially the Calvinist doctrine of total human depravity.

Liberalism sometimes means freedom from prejudice and a readiness to welcome new ideas and progress in religion. By this criterion one can find liberals in all churches: Catholic, traditional Protestant, and Evangelical. *Liberal Protestantism* usually refers to an understanding of Christianity that emphasizes its humanitarian impulses rather than dogmatic propositions or emotional conversion. It is, accordingly, an often misunderstood term and frequently used to criticize people for being insufficiently religious in a traditional sense.

Communitarian Groups

A variety of religious experiments flourished in the climate of religious freedom of nineteenth-century America. The communitarian impulse derived from the early Christian tradition of members sharing their goods and living a common life (see Acts 4:32–37).[4] The monastic tradition (as we have seen in Chapter 4) sprang from the desire to live a life of perfection and to do it in a community. Throughout history there have been communitarian groups drawn together for these general reasons: for example, the Waldensians were a twelfth-century group that gathered around Peter Waldo (ca. 1176) in order to live in apostolic poverty.

We have already seen that groups can split from a major Christian denomination to form a separate religious entity (the Amish splitting from the Mennonites, for example). Communitarian groups sometimes split from a parent group and sometimes were an entirely new creation. In America, many of them were drawn together by their belief in the Second Coming of Christ. Whatever their beliefs, they were usually founded by a strong leader, and lived together in separate villages or communes, often with some distinguishing practice or belief. There were groups inspired by perfectionism and made up almost entirely of intellectuals and literary people (like the Brooke Farm Movement), and groups inspired by German Pietism who practiced celibacy and waited for the world to be restored to harmony (like the Rappites, also known as the Harmony Society). Some of the products we use today (or brand names we know) were originally associated with nineteenth-century communitarian groups, like Amana appliances, connected to Amana Church Society in Iowa, and Oneida silver, connected to the Oneida Community founded in New York by John Humphrey Noyes (1816–86). Let us look more closely at two of these groups.

The Hopedale community. This group was founded in Massachusetts in 1842 by Adin Ballou (1803–90), an American Universalist preacher. It was a nonviolent utopian community that required no common beliefs, but did require members to refrain from violence, taking oaths, and intoxicating drinks. It disintegrated as a community in 1857, but the Universalist movement—for which Adin Ballou was a preacher and with Hosea Ballou (1771–1852) one of its most important leaders—continued, became the Universalist Church of America, and merged with the American Unitarian Association in 1961 to form the Unitarian Universalist Association. Universalism is the doctrine that affirms the salvation of all people; God's love for everyone and desire for the salvation of all souls accomplishes this universal saving action.[5]

The Shakers. The United Society of Believers in Christ's Second Appearing is the official name of the Shakers, a group of "Shaking Quakers" led to New York by Mother Ann Lee (1736–84) in 1774. Shakers believed that God was manifested in male form in the person of Jesus Christ and in female form in the person of Mother Ann Lee. In New York, they established a community of celibacy, pacifism, and cooperative living. Some Shaker communities still exist—in Canterbury, New Hampshire and in Sabbath Day Lake, Maine—though most have disappeared. They were the largest of the communitarian groups and are remembered historically for their ritualized ecstatic dancing, their distinctive architecture and furniture, and their theological innovations, specifically for their belief in a female manifestation of God.

Most of these communitarian groups have ceased to exist, but many of their settlements are preserved as historical sites and they continue to be remembered for their experiments in community living.

Millennialist Groups

From the New Testament we can see that Christians have, from the beginning, thought about the Second Coming of Christ. If we think about the return of Christ, certain questions occur to us: *When* will he return? *What will happen* when he does? Some Christians, reading Revelation 20:1–10, believe that Christ will establish a thousand year period of bliss, and so wait joyfully for the millennium (millennium means a thousand-year period). Most Christians believe that Christ will return to judge the living and the dead, but they do not all attempt to predict the time of the Second Coming. Millennialist groups in the nineteenth century were preoccupied with questions about the Second Coming and very much involved with interpreting the signs of the times so as to maintain a high level of expectation about the imminence of Christ's return. The three most significant groups of millennialist Christians formed in the nineteenth century are the Adventists (represented here by the Seventh-Day Adventists, though there are other adventist groups),[6] the Jehovah's Witnesses, and the Dispensationalists.

Seventh-Day Adventists. Adventism, as a movement, originated with the prophecies of William Miller (1782–1849) about the end of the world. Miller, a lay preacher in the Baptist church, concentrated on the books of Daniel and Revelation and devised a way to tell when the end of the world was coming. In 1831 he began to preach that Christ's Second Coming was to be expected in 1843. His preaching was apparently convincing since more than seven hundred ministers of various denominations welcomed him to their pulpits and helped him to spread the word. When Christ did not return in 1843, Miller recalculated and predicted two dates in 1844, by which time between fifty thousand and one million people had left their congregations to wait for the coming (advent) of Christ. When Christ did not return on the second set of dates, some of these people left their churches altogether, some returned to their own congregations, and still others formed splinter adventist groups.

In general, Adventism is the belief that Christ's Second Coming is at hand, that the wicked are soon to be punished and the good rewarded. The largest and most famous of the adventist groups is the Seventh-Day Adventist Church founded by Joseph Bates, James White, and his wife, Ellen Gould White (1827–1915), who is considered the prophetess of the Seventh-Day Adventist Church. The first conference of the new church was held in Battle Creek, Michigan, in 1863; Ellen White's numerous visions were crucial in resolving early questions of doctrine and practice. Seventh-Day Adventists observe Saturday (not Sunday) as the proper day of Christian worship; they accept the Bible as the only authoritative rule of faith and interpret it literally. They also affirm the prophecies of Ellen White and believe that the spirit of prophecy is present in their church. They are strict sabbatarians and follow many Old Testament dietary laws; they wait for the Second Coming of Christ, but do not attempt to predict an exact time for it. They believe Christ *began* his judgment in 1844 (the date Miller set for the Second Coming), and will finish it in his own time.

Jehovah's Witnesses. The Jehovah's Witnesses were founded by Charles Taze Russell (1852–1916) who studied the Bible and became convinced by 1872 that Christ would return secretly in 1874 and that the world would end in 1914. His published opinions secured a large following and from 1879 he established himself as pastor of an independent church in Pittsburgh where he published *The Watchtower*. His followers were known by different names, including the Watchtower People. They were named Jehovah's Witnesses by their second leader, Joseph Franklin Rutherford (1869–1942). The sect grew from a few thousand to 106,000 during Rutherford's lifetime and today claims more than a million members in various countries.

Jehovah's Witnesses believe that only the elect of Jehovah (a form of the Hebrew name for God) will get into the kingdom of God. The present world, according to them, is ruled by Satan and all government, business, and organized religion is in league with the devil and in conflict with the will of Jehovah. They consider themselves part of a theocratic kingdom and, accordingly, will not serve in the armed forces, salute any flag, or hold political office. They avoid the ways of the world and traditional religious feasts, refusing to celebrate Christmas or Easter. Based on the books of Daniel and Revelation they believe that only Christ and 144,000 elect have immortal souls and that everyone else has a mortal one, but will be given a second chance during the millennium. At that time the just will reign and the wicked will perish.

Dispensationalists. Dispensationalism is a system of biblical interpretation that divides all time from the creation of the world into units called dispensations. In each dispensation God is revealed in a new way and treats people differently. The first five dispensations refer to periods in the Old Testament, the sixth is the time of the Christian church, and the seventh is the coming of the kingdom. If Christians are now living within the sixth dispensation they are, in a sense, living at the edge of the kingdom and should expect the return of Christ soon. Dispensationalists read the Bible from this perspective and interpret its prophecies to support their beliefs. Twentieth-century American Dispensationalists use the Scofield Reference Bible, edited by Cyrus I. Scofield (1841–1923), which offers a dispensationalist key to the interpretation of Scripture.

New American Religions

Most "new" religious groups were formed from a particular established church, or established on the basis of a generalized belief—such as nineteenth-century Adventism—that swept through all churches. Two religious groups founded in the nineteenth century, however, were *really* new: they did not spring from established churches or movements, and they were specifically American, with distinct aspects growing out of the American context. These were the Mormons and the Christian Scientists.

Mormons. The Church of Jesus Christ of Latter Day Saints (the Mormons) was founded in New York by Joseph Smith (1805–44) in 1830. Smith had a revelation experience: he was led by an angel to discover the Golden Plates, which contained "the fullness of the everlasting Gospel." According to Mormons, the Book of Mormon was translated by Smith from the Golden Plates; it is approximately five hundred pages long and is divided into books like the Bible. The Book of Mormon describes the lives of the "lost tribes of Israel" who migrated to America; it covers the years 600 B.C.E. to 421 C.E. According to the Book of Mormon, Jesus appeared to these people after the Resurrection and established a church among them; it is this church that Smith claimed to revive. According to Smith, all other churches have no divine authority; his authority came directly from God and he was ordained by John the Baptist.

Smith and his followers moved to Kirtland, Ohio, where an entire congregation joined them. From there they moved to Missouri, then to Illinois where they prospered but aroused their neighbors' animosity. Smith was killed by a mob in Illinois in 1844. When Smith died, the church divided into several groups, two of which are particularly important. The largest group followed Brigham Young (1801–77) to Salt Lake City, Utah. There they established a theocracy and openly practiced one of the doctrines of their faith—polygamy—from 1852 to 1890. According to Smith, marriage was important for salvation—singlehood and celibacy were considered to be against God's will—and plural marriage a revealed doctrine.

In Mormon theology God was once a man, who later achieved divinity, as can any man. Mormons say, "What man is now, God once was; what God is now, man may become."[7] A man becomes a god by successfully living through the testing period of mortality on earth; if he does well he can become a god presiding over his own world; there are many worlds and many gods. In Mormon belief God is the literal father of human souls; God is a polygamist who mates with female deities to produce an abundance of spirits or souls. In order for those souls to have an opportunity to become divine they must become embodied, be born as human beings. Thus Mormons regard it as a duty to have as many children as possible, to embody as many souls as possible. The practice of polygamy enabled more souls to become embodied.

The other significantly large group of Mormons is the Reorganized Church of the Latter Day Saints (1852). It considers itself the legitimate successor of Smith's church and repudiates some of the later doctrines, especially polygamy and polytheism. Theologically this body resembles traditional Protestantism. It is headquartered in Independence, Missouri. Joseph Smith Jr. (1832–1914) was the original president, and this group owns the original church in Kirtland, Ohio, and the original manuscript of the Book of Mormon. Millennialism is an important part of all Mormon belief.

Christian Scientists. The Church of Christ, Scientist was founded by Mary Baker Eddy (1821–1910) in 1875. Most of her life she had been unhappily married and critically ill, but her life changed radically in the 1860s when she met Phineas Parkhurst Quimby (1802–66), a mental healer. After a healing experience with him she developed her own system; in 1866 when she was seriously ill, she read the account of Jesus raising the daughter of Jairus (Luke 8:40–56) and was cured. This was a decisive experience for her. She had discovered the real meaning of the Gospels: that Christ healed by spiritual influence.

According to Eddy, Jesus taught people the power of the mind to eliminate the illusions of sin, sickness, and death. All people, she taught, can be loving, confident, and well instead of hateful, fearful, and sick if they simply understand the spiritual nature of all reality: God is a spirit or *idea* and God is everything. Human beings, as a reflection of God, are also spiritual and good. The role of Christ is to bring people to this understanding. Eddy wrote *Science and Health* in 1875 and added to it "A Key to the Interpretation of Scripture"; this book, according to Christian Scientists, presents the *only* way to read the Bible. In following it, people find that the only reality is *ideas* and that matter does not exist; God is all good and there is no room for sickness; the cure comes when one can perceive this fact. In 1877 Eddy opened the Massachusetts Metaphysical College where she trained healers. By 1886 these healers were so successful that the National Christian Science Association was founded. By 1900 there were over one hundred thousand Christian Scientists.

Christian Science was one part of a larger intellectual and emotional movement known as New Thought. Mental healing was popular and influential in the late nineteenth century, and its teachings appealed to members of many different Christian denominations. According to the followers of New Thought, God is a life principle; salvation is happiness here and now; the absence of sin makes repentance unnecessary; and Jesus Christ is the symbol of the divine spark of goodness in everyone. New Thought promises secret inner power and a "real" understanding of Christianity to its followers. While there are certain common beliefs in New Thought—spiritual healing and the creative power of thought, for example—it was never an organized denomination. At the same time, as a healing movement, it influenced people like Mary Baker Eddy who did found organized churches.

Americanization and the Churches

English-speaking denominations in some ways set the pattern for American religious development. Non-English-speaking groups—especially German Lutherans and European Catholics—had some trouble determining how American to become. Catholics had the added difficulty of being perceived as a church dominated by a foreign power.

Lutheranism. Lutherans from Germany, Austria, and the Netherlands began to immigrate to America in the seventeenth century, but never were well organized as a confessional group. In the eighteenth century a German missionary, Henry Melchior Mühlenberg (1711–87), came to America to minister to and organize American Lutherans. He organized the first synod (group of Lutheran congregations) and by 1770 eighty-one Lutheran congregations existed in Pennsylvania alone. By the nineteenth century many more Lutherans had come and were spread out over a wider territory. Many of them were German. One question that arose in the minds of many of these people concerned the relationship between their ethnic and their religious identity. They wondered whether to maintain their German heritage or to become more thoroughly American in language and custom; they wondered how much being Lutheran had to do with being German.

The dilemma of Americanization gave rise to three general solutions. The wholeheartedly pro-American option was defined by Samuel Simon Schmucker (1799–1873). He urged Lutherans to band together into one American Lutheran church and to dissociate themselves from ethnically defined churches; he hoped to build a church without ethnic barriers. Schmucker had been touched by American Evangelicalism and his plan was based on some doctrinal compromise; he was willing to abandon some traditional Lutheran positions in order to become more American. The conservative reaction to Schmucker's position was led by Carl F. W. Walther (1811–87) who supported strict confessional Lutheranism (giving nothing to American evangelicalism) and German ethnic heritage. Walther's group formed a German Lutheran Synod in the 1840s, which eventually became the Lutheran Church-Missouri Synod. The middle-of-the-road alternative was defined by Charles Porterfield Krauth (1823–83) and became the basis for the Lutheran Church of America. Krauth supported the traditional Lutheran confessionalism of the conservatives, but also advocated an American Lutheran identity as urged by Schmucker; his group maintained its Lutheran doctrines and also abandoned Old World ways. As more Germans entered the country, these arguments continued; the three main branches of the Lutheran church in the United States reflected the divisions and arguments.

In 1974 there was a major schism within the Missouri Synod, which resulted in the Association of Evangelical Lutheran Churches. The dividing issue was the interpretation of Scripture; the new group adopted methods and positions often associated with more liberal viewpoints. In 1982 the Lutheran Church of America, the American Lutheran Church, and the Association of Evangelical Lutheran Churches voted to merge into a single new church. This merger, which should be completed by 1987, marks an important step not only in Lutheranism (making it the third largest Protestant denomination in the country, after Baptists and Methodists) but in American religious history.

Roman Catholicism. Roman Catholics encountered two problems related to their Americanization. Internally there was a division between the more liberal Irish bishops who pushed for Americanization and the more conservative German bishops who wished to avoid Americanization in favor of preserving their ethnic identity.[8] Externally, hostility from a variety of anti-Catholic nativist movements followed Catholics up to the second half of the twentieth century. The English colonies had never welcomed Roman Catholics nor made them very comfortable; Catholics suffered from a variety of social and legal restrictions and a lack of religious freedom. During the colonial period few Catholics came to the colonies, but from the 1820s to the 1870s the Catholic population increased from 195,000 to 4,504,000; most of them were immigrants. The rapid increase in the Catholic population and their foreign connections (by birth or church affiliation) inspired the rise of nativist movements.

Nativism is intense suspicion and dislike of any foreigner, especially a Roman Catholic. Revivalist preachers and nativist publications warned Americans against the "international conspiracy" of the Roman Catholic church. Catholics, they said, were under the domination of a foreign monarch (the pope) and were by definition (as members of a hierarchical, nondemocratic church) unable to support American freedoms. In the early part of the nineteenth century people were easily convinced that Catholics were a menace, that convents were dens of iniquity, and that there was a Roman conspiracy led by the pope and managed by the Jesuits. In some anti-Catholic riots people were killed and convents burned.

From the 1850s to the present there have been nativist movements. The Know Nothing movement (so-called because members always claimed to know nothing about their secret activities) was founded in the 1850s as a secret political society. In 1854 they formed the American Party to combat foreign influence, popery, Jesuitism, and Catholicism. Their political aim was to exclude all Roman Catholics from public office and in 1856 they gained 25 percent of the popular vote. The Know Nothings disappeared after the Civil War partly because of their alliance with the proslavery movement, but nativism did not disappear. In the 1880s new waves of eastern and southern Europeans, predominantly Catholic, immigrated, and the American Protective Association was formed in 1887 to limit the Catholic population with a stringent immigration quota system. By 1896 the American Protective Association had a million members; it lingered as an association until 1911. In the 1920s the Ku Klux Klan was revived against blacks, Jews, and Roman Catholics; Klan policies against foreigners were supported by a systematic use of terrorism.[9] The Klan gained political power and was able to support legislation that restricted immigration of eastern and southern Europeans. The revival of the Klan in the 1970s is a modern example of nativism as directed against foreigners.

Catholics responded to nativism with withdrawal and patriotism. On the one hand they pulled back from the mainstream of American life, founded a separate, extensive private school system, and organized Catholic neighborhoods and social units. When necessary, however, they exhibited intense patriotism—as if to prove that Catholics were especially good Americans. The most significant response to nativism, however, led to the most divisive argument within the American Catholic church in the nineteenth century.

The two predominant groups of Roman Catholics in nineteenth-century America were Irish and German, with church leadership in predominantly Irish hands. German Catholics settled into the so-called German Triangle defined by Milwaukee, Cincinnati, and St. Louis, where they hoped to live quietly and continue to retain their ethnic identity and the German language and customs they believed to be so superior to American or Irish Catholicism. A group of liberal bishops—John Ireland (c. 1838–1918), John J. Keane (1839–1918), and John Lancaster Spalding (1840–1916)—who were more enthusiastic about American pluralism, urged an American Catholicism without ethnic divisions. Through a series of conflicts and misunderstandings centered more in Europe than in the United States, the pope condemned "Americanism" in 1899. The papal condemnation was based on an inaccurate understanding of the American situation, but tended to dampen all efforts toward liberalization within the American Catholic church. The American Catholic experience in the 1890s set the tone for the conservative isolated Catholicism of the early part of the twentieth century.

Catholics deplored the tactics and theological positions of American Evangelicalism; they stressed the importance of the organized church and the sacraments as opposed to emotional conversions and reliance on subjective religious experience. Still, revivalism did influence the Roman Catholic church's concept of missions.[10] Specially trained priests moved from parish to parish preaching missions which were intended to strengthen Catholic identity and renew religious experience. Their style was not that of revivalist preaching in the American evangelical churches, but the desired goal was similar. Revivalist preachers aimed at conversion as manifested in response to an altar call; Catholic mission preachers sought to engender deep feelings of repentance manifested by an increased use of the sacrament of penance and a marked increase in devotional fervor.

Growth and Division within Christian Churches

The ethnic and ideological complexity of America inspired an enormous growth and division within the churches. Nearly every Christian church divided over slavery during the Civil War, and most churches suffered some division over the evangelical impulse. As happened during the Reformation, divisions continued over internal church polity. The melting pot image of America never quite took hold of the ethnic imagination—at least not during the nineteenth century—and many specifically ethnic churches and church groups remained. The so-called Restoration movement attempted to unify like-minded people into one "Christian" church.

Roman Catholics remained united as a single church while most other Christian groups experienced major schisms. Those divisions were sometimes over what were considered to be innovations (Sunday school, or a paid professional ministry), sometimes over major national conflicts (slavery), and sometimes were continuations of earlier arguments (the appropriateness of evangelical preaching). In many churches most members were willing to accept a particular progressive teaching or arrangement and a small group split from them to be faithful to their understanding of the original vision of the group. Many churches split along North/South lines during the Civil War—American Baptists and Southern Baptists; United Presbyterian Church (Northern) and Presbyterian Church in the United States of America (Southern); the Methodist Episcopal Church (Northern) and Methodist Episcopal Church of the South—and reunited in the twentieth century (though some groups are still attempting reunification).

Within the variety of Christian responses to the challenges of the late nineteenth century, three significant movements occurred: the Holiness movement, Pentecostalism, its lineal descendant, and the so-called Restoration movement. We will look at each of these movements briefly before drawing conclusions about religious diversity in nineteenth-century America.

The Holiness Movement. After the Civil War a series of Methodist revivals were preached stressing a return to holiness and emphasizing "entire sanctification." Wesley believed that there were two distinct blessings in the Christian life: justification (which changes the condition of one's life because God forgives one's sins and restores fellowship), and sanctification (which changes one's nature and helps a person to live a life of perfect love). Sanctification or Christian perfection does not mean freedom from mistakes or illness, according to Wesley, but is freedom from sin. The grace of God enables a person to love God so wholeheartedly that all that person's actions, thoughts, and words will be directed by love. The pivotal question is how sanctification is interpreted with regard to *time:* for the Methodists sanctification is a gradual process attained throughout the Christian life. Those who became part of the Holiness movement, however, believed sanctification was a sudden acquisition by the action of the Holy Spirit. Within the Holiness movement people expected to receive entire sanctification—instantaneous holiness—at revival meetings. In 1867 a group of like-minded individuals formed the National Camp Meeting Association for the Promotion of Holiness. From this came an interdenominational movement and the formation of separate Holiness churches.

Churches of God are more than two hundred separate denominations in the United States. The first impetus for their formation was the revivalist work done in German American communities in the first part of the nineteenth century; there was some spillover from this movement into several denominations. The second major group of members of Churches of God were from the Holiness movement: many of the Churches of God are Holiness churches. The oldest is the Church of God (Anderson, Indiana), which became a separate church because of its acceptance of the doctrine of entire sanctification as proclaimed by Holiness churches. The largest Holiness church is the Church of the Nazarene (1908). Holiness churches are usually evangelistic and fundamentalist; they stand for what is known as the Four-Square Gospel: that Jesus is the savior, the sanctifier, the healer, and the coming Lord.

Pentecostalism. The lineal descendant of the Holiness movement was the Pentecostal movement. Pentecostals believe in entire sanctification, but as a gradual—not instantaneous—process initiated by baptism in the Holy Spirit (often referred to as the Holy Ghost). Baptism with the Holy Ghost is manifested in the gift of *glossolalia,* according to Pentecostals: those who receive the Holy Ghost will speak in tongues. According to Pentecostals, the Christian experience at Pentecost—the coming of the Holy Ghost, the gifts of glossolalia, healing, and prophecy—should be a continuing and normal experience within Christianity.

Pentecostalism began in Kansas in the early part of the twentieth century. Charles Fox Parham (1873–1937), a preacher in the Holiness movement, convinced his followers that the baptism of the Holy Spirit required for salvation was essentially connected with speaking in tongues. One could determine whether or not one had received the Holy Ghost on the basis of a particular gift: only if the person spoke in tongues was it certain that he or she had received Spirit baptism. The most important source of Pentecostalism was the Azusa Street Revival held in Los Angeles, California, in 1906 by W. J. Seymour, a Holiness preacher.

Pentecostals are united in their belief that baptism in the Spirit and speaking in tongues are necessary signs of holiness; they are fundamentalist in their interpretation of Scripture, have strong dispensationalist leanings, and are strong believers in the imminent Second Coming of Christ. Pentecostals differ on matters of doctrine—some of them do not believe in the Trinity but see the Father, Son, and Holy Ghost as different manifestations of God in history—polity, and practice. The largest Pentecostal group is the Assemblies of God, an organization established in 1914. The United Pentecostal Church is the largest "Jesus name" (non-Trinitarian) group; baptism is administered in the name of Jesus Christ, not in the name of the Father, Son, and Holy Ghost.

A movement that has touched all other Christian churches and that is in some ways associated with Pentecostalism is Neopentecostalism or Charismatic Renewal. Christians in nearly all denominations, including Roman Catholics, have sought to experience the gifts of the Holy Spirit outside the context of classical Pentecostalism. These people are not usually motivated by a desire for the sign of *glossolalia,* but do hope to have some tangible experience of God, some manifestation of the Holy Spirit in their lives, without separating themselves from their particular churches. They do not want to agree to some of the doctrinal and behavioral principles of classical Pentecostals, but do share with them a desire for an experience of the Holy Spirit.

The Restoration or "Christian Church" Movement. The Restoration movement or New Reformation of the nineteenth century was an attempt to combine efforts for Christian unity with a return to simple, New Testament Christianity. Some people believed that Christians were unnecessarily divided over issues of polity, practice, and creeds, so they espoused a noncredal New Testament-based Christianity. One leader of this movement was Barton Stone (1722–1844), who participated in the Cane Ridge Camp Meeting (1801) and was led to dissolve his Presbyterian congregation so that they could be "simple Christians"; James O'Kelly (ca. 1735–1826) led a group of congregational Methodists to accept the Bible as their only creed. Other leaders were Thomas Campbell (1763–1854) and his son Alexander (1788–1866). Thomas Campbell left the Presbyterian church to found the Christian Association to promote unity among Christians. His son Alexander worked within Baptist associations and then founded a separate community that supported a rational, biblical, practical approach to Christianity. He avoided theological disputation and subtlety, on the one hand, and emotional revivalism on the other.

Alexander Campbell called his followers the Disciples of Christ and their churches were known as Churches of Christ. A conservative splinter group opposing non-New Testament innovations like Sunday school, instrumental music in worship, and missionary activity took the name Church of Christ for itself and was recognized as a separate body in 1906. The Disciples of Christ are members of the Christian Church.

Conclusion to Nineteenth-Century Christianity

The nineteenth century was one of enormous growth and diversity within the Christian churches of America; by the end of the century a widespread spectrum of belief and practice was manifested in a multitude of American Christian groups.[11] Throughout this time and into the twentieth century groups of Christians split and regrouped under different banners, a tendency that may attest to the dynamism within Christianity and the human need to join like-minded groups. By the middle of the twentieth century, many of the divided clusters had joined with others and merged to form large united churches like the United Church of Christ and the United Methodist Church. Some groups continued to maintain themselves as small churches. For the most part, however, the growth and diversity experienced in the nineteenth century gave way to movements of unity and cooperation in the twentieth century.

THE TWENTIETH CENTURY

Optimism and a belief in human progress characterized the first part of the twentieth century. American Protestants entered into the spirit of the times with plans to improve themselves (by way of the temperance movement, for example), while Roman Catholics put an enormous amount of energy into building and maintaining their own school system and network of hospitals, newspapers, and charitable and religious institutions.[12] The feeling of manifest destiny, which supported the idea of American democracy as capable of saving the world, was often given religious formulation by the churches, and a broad-based missionary movement was designed by the evangelical center of American Protestantism.[13] All these noble adventures, begun in the enthusiasm of the new century, had been abandoned by the 1930s: the Eighteenth Amendment (Prohibition—passed to stop the consumption of alcohol) was repealed in 1934 because it had been a massive failure; American nationalistic fervor cooled when World War I ("the war to end all wars") did not end human warfare; and the worldwide missionary movement, begun in the nineteenth century, collapsed for lack of cooperation.

The 1940s focused the nation's attention on the Second World War and its aftermath. There was a resurgence of monastic life in the Roman Catholic church right after the war,[14] and renewed interest in religion in general. The 1950s were times of extraordinary success for almost all churches: more than 70 percent of the American population considered themselves to be religious and almost all Christian groups were busy building new churches, schools, fellowship centers, and other structures. If the 1950s were a boom time for religions, the 1960s were a down time. For a number of reasons (related to the war in Vietnam and its attendant unrest, both personal and social), church attendance declined markedly, fewer people supported their churches financially, and most churches went into debt. Most Protestant churches went into a decline, the Roman Catholic church began to experience the unsettling reform attempts of the Second Vatican Council,[15] and some of the newer Christian churches (Mormons and Pentecostals, for example) were growing at enormous rates. The 1970s cannot be easily characterized, nor should they be at this point of insufficient historical distance, though we can relate some of the contemporary issues within American Christianity to older and perhaps deeper issues. But for background, we step back again to the beginning of the century and to the battle between two distinctly different religious views.

Fundamentalism versus Liberalism: The Battle of the Century

As we have seen, Christians in the modern period did not divide neatly along denominational lines, but were inclined to group together on the basis of shared beliefs or theological convictions. Many of the beliefs and practices in nineteenth-century American Christianity had repercussions in most of the churches: Adventism, Evangelicalism, Pentecostalism all inspired the formation of separate churches, but they also precipitated groups within churches that did not split from those churches. The contemporary context, therefore, is genuinely pluralistic, and modern Christian churches often have a surprisingly wide range of opinion represented within them.

One of the main dividing issues in twentieth-century Christianity is *orthodoxy*. What are the "right" beliefs for Christians? As you can imagine, there are many answers to that question, all of them grounded on specific denominational histories. But let us make a broad generalization and divide Christians into two main groups: those who have welcomed the discoveries of the age and sought to use scientific insights and methods within Christianity, and those who have scorned or shunned new ideas in order to stay deeply in touch with the "old time religion." Neither of these groups can be adequately described, but they stand at the limits of the argument, fundamentalists on the one hand and liberals on the other. Both words have been used as terms of derision and as badges of righteousness.

Orthodoxy is a question of right belief. What must a Christian believe? A certain theological orthodoxy had developed over many centuries and could, it was felt, be outlined in some basic (or fundamental) positions. Christians ought to believe in the Resurrection, in Christ as Savior and Lord of the world, in grace as a power of forgiveness and enablement (the power to do good), in the Trinity (three persons in one God, as defined by the ancient church), in the statements of the Apostle's Creed (see Appendix 5), in Original Sin and inherent spiritual weakness. To these central doctrines Protestants added some of the insights of the reformers: the priesthood of all believers, the salvation in Christ through faith alone, the sufficiency of Scripture as a religious authority, the sovereignty of God, and predestination. Catholics denied the Protestant insights and added instead the positions of the Council of Trent.[16] The argument I am now describing, however, is a Protestant one for the most part and what I say here relates to a debate within the Protestant church (one which the Catholic church would face in a different way and solve in a different way later in the century).

Important for Christian orthodoxy was the theory of the atonement. The orthodox Protestant position up to the nineteenth century was that of substitutionary atonement. This doctrine says simply that human sinfulness demanded a payment, that Jesus paid the price (substituted for humanity), which satisfied the demands of divine justice, and that because of his work, death, and resurrection, people can be saved. All these points of orthodoxy derive from the Bible.

The orthodox view did not endure without challenges (in the Enlightenment, for example). Modern scientific discoveries were often at odds with established religious beliefs, and in the nineteenth century a whole new scientific method of textual analysis presented Christianity with its most difficult modern challenge. For a number of reasons, scholars became interested in biblical texts. Some wanted to find the most accurate version of the Bible (the earliest translation, or the one least tampered with) and to revise the Bible people used in the light of new discoveries.[17] Some wanted to read the Bible differently. They were not so much interested in its devotional message as they were in trying to discover what the biblical authors really meant in the text. They studied the history and archeology of the biblical period to see what they could discover about those people and were able, they thought, to shed new light on biblical stories and figures. Some of the conclusions of these scholars were threatening to traditional Christian beliefs. Most Christians had always believed that Moses wrote the first five books of the Bible, that the Gospel of John was an historically accurate picture of Jesus, and that no matter what else one could find in Scripture, there were no mistakes.

You can imagine how threatening it was (and still is to some Christians) to see these beliefs challenged. If Moses did not write the first five books of the Bible, then who did? What did one do with the theory of inspiration that said God dictated those first five books to Moses? If the Gospel of John was not a historically accurate picture of Jesus, what was? Who was the *historical* Jesus? Did he really work miracles? Did he know he was the Messiah? Did he really think the end of the world was coming? Are his ethics really meant to be lived by people now, or were they meant to be an interim ethic based on his belief that the world would soon end? Finally, if there were mistakes in the Bible, what happened to the whole concept of revelation, of God's authorship of Scripture? Surely, God did not make mistakes?

All these questions—originally posed by scholars in Europe—made their way into American Christianity and became the backbone of American Christian Liberalism. The American context provided a congenial atmosphere for such questions: people were much more ready to believe in natural human goodness than they were to welcome theories of human depravity and predestination, and perhaps this new scientific method could provide a new way to understand and embrace the Christian faith.

The pivotal issue was the *authority of the Bible*. Let us review this issue a little bit. Before the Reformation there were profound differences of opinion about the Bible. Some parts of it were valued more highly than others. Luther judged the books of the Bible with reference to the norm of salvation by grace through faith, and so had little good to say about the Epistle of James with its emphasis on good works. He was not worried about the infallibility of the Bible. Later, however, people wanted to be able to place more authority in Scripture, to cite the authority of God (as written down in Scripture) against the competing authority of kings or popes or new religious views. In the seventeenth and eighteenth centuries some people went to extremes in their defense of biblical infallibility, arguing that even the *punctuation* of the Bible was infallible and could not be questioned or changed.

Fundamentalists inherited these conservative views about biblical authority, and held fast to a belief that Scripture was infallible. It is not fair to characterize all of them as extreme literalists or to picture them as closed-minded. The term *fundamentalist* comes from their belief that there is an irreducible minimum of belief without which one cannot claim to be a Christian, and one of those beliefs is in the inerrancy of the Bible.[18]

The heart of Fundamentalism is a concern for salvation. The key question for them is simple and direct: "Have you been saved?" But, how is one saved? According to orthodox Christian beliefs one cannot save himself or herself; God must act to do it. And God has done it in Christ, who atoned for human sinfulness, but that atonement cannot work for a person unless she or he accepts Christ. Once one accepts Christ as the son of God and Savior, that person is assured of heaven and receives the grace of God as a power to overcome sin. How does a person know this message or scenario to be true? Because God has said so: because it can be found in the Bible, which is God's infallible word and gives assurance to this position. Fundamentalists are concerned, therefore, to assert the infallibility of Scripture in order to protect what they see as the essential message of the gospel.

An *extreme fundamentalist* believes that there are no mistakes in the Bible and that every word means exactly what it says: the Bible is to be read as fully and literally true. An *extreme liberal* admits that there are mistakes in the Bible, sees much of it as metaphor, and argues that the Bible should be read as an ethical guide for human life. Most of the people who tend to one or the other end of this spectrum are not extremists, and that makes the problem of interpretation more difficult. Conservatives or *neoevangelicals* are descended from the fundamentalist position, but have moved away from it in order to meet scientific and biblical criticism part way: they support their traditional views by way of scientific methods. They do not condemn biblical criticism as the work of the devil (as some extreme fundamentalists do), but neither do they accept the basic presuppositions of liberals. Neoevangelicals accept the supernatural world as a reality and are not constrained to explain divine intervention in the world; at the same time, they are willing to defend their views with reason and logic. They combine traditional orthodoxy with social activism and scholarship.

After a stormy history in the early part of the twentieth century *neoliberalism* emerged in the 1940s. Harry Emersom Fosdick (1878–1969) elaborated some key tenets of it in a 1935 sermon: it is necessary to adapt Christianity to the modern world, but not by diluting the concept of God. Neoliberals are not overly optimistic about human nature (as earlier liberals, especially before the First World War, may have been); they are willing to admit that the human situation is a predicament. People, they say, are sinful and there are no simple solutions; and people need more than ethics: they need to find themselves driven to God. Neoliberals affirm the importance of the church as a living society and a divine institution (old liberals often looked at the church as no more than a social institution), and they affirm the necessity of repentance (some old liberals were not convinced of the reality of sin).

A tradition with some of its roots in Liberalism but at the same time essentially convinced about the primary insights of the Protestant reformers about God, human nature, and the Bible, is *neoorthodoxy*. Most neoorthodox theologians have been suspicious of Fundamentalism, yet convinced of the sovereignty of God, the power of sin, and the importance of the Bible for a realistic appraisal of human nature. The most important proponent of neoorthodoxy was Karl Barth (1886–1968), a Swiss theologian who has made a major impact on twentieth-century Protestant theology. The strongest American advocate of neoorthodoxy was Reinhold Niebuhr (1892–1971). Neoorthodoxy is socially and politically liberal yet theologically conservative. It requires a special social activism based on a committed Christian life. Neoorthodox theologians have a renewed appreciation of the church as a collective group or community, and they support the concept of a worldwide church and give strong support to the ecumenical movement.

Contemporary Issues

Today Christians face similar issues of biblical authority, orthodoxy, Fundamentalism, and social activism, and they do so in a pluralistic context, and often as part of larger social or political movements. Religious positions or controversies are no longer confined to denominational arguments, or even theological arguments: many of the ways Christians respond to their religious impulses today have worldwide consequences or roots. Since many of these areas are changing almost constantly and since I find them too close and complex to present in any detail, I will simply make some suggestions about contemporary issues and urge you to read and reflect further.

There are at least four areas of contemporary Christianity that carry on some of the developments we have been talking about. Some of these will be discussed in the next two chapters and some of them alluded to in footnotes, but let us look at them briefly as a way to think about modern Christianity. In terms of *biblical authority,* we have to take cognizance of the issues raised by feminist theologians; in terms of *orthodoxy,* we will look at liberation theology; we can get a different picture of *Fundamentalism* by looking briefly at the so-called electronic church; and we will talk about *Liberalism* in terms of new lines of social activism (especially related to nuclear power and war) in the churches.

Part of the task of the women's movement has been to point out that women's experience has been left out of history books, political considerations, literary criticism, psychological theory, and religious development. In almost every area of human life and thought women are working to change that situation. In Christianity women point to what they consider to be omissions and abuses in the Christian tradition: they point to patriarchal presuppositions of the tradition, exclusion of women from ordination on the basis of sex, and the use of sexist language in Scripture and worship. The language of the Bible is masculine, but does that mean that God is masculine? Does it mean that the systematic exclusion of women from religious rites and power is divinely intended? In asking these and other questions, women question biblical authority and the fixity of revelation. Can the *language* of revelation be limited, or mistaken? Can traditional concepts of God be inadequate? Has Jesus's startling treatment of women in the New Testament been fully exploited? If apostles were those who had an experience of the risen Lord, why were no women recognized as apostles? These questions are current: they are being raised from all sides and "answered" from all sides. My intention in raising them here is to show that for some Christians the question of biblical authority is not closed.

Liberation theology begins not with right belief (orthodoxy) but with what liberation theologians call right practice (orthopraxis). Based on a reading of the Bible in which God's most pressing concern is with the poor, and God's most significant action is liberation (from captivity, exile, sin), liberation theologians from Latin America (mostly) are offering a new challenge to the traditional way Christians have of "doing theology." They do not begin with a doctrine (a belief) about God, but begin with their experience (living with the poor) and build up a theory that God is presently being revealed in situations of oppression. Liberation theologians call on Christians to develop a whole new approach to theology and, accordingly, offer whole new versions of orthodox Christian doctrine.[19] Liberation theology is complicated and new: each year several more major texts are translated into English, and each year the *political* implications of a particular theological position are advertised by these theologians. As American Christianity begins to take this new theological impulse seriously, the parameters of orthodoxy may change.

From the early 1920s Christian preachers have taken advantage of new communications technology: radio evangelism was an important part of almost all Christian churches in the 1930s and 1940s and represented denominational interests. In the 1950s, with television, religious personalities emerged who were attached to a denomination, but were also interested in appealing to a wide audience with a specific kind of religious message. In the computer age, beginning in the 1970s, with new possibilities for mass mailing and marketing, a whole new kind of religious media use has begun to occur. Preachers today often use air time not just for a religious message, but for a political one as well. In the process, the old Fundamentalism is being enlarged to include political views: a fundamentalist, according to some interpreters, needs not only to believe in the atonement, but also in the conspiracy theory of communism versus American (Christian) life.[20] It is instructive to spend a few hours watching Sunday-morning television, especially to compare the "old time religion" of the 1920s with the old time religion being offered today. The changes in tone and emphasis may tell us something about developments in fundamentalist Christianity.

If conservative ministers have taken up conservative politics as part of their religious message, liberals have taken up issues of social justice as part of their understanding of religious commitment. There is nothing new in this, but there may be something new in the fact that many of those espousing liberal political views (or views aimed against present American military policy) are *not* just liberals. The volatile political climate and the issues of nuclear war and nuclear power have activated a left wing in almost all the churches and have made definitions of religious Liberalism very difficult to devise. The coalitions of activity change with the issues, as do the arguments. Is it acceptable for Christians to get involved in politics? Pay some attention to who asks and who answers that question. Old civil rights liberal Christians in the 1950s and 60s said yes while some conservative Christians said no; but when a conservative religious coalition backed Ronald Reagan for president, old liberals decried the union of religion and politics. I do not mean to do any more here than raise an interesting issue of definition and judgment which, I suspect, will be with Christians for a long time.

Finally, let us speculate about the hopes some have for a worldwide Christianity. On what basis could such a worldwide church develop? Are Christians increasingly united in matters of doctrine? Have the scars of the Reformation healed? Can Christians agree on the primacy of the Bible in their lives? Even if the answer to these questions were affirmative, does that solve the issues, or have the arguments simply shifted to a different ground? The next two chapters attempt to pose these and other questions so that you can look at Christianity from a different perspective.

In some senses we have been talking about a worldwide Christianity all along, even though we have centered our attention on the American scene. The issues of biblical authority, orthodoxy, Fundamentalism, and Liberalism change somewhat according to context, but the basic arguments are probably similar. The problems raised as contemporary issues all reflect a worldwide movement in some ways. The women's movement in its religious embodiment is challenging traditional religious authority not only all over the Christian world, but in non-Christian religions as well. Liberation theology, rooted in a Latin American experience, has reverberations in Africa, parts of the Third World, and even in some of the depressed areas of American life. Mass communications technology as it relates to religion (whether it is fundamentalist or not) reaches all parts of the globe and raises new possibilities for missionaries and religious educators. The various manifestations of the peace movement (whether they come from religious liberals or political radicals) have called forth reflections on peace and justice that transcend national and religious boundaries.

CONCLUSION

I hope that from this chapter (and from the whole of Part Two) you have seen that the complexity of the arguments and the peculiarities of denominational history, even in American culture, make it nearly impossible to make simple characterizations of particular groups. Add to this the enormity of some of these contemporary issues, and I hope you will see how much caution needs to be exercised before making sweeping statements about any Christian group.

Christianity—in America and in the world—is not simply made up of a variety of churches or denominations; it is also characterized by specific beliefs, questions, and actions. The purpose of this chapter has been to show how difficult it is to know exactly what we mean when we say that someone is a Methodist or a Catholic: there are wide differences of opinion within single denominations. It is also extremely hard to know what we mean when we say evangelical or liberal or fundamentalist. The words have been used by one group to dismiss the importance of another one. We should be careful and generous, therefore, when using them descriptively. When we move into contemporary issues we may be inclined to see either fractionalization or richness, depending on our proclivities and our background. Whatever we see, we have seen it coming: the early church began in variety and diversity, it was politically involved as soon as it was able to be in a power position, it responded to serious controversy and reform from within, survived some challenges and re-formed on the basis of others, and has demonstrated extraordinary adaptability.

CHAPTER 7 NOTES

1. For a description of a camp meeting and some of its religious exercises, see Alice Felt Tyler, *Freedom's Ferment: Phases of American Social History from the Colonial Period to the Outbreak of the Civil War* (New York: Harper & Row, 1944), pp. 35–42.

2. The Evangelical Covenant Church of America (1885), the Evangelical Free Church of America (1885), and the Missionary Church Association, a union of independent evangelical churches organized in 1898, are some examples of specifically evangelical denominations.

3. Fundamentalism (discussed later in this chapter) is a post-Civil War movement that attempted to define those fundamental characteristics or beliefs that a Christian must adhere to.

4. For a short, readable account of the communitarian impulse see Mark Holloway, *Heavens on Earth: Utopian Communities in America 1680–1880,* rev. ed. (New York: Dover, 1966).

5. Do not confuse this universalism with the universal mission discussed in Chapter 3.

6. The Advent Christian Church (1860), for example, or the Church of God (Abrahamic), a non-Trinitarian group organized in Philadelphia in 1888.

7. This summary of Mormon doctrine was passed on to me by my colleague Jan Shipps, who heard it from a president of the Mormon church. The word *man* here is intentional: women are saved along with their husbands. Single men and women can be saved but not "exalted"; they remain in the lowest heaven in a state of suspended animation. For an excellent look at Mormon belief see Jan Shipps, "Mormons: Looking Forward and Outward" in *Christian Century* 95 (16–23 August 1978), 761–6.

8. For a provocative, pro-Americanist (but not always accurate) account of this chapter in American Catholic history see Andrew M. Greeley, *The Catholic Experience* (New York: Doubleday, 1969).

9. A short, engagingly written account of the Klan as experienced by a Catholic at the time is Robert Coughlan, "Konklave in Kokomo" in Isabel Leighton, editor, *The Aspirin Age: 1919–1941* (New York: Simon & Schuster, 1949), pp. 105–30.

10. For an historical analysis of the Catholic revivalist impulse see Jay P. Dolan, *Catholic Revivalism: The American Experience 1830–1900* (Notre Dame, Ind.: University of Notre Dame Press, 1978).

11. Virtually all Christian churches experienced growth and division during the nineteenth century, but a full listing would be confusing and probably counterproductive. Let me give you some examples, however, so you have some sense of the diversity. A schism in the Roman Catholic church resulted in the Polish National Catholic Church (established as a separate group 1897–1900). Lutherans divided into more than the three main groups I discuss here—one can find many independent synods, like the Wisconsin Evangelical Lutheran Synod (1849). Radical Reformation churches split many times, usually over issues of purity or discipleship, but sometimes over what appear to be small matters (Black Bumper Mennonites, for example, think it is acceptable to own cars, but not adorned with chrome bumpers); it is not unusual to find many different kinds of Brethren, Amish, and Mennonite churches. Calvinist churches already had branches (Dutch Reformed and Presbyterian, for example) and those split, too, into other churches. Baptist churchs tended to split easily over issues so that major arguments about revivalism, pacifism, the missionary movement, and so on, all tended to produce separate Baptist groups (Hardshell or Primitive Baptists, for example, oppose sending missionaries anywhere). Methodists divided into Wesleyan Methodists, Free Methodists, Evangelical United Brethren, and so on, many of which were drawn back together with the establishment of the United Methodist Church. There are virtually hundreds of different Holiness and Pentecostal churches and thousands of independent churches that have no formal affiliation with anyone.

12. See John Cogley, *Catholic America* (New York: Doubleday, 1974).

13. For a readable introduction to worldwide expansion and missionary activity see Stephen Neill, *A History of the Christian Missions* (London: Penguin, 1964).

14. The clearest impetus for this may well have been Thomas Merton's *The Seven Storey Mountain* (New York: New American Library, 1943). Merton (1915–68), a young, sophisticated writer, left it all behind to join a Trappist monastery in Kentucky; his autobiography had a tremendous impact on the American Catholic church and on monasticism in the postwar period.

15. There are many books on the Second Vatican Council. One good introduction to the council itself is Gary MacEoin, *What Happened at Rome?: The Council and Its Implications for the Modern World* (New York: Doubleday, 1967). One that captures the challenges for American Catholics is George Devine, *American Catholicism: Where Do We Go From Here?* (Englewood Cliffs, N.J.: Prentice-Hall, 1975).

16. See Chapter 5 for a discussion of the Council of Trent.

17. The scholars' version of the Bible is the Revised Standard Version (RSV), which is rejected by fundamentalists precisely because it was done by scholars rather than by "inspired" or holy persons. According to them, the Holy Spirit (not scholarship) was behind the King James Version (KJV) and they hold to that as their official text.

18. Originally there were five fundamentals: inerrancy of the Bible, substitutionary atonement, the future Second Coming of Christ, full face value of biblical miracles, and the divinity of Christ, including his physical Resurrection.

19. One example of this is the new Christologies coming out of Latin America. Jon Sobrino, *Christology at the Crossroads* (Maryknoll, N.Y.: Orbis Books, 1978) shows the connection between the suffering poor and Jesus, and begins from a reflection on the experience of the oppressed. His Christology, rooted in the experience of the historical Jesus, has a different emphasis and purpose than traditional Christologies that begin with doctrinal definitions of Jesus Christ as the God-man now seated at the right hand of the Father. Leonardo Boff, *Jesus Christ Liberator* (Maryknoll, N.Y.: Orbis Books, 1979), does a conscious rereading of New Testament texts based on the Latin American situation of poverty and oppression.

20. Reverend Greg Dixon, national secretary of the Moral Majority, claims there are now twenty-one fundamentals including the Christian academy movement, anticommunism, and antiwelfare ideas (this was said to me in conversation with Reverend Dixon in 1980).

SUGGESTIONS FOR FURTHER READING

1. For more on specific denominations or general Christian history in America and the modern period, consult the bibliography at the end of the book.

2. Liberation theology, as I said, is a whole new way of "doing theology." There are no easy introductions to it but a clear, though perhaps too simplified, summary of it appears in L. John Topel, *The Way to Peace: Liberation Through the Bible* (Maryknoll, N.Y.: Orbis Books, 1979), pp. 146–56. One of the first (and now classic) books is Gustavo Gutierrez, *A Theology of Liberation* (Maryknoll, N.Y.: Orbis Books, 1973). An excellent series of essays is Rosino Gibellini, editor, *Frontiers of Theology in Latin America* (Maryknoll, N.Y.: Orbis Books, 1979). If you check through a catalogue from Orbis Books (probably the largest publisher of liberation and Latin American theology) you will see some of the directions and questions, and if you look through religious periodical literature from the last few years you will see how much of an argument has been raised in the scholarly community about its validity, intentions, and directions.

3. A feminist critique of Christianity is not new: see Elizabeth Cady Stanton, *The Woman's Bible* (Seattle: Coalition Task Force on Women and Religion, reprint 1974), which was originally published in the 1890s. For a survey of Christian attitudes toward women (especially in the Roman Catholic church) see Mary Daly, *The Church and the Second Sex,* 2nd ed. (New York: Harper & Row, 1975), which was originally published in 1968 and was the first to raise the modern cry against sexism within the churches. For an interrelation of feminist and liberation theologies see Rosemary Radford Ruether, *New Woman New Earth: Sexist Ideologies and Human Liberation* (New York: Seabury Press, 1975), and check into other books written or edited by Ruether. For a feminist reinterpretation of early Christianity by a New Testament scholar see Elizabeth Schüssler Fiorenza, *In Memory of Her: A Feminist Theological Reconstruction of Christian Origins.* (New York: Crossroad/Continuum, 1983). For an overview of feminist thinking in religion see Carol P. Christ and Judith Plaskow, *Womanspirit Rising: A Feminist Reader in Religion* (New York: Harper & Row, 1979).

4. The "electronic church" phenomenon has caused a great deal of turmoil within the churches on various issues (Is it all right to do it? Does it harm regular church attendance? Does it present the heart of the Christian message?), which you can find by way of periodical literature. Books on this phenomenon are just being published and so the main source at this point is still periodicals. See, for example, Jeffrey K. Hadden,

"Soul-Saving via Video," *The Christian Century 97* (28 May 1980), 609–13. The *political* implications of television evangelism are associated perhaps most strongly with Jerry Falwell and the Moral Majority. See "Born Again Politics" in *Newsweek 96* (15 September 1980), 27–36; and Frances Fitzgerald, "A Disciplined, Charging Army" in *The New Yorker 57* (18 May 1981), 53–141.

5. For an introduction to some new developments in Christian practice throughout the world, see Gerald H. Anderson and Thomas F. Stransky, editors, *Mission Trends No. 3: Third World Theologies* (New York: Paulist and Grand Rapids: Eerdmans, 1976), which contains excellent essays about Christianity in Africa, Latin America, and Asia. The same editors also edited *Mission Trends No. 4: Liberation Theologies* (1979), which focuses on Christian missions among blacks, women, Hispanics, Native Americans, and Asians, and shows the importance liberation theologies are having in North America. For more on a worldwide network of nonviolence and its influence in Christian churches see Marjorie Hope and James Young, *The Struggle for Humanity: Agents of Nonviolent Change in a Violent World* (Maryknoll, N.Y.: Orbis Books, 1977). For an introduction to a Latin American strategy that is having an impact on Christian communities of all kinds all over the world see Sergio Torres and John Eagleson, editors, *The Challenge of Basic Christian Communities* (Maryknoll, N.Y.: Orbis Books, 1981); it features essays on Christian presence in situations of domination and also personal reflections on basic communities, liturgies, and popular practice.

PART THREE

Christian Life and Worship

T HE FIRST TWO parts of this book have dealt with the biblical back-ground and historical diversity of Christianity. Part Three presents some of the ways Christians relate to the world and to their culture, and describes the variety of Christian polity and worship. Chapters 8 and 9 focus on typical Christian responses to the world and to American culture by suggesting the alternatives of withdrawal, domination, adaptation, and nonconformity. The alternatives can be visualized as shown in the diagram below. I developed the diagram to be not a perfect delineation of Christian possibilities, but a suggestive configuration by which one can begin to discern some of the differences among Christians in their attitudes toward the world and their culture. Many Christians feel a tension between the lure of the world on the one hand and the attractions of the church on the other. The postures of withdrawal and domination stand outside the tension as attempts to avoid it; the postures of nonconformity and adaptation exist within the tension as attempts to cope with it. The diagram is explained fully in Chapters 8 and 9.

Chapters 10 and 11 outline varieties of Christian polity and worship, and are meant to present information rather than to raise questions. Since Christians usually discover and celebrate their religious identity within a community context, it is important to take note of the different kinds of community *structures* they have developed. Once we have some understanding of different polities, we can look at the ways Christians celebrate their beliefs in worship. These chapters focus on diversity (in structural arrangements) and unity (in intention), on emphatic differences (in ways of worship) and similarity (in desire).

We have seen that Christianity arose within a complex historical milieu and developed into a pluralistic religion with a wide variety of doctrinal and behavioral expressions. In looking at different Christian polities, we can see how different understandings (of divine authority) and historical experiences shaped these polities; in examining Christian worship, we can see how differences have been expressed liturgically. Despite all the differences that do exist, however, one can still find a unity of purpose within Christianity. It may find expression in different ways, but Christians do strive to organize themselves into a community in which the authority of Jesus and the presence of the Holy Spirit can be experienced and followed. Despite differences in ways of worship, they share some common ideas about the importance of sacraments, prayer, preaching, and singing.

Incompleteness is the necessary companion of broad ambition; I cannot discuss the positions of all Christian groups on every issue. Nor is it possible to pursue topics in any depth. The purpose of this final part is simply to stimulate discussion by introducing questions, and to describe differences and common purposes in Christian behavior.

CHAPTER 8

Christians and the World

T he Bible and history reflect a tension believers have often experienced between the demands of faith and the demands of life in the world. Christians have been warned to avoid the allurements of "the world, the flesh, and the
devil." The meaning of these words—*world, flesh, devil*—has not always been
clear, although people often have had more trouble describing *the world* than the
other two. Sometimes *the world* is understood to include sinful enticements of
the flesh and devilish preoccupations of pride, as well as temptations of power
and greed. In this framework, a major tension exists between the values of the
Christian faith or church and the values of the world. Some Christians regard
the tension between the church and the world as no more than a reflection of the
Christian belief in Original Sin; it simply points to an internal individual battle
between good and evil desires. Whatever the understanding of the tension—and
by all accounts the understandings are ancient—it has figured prominently in
Christian experience.

A simple way of diagramming this idea is this:

Church World

The jagged line represents tension. There are many different ideas about the
nature of the church and the world. For purposes of our discussion, *church* is
linked to the values of the Bible or Christian tradition, and *world* refers to the
values of the surrounding culture. Individual denominations feel a pull from

both sides just as individual believers do; different religious denominations take significantly different positions within the tension. Because religion does not exist in isolation, but within a community of believers who live in the world, the community feels the tension between the attractions of the church (spiritual values, love of God and neighbor, specific moral values, and the hope of future happiness) on the one hand, and the lures of the world (worldly values, material goods and power, love of oneself or one's culture, and satisfaction with the here and now) on the other. If the two poles of the tension can be said to set limits, the diagram of possibilities might look like this:

Here *church* is idealized and never perfectly realized and *world* encompasses a wide range of meanings, some positive and some odious. Most religious denominations work out their existence within the boundaries of the tension and take different positions within the middle area of the diagram. But this chapter, describes two attitudes toward the world that support positions—radically different from one another—outside the limits of the tension.

Group 1 in the diagram represents a position of withdrawal from the tension and group 2 represents a position of domination. Group 1 is placed on the *Church* end of the scale because the motivation for it usually derives from religious purity or perfection and a longing to achieve the ideal; group 2 is placed on the *World* end of the spectrum because its tactics and strategies often derive from worldly or political power. Both groups have definite attitudes toward the world—usually negative ones—and both seek to avoid or live outside the tension between the world and the church. Those who withdraw from the tension usually create their own worlds within the church and therefore widen the space between the limits of church and world. They respond to the tension by pushing the world far away. Those who take a position of domination usually extol the values of the world insofar as those values can be controlled by the church. They reduce the space between the church and the world—may even obliterate it—by imposing church values on the world.

GROUP 1: WITHDRAWN COMMUNITIES

Groups that withdraw from the tension want little or nothing to do with the world; they think of themselves as removed from the world or standing entirely against its values. At least three forms of withdrawal are possible: physical, cultural, and psychological. Any of these forms may allow for some interaction with the world, but that interaction is perceived as an unwelcome necessity.

Members of all these groups are united in their belief that the world interferes with their religious lives.

Why would a religious group choose to withdraw from the world? There are at least two general aims: purity and perfection. Perfection is a positive striving toward a spiritual ideal, while purity here means seeking to defend one's values and culture from the harmful ways of the world. Some believers, in order to keep their beliefs, practices, and lives free from taint, separate themselves from those who do not share their convictions and concerns. The less contact they have with people in the world, the more likely, they feel, is their religious life to remain constant and pure. Another reason for withdrawing to attain purity derives from a perception of the world as an evil place, a den of iniquity and a hotbed of temptation. According to this view, the world is the place of the flesh and the devil; it feeds on vice, narcotics, gambling, and prostitution; one keeps pure and out of the reach of temptation by staying away from the world.

A second aim of withdrawal is perfection. Some groups feel called to live a more rigorous, more communitarian, or more "perfect" life than can be lived in the world. Jesus commanded people to love one another, but also added these challenging words: "If you would be *perfect*," (Matt. 19:21) he said, then sell all you own, give the money to the poor, and follow me. Some people have believed that following Jesus means withdrawing from the world. The monastic vows of poverty, chastity, and obedience (discussed in Chapter 4) have often been called counsels of *perfection* and they have been built upon a strategy of withdrawal from the world. Some withdrawn communities have been separate religious entities and have been physically, culturally, and psychologically withdrawn from the world. Nineteenth-century communitarian groups (discussed in Chapter 7) were often withdrawn at all levels and lived out their specific interpretations of the Christian life as separate, intentional communities.

Physical Withdrawal: Monastic Communities

Often withdrawn groups are parts of larger communities of faith. Monastic communities represent a specific vocation within a particular kind of Christianity and are usually a small part of the larger religious group. They are not separated from the larger group by differing beliefs but as a special way of life within that larger community. Monks and nuns are a significant part of Orthodox Christianity, Roman Catholicism, and Anglicanism. The monastic vision has been discussed already (in Chapter 4) and need not be repeated here. Monastic life is an example of physical withdrawal from the world. Monks and cloistered nuns live in self-contained communities apart from the world and often in isolated places. Monasteries have existed from very ancient times and some contemporary monasteries provide a way of life that has not changed much in centuries. Some modern monasteries are a blend of the old and the new: they trace their origins back to ancient religious communities but also embrace some contemporary ideas. Ecumenical monastic experiments embrace a variety of believers in physically withdrawn settings.[1] Monasteries usually are a world unto themselves, and often are self-contained places that provide for their own physical needs. Monastic separation from the world is supported by non-monastic believers in the same denomination and is seen as one valid embodiment of the Christian life.

Cultural Withdrawal: The Amish

Sometimes a withdrawn community expresses the pure extreme of a particular religious viewpoint, which itself has undergone some significant changes; it is separated from the world and, in some senses, from its parent group. The Amish are an example of cultural withdrawal: they share a sectarian viewpoint with other Radical Reformation groups, but have separated from those groups precisely over the issue of involvement in the world.

A word about sectarianism. Sociologist of religion Ernst Troeltsch (1865–1923) distinguished between church and sect and characterized sect-type Christianity as emphasizing an individual religious experience, voluntary membership, and radical obedience to Christian ethics as specified in the words of Jesus.[2] It appeals to the life and beliefs of the primitive church and specific attitudes toward the world. Sectarians aim at personal fellowship and inward perfection and have no desire to dominate the world; they are indifferent or even hostile to the world and tend to be suspicious of worldly ways. Troeltsch's distinctions cannot adequately describe the American religious situation—some groups that otherwise fit his "sect" category are not withdrawn from the world and are not necessarily hostile to the political order—but they do serve to describe the Amish viewpoint.

In some senses the Amish have built a world of their own, but not for monastic reasons. Monks and nuns are often willing to adopt some of the conveniences of the modern world; their withdrawal does not necessarily reflect a negative judgment of surrounding culture, though their lives are decidedly simple. The Amish refuse to be part of the general society—the world—and they refuse to conform to cultural values or adopt modern conveniences. To their way of thinking, God's law has a specific rhythm that cannot be interrupted by the contrivances of the modern world. They do not drive cars but continue to use horses and buggies. They have nothing against the gasoline engine—indeed, they will ride in other people's cars, and one can sometimes see an Amish farmer using a horse-drawn wagon and a gasoline-powered cutting machine—but have a sense of life's pace that will not be hurried or overwhelmed by modern gadgets. They have no electricity—except in places where Amish bishops have deemed it acceptable as a way to cool milk and comply with state dairy laws—and are not disturbed by television and radio. The values of the world are not automatically adopted as their values, and their cultural and religious ways—

styles of life, patterns of worship, language, and dress—have remained much the same for centuries.

The Amish are a small group, withdrawn from the world; they have definite and rigorous qualifications for admission. Their idea of community is intimate and physical: they believe that one must identify with a concrete local group. They are, accordingly, perfectly sectarian, but have also chosen to remain culturally withdrawn—unconformed—as well. Some groups that were originally sectarian were slow to change and to adapt to new ways, but have adapted to the society in which they live. The Amish, on the other hand, are bound to their withdrawn position by their understanding of the world and its culture as inherently destructive of their religious life.

Psychological Withdrawal: Millennialist Christians

Many Christian groups—especially those with highly developed eschatological consciousness, those anticipating the end of the world in their lifetime—are withdrawn from the world in mind and heart only. They live and work in the world, do not establish themselves as isolated communities (like monks and nuns) and are not hostile to modernity; yet they create worlds of their own in such a way that they exemplify psychological withdrawal. All these groups—Adventists, Pentecostals, Jehovah's Witnesses, some fundamentalist Christians, and Dispensationalists—share certain attitudes about the world: they perceive the world as an evil place and tend to see all others as outsiders in relation to their own world in the church.

Most of the individuals in these groups take a dim view of the world; it is a place of seduction by alcohol, drugs, or sex.[3] They work in the world but are mentally and behaviorally removed from it. A rousing hymn states the theme: "Take the world but give me Jesus, I won't go back [to the world and its vices], I won't go back." Testimony during religious services often takes a world-disparaging form: "When I was in the world I drank [or gambled or was unfaithful] but now that I am here [in the church] I am free from those things."[4] Preaching compares those in the church with those in the world in such a way that the worldly ones are invariably wicked, misguided, and not worthy to be part of God's entourage when Jesus comes again.

Most of these millennialist Christians live their lives within the framework of their organization: Bible study meetings, working for church concerns, social events within the churches, and various missionary enterprises (in the case of Jehovah's Witnesses, going door-to-door with a religious message) take up much of their lives outside work and family time. Their friends and family are (ideally) church members, and their reading and interests are very much defined by their religious preoccupations. Often television and movies are denigrated and drinking, smoking, and dancing forbidden entirely.

These groups are united primarily by their millennialist views. They eagerly await the end of the world and interpret political events and worldly happenings predictively, as part of God's plan. They build upon an apocalyptic scenario culled from the Bible, especially from some chapters in Daniel and from the Book of Revelation. In the apocalyptic vision set forth in those books one can find a general plan: the world is dominated by an evil power (often shown as a beast or a tyrannical ruler); that evil power persecutes the saints and treats them shamefully; suddenly the saints are able to rise up and overthrow the beast or evil potentate; and the saints inherit the earth or reign in heaven. In that vision no one wants to be on the side of the world. *All* Christians are enjoined to remember that no one knows the day or the hour when Jesus will return and they are, accordingly, supposed to be always ready. In many millennialist groups, however, the readiness goes hand in hand with fear and/or assurance; in both cases the world factors heavily as an evil place.

Summary of Withdrawn Communities

All these various religious groups—monks and nuns, the Amish, Adventists, Pentecostals, Jehovah's Witnesses, dispensationalist Christians and some fundamentalist Christians—differ from one another theologically, historically, and in terms of doctrine and practice. But they are bound together by their relationship to the tension between the world and the church; they all seek to avoid that tension by withdrawing from the world. All see the necessity of being in some way separated from the world, but they differ about how and why that separation should occur. They are united in believing that the world interferes with their goals of purity or perfection, but they have different attitudes toward that interference and toward the world itself.

Monastic life is built on the notion of withdrawal from a *distracting* world. Monks and nuns do not hate the world, but choose to withdraw from it in order to "pray without ceasing" (1 Thess. 5:17) to pray for the world and the people in it even while they pursue their own spiritual journeys. The religious traditions that support monastic life—Orthodox Christianity, Roman Catholicism, and Anglicanism—all believe that the world, created by God, is good and not evil. They may quarrel with specific worldly positions but they do not, by definition, hate the world. Monasteries stand as a witness to a specific way of Christian life. The desire to leave the world, monks and nuns believe, is the result of a distinct and special call by God to an individual; other individuals are called to life in the world.

The Amish withdraw from the world because the world is a *threatening* place where the time-honored ways of their ancestors are not respected. The world is a place of change—not fundamentally motivated by religious concerns—and their policy of cultural withdrawal is based upon their own needs for preservation; they hope to conserve their culture and way of life, which they believe is better suited to the commands of Scripture. Many of them have a hostility toward the world and tend to see it as irredeemable and not worth bothering with; in that way they reflect something of the spirit of sectarianism. There is no need, in a sectarian model, to get involved with politics or other worldly preoccupations. The life that matters is the life of the church, and the church exists in the small group that lives out its convictions without reference to the world. The Amish do not make much attempt to draw others into their life despite the active missionary stance of their Anabaptist predecessors. To a great extent, one is born into an Amish way of life and then is asked to choose whether or not to accept it when one gets to be an adult. Those who reject it often must leave farm, family, and the whole way of life.

Millennialist Christians view the world under the influence of their apocalyptic understanding as an *evil* place dominated by evil powers. By virtue of their hopes and beliefs they tend to hate the world and to denigrate its ways. The world is not simply distracting or threatening to a specific way of life, it is evil and predatory and to be avoided at all costs. Unlike the Amish and monastic communities, most millennialist Christians proselytize with vigor. Withdrawal from the world is not a matter of vocation or of birth, but a matter of perceiving the state of things and asking for admission into the group that stands ready and waiting for the return of the Lord. Jehovah's Witnesses, especially, are tireless in their door-to-door ministry and many other groups, such as Pentecostals, support a wide network of local and foreign missionary activity. Assurance of salvation and methods of increasing church membership differ among them, but they are all zealous to draw as many as possible into the church and away from the world.

All of these groups build their own worlds in some ways. Monks and nuns build a physical world of their own in order to pursue their relationships with God apart from the distractions of the world. The Amish live in their own cultural world and live on their own terms and at their own pace so that their religious beliefs are not threatened by modern conveniences, language, and ideas. Millennialist Christians build their own worlds psychologically in their churches; the church is the social and religious center of their lives, a place safe from the dangers of the outside world.

GROUP 2: DOMINATING POSTURES

Another way to avoid the tension between the church and the world is to obliterate it by making one's religious views predominate in a society. Those who master the tension do so by conquering the world with a religious point of view, by attempting to shape the life and values of the world in a particular religious way. If a society is dominated by Christian values, Christians do not feel the tension; the sacred so imposes itself on the secular that they become identified. Theocratic states operate on this principle; they are governments by

God administered through a church or one of God's special agents. Calvin's experiment in Geneva is one historical example of domination; the medieval papacy of the Catholic church is another.[5]

Why would a religious group seek to avoid the tension by dominating the general society? There are probably many reasons and most of them derive from negative views of the world or highly optimistic evaluations of human potential within the world. The medieval popes saw worldly princes as dangerous to the aims of religion; one way to understand the designs of Pope Gregory VII is through the slogan: "Dominate or be dominated." Gregory inherited an abysmal situation[6] in terms of power politics, and the church/state arguments that plagued the Catholic church from the eleventh through the nineteenth centuries in some ways reflected his hope to dominate opposing rulers in order to make the world ready to hear the gospel. Some nineteenth-century religious leaders were so enamored of human progress and the power of the gospel that they hoped to build the kingdom of God on earth. This plan presupposes that the general society ought to be shaped into that kingdom, to be dominated by a particular religious view whether the society is willing to be shaped to that vision or not. Some groups want to assume political power for themselves in order to establish what they perceive as a more Christian society.

No one Christian group can dominate American society and there is little point in worrying about the renewal of medieval papal policies or Calvinist theocracies in the contemporary world. The *mentality* of domination, however, does survive in the least two ways: politically and financially. Since these ways take in a broad range of activity, they cannot be primarily associated with particular Christian groups and will be discussed here more as attitudes present in many different Christian communities and embodied in certain plans or movements. Like the discussion of the withdrawal mentality, this one gathers disparate groups together that otherwise would not be discussed in the same chapter, in an attempt to look at a range of Christian groups with a different lens.

Political Domination

Political domination as a religious strategy is a willingness to use political means to impose a religious viewpoint on everyone. Historically it was adopted by the Roman Catholic church and, later, by Calvinists, Anglicans, and Lutherans. One of the wrenching arguments of the Reformation was over the appropriateness of the Christian desire for political support of its views; much of the hostility of all Christians toward sectarian or radical reformation groups derives from the sectarian unwillingness to be allied with the political order. Groups that subscribe to political domination usually want some sector of the government or the society at large to conform to their particular religious interpretations; they hope to link a religious position to a political one and to pursue them as a single (usually religious) entity. We will look at three contemporary manifestations of the religious strategy of political domination here: liberation theology, the antiabortion amendment, and "Christian" political solutions.

Liberation theology. The theology of liberation is based on a reading of the Bible in which God is perceived as a liberator of captives (in the Exodus) and Jesus as identified with the poor.[7] According to this view, God's primary interest lies with the poor: they are the objects of divine concern in the Old Testament (see the Prophets, especially), and the ones to whom Jesus brings the message of salvation. It is argued that all Christians who want to imitate Jesus should work for the elimination of oppression, a task that may mean working to overthrow corrupt and exploitative political structures. Liberation theology is not entirely clear on its relation to violence: some who accept the premise that God has a preferential option for the poor also believe that nonviolent means are the only appropriate ones for a Christian; others believe that the abuse perpetrated by economic or political systems upon the poor cannot be changed except through violent revolution. Whatever its position on violence, liberation theology is usually revolutionary: its adherents seek to replace an existing regime with a different, more "Christian" one. Liberation theology has found its most fervent adherents in Latin America—indeed, liberation theology may be seen as a creative contribution to world Christian thought from Latin America and parts of Africa—where totalitarian governments and multinational corporations are regarded as exploitative institutions that undermine more "Christian" socialist experiments. Liberation theology uses a combination of religious and political methods, methods that change according to the particular situation, to achieve its aim. The aim is consistent and clear: to bring what is perceived to be God's love for the poor into the political realm as the primary agenda.

The Antiabortion Amendment. Some religious groups use *constitutional* power to promote their views in order to dominate the entire society with them. The campaign on the part of a variety of Christians—Roman Catholic, fundamentalist, and conservative Christian churches—to secure a constitutional amendment against abortion is an example of this strategy.[8] The point to my inclusion of them here is not their belief that abortion is a sin, but their willingness to use political means to get all of society to behave according to their views. Other Christians may perceive abortion as wrong, but also see it as the proper concern of the church, not the state. The purpose of the amendment strategy is to make abortion a crime, to put the state in a position to punish those who commit what these Christians perceive as a grave sin.

"Christian" political solutions. Religious groups on both the right and left wings of the political spectrum can seek to enforce their religious views *politically* in the belief that society will be better if all people live according to their ethic—willingly or unwillingly. Some right-wing Christians—for example, members of the Moral Majority—have identified their religious beliefs with conservative

political views and have linked Christianity itself with a specifically conservative political agenda. These Christians take political positions—against communism, against welfare, in support of capital punishment and conservative fiscal policy—and tie them up with God's will or the gospel. Their reading of the Old Testament and the words of Jesus leads them to a political-religious viewpoint that is essentially right-wing. On the other end of the spectrum, some large church organizations—the World Council of Churches, for example—have been dominated in recent years by liberal or left-wing political viewpoints. In some ways they have identified their religious beliefs with select revolutionary movements, and have given financial support to aid victims of "liberation movements" (like the revolution in Zimbabwe). Their reading of the Old Testament and the Gospels leads them to a political posture that is left-wing. In both cases—from the right and from the left—churches and church members have been asked to endorse political viewpoints as if they were both the clearest readings of the gospel and the best course for worldly governments.

Financial Domination

Financial domination is the propensity to tie the Christian message to money in such a way as to control the society. What does one find in the Gospels about money? In the synoptic Gospels we find a story about a rich man who wished to follow Jesus. He had kept all the commandments and wondered what else he should do. Jesus told him to sell everything, give the money to the poor, and follow him, whereupon the rich man changed his mind and went away. His inability or unwillingness to do as Jesus asked inspired Jesus to say, "It is easier for a camel to go through the eye of the needle than for a rich man to enter the kingdom of God" (Mark 10:25). What do these words mean? If fidelity to God's law is bound up with justice, sharing, and concern for the poor—there is also Old Testament evidence for this—then it seems Jesus means that it is virtually impossible to have much money and be faithful to God. On a literal level the words mean what they say: being rich is dangerous and keeps one away from the kingdom of God. On an allegorical level, however, one can say that Jesus asked the young man to get rid of his *attachment* to money; one can be rich, but cannot be obsessed with riches.[9]

The question turns, to some extent, on what one thinks about poverty. On a practical level people cannot "feed the hungry" if they are poor themselves; on the other hand, Jesus seemed sometimes to have a particular concern for the poor. The Beatitudes reflect Christian ambivalence: in the Gospel of Luke, Jesus says, "Blessed are the poor" (6:20); in Matthew's gospel, Jesus says, "Blessed are the poor *in spirit*" (5:3).

We have already seen that poverty was accepted as a value in monastic life and understood as one of the counsels of perfection. In the Middle Ages new religious orders were founded—the Franciscans, for example, founded by Francis of Assisi (1182–1226)—that valued poverty for its own sake; church laws protected the poor and reminded the rich of their obligations to all people who lived in poverty. Poverty became a pressing religious issue during the Industrial Revolution from the mid-eighteenth to mid-nineteenth centuries. The Salvation Army, founded by William Booth (1829–1912), was a specifically religious response to poverty in England.

American Christianity in the nineteenth and twentieth centuries took two fundamentally different positions on poverty: the Social Gospel and the Gospel of Wealth. One extolled collective responsibility and the other advocated self-help; both grounded themselves on an interpretation of Scripture. Social Gospel, a theory associated with the teachings of Walter Rauschenbusch (1861–1918) offered a theological justification for collective responsibility for the poor. Poverty, Rauschenbusch believed, was a disgrace and a blight on the Christian conscience that ought to be addressed by Christians in terms of building the kingdom of God on earth. The Gospel of Wealth, rooted in American self-confidence and the work ethic, offered a theological justification for self-help: the poor were exhorted to change their lives and to pull themselves up by their bootstraps, and Christians were absolved of obligations to change society or to work for the elimination of poverty. Both were religious responses to the social conditions of the nineteenth century and both were colored by strong feelings (in different directions) toward the rise of American capitalism. In some ways this argument about poverty and social ills reflected a fundamental argument in Christianity between personal salvation and the regeneration of society. Are Christians bound to look after the society in which they live, or are their efforts to be primarily directed at their own personal salvation? The conflict between the Social Gospel and the Gospel of Wealth did not settle that controversy: it continues down to our own day.

The Social Gospel. Rauschenbusch argued, in a series of books and articles, that capitalism and individualism had numbed the Christian conscience. Poverty was not a divine curse (as some had suggested), but was a result of human exploitation. The poor, said Rauschenbusch, were victims, and Christian men and women had an obligation to care for them. He believed that the church was the vehicle to be used for spreading the kingdom of God on earth, and he perceived the kingdom of God to be concerned primarily with social justice. Rauschenbusch tried to combine both sides of the argument: he did not think that external improvements by themselves were sufficient, but believed that social or collective concern was related to personal regeneration as well. One was truly Christian only insofar as he or she was concerned both for personal salvation and for changing the societal structures of oppressed peoples.

Social Gospel, as espoused by most of its adherents, belongs in the category of domination because it was a justification for imposing a specific vision of God's will on the churches and, through them, to "Christianize" all of society. Rauschenbusch's followers hoped to establish the kingdom of God on this earth, by which they meant that they wanted the churches to change the social order by supporting a specific political program. The Social Gospel understanding of Christianity was essentially collective: it hoped to use the churches and the political structure to put this view (with its economic ideas) in practice in the general society.

The Gospel of Wealth. Many Christians, however, had a quite different idea about responding to poverty. Led by their belief in individual salvation, they argued that one did not change social structures but tried, instead, to change human hearts. The Gospel of Wealth also reflected some other theories current in the nineteenth century, though its basic belief was in the necessity of individual salvation. The doctrine of predestination as accepted by some Christian churches led them to believe that God was only interested in the elect and that poverty was a sign that a person or a family was not part of God's chosen few. The work of Charles Darwin (1809–82) on the evolution of the species and the popular slogan about the survival of the fittest led many people to look upon the poor as morally unfit, a position known as Social Darwinism. Sociologists linked poverty with crime as surely as some church members associated it with sinfulness.[10] Some Christians saw poverty as a divine curse or punishment for sin, and if poverty were a divine curse, then it was the will of God, and working to eliminate poverty was tantamount to opposing God's will. These Christians took the words of Jesus, "The poor you will always have with you" (Matt. 26:11) as a mandate to leave the structures of poverty in place while, at the same time, exhorting the poor to move up out of them. Some Christian preachers saw riches as a sign of God's favor and the kingdom of God as a kingdom of wealth, as a place where the morally fit should be allowed to make money. Rich Christians acknowledged their great wealth as a sign of approval by divine providence.[11]

In contemporary terms, a version of the Gospel of Wealth is supported by some conservative Christians who think Jesus would have supported the American dream had he known about it. According to them, the economic system of America is bound up with God's plan: preachers assure their members that God wants them to be rich, that a believing Christian will never go under financially. In some ways they hope to demonstrate that it "pays to believe in Jesus." The sign of salvation for these preachers—who can be seen regularly on television— is prosperity. The Gospel of Wealth belongs in the category of domination because it adopts the financial values of the culture and equates them with the values of religion: it avoids the tension between the secular and the sacred by imposing religious approval on a particular economic system.

Financial perspectives from the left (collective) and from the right (individualist) both tend to associate economic positions with God's will. Both ground their beliefs on a reading of Scripture and believe that they have rightly interpreted the divine will. Both want the society at large to conform to an economic stance they regard as "more Christian."

Summary of Dominating Postures

All these religious attitudes—liberation theology, support of a constitutional amendment against abortion, varieties of "Christian politics," the Social Gospel and the Gospel of Wealth—differ from one another radically in terms of religious interpretation and ultimate goals. But they are bound together by their desire to eliminate the tension between the church and the world by imposing a specific religious perspective on the general society. All of them consider it appropriate for Christians to impose a particular viewpoint upon all members of a society, though they employ different strategies in pursuit of that imposition. Most of them can be classified on either the right or left wing of the political spectrum, and in that way they reflect perennial arguments within the society.

Liberation theologians have been active mostly in Roman Catholic countries and reflect a serious pastoral problem within Roman Catholicism as that church relates to its members in Third World countries. It is usually a left-wing, socialist movement attempting to work out the doctrines and practices of the Roman Catholic church in repressive political climates. The coalition that supports a constitutional amendment against abortion is made up of conservative church members from a number of denominations. It is heavily Roman Catholic, but had strong support from Baptists, evangelical Christians, and fundamentally conservative Christian groups. Specifically "Christian" political ideologies manifest themselves as right-wing political attitudes in some sectors of the evangelical churches and have been active to some extent in the attempted politicization of such organizations as the Campus Crusade for Christ. They have taken on left-wing or radical political embodiments in large interchurch groups like the World Council of Churches. One of the results of this overt political activity among Christians has been a new wedge of divisiveness among Christians: they are no longer divided simply along denominational lines; now those denominational lines have political agendas as well. Some conservative or right-wing evangelical Christians tend to adopt the attitude of the Gospel of Wealth. Modern adherents of the Social Gospel theory tend to be left-wing or socialist Christians. All of them perceive their position as the one sanctioned and supported by the Gospels.

All of these groups hope, in some way, to alleviate problems within society and all of them hope to do that on "Christian" grounds. Their strategies are those of domination—all hope society (or the political structure) will be run according to their reading of the Gospels.

QUESTIONS RAISED BY THE POSTURES OF WITHDRAWAL AND DOMINATION

The reason for making these general interpretations of some Christian attitudes about the world is to see what kinds of questions can be raised by such radically different attitudes and ideas. All of these groups, whether they adopt a strategy of withdrawal or domination, take their positions on the basis of their readings of Scripture. The life and words of Jesus provide the support they need for their positions. The very notion that such different attitudes are legitimate embodiments of the Christian vision, however, raises interesting questions.

Consider the question of the church and the world, especially in terms of political action. If the church is made up of members who believe that they in some way understand God's will and corporately reflect God's intentions, words, and actions, then we must first speculate a moment about God. According to the Bible and traditional Christian belief, God is perfect, eternal, invisible, and the source of absolute truth. How do these attributes correspond with the political order of the world? God is perfect, yet societies are imperfect; does an attempt to raise them to perfection—to an embodiment of divine will—invite frustration and violence? Or is it a real possibility that Christians have an obligation to pursue? God is eternal and invisible, yet societies are visible and continually changing; does a Christian political vision deny the necessity of change to societies? God possesses absolute truth, yet societies can only reflect relative truths; does a Christian approach to the situation obviate the room for disagreement that has historically been a part of all societies? These are general questions, but there are more specifically religious questions as well.

In What Sense Is Christianity Political?

The first question within this question is definitional: What does *political* mean? If it means "worldly" politics, some Christians would answer that Christianity is not at all political and should not be. These believers might cite the words of Jesus, "Render therefore to Caesar the things that are Caesar's and to God the things that are God's" (Matt. 22:21), and argue that Jesus was more interested in changing people's minds and hearts than he was in changing political structures. Others might wonder how it is so clear what things belong to Caesar and what things belong to God and argue from the Bible that God loves the weak, clothes the naked, visits the sick, comforts the afflicted, cares for widows and orphans, feeds the hungry, and buries the dead, and that Christians must work toward those ends—even politically—within the society.

If politics can be described broadly as the way people deal with the structures and affairs of the government (or state), then some people might argue that "Christian" politics do not correspond to the aims and tactics of traditional politics. The politics of Jesus, they might say, are revolutionary because they attempt to deal with political questions in fundamentally new ways.[12] Christians, according to this view, are enjoined to behave differently from everyone else: they are to follow Jesus's words and example by turning the other cheek, doing good to those who persecute them, and loving their enemies. If this is the case, then the political action of Christians becomes a way of life inherently different from and in some ways hostile to the political action of the state; the ethic of the church is an alternative to the ethic of surrounding society. On these grounds some Christians refuse to support wars and violence, and manifest their political consciousness precisely by embodying a different sort of society from the one embodied in the surrounding culture.

What Is the Church?

The same sorts of arguments arise with this question. Is the church an agent to promote societal change and to create a better life for all? Or is it the kingdom of the saved, the fellowship of personal regeneration, with no obligations to the larger society? Is the church a small body of believers who embody the kingdom of God and invite other people to become a part of it? Or is it a large organization that uses its power as an aggressive social agency? Does the church transcend the world in such a way that it must refuse to become involved in secular values and questions? Or is it necessarily involved in the world and somehow responsible for its values?

Is the church a prophetic fellowship that speaks out on injustice but leaves the remedy of injustice to secular agencies? Or are church members to take a prophetic stand within the secular world by working for specific political goals? Is the church a moral educator responsible for raising the consciousness of its members and other people by working for a better world? Or is the church the kingdom of God already come and yet still waiting to become the kingdom, the place in which one should be born again and wait for the coming of the Lord? Is the kingdom of God within the individual believer? Or is it a possible model for the general society? How does the kingdom come? Do believers create the kingdom on earth by virtue of their own works and political vision? Or is it entirely an act of God that makes human efforts worthless?

What Is the Christian Vision of Jesus?

We have already seen that presuppositions about Jesus color the way one interprets the Christian vision. The question of who Jesus was and what he hoped for are crucial to this issue. Was Jesus primarily a man of prayer who inspired people to withdraw from the world in order to pray for it? Was Jesus a revolutionary interested in the political order? Was he concerned primarily with the individual believer? Or was his concern primarily for the future of his movement, and not for the general society? Did Jesus speak as a political figure and imply that Christians are competent to speak out on political issues? Or was Jesus manifestly not interested in political values, implying that Christians ought only to be interested in their personal relationships to God through him?

If believers take a purely social-reform approach to Christian life, do they ignore the underlying issues of temptation/greed/evil in the human heart? Is a purely political approach naive, acting as if the elimination of poverty and injustice also eliminates people's grasping and selfish interests? Must one also seek spiritual elevation and moral earnestness? If believers take a purely evangelical approach to Christian life, is that enough? Is there a valid point in the historical example of converted Christians with good hearts and good intentions who continued to own slaves and to participate in the workinghouse abuse of women and children? Is there a way to both be personally converted to Jesus *and* to work towards a better society? Was Jesus socially conscious—eager for the welfare of the weak—as well as interested in the personal conversion of his followers? Does faith in Jesus require service in the world?

CONCLUSION

None of the questions this chapter raises about the relationship of Christians to the world can be answered simply. Those Christians who take a position of withdrawal or a position of domination have different answers, all of which are based on a careful reading of the Gospels and a thoughtful understanding of Jesus and his desires. How people can read the Gospels so differently is one of the continually perplexing questions in Christianity. The questions have not been raised here in order to confuse you, but as an attempt to broaden your understanding of the complexity of Christian belief and behavior. Other questions could also be raised; but there are enough here to indicate that there is no single Christian position on these issues, and that the arguments within the Christian community are worthy of consideration.

CHAPTER 8 NOTES

1. One experimental group that has been in existence for more than twenty years is the Spiritual Life Association of America in Sedona, Arizona. It was begun by a Carmelite monk, William McNamara, as a contemporary ecumenical community of men and women living in the desert according to a modified monastic rule. See Walter Burghardt, "Without Contemplation the People Perish," *America* 127 (22 July 1972), 29–32.

2. Troeltsch's work is dated and is not meant to be a last word here but is offered as a clear, general view. See *The Social Teachings of the Christian Church* (London: Allen & Unwin, 1931), pp. 331–43. For a more thorough understanding of the complexities of sectarianism see Bryan R. Wilson, *Patterns of Sectarianism* (London: Heinemann Educational Books, 1967).

3. One can find this view exposed by an ex-believer in Barbara Grizzuti Harrison, *Visions of Glory: A History and a Memory of Jehovah's Witnesses* (New York: Simon & Schuster, 1978). Like many ex-believers, Harrison has an axe to grind and you should read this book with a clear understanding of her presuppositions: it is *not* an objective history of the movement. I cite it here because she captures the "world-hating" posture clearly (see pp. 213–20).

4. These quotations—from songs, sermons, and testimony—are ones I have picked up by attending various churches in Southern Indiana, Mississippi, Ohio, and Texas over the last few years. I take them to be typical.

5. A contemporary non-Christian example is present-day Iran under the leadership of the Ayatollah Khomeini.

6. For some indication of how bad a state the papacy was in when Gregory became pope, read about the House of Theophylact in E. R. Chamberlin, *The Bad Popes* (New York: New American Library, 1969), pp. 35–83.

7. See the discussion of liberation theology in Chapter 7.

8. Not all Roman Catholics support a constitutional amendment against abortion. Catholics for a Free Choice, with national headquarters in Washington, D.C., represents those who do *not* agree with the position and strategy of the Catholic Bishops on the abortion issue.

9. This is the position of Clement of Alexandria (d. 215), one of the early Christian writers (see Appendix 3) whose sermon on the text from Mark 10:17–31 gives a symbolic or allegorical interpretation of the passage rather than a literal one.

10. Robert Dugdale (between 1874–6) devised a criminal theory that linked crime, poverty, and heredity. For a discussion of his theory in an unusual and fascinating setting see Michael Lesy, *Wisconsin Death Trip* (New York: Random House, 1973), the conclusion (not paginated).

11. See, for example, Russell H. Conwell, *Acres of Diamonds* (New York: Harper Brothers, 1915). On another level, a rich person like Andrew Carnegie could satisfy his Christian duty *not* by giving money to the poor, but by endowing libraries where they could further their educations and lift themselves up.

12. For a further explication of this position see John Howard Yoder, *The Politics of Jesus* (Grand Rapids: Eerdmans, 1972).

SUGGESTIONS FOR FURTHER READING

1. For more about the influence of Social Darwinism, see Richard Hofstadter, *Social Darwinism in American Thought* (Boston: Beacon Press, 1967).

2. For a survey of social ethics with some of the texts and problems incorporated in this and the next chapter, see George W. Forell, editor, *Christian Social Teachings: A Reader in Christian Social Ethics from the Bible to the Present* (Minneapolis: Augsburg Publishing House, 1966).

3. For a fascinating (though not simple) history of the influence of apocalyptic literature on people see Norman Cohn, *The Pursuit of the Millennium* (Oxford: Oxford University Press, 1970). Related to this, and a book you should be aware of as both controversial and brilliant, is Robert Mapes Anderson, *Vision of the Disinherited: The Making of American Pentecostalism* (New York: Oxford University Press, 1979), which relates the rise of Pentecostalism to certain class and economic factors.

4. For more on the Social Gospel see Charles H. Hopkins, *The Rise of the Social Gospel in American Protestantism, 1865–1915.* (New Haven: Yale University Press,

1967). You might be particularly interested in pp. 143–48, an analysis of *In His Steps,* a novel written by Charles Sheldon and made into a movie in 1936. Every chapter of the novel begins with a biblical quotation and the central question was: "What would Jesus do?" Would Jesus advertize liquor in local newspapers? Would Jesus report prize fights? The answer is always no, and Sheldon's point is that Christians are to walk "in his steps." The book and its examples are dated, even quaint, but the question and the way of posing it is current in some ways.

5. For a look at the religious right, see Edward E. Plowman, "Is Morality All Right?" in *Christianity Today* 23 (2 November 1979), 76–85. The religious right, especially the Moral Majority, has created a contentious environment for discussion and you should exercise caution when reading about it: finding objective studies in a heated atmosphere is difficult. Daniel C. Maguire, *The New Subversives: Anti-Americanism of the Religious Right* (New York: Crossroad/Continuum, 1982) is too negative. Jerry Falwell, *Listen, America* (New York: Doubleday, 1980) is too positive.

CHAPTER 9

Christians and Their Culture

This chapter deals with two options some Christian groups have chosen in order to live *with* the tension between the world and the church, rather than outside it. The two groups may be represented on the diagram like this:

Recall that the broken lines represent tension between the values of the church and the values of the world, and that these interpretive descriptions allow us to raise some religious issues in ways that would not be possible if we were content simply to understand Christian groups in terms of denominational lines. Since the culture and values described here are American, the issues and examples have a particularly American flavor in most instances. The postures themselves, however, could be used to describe the varieties of Christian response to the world and church within other cultures as well.

Group 4 represents a stance of nonconformity to the world within the limits of the tension; group 3 represents the position of adaptation to the world and its values, or a willingness to be associated with the norms of the society. Nonconformists consciously reject some of the values of the culture they live in, but are not so alienated that they withdraw from the tension. They understand themselves as embodying a small but persistent witness to the values of the gospel insofar as those values are at odds with the values of the society. Those in group 4 tend to be part of large, established churches who have, for a number of reasons, accommodated themselves to the values of the society. They are not so identified with the general society that they wish to impose their values on everybody (the position of domination). They may lobby for a particular religious position—the abolition of the death penalty, for example—but they tend to do it in more culturally acceptable ways, as in appealing to humanitarian values through a Washington-based lobby supported by a coalition of people who share similar views.

GROUP 3: THE POSTURE OF ADAPTATION

Christians who choose to adapt have adjusted to their environment; they have conformed or modified themselves in order to be more intimately a part of the culture. In America, a pluralistic environment, one is free to adopt almost any religious posture. That has not always been the case, however, in America or in Christian history. The early Christians had a chance to adapt themselves to Roman culture—to be free to pursue their own religious preoccupations so long as they would occasionally offer sacrifice to the pagan gods—but they refused. Their understanding of Jesus and the gospel made them radical monotheists who would not offer sacrifice to pagan gods. They would not conform, adjust, or adapt. The response of the government to their intransigence was persecution; Christians were burned, maimed, tortured, and harrassed. And the Romans made periodic efforts to destroy the movement altogether.

In times of persecution the choice for the Christian was stark: be faithful (and perhaps die miserably) or repudiate your beliefs (and be damned). Within this difficult choice some Christians discovered a compromise: they bribed officials to certify that they had sacrificed to the gods when, if fact, they had not. The early church came to regard this practice as apostasy. Deciding how to treat people who had denied their faith either directly or by using this method was an enormous pastoral problem in the third and fourth centuries. The compromise position illustrates the *mentality* of adaptation. In this line of reasoning one desires to be a Christian but does not understand Christianity as necessarily exacting such a great price; a believer ought to be able to adapt to the needs of the time, cooperate a little more with outside forces and so avoid persecution and martyrdom.

With Constantine the situation changed dramatically; his reign marked the beginning of the end of persecution and antagonism between church and state. Persecution—and the problems of adaptation under those circumstances—was not a major problem in the West again until the Reformation. We have already seen that one of the results of the Reformation was a series of religious wars in which Catholics and Protestants fought each other in the name of Christianity. Those wars and the peace that followed them raised a new set of questions about adaptation. What should a Roman Catholic in a Protestant country do? Or a Protestant in a Roman Catholic country? Should one withdraw and hide away or be a public witness to a particular religious view? Openly advocating a religious view different from the officially sanctioned one often ended in a gruesome public execution for the preacher. Should one move to a more congenial place? The mainline Reformation did not change the assumption that religion and culture were identified, but the Anabaptists did. They believed that Christian faith and the culture should not be identified; their sectarian stance was offensive to both Roman Catholics and Protestants precisely because it divided religion from culture.

Thus during the Reformation people began to find ways to adjust or adapt to their situation if they could not move away from it. Various religious undergrounds came into being and some groups had to hide in order to survive: in the mountain area of Switzerland and Italy, the Anabaptists took refuge from persecution from all sides. In America, religious pluralism eventually prevailed; the attempt by one group to dominate the religious life of all Americans failed. Still, in some areas religious persecution persisted, especially of non-English-speaking Christians and Roman Catholics. For a while both groups drew back into their own communities separated from the mainstream of American culture.[1] As time went on, however, and people were no longer barred by language or education from participation in the American experiment, more and more formerly isolated groups joined the mainstream.

Roman Catholics had special problems in adapting to American pluralism. They were separated from their Protestant neighbors until the mid 1960s on several levels: they celebrated their liturgy in a foreign language (Latin) and visitors usually did not know what was happening in Catholic worship. Their political loyalties were questioned because they owed allegiance to a foreign monarch (the pope); and their behavior set them off from other people because they observed dietary laws and fasts. Catholics were also different from the rest of the culture because they were forbidden to practice birth control; they often had large families and were expected to marry within their faith. Some of those differences have been obliterated officially: Catholic liturgy is now celebrated in the vernacular and Catholics are no longer rigidly bound by dietary laws. Some differences have been minimized because individual Catholics, contrary to the official teaching of their church, have adapted to the culture around them: Catholics no longer tend to have large families and many are practicing birth control in opposition to official teaching but in conformity with their understandings of themselves within this culture.

Roman Catholics have adapted to American culture partly as a result of persecution and bigotry; persecuted groups often labor to prove that the surrounding culture is unjustified in discriminating against them. Other religious groups are increasingly adapting to American cultural values because they are losing their ethnic distinctiveness. Some Radical Reformation groups like the Mennonites are no longer simple rural folk; many have become professionals and have moved to urban areas where they have lost the trappings of their ethnic distinctiveness.

Adaptation is the posture many groups throughout Christian history have adopted. In the American context of religious pluralism adaptation involves taking on an attitude of religious toleration: groups recognize that people of other beliefs may possess no less truth, may in fact be just as likely to be "saved." In the context of the American dream of upward social mobility, these Christians live comfortably within the culture.[2] Finally, adapted church groups cooperate with the government and often perceive their own aims as compatible with those of the government.

GROUP 4: THE POSTURE OF NONCONFORMITY

Nonconformity is a failure or refusal to conform or adapt to the established order. Nonconformists believe that the church must be clearly distinguishable from the state. Sometimes, they believe, the values of the church are in conflict with those of the world around; at those points they must not conform to the surrounding culture. They share some of the assumptions of the adapted Christians. They may recognize that people in other religions can be "saved" (endorsing religious pluralism), and they may sometimes be active in political matters, sometimes cooperating with government agencies in pursuit of a specific goal. Their main point of difference lies in their willingness to criticize the policies and pursuits of the establishment, whether that establishment is political or religious or both.

Unlike adapted groups, nonconformists do not assume that their religious beliefs are compatible with the values of the general society or the policies of the government. Unlike withdrawn groups, they are not so pessimistic or apolitical as to write the culture off as entirely evil or irrelevant to their belief. Rather they accept and adopt some aspects of the culture, but maintain the importance of some critical distance from it, emphasizing the need to discern between what suits their convictions and what undermines or runs counter to them.

These postures are easier to describe in terms of specific issues than they are in isolation. Nonconformity changes as the society changes: in the second century it might have meant sure martyrdom; in the seventh it might have inspired a monastic life; in the thirteenth century nonconformists might have joined the communities of Francis of Assisi in order to live in "holy poverty", and in the sixteenth century nonconformity might have meant risking one's life in pursuit of the Anabaptist vision. In the twentieth century nonconformity means a number of different things depending on the cultural context and the religious alternatives available.

RELATIONSHIP OF THE TWO POSTURES TO VITAL ISSUES

The positions of adaptation and nonconformity are clearer when understood in relation to specific issues within the culture. No more than a sampling of groups and their response to issues can be presented here; this treatment is not intended to be complete. Here we discuss these two different attitudes as they relate to concrete problems of war, poverty, and racism.

Problems of War and Peace

War has historically been part of the human experience; hostility and violence seem to be a constant part of the human condition. How might one think about war? On the one hand one could hold that every war that serves someone's legitimate interests is acceptable: war is simply another way of doing politics and if the cause is justified, then the means used to pursue that cause are necessarily justified as well. On the other side of the question one could say that all wars are wrong: every war, even a war of self-defense, is unacceptable because bloodshed is always evil. The two extremes of the argument are these: war is always right and war is always wrong.

Most Christian churches have adopted a position somewhere between these opinions. Peace, they say, is to be preferred, but is not always possible. Because we live in a sinful world, sinful, unscrupulous people will attempt to involve a society in dangerous, criminal ventures. Experience shows, the argument continues, that only violence can stop violence. Here Christian participation in war is permitted, but only under certain circumstances. The theory of *just war* specifies the conditions under which Christians may wage war. To be justified in waging war, a group:

1. Must have just cause (one side must persist in unjust aggression).
2. Must exhaust all peaceful means first (so war is a matter of legitimate self-defense regretfully taken up when negotiations have failed).
3. Must have reasonable hope of success (a tiny country should not sacrifice its people in a hopeless war against a superpower).
4. Must use proportionate means (one side cannot use guns when the other side is just using swords and spears).
5. Must observe noncombatant immunity (violence may not be directed against civilians).

Almost all American Christian groups have adopted this theory in some form and members have distinguished themselves in every American war as soldiers, chaplains, nurses, and so on. Adoption of just war theory is one form of adaptation because it enables Christians to sanction warfare.[3]

The nonconformist position on this issue is taken by the "peace churches," those churches that consider pacifism and nonresistance a Christian obligation. The historic peace churches have been Anabaptist groups (Mennonites, Amish, Hutterites), the Religious Society of Friends (Quakers), and Churches of the Brethren. In recent years they have been joined by Christians from other churches who are convinced that the peace churches have a valid reading of the Bible and a valuable position of witness on this question.[4] Peace churches are opposed to Christian participation in all war, no matter what the circumstances. They argue that experience does *not* teach us about the efficacy of violence but about its uselessness; violence, they argue, breeds violence. Jesus meant what he said about loving one's enemies and turning the other cheek. They say that nonviolent means have never really been tried and taken seriously. More importantly, the peace churches argue that Christians must be nonviolent whether nonviolence works or not: their position is not based on a pragmatic judgment about the possible good outcomes of the position, but is based upon Jesus's words and his way of dealing with violence. These people believe that being faithful is more important than determining by violent means what kind of government they will live under.

Many members of the peace churches are absolute pacifists: they will not fight in a war, nor will they contribute to the war effort in any way (for example, they will not take a desk job in the army which then frees someone else to carry a gun). Some may help the wounded, but they are as willing to nurse the "enemy" as their compatriots. Some peace church agencies were severely criticized for providing vitamins and medicine to children in North Vietnam during the Vietnam war. Peace church members have been involved in relief work in the aftermath of war: Mennonites, Quakers, and Brethren poured into Europe after the Second World War in order to clean up the rubble, distribute food and clothing, tend the wounded and homeless. Quakers won the 1947 Nobel Peace Prize for their work in relief, reconstruction, and international services during the war.

Some peace church people now are trying to discover the meaning of peacemaking in a country that is not at war but that spends half of its budget for national defense. A New Call to Peacemaking movement sponsored by the historic peace churches has been established to introduce conversations about peace into all the churches. Consciousness raising about issues of war and peace have also spilled over into issues of nuclear weapons and the arms race. Pacifist Christians have been active in nonviolent demonstrations at plants where nuclear weapons are constructed; some are engaged in various forms of tax resistance, to show their opposition to what they regard as excessive defense spending. They publish pamphlets and books on the peace issue and work to raise the consciousness of other Christians on issues of peace. Members of the peace churches have traditionally provided counseling services for young people about draft resistance and conscientious objection.

In all these ways the peace churches do not conform to the cultural assumption that war is sometimes necessary. As such they witness against a major government policy and against those churches that accept and support that policy. Christians with a pacifist position have not always been welcome in American culture, especially in times of war. Their position assumes a willingness to spend time in jail, and during every American war some members of peace churches have spent time in prison and some have been harrassed by their neighbors. Because of the efforts of the historic peace churches, the American government made a legal provision for alternative service and conscientious objection.

Problems of Poverty and Life-style

The poverty issue surfaced in the last chapter in the discussion about financial domination. Scripture focuses on two concerns: the needs of the poor and the appropriateness of accumulating personal wealth. Some Christians have tied the message of Scripture to wealth and capitalism while others have linked it with socialism and a distribution of goods and properties. Christians use Scripture to justify both extremes. But what about poverty itself? If one maintains that feeding the poor is a primary New Testament value, then one can argue that some private wealth is necessary to perform this service. Christian churches can have money and individual Christians can accumulate wealth as long as they attend to their obligations to the poor. Nonconformists see the issue not simply as one of caring for the poor; they regard accumulating personal wealth as contrary to their calling. The questions, from their perspective, cannot be separated: Christians have an obligation to help the poor by identifying with their state; Christians should stand as a witness against the American values of accumulation and upward social mobility. Nonconformist Christians identify with the poor, moving into their neighborhoods, living at their standard of living.

One Christian denomination founded specifically to minister to the poor is the Salvation Army (mentioned in Chapter 7). Two other groups that illustrate this position are both affiliated with larger Christian groups. The People's Christian Coalition, sometimes called the Sojourners Fellowship because the magazine they publish is called *Sojourners,* is rooted in the American evangelical tradition.[5] The Catholic Worker Movement is rooted in American Catholicism.[6] The Sojourners group is relatively young; it began in the early 1970s and moved to its Washington, D.C. address in 1975. The Catholic Worker was founded in 1934, enjoyed a considerable success at one time, but has dwindled in recent years; it continues, nevertheless, to pursue its goals. Both groups read the Gospels in such a way that they believe it is necessary to identify with the poor, not just provide food for them. Both groups have been active in peace movements, oppose nuclear armament, and serve as advocates for left-wing political causes.

The Sojourners Fellowship began when a small group of young evangelical seminarians in Chicago prayed together and began to look for a place to live according to their interpretations of the gospel: in poverty, helping the poor, widows, orphans, and other disenfranchised peoples. After some initial experiments in the Chicago area they moved to Washington, D. C., found a large house near the so-called riot corridor (a slum neighborhood, mostly black and very poor), and moved in there as a group. They did not immediately design programs or enlist government aid, but simply went out into the street each evening and invited people without places to go to come in for dinner and a place to sleep. Their community has grown, as has their magazine's circulation. Members live in several households in one neighborhood, in a conscious attempt to offer an alternative to American values of consumption, accumulation, and upward social mobility. Accordingly, they feel called to demonstrate and write against the arms race and American defense policies. In addition to spirituality and Christian nurture, their magazine deals with poverty, peace, the arms race, political repression, and so on. The publication has become a forum for other like-minded groups; their movement is not unique, but exemplifies one type of nonconformity in the area of poverty and life-style.

The Catholic Worker Movement was founded by a young, well-educated Roman Catholic convert and a French peasant with ideas about agrarian reform and Christian poverty. Dorothy Day (1897–1980) had been a young socialist at the University of Illinois who rejected religion as poppycock even as she continued to read evangelical sermons. She was drawn to the Roman Catholic church because of its teachings about poverty—the social encyclicals of the late nineteenth century[7]—but found those teachings were not often implemented within the church. She could not understand piety that did not help poor people. Peter Maurin (1877–1949), a French agrarian anarchist disdainful of modern technology and urban middle class values, gave her the impetus she needed; together they founded the Catholic Worker Movement.

They set out to practice a kind of Catholicism that did not conform to the general norm: they were socialists when most Catholics were staunchly anticommunist, pacifists when Catholics were strong supporters of the just war theory, and they opposed big government when some of the principles of the New Deal echoed modern Roman Catholic social theory.[8] Their fundamental principle, derived from their reading of the New Testament, was subsidiarity: what a small group can do, it should do; people ought to do what they can to look after one another, however small the scale. Catholic Workers perceive government policies like social security as an indictment against churches, which are not fulfilling their obligations to the poor, widows, orphans, and the elderly. With headquarters in New York City, they operate a soup kitchen and shelter in the Bowery. They publish a newspaper, *The Catholic Worker,* that has sold for a penny per copy since its beginnings.

Both Sojourners and the Catholic Worker Movement are examples of nonconformity in poverty and lifestyle. Both have moved into poor neighborhoods in order to identify with the people to whom they are ministering. For both groups community life and prayer are an important part of their Christian self-understanding. That prayer life takes evangelical form in the Sojourners community and traditional Roman Catholic form at the Catholic Worker.

Churches with more conventional views have addressed the issues of poverty in a different way. They set aside a portion of their budget to give to the poor, unite in groups to establish programs for the forgotten members of society, and support missions in poor neighborhoods to care for and preach to the poor. They do not feel compelled, however, to move into those neighborhoods or to identify with the poor by living at the same income level. Ecumenical groups have funded organizations to lobby for legislation for the poor and the powerless; their organizations in Washington try to influence congressional decisions on the one hand and raise the consciousness of Christians within their constituent churches on the other.

Problems of Racism

The belief that one race is inherently inferior to another has sometimes led Christians to violent exploitation of other peoples. The postures of nonconformity and adaptation can be delineated on the issue of racism—especially white discrimination against blacks—in its most virulent form, slavery. From the seventeenth through the nineteenth centuries black Africans were systematically uprooted from their own civilizations and religions and sold into slavery. Their culture was destroyed and their religion replaced with a form of Christianity designed as a means of social control. The New Testament injunction, "Slaves, obey . . . your earthly masters" (Coll. 3:22) was pushed to its limits as a theoretical justification for slavery. Nevertheless, people soon began to ask, "If slaves have been baptized into the body of Christ, does that mean they must be set free?"

Only one nonconformist group made a concerted protest against slavery. Quakers were the first Christians to condemn slavery systematically; they were united and firm in their protest. When Thomas Jefferson and George Washington still owned slaves, a Quaker preacher, John Woolman (1720–72), traveled up and down the colonies speaking against it. Quakers formed an important part of the "underground railroad," which provided an effective escape route to the North for runaway slaves.

By the mid-nineteenth century American Christians were at a moral impasse about slavery. Three major American churches split precisely over the issue: Methodists, Baptists, and Presbyterians divided along North/South lines when each group adopted the predominant position of its culture on the issue. John Wesley, founder of the Methodists, opposed slavery, but by the 1840s, American Methodists had divided over the right of the clergy (especially bishops) to own slaves.

We have already seen that one product of the Second Great Awakening was an informal coalition of evangelical Christians united by their conversion experience and prepared for a life of action. The American Bible Society and the American Temperance Union were two projects supported by the evangelical alliance. The American Anti-Slavery Society was also part of the evangelical alliance, but it did not succeed in uniting all evangelical Christians for the abolitionist cause. The great revivalist preacher Charles Grandison Finney sympathized with antislavery views and influenced the revivalist movement significantly. One of his disciples, Theodore Dwight Weld (1803–95), became a leader of the antislavery movement and a founder of the Anti-Slavery Society. Agents selected by the society spread abolitionist views along with evangelical Christianity. Weld influenced politicians in the North and shaped public opinion on the issue. His book *Slavery As It Is* (1839) inspired Harriet Beecher Stowe's novel *Uncle Tom's Cabin*. Those two books were the most important antislavery works written in the United States. Stowe's novel is clearer in its opposition to slavery than to racism in general. She assumes racism will continue: freed blacks will want to be *separate*. In this view neither the gospel nor abolition require fellowship with blacks. Stowe could, therefore, imaginatively enlist white evangelical preachers in the cause of abolition without challenging them to speak for integration.

The division within the churches reflected a division within the society. Apart from the Quakers, the abolitionist cause had few advocates in the eighteenth century. The American constitutional principle that all men are created equal did not apply to slaves; each slave counted only as three-fifths of a human being in early census figures. The liberal positions of the time were shaped by antiblack stereotypes almost as much as by proslavery arguments. Liberals aimed at finding a cure for blackness (as if it were a disease) or a way to surmount the problems of black genetic "inferiority." The religious viewpoint was shaped, in part, by an acceptance of slavery as part of God's plan: God created black people for a reason—to be slaves. Many ministers argued that blacks could not be set free because freedom would violate a divine design. (This argument, as we have seen, was later extended to speak to the problem of poverty).

By the early nineteenth century people began to be more bothered by slavery; the situation approached crisis proportions. A swelling tide of humanitarian reform inspired solutions to the slavery problem: some people thought blacks ought to be free to emigrate elsewhere to form their own colonies; others joined in the abolitionist movement and hoped to free all slaves and so destroy the institution of slavery. Finney and the American Evangelical Alliance adopted an antislavery position and disciples like Weld carried it forward. The revivalist movement was strong in the 1830s, a period when the seeds of division began to take root. The Nat Turner rebellion in 1831 unleashed latent fears in the South and precipitated a tightening of the slave code. William Lloyd Garrison (1805–79), a strong abolitionist, founded *The Liberator,* a proabolition newspaper. His editorial policy led to increased hostility between North and South. By the end of the 1830s the South had rallied to support slavery both theologically and with their own distinct form of revivalism. The splits within the Methodist, Baptist, and Presbyterian churches reflected this growing gap between South and North.

Southern Christians used the Bible to support slavery. Since slavery was mentioned in the New Testament and not specifically condemned there, the churches argued that baptism meant only that slaves were set free in the Lord. Their freedom consisted in the ability to obey their masters willingly and cheerfully in order to secure a place for themselves in heaven. Segregation was extolled as a sensible arrangement and projected into the future. One white minister told a slave congregation they would reach heaven if they were docile and obedient, but that even in heaven they would not mingle with the master and mistress; they could look forward to a heaven with a dividing wall.[9] Northern Christians also supported their abolitionist views with the Bible. The theological stance of both Northern and Southern Christians reflected their differing cultural and political beliefs.

In the twentieth century American Christians—North and South—have not distinguished themselves for their antiracist beliefs. A number of specifically black churches were formed in the eighteenth and nineteenth centuries within mainline Protestant Christianity in America. Black churches often existed as segregated adjuncts, represented as such. Catholics, too, supported a policy of separation with black seminaries, church organizations, convents, and schools. For most Christians no obvious "Christian" alternative to segregation presented itself; the culture only assumed a position of "separate but equal" after Supreme Court rulings. The churches did not lead people to consider black equality or integration. When Martin Luther King, Jr. (1929–68) led civil rights protests in the 1950s in the name of Christianity, church leaders cautioned that his protests and actions against segregation were "unwise and untimely."

Racism is supported by negative presuppositions about other people. One modern religious experiment that has attempted to challenge those fundamental presuppositions is Koinonia Partners of Americus, Georgia.[10] The Koinonia group—a nonconformist experiment in Christian living—was founded in 1942 by Clarence Jordan. This community has a twofold goal: to live together as an integrated fellowship sharing wealth and labor; and to assist local farmers by introducing scientific farming methods so that poor farmers can make their land more fruitful. The group had to withstand mounting hostility in the 1950s when racism and segregation were particularly sensitive issues. Their locally supported chicken and egg business had to shut down because of racial prejudice and they began a mail-order pecan business, which had a broader base of support. The mail-order operation allowed them to extend *koinonia*—fellowship—to Christians all over the world. The partnership with those Christians, they said, reflected their own partnership with God. Koinonia continues to exist as a commune in partnership with people; their activities include providing housing for poor people, child development, and small industries. Their common life involves a wide variety of people in a fellowship they believe to be similar to the kingdom of God they await. Their first interest is not to inspire people to live in communes, but to encourage them to adopt a new way of seeing other people.

QUESTIONS RAISED BY THE POSTURES OF NONCONFORMITY AND ADAPTATION

Although these brief glimpses into the problems of war, poverty, and racism do not shed light on the issues as such, they clarify the distinction between nonconformist and adapted Christianity. Examining the postures within the context of specific cultural issues permits a view of their interconnectedness with society. Some of the general questions raised in the last chapter are important here as well; the same questions about the churches and the political order are raised within the framework of these alternatives of nonconformity and adaptation.

In What Sense Is Christianity Political?

Christian understanding of the church's role in the political order varies according to the definition of politics different groups adopt. Nonconformist Christians take politics to be broader than the accepted life of the society, its government, and public institutions. Their political stance rests on the assumption that the Christian community is inherently different from the state; in some cases the church provides an alternative to the established order. Christians in this group limit their cooperation with the state on the grounds that its values and policies are sometimes different from and even hostile to the values of the church. Their loyalty to the distinctive witness of the church, they believe, prevents them from fully endorsing the values of the culture. Christians in churches that are more adapted accept more of the values of the culture; they tend to see the aims of the state as coextensive with the aims of the church. Adapted Christians usually see no reason, *in principle,* to oppose the goals and policies of the state; they minimize areas of possible conflict between the aims of the society and those of Christian truth.

Whether Christianity is concerned primarily with personal regeneration or with restructuring the society is not the fundamental issue between nonconformity and adaptation. The argument, to some extent, is part of Christianity in whatever form it takes; both nonconformist and adapted Christians would see need for both personal regeneration and efforts for social change. The difference between the positions lies in the way they conceptualize the church and its role in society. Nonconformists tend to see the church as fulfilling an important prophetic function in society; they regard the church as the locus of strong social critique and witness to a radical alternative. Adapted Christians tend to see the church as moral educator and helper; they are often more willing to proceed slowly towards change because they regard the church as an institution in fundamental cooperation with the state. Their confidence in social structures is manifested by their willingness to change society by their votes and by participation as candidates for public office.

What Is the Church?

Sociologists of religion sometimes distinguish between "church-type" and "sect-type" Christianity.[11] According to this distinction sectarian Christians identify the church as a small group of believers whose values differ from those of their culture; their life-style is often rigorous and they do not expect to attract many followers or to see their views adopted by the society in general. Christians with a nonsectarian perspective see the church as a large institution whose values contribute to the stability of the society as a whole. They expect to be socially acceptable, with many followers, and to exert a positive influence on society. They expect to see their views sanctioned by the culture in which they live.

Were the words of Jesus, which are taken seriously by many sectarians— about loving one's enemies, for example—meant to apply for all times? Or were Jesus's ethics meant to be for the interim: did Jesus expect the world to end so soon that he formulated positions to be adhered to only for the short interim between his death and the end of the world? These serious theological questions and issues of scriptural interpretation are reflected in the differences between the nonconformist and adapted positions on some of the issues outlined above.

The questions raised by an argument between sectarian and nonsectarian perspectives often lead to self-righteous judgments on the part of one group or the other. Both groups can perceive themselves as the locus of true Christian conviction. Sectarians often see themselves as more righteous or more faithful to the commands of Jesus; they may condemn the nonsectarian position as secular and perceive the churches as interested in the salvation of the world on the world's terms. Sectarians may see the church as no longer motivated by divine ideals, but moved by the business of the world while sectarians provide the witness of the faithful remnant. Nonsectarians often understand themselves as more realistic interpreters of the gospel because they do not present the message of Jesus in such stark terms; they may condemn sectarians for being socially ineffective and alienating. Church-type Christians may see sectarians as narrow and unnecessarily hostile to the world while the churches provide an effective Christianity attractive to the modern world. Church-type Christianity can be universal, reach out to large numbers of people, and bring its influence to bear on social and political problems. Sectarian Christianity can remind people of the demand for personal commitment. Together they reflect the range of opportunities within the Christian experience.

How Should the Bible Be Interpreted?

As with the options described in the last chapter, adapted and nonconformist Christians support their positions with their reading of the New Testament. Does their use of the New Testament to support fundamentally differing views mean that the message of the New Testament is not clear with regard to racism, violence, and poverty? Does the New Testament itself reflect differences or disagreements already present in the early Christian community? Or is the New Testament perfectly clear on every issue and do some Christians willfully misunderstand it? Did the cultural context in which the Bible was written shape its message? Does their cultural context shape the way North Americans read the Bible?

Most Christian groups agree that Scripture is normative, but how, exactly, does it bind people? Are only the general principles found in Scripture—for example, to love God wholeheartedly and one's neighbor as oneself—binding? Or are specific injunctions addressed to a particular cultural context—"A woman ought to have a veil on her head" (1 Cor. 11:10)—equally binding? How does one discriminate? Should Christians conform their behavior to descriptive statements in the Bible—for example, that Abraham had slaves? Or are they bound only by prescriptive statements like the Ten Commandments? How do they decide about these matters? Must Christians do only what the Bible commands? Or may they do anything not specifically forbidden—for example, since Jesus said nothing about slavery, can one assume owning slaves is acceptable?

Are some parts of the Bible more important than others? In the Old Testament God urges people to go to war and often supports their efforts to conquer another nation; in the New Testament Jesus enjoins his followers to love their enemies and to put away their swords. How do Christians decide which texts are more important in times of war? Most Christians use the New Testament as an interpretive key to the Old Testament: they see God's words and actions in the lives of the Jewish people as pointing directly toward Jesus. Does that mean that the words of the New Testament must always supercede those of the Old Testament? Within the New Testament how does one resolve differences in wording, as between being poor and being poor "in spirit"? Are some parts of the New Testament more important than others? Are the words of Jesus more binding than the teachings of Paul?

All these questions occur in the differences between nonconformist and adapted perspectives on particular issues. They are usually answered with the context of the believing community's historical experience and tradition. Can those answers change? Will textual criticism and biblical scholarship help people to answer these questions more clearly? Or does biblical scholarship threaten the inerrancy of the Bible? Will cultural attitudes be the major interpretive framework in which such questions are answered? Or is it possible to read the text purely, without being influenced by the cultural context? Does a literal reading of the New Testament lead to clear interpretations? Or does that reading tend to reduce issues to a simplicity they do not have?

CONCLUSION

None of the questions raised in this chapter or the previous one can be answered simply; they reflect ancient disagreements and contemporary problems of interpretation. The four postures outlined—withdrawal, domination, nonconformity, and adaptation—do not describe particular groups in an iron-clad way, but suggest some pressing theological issues underlying a wide range of Christian belief and behavior. As Christians continue to be challenged by problems within the world and their culture—nuclear power and weapons, sexism, multinational corporations in Third World countries, worldwide poverty, the emergence of new nations in Asia and Africa—most will not find simple solutions. They will continue to seek answers within the tension between the church and the world and beyond its bounds.

CHAPTER 9 NOTES

1. Religious persecution was part of the American scene almost from the beginning, and was energetically anti-Catholic throughout much of the nineteenth century in various nativist movements, as mentioned in Chapter 7. See John Higham, *Strangers in the Land—Patterns of American Nativism 1860–1925* (New York: Atheneum, 1977).

2. There may even be an "American civil religion": a general kind of religious ethos that transcends specific denominations. For a statement of this social theory see Robert Bellah, "Civil Religion in America," *Daedalus* 96 (1967), pp. 1–21: also, G. Bedell et al., *Religion in America* (New York: Macmillan, 1975), pp. 14–68.

3. One modern consideration turns on how to apply just war criteria to the possibility of nuclear war. An opinionated but thorough book on this subject is William V. O'Brien, *The Conduct of a Just and Limited War* (New York: Praeger, 1981).

4. The peace movement has grown in other churches since the war in Vietnam, and nuclear war discussions have activated Christians in almost all denominations. One group that is causing quite a stir with its emerging protest against nuclear arms is the Roman Catholic church. In 1976 the American Catholic bishops in a pastoral letter questioned the morality of modern war; in 1979 they declared that a nation could not, in conscience, use or *intend to use* a nuclear weapon. This latter position raised serious questions about deterrence and American military policy, and the Catholic bishops received both criticism and support for their views. In 1981 a committee headed by Archbishop Bernardin of Cincinnati (later Cardinal Archbishop of Chicago) began to draft a pastoral letter on nuclear war: the committee represented a broad spectrum of Roman Catholic opinion on the issue, held fourteen hearings, interviewed thirty-six witnesses (including the Secretary of Defense) and began to draft the letter. In June 1982 word leaked out that the pastoral letter was decidedly "dovish" in tone and emphasis, and the controversy surrounding the issue grew more intense. By the end of 1982 the bishops had become a hot topic for the media; see, for example, the cover story in *Time 120* (29 November 1982), pp. 68–78.

5. An article about the beginnings of this community can be found in the magazine, *Sojourners* 6 (January 1977), 14–31. Looking through the magazine will help you see the kinds of concerns they have and also will give you some indication of the other like-minded groups that have sprung up in the United States in recent years.

6. The best study of the movement is William Miller, *A Harsh and Dreadful Love* (New York: Image, 1974). Miller has also written a biography of Dorothy Day, one of the founders, called *Dorothy Day: A Biography* (New York: Harper & Row, 1982), but one would do better to turn to Day's own autobiographical work, especially *The Long Loneliness* (New York: Curtis Books, 1952).

7. Leo XIII (pope from 1878–1903) wrote a ground-breaking social encyclical (letter to the whole world) in 1891, *Rerum Novarum;* it set a pattern for Roman Catholic social thought for the next fifty years. See Aaron I. Abell, *American Catholicism and Social Action: A Search for Social Justice 1865–1950)* (Notre Dame, Ind.: University of Notre Dame Press, 1963), for a history of Catholic social thought and for some indication of why Dorothy Day might have found such things exciting.

8. One Roman Catholic social reformer, Monsignor John Ryan (1869–1945), was the author of the American Catholic Bishops' Program for Social Reconstruction (written in 1919); many of the suggestions it offered were also part of President Franklin Roosevelt's program. Ryan's biography is subtitled *The Right Reverend New Dealer.*

9. See Martin Marty, *Righteous Empire: The Protestant Experience in America* (New York: The Dial Press, 1970), p. 33.

10. A good book on Koinonia, with pictures, is William Hedgepeth, *The Alternative: Communal Life in New America* (New York: Macmillan, 1970).

11. I am using the same general distinction I used in Chapter 8 from Ernst Troeltsch, but see also Note 2 to that chapter.

SUGGESTIONS FOR FURTHER READINGS

1. For more on the black Christian experience see C. Eric Lincoln, *The Black Church Since Frazier* and Franklin E. Frazier, *The Negro Church in America,* combined in a single volume (New York: Schocken Books, 1963).

2. For documents on American religious history that will deepen your understanding of both Protestant and Roman Catholic adaptation see George Bedell et al., *Religion in America* (New York: Macmillan, 1975).

3. Any of the peace churches will be able to give you information on the current activity within the peace movement, not only within their churches, but worldwide. Since this is a changing and contemporary movement, consulting them might be better than any book or article I could cite.

CHAPTER 10

Christian Community and Polity

M ost Catholics and Protestants agree that Christian commitment involves membership in a body of believers, a congregation, but they disagree about how that body mediates God's presence to them. One might regard the life of the church from at least two different perspectives: by examining structures—how various church groups are organized—or by examining what they do when they gather as a body, their worship. These two dimensions are related, but are treated separately in the next two chapters. This chapter deals with church polity, the internal government and organizational structures of the church.

Some revivalist and evangelical Christians have so stressed individual religious experience as to underplay the importance of the church. Some mystics and independent prophets understand Christian faith as a personal relationship with God apart from any community context. Still others believe that the true church is invisible—one cannot know now who will ultimately be saved and who will be damned—yet those Christians see the need for an interim visible structure. Apart from these minority positions, throughout history the weight has been on the side of those who see church as more central than salvation or religious experience outside of a community. The traditional understanding of Christianity—Catholic, Orthodox, Protestant, Anabaptist—has always been bound up with the church and Christian experience with a body of believers. Enormous differences of opinion exist about the nature of the church and the requirements for membership, but there is general agreement that the church is a necessary part of the Christian life.

Christians share an understanding that the church is guided by the Holy Spirit but they divide over the issue of the Spirit's function within the church. This division is especially apparent in the practical issue of church authority, an issue that can be delineated by examining various church structures or polities. In *episcopal* structures spiritual authority moves from the top down; in *congregational* polities it operates within the local community; in *presbyterian* models it moves both up and down through specified levels of organization. The Spirit operates directly in Pentecostal communities to sanctify individual members; in Independent churches[1] the Spirit inspires the prophet who leads the church by means of special insights, dreams, and visions. Sometimes the power and authority of the Spirit rests with a charismatic individual who leads a community; often that community ceases to exist or changes its form significantly when the charismatic individual leaves or dies without provision for succession. After some general remarks about community, we will look at the varieties of Christian polity and then use the differences among them to raise some ecclesiological questions.

CHRISTIAN COMMUNITY

A primary source for understanding God's word and will is the Bible. We have already seen that God spoke and acted in the lives of a particular people in the Old Testament and that Jesus gathered a community around him and enjoined his followers to make disciples from all nations (Matt. 28:19). Most Christians believe that the words of the Bible, spoken for a particular people in an ancient time, are also significant for them, and that God continues to act and speak through the Holy Spirit. Some Christians look back over the history of the church and interpret certain developments as guided by the Holy Spirit; they accept parts of their history as significant and binding. This position—the concept of tradition—was discussed in Chapter 4. Other Christians do not interpret tradition as binding, but position themselves so as to be moved by the Spirit as the Spirit moves and acts in the present. Still others try to strike a balance between tradition as binding and openness to the Spirit within the local community.

Whatever concept Christians have about tradition or the activity of the Spirit in the present, however, they share the belief that the Spirit operates in the life of the church, and believe that the community of believers is a crucial aspect of Christian life. Jesus gathered a group of followers around him during his public life; he promised to send the Spirit to them as a guide and a continuation of his presence among them (see John 16). The early Christians apparently lived together in groups and met regularly to worship and remember Jesus. During his lifetime Jesus promised to be present when two or three were gathered in his name. The idea that Christians ought to come together as a group, therefore, is one with strong roots in the New Testament. Its roots go beyond the New Testament into the Jewish understanding of people of God.

Any community—family, sorority or fraternity, political party—offers its members at least three things: a sense of identity, a source of security, and a way to participate in its corporate life. Identity is unity and persistence of personality, the trait that makes an individual a consistent person. Most of us have several parts to our identity and may choose to feature one or another of them depending on the context: we may identify ourselves by nationality when abroad, by political party when we are in a political argument, and by year of graduation at a school reunion. When people identify themselves religiously they can do so generally (Christian) or specifically (Southern Baptist or Russian Orthodox); the more specific their self-identification, the more we know about their beliefs and practices. Identity not only tells the outsider who people are; it provides people inside with a clearer sense of who *they* are. Those willing to identify themselves with a particular group are willing to answer to the description of that group and to own its beliefs and practices. Disagreements may exist among members of a particular community—individual Republicans might disapprove of their party's presidential candidate, for example—but finally a person prefers the beliefs, policies, and practices of that group to those of another one.

Community also provides members with a sense of security. Knowing one is part of a community that has a history, has weathered storms in the past, and is still alive gives a person a sense of safety, of being part of something larger and more lasting than the individual alone. Community gives one a sense that one is not alone in the world; in a religious group or community a person is able to share the values and experience of other believers and to speak a common language.

Finally, a community offers members a way to participate in its life. Members of sororities and fraternities have rituals, traditions, reunions, and rules designed to enhance the community life of the group on local and national levels. The religious community, too, has rituals, traditions, and rules that support community life and offer a person a way to be part of a group; these rituals also attract because they are seen as bound up with God's will. Though Christian communities differ in their worship and practice, all offer some way for their members to participate in Christian life as they believe Jesus intended it to be lived.

A necessary connection exists between community identity and responsibility. Communities make demands on their members; believers must do certain things in order to remain members in good standing. Membership becomes a contractual understanding between the individual and the larger community. In general, what is the connection between the promises of the New Testament and its demands? If the New Testament offers the believer a new life, a place in the kingdom, fellowship, and eternal life, what does it require? Christians believe they have some responsibility to witness to the gospel in their lives, actions, and words, but they have no unanimously held conviction about the nature of that responsibility. The variety of ways Christians actually fulfill their responsibilities testifies to the vitality of the concept and the complexity of Christian history and understanding.

Churches differ in their ongoing expectations of their members. Some Christians attend church once or twice a year and otherwise do not involve themselves in the life of the community; others attend services and meetings several times each week and are intimately involved in the life and growth of the community. Churches require different levels of participation. Some churches require a certain level of financial support; others require regular attendance and prayer on behalf of the group; still others may require members to adhere to strict codes of dress and behavior, attend business meetings, and give counsel there. Christians fulfill the requirements of membership in various ways and in a variety of denominations or communities. Those communities have different polities, different organizational models and structures.

CHRISTIAN POLITY

Christians believe that the Holy Spirit is present in the church, but they differ about the locus of that presence and its implications for church authority; they also differ in their interpretation of New Testament passages on issues of organizational structure and authority. Does authority rest with a few officials who are modern successors of the apostles? Or does it belong to every baptized member of the community in some way? Is authority shared among members or vested in certain offices within the community—minister, deacon, elder? Is the church a highly organized institution founded by Christ with definite patterns of worship and authority? Or is it a loosely structured community of believers who come together to share fellowship and mutual belief? Varying answers to these questions are reflected in the different structural arrangements one can find within Christianity. There are three common polities—episcopal, congregational, and presbyterian—and some less usual ones.

The Episcopal Structure

Episcopal comes from the Greek word for overseer; it is translanted into English as *bishop*. An episcopal polity, therefore, is a system of church government by bishops. Traditional episcopal polities are based on apostolic succession as the legitimation of their system of church government. Some post-Reformation churches, on the other hand, are presided over by bishops (or superintendents or overseers) who are essentially administrative officers and not understood as the successors of the apostles. One can find the word *episcopoi* (overseers/bishops) in the New Testament, though it is not clear to biblical scholars that its meaning differs from the word *presbytoi* (elders). Still, by the year 100—in the writings of Ignatius of Antioch,[2] for example—three clearly distinct offices had emerged within the Christian church: bishop, presbyter (or priest), and deacon.

Traditional episcopal churches—Roman Catholic, Eastern Orthodox, Anglican, and Old Catholic—agree that the Christian clergy are divided into a hierarchy of order: bishops are the highest order of ministers, followed by priests, and then deacons. The hierarchy of order is supported by a corresponding hierarchy of powers: deacons have some sacramental and ecclesiastical powers (they can preach and baptize), priests share in more of the sacramental power of the church (they can celebrate the Eucharist and forgive sins), and bishops have full sacramental and ecclesiastical powers (they can ordain priests and administer the sacrament of confirmation). These same churches agree that bishops are the successors of the apostles and derive their authority from that succession; they share in the power and authority of the apostles as that authority was conferred on them by Christ. Nontraditional episcopal churches—Methodist, Church of the Nazarene, some Lutherans and Evangelicals—deny the importance of literal apostolic succession, but understand bishops as historically important figures within the Christian church since New Testament times.

The episcopal or hierarchical structure is a pyramid. According to the assumptions underlying this model, Jesus invested his divine authority in the apostles, whose modern successors are the bishops. The authority of the Holy Spirit rests, for the most part, with the bishops; authority in the church flows from them at the top of the pyramid through the priests to the members of the congregation at the bottom of the pyramid.

In traditional episcopal polities, bishops, as successors of the apostles, are invested with powerful symbols of their office. The *cathedra* is the bishop's chair or throne and the cathedral church is the building that contains the bishop's chair. A cathedral is not always the biggest church in the diocese (the bishop's jurisdictional territory), but it is usually grand. A bishop wears a mitre (from the Greek word for turban), a special headdress; Orthodox bishops wear crowns. Bishops carry a pastoral staff (sometimes called a crozier), which is often made of gold and richly ornate; it is shaped like a shepherd's staff with a crook at the top (for collaring lost sheep). They wear a pectoral cross made of precious metal as a sign of the dignity of their office, and a ring as a sign of their marriage to the church. Bishops inherit the powers and functions of the apostles, and embody three of Christ's titles in their work: bishops are expected to be *priests* (sanctifying the church and possessing full sacramental powers), *prophets* (teaching and interpreting doctrine and discipline), and *kings* (ruling or administering their dioceses).

Three things are necessary for a man to become a bishop.[3] He must be *elected*, have a *mission*, and be *consecrated*. A bishop must be elected or chosen from a list of suitable candidates: he must have attained a certain age and served as a priest for a number of years; in Orthodox Christianity bishops must be celibate and are therefore almost always chosen from monasteries. Who elects the bishop? In the early church each congregation selected its own bishop.

During the church/state controversies of the Middle Ages, secular rulers vied for the power to appoint bishops of their choice within their countries; they were opposed by the pope, who elects bishops within the Roman Catholic church. In the contemporary Roman Catholic church, the members of a diocese are asked to submit names of candidates (to advise the pope), but the pope has final authority and appoints the bishop of his choice. Orthodox bishops are appointed by the patriarch of Constantinople/Istanbul, except in those churches where the state has the authority to appoint bishops. The most recent appointment of a new archbishop of Cyprus (1977) led to a struggle between the patriarch and political leaders and reflects a continuing church/state conflict over the election of bishops. In the Anglican church a bishop is elected by a diocesan convention made up of members from local churches; his election is confirmed by a majority of other bishops and a majority of the standing committees of the other dioceses.

A bishop must have a place to exercise his power, a mission. After consecration, the bishop usually "takes possession" of his diocese. In the Roman Catholic church the pope gives the mission to the newly consecrated bishop and each bishop must come to Rome every five years to report on the state of his diocese. The powers of a bishop vary in each church. Orthodox bishops exercise absolute, exclusive religious authority in their dioceses. Roman Catholic bishops used to be defined only as pastors of their dioceses and subordinate to the pope. Since the Vatican II definition of collegiality, however, bishops are defined as members of a group that governs the whole church. Bishops, therefore, *share* in the pastoral responsibility of the whole church (along with the pope). On a diocesan level, priests share with their bishops the pastoral responsibilities of the diocese, and parishoners share with their pastor the pastoral administration of the local parish. The extent to which this theory of collegiality has actually been embraced in the Roman Catholic church varies with different dioceses.

Bishops are overseers of a diocese; they supervise the clergy, preside over meetings and synods, and rule over the diocesan court (which includes a marriage tribunal and hears specifically ecclesiastical grievances). The bishop must see to the spiritual welfare of all the people of his diocese, and be responsible for the selection and ordination of people for the offices of priest and deacon. Bishops are helped in their duties by assistant bishops, administrative staffs, seminary faculties, and advisory boards made up of members of local churches.

A bishop is usually consecrated by a metropolitan bishop and at least two other bishops. Because the early Christian church was organized like the Roman Empire, each city was governed by a bishop and each province had a chief bishop or metropolitan who had some jurisdictional rights over his brother bishops. Those rights began to be defined legally at the Council of Nicaea. The metropolitan was responsible for presiding over provincial meetings (synods), for visiting the dioceses within his province, and for supervising the bishops within his province. When Diocletian reorganized the Roman Empire in the late third century, metropolitans were made subordinate to patriarchs. Patriarch is a sixth-century title for the bishops of the five ancient sees (seats of bishops): Rome, Constantinople, Alexandria, Antioch, and Jerusalem. Patriarchs were able to ordain metropolitans and had jurisdiction over all the adjoining territories and provinces of their city. The old office of metropolitan survives today as the office of archbishop.

Bishops have the power to teach and have structures within which they can deliberate about doctrine and amend Christian teaching. In Roman Catholicism the chief bishop (bishop of bishops) is called the pope (the history and claims of the papacy were discussed in Chapter 4). According to Roman Catholic belief, the pope can call an ecumenical council—a meeting of all the world's bishops—to discuss doctrinal and disciplinary matters. Eastern Orthodox Christians do not believe they can call a council so long as they are not in communion with Rome, nor do they accept the pope's claim to be able to call councils. Accordingly, they are bound by the tradition as it developed up through the last ecumenical council recognized by them, held in Nicaea in 787. In the Anglican church the means are provided for democratic participation in the government and teaching of the church. The communicants of each local church elect local representatives (vestries) who in turn elect representatives to the diocesan convention. Vestries attend to the business of the local church, while the diocesan convention helps the bishop preside over diocesan matters. Provincial (regional) synods and the general (national) convention are bodies made up of bishops and elected laity and clergy from each diocese. Bishops derive their authority from apostolic succession and from the consent of those who are led.

Traditional episcopal polities rest on the claim of apostolic succession. Orthodox Christians and Anglicans deny that apostolic succession grants any personal primacy to a chief bishop or pope. Roman Catholics argue that Jesus not only vested authority in the apostles but made Peter head over all other apostles; their claim rests on their notion that the popes are the successors of Peter. All of these churches have pyramidal models where authority flows mainly from the top whence it is derived from Jesus through the apostolic succession.

In some churches the title of bishop has survived without any of the hierarchical structures or powers. One can find Lutheran bishops—sometimes even those who claim apostolic succession—who are basically administrators; they do what traditional bishops do—ordination and visitation—but they have no more power than pastors. In some Christian churches, bishops have special powers and function as spiritual leaders. Moravian bishops are spiritual leaders who ordain ministers and advise the church on spiritual matters; their functions are more spiritual than administrative. Amish bishops preside over a church district, over the families that can be accommodated at a preaching service held in a home (sometimes in the barn). The bishop has full powers to lead the congregation; administer Communion, baptism, and marriage; declare excommunication; receive members back into the church; and supervise and ordain ministers. The bishop must obtain the consent of the members on some issues and is subject to the vote of the church; no one can be excommunicated or accepted back into the church, for example, without the vote of all the baptized members of the church. The bishop is assisted by preachers (ministers of the book) and deacons (ministers to the poor). Deacons and preachers are chosen by lot or nominated from the congregation; bishops are ordained from among the ordained preachers to serve for life. There is no central organization in Amish churches. Each district is a self-contained unit, though unofficial meetings may be held among bishops in a territory heavily populated with Amish— parts of Pennsylvania, for example—for purposes of communication and fellowship and to discuss pressing problems.

Some Christians—some Evangelicals and Methodists—retain the title of bishop to designate the overseer of church business; Nazarenes do not use the title of bishop, but their district superintendent functions like Methodist bishops do. These churches recognize the importance of the office of bishop, but do not invest it with any special sacramental power, nor do they recognize the need for apostolic succession. Oftentimes their polities are a mixture of congregational or presbyterian ones on the level or representational government, but the retention of the office of bishop suggests that their primary polity—albeit in modified form—is episcopal. In their understanding, bishops functioned in the early church as administrative overseers. Their bishops are members of a council of bishops (usually governing a geographical region), which presides over the general life of the church; within their own districts they are recognized for their spiritual gifts and leadership ability and have broad powers of an administrative, not doctrinal or sacramental, kind. They cannot change the beliefs or structures of the church, but their recommendations for a particular ministerial appointment carry weight. In the Church of the Nazarene, district superintendents are elected every four years and can be reelected continuously until they pass the age of sixty-eight.

Methodists are organized into conferences: the local church is called the *quarterly* conference, and the *district* conference is made up of several local churches. The *annual* conference is regional—taking in several districts—and the *jurisdictional* conference—five in the United States—meets every four years. The worldwide *general* conference also meets every four years. Methodist bishops are elected by the jurisdictional conference to serve within that jurisdiction. Within their jurisdiction, they have the power to appoint people to their work— to transfer ministers from one church to another—but have no authority in matters of dogma. Their territory is larger than a Catholic diocese and their powers, therefore, extend further. In all these churches, bishops have power over large segments of the church and hold sway in appointments and other administrative matters. Representational participation exists at a number of levels from the local church to the international body.

The Congregational Structure

The congregational polity, modeled on the New Testament concept of a house church (a small local body of believers gathered together in a home in the name of Jesus), makes the local congregation supreme. The ministers, deacons, elders, and other officers all come from within the congregation. The gathered group of believers *is* the church and as such is guided by the Holy Spirit. Those who espouse congregational polity defend private judgment and interpretation of Scripture, but they believe that the gathered body of believers is a place where matters of worship, belief, and practice are discussed and decided on.

The congregational structure is circular. According to this model, Jesus sent the Holy Spirit to the church, to the gathered Christian believers, not to a few leaders and administrators. The Holy Spirit guides the local church and authority flows throughout the congregation. The local church does not need external or hierarchical authority since the power of the Spirit is present in all and since the word of God in the Bible is equally accessible to everyone. While congregations may appoint pastors, deacons, elders, or teachers, those offices designate people's differing functions/gifts but do not create differences of status within the group.

Two types of congregational polity need to be distinguished. Pure/independent congregationalism is just that: the local church sets its own theology, doctrine, practice, and internal life without responsibility to any other group. Associational congregationalism recognizes local church autonomy but also acknowledges the need to relate to the larger body of believers. In associational congregationalism, theology and doctrine are guarded by the developed tradition; the local congregation is not free to determine its own theology and doctrine. Independent Christian churches, some storefront churches, and some other groups follow a pure congregationalism. Most traditional congregational churches—Baptist, United Church of Christ, Brethren, Mennonites—adhere to an associational congregationalism of a kind and provide ways for their members to meet with other church members so that decisions about behavior and interpretation are made within a broader-than-congregational frame of reference.

Associations are agencies of interdependence within Baptist churches that take cognizance of the obligations local churches have to one another. Within congregations people relate to each other as members of one body under Christ and, by analogy, various churches associate with one another as parts of one body. The first Baptist Association in the United States was formed in Philadelphia in 1707 to promote doctrinal unity, to settle disputes, to help churches find suitable ministers (sometimes by supporting seminaries or colleges), and to promote missionary activity by collecting money and supervising missionary agencies. Associations have no juridical power and Baptists are not required to cooperate with them; congregational relationship to associations is voluntary.

Baptists are also united in conventions, which are state or national organizations of cooperation—for example, the Southern Baptist Convention—that meet annually. They may make recommendations about an issue—for example, they may suggest that ministers ought to have a college degree and a seminary education—but the local church is still free to follow its own lights on the matter. No association or convention has any legal power over the congregation.

The Congregational church began precisely because certain Christians preferred a congregational polity to an episcopal or presbyterian one (see Chapter 6). Like all congregational polities, Congregationalists encouraged lay involvement in the life of the local church and were governed by members' meetings. Originally, congregational autonomy arose because episcopal (and papal) structures were perceived as extreme and evil: one Reformation complaint was that the Roman Catholic church structure was not biblical. Luther's doctrine of the priesthood of all believers and salvation by grace through faith minimized the need for episcopal structures and reduced the power of the priesthood. Luther, however, did not establish a particular Lutheran polity and one can find many different kinds of polity within the Lutheran church. Congregationalist churches began in protest against episcopal and presbyterian polities in England, and hoped to be free from credal uniformity and from interference in the life of the local congregation by either the church hierarchy or the state.[4]

In the United States, Congregationalists made efforts to unify themselves by forming organizations for cooperation and fellowship. The National Council of Congregational Churches was formed at Oberlin, Ohio, in 1871, to provide opportunity for local churches to cooperate in matters too broad for them individually: administration of missionary work, colleges and seminaries, and so on. These national organizations—and international ones, like the International Congregational Council founded in 1948—have no juridical power over the local congregation. Local congregations *are* the church; they are not *part* of the church. They may participate in national organizations, but have no obligation to do so. Like the Baptists, they are associational. Congregationalists have worked for Christian unity, but always with the intention of maintaining the importance of the life of the local church and its essential independence.

Some churches with a congregational polity operate on a consensus model for making decisions; every member of the local congregation must agree to a policy before the church pursues it. When difference of opinion is present, members listen to all dissent; their belief in the Holy Spirit's presence in the local community suggests to them that a dissenting voice is as valuable in a discussion as one of agreement.

Other churches have congregational structures and representatives elected by the congregation to make decisions, present them to the church, and proceed if a majority vote favors the proposal. In Mennonite and Brethren churches, annual conferences can be attended by all members of the denomination; the purpose of the annual conference is fellowship, growth in mutual understanding, and deliberation on matters of discipline or policy of broad interest. In all these cases the locus of the continuing presence of the Holy Spirit is the congregation; the church is understood to be the gathered community.

The Presbyterian Structure

According to the model followed by Presbyterian and Reformed churches, authority rests with a group of elected elders—the Greek word for elder is *presbyter*—not with a single authority figure (the bishop) nor entirely with the local congregation. The presbyterian model, based on New Testament offices of elder, deacon, and so on, combines some characteristics of both episcopal and congregational structures in an attempt to reflect the organization of the early church. Presbyterianism is based on Calvin's doctrines and organizational models. According to Calvin, the church possesses divine authority, but is also *semper reformanda*, always needing to be reformed, and therefore has no final and perfect form, no structure presented to it by divine design. One can, however, work out from the New Testament a set of offices and functions within the church.

The presbyterian model, which is basically elected constitutional government, operates very much like the United States' constitutional government. It might best be represented as trapezoidal; it has an authoritative body, not an individual, at the top (like the episcopal structure), but also provides for local initiative and governance (like the congregational model). Authority circulates within the structure and moves from the bottom up (by way of suggested agenda) and from the top down (by means of the decisions of the general assembly agreed upon by the presbyteries). In this polity the local church (called a *session*) is administered by the pastor (who is a *teaching elder;* all ordained ministers are teaching elders, but not all are pastors) and a certain number of *ruling elders* elected by the congregation. The pastor is the moderator of the session; the number of ruling elders depends on the size of the congregation and can vary from three to more than twenty. The task of the session is to maintain the spiritual government of the local church. The session can receive and dismiss members of the church, examine and ordain ruling elders, and supervise the educational work of the church. The session also regulates times and places of worship. Session meetings must occur at least four times each year, though some sessions meet more frequently.

A number of sessions (at least twelve) together form a presbytery, which is a district body presided over by an annually elected moderator. The presbytery has legislative, executive, and judicial powers. Ministers are not subject to the session, but to the presbytery. All the teaching elders (ordained ministers) in a session are part of the presbytery. Not all teaching elders are involved directly in the session—they may teach in nearby colleges, or have some other job—but they are, by virtue of their ordination, part of the presbytery and may participate in it if they wish to. Each session also sends ruling elders to the presbytery;

The episcopal polity

The congregational polity

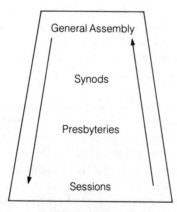

The presbyterian polity

ideally there should be an equal number of teaching elders and ruling elders from each session at the presbytery. The presbytery is a kind of corporate episcopacy: it receives candidates for ministry and sanctions the call of a congregation to a minister by ordaining and installing him or her. The presbytery can dismiss, judge, and remove ministers and can organize and divide local sessions. All delegates sent to synods and to the general assembly are elected at the presbytery level. They can be elected from the general membership in various sessions; they do not have to be ruling or teaching elders. The presbytery also initiates the business of the general assembly. The questions and issues decided higher up, therefore, are generated from the district level. If the general assembly proposes some change in government, their proposal has to be passed by a certain percentage of the presbyteries.

Many presbyteries—the number depends on the number of Presbyterians in a given geographical area—combine to form a *synod*, a regional body presided over by an elected moderator. The synod, an American addition to or refinement of presbyterianism, is a governing body made up of representatives of teaching and ruling elders from the various presbyteries. They meet annually to handle appeals from the presbyteries and to coordinate educational projects and financial cooperation for various projects. The synods are often less important in practice than the presbyteries; they provide resources to enable the presbyteries to carry out their work.

The *general assembly* is a national body made up of members elected by the presbyteries and presided over by an annually elected moderator. The general assembly represents the whole church and is responsible for matters of faith and order. It institutes and supervises agencies for education, missions, and ecumenism. It meets annually and can advise the presbyteries—on issues like ordination of homosexual ministers, for example—and can amend some things; but all changes in traditional documents or beliefs have to be passed by the presbyteries, and all questions of policy and items for discussion must be initiated by a presbytery. There is a World Alliance of Reformed Churches, but it has no jurisdiction; the main juridical body within this system is the general assembly, working in cooperation with the presbyteries.

The three common forms of church polity—episcopal, congregational, and presbyterian—are represented in the diagrams on the facing page.

Other Polities

Some Christian communities—including many nineteenth-century communitarian groups—have been founded by single charismatic individuals and often disband when that leader leaves or dies. Other groups founded by a charismatic leader—the Church of Christ, Scientist, for example—continue to be "led" by that individual. Christian Scientists have no local or regional organization; all decisions about policy and teaching come from the "mother church" in Boston. But the mother church has no power to make changes or introduce new ideas; it follows the *Manual of the Mother Church* written by Mary Baker Eddy. Decisions are administered according to her will and direction.

Mormons follow the organization of the early church as they understand it; their structure includes apostles, a prophet, and elders. Their chief officer is the First President, who is also a "priest of the order of Melkisedek" (see Heb. 5:6 and Gen. 14:18), he is assisted by two counselors. The president is also a prophet who Mormons believe receives the ongoing revelation of God. He is elected for life. Assisting these officers is the Council of the Twelve Apostles, chosen on the basis of revelations received by the president. New decisions arise from new revelations: for example, black males were admitted to full priesthood in 1978, when the prophet received a revelation that said they could be included.

Quakers began with a belief about the centrality of an Inner Light in each person, not mediated by church membership, sacraments, or a particular polity. By 1668, however, George Fox developed the *Rules for the Management of a Meeting* and an organizational scheme to go with it. Friends meet weekly for worship and monthly for business; the monthly meeting is either local or regional. Quarterly and yearly meetings take in wider geographical areas and include more people. No voting occurs at meetings because the Quaker doctrine of the Inner Light upholds the notion that members seek to discover God's will by deliberation. The decisions of the yearly meeting have the highest authority within the church. Friends have also organized for specific purposes beyond the scope of the local meeting. The American Friends Service Committee, for example, unites Quakers in peace and humanitarian efforts throughout the world.

Not all Christians are comfortable with these models; contemporary dissatisfaction with all these polities may lead to experimentation with new models. Some Christians display an anti-institutional bias and others have a strong desire for interdenominational fellowship and worship; some form groups around specific issues of social justice. Within this mixture of discontent and desire some Christians have abandoned old structures altogether in favor of new ones or modified ones, and others have supplemented old polities with new experiments in Christian living. New experimental structures include small groups that meet weekly for worship and fellowship; house churches that gather members together for worship and sharing in homes rather than the more formal atmosphere of church buildings; "floating parishes" where people meet to celebrate the Eucharist in smaller, more informal settings; and Christian communal groups, like Koinonia Partners in Georgia.[5] Any of these might be interdenominational; most of them have some form of congregational polity.

QUESTIONS RAISED BY DIFFERENCES IN POLITY

Clearly, most Christians maintain their religious identities within a community. A group seems almost automatically to develop structures to insure the continuance of its life. Early Christians developed some patterns to perpetuate their faith. How were those structures derived? Did early Christians derive their organizational model from Jesus's words or practice, or did they modify existing Jewish or Hellenistic or Roman structures to suit their new faith? Were they led by the Holy Spirit to develop models of community that were entirely new, or did they adopt structural insights from a number of different places? When a group adopts a polity they believe Jesus commanded, are they bound to it in an absolute and permanent way, or may they modify it to fit contexts different from first-century Palestine? How would a group decide about that? If a group adopts a model for avowedly practical reasons, what guidelines might be used for continuing modification? Is practicality itself an adequate norm for a given group or must it justify its model with reference to some biblical framework? If the presence of the Holy Spirit led to new structures in ancient times, can one assume new structures are possible in modern times as well?

What attitudes do various groups take toward their polities? Do they regard the organizational structure of the church as absolute, or can it be varied? Christian missionaries struggle with questions of adaptation when traditional Christian polities do not seem to fit the needs of a particular people. Is it appropriate to make room for a charismatic leader and some tribal styles of government and participation, or must a missionary impose a more rigid and self-perpetuating structure on people unaccustomed to such forms?[6]

We noticed in Chapter 5 that the reformers patterned their churches on what they believed to be New Testament models, and in opposition to what they considered to be nonscriptural Roman Catholic polity. Yet, Catholics claim that they derived their episcopal structure from Jesus's words to Peter: "You are Peter, and on this rock I will build my church, and the powers of death shall not prevail against it" (Matt. 16:18). None of the Christian churches during the Reformation or after believed they were acting contrary to scriptural directives; all of them believed their polities were present in the New Testament. Is the New Testament unclear on this issue, or multi-dimensional? Can one find evidence for many different polities within the New Testament: small house churches; congregational structures; charismatic groups that gather to celebrate and share the gifts given all of them by the Holy Spirit; presbyterian models with elders and deacons carrying administrative duties; and hierarchical models with definite patterns of authority culminating in a single leader? Are the various ministers all named in the New Testament? Can one find mention of bishops, elders, deacons, teachers, prophets, healers, and priests? Those who defend congregational or presbyterian polities do so on New Testament grounds, but so do those who follow charismatic models or ones derived from apostolic succession. Beneath their differences we can see that most Christians agree that the church needs to have a leadership structure based on early Christian practice and New Testament ideas.

Christians also agree that the church should provide members with an identity and a sense of mission; they agree that the church ought to foster virtues of faith, hope, charity, repentance, and honesty. All of these models are meant to support Christians in their lives in Christ by offering them ways to experience God's graciousness as part of a community of fellow believers. Some polities aim to enhance Christian life by providing avenues where administrative matters are dispatched with maximum efficiency, where patterns of worship and authority give a sense of order and stability and permanence. Some models hope to sustain Christian life by offering members a forum for theological and practical discussion; the church provides ways for members to participate in decisions about virtually all church matters.

Polities can be used by church members to sustain their own theological preoccupations; they can be adapted to new situations or they can refuse to compromise with the challenges of the world; they can be used to foster interdenominational cooperation, or to quell it; they can conceptualize themselves as eternally binding and unchangeable or as flexible, provisional, situation-specific. What is the relationship between social context and church polity? Will contemporary dissatisfaction with old forms result in the emergence of entirely new polities that will stand the test of time? Will traditional polities be modified to suit contemporary needs? Or are experimental polities a fancy that will pass and be replaced with traditional models again?

CONCLUSION

We can learn about Christian groups from their polities and from their descriptions about themselves as churches. Various descriptions include understandings of the church as the body of Christ, a pilgrim people, an institution founded by Christ, a fellowship of the elect, the kingdom of God on earth, a community of believers, a gathering of believers, the people of the name of Jesus, the believers' church, a community of love, a fellowship of hope, a congregation of saints, a community of sinners, a mystery. All of these descriptions go beyond polity into the center of Christian identity, and all of them testify to the central importance of church in Christianity. Whatever the differences in historical understanding and contemporary polity—and they are numerous—Christians are united in believing that the church is the center of community life and that the community is the primary locus of new life in Christ.

CHAPTER 10 NOTES

1. One example of independent churches can be seen in Africa. The spread of Christianity in Africa has not resulted in a *few* different Christian denominations, but in more than five thousand independent Christian churches, often associated with specific tribes or individuals. Each church accepts Jesus as savior and Christ, but otherwise follows a Christianity made up of an amalgam of Christian teachings and native beliefs. See Bennetta Jules-Rosette, *African Apostles: Ritual and Conversion in the Church of John*

Maranke (Ithaca: Cornell University Press, 1975), and Nathaniel I. Ndiokwere, *Prophecy and Revolution: The Role of Prophets in the Independent African Churches and in Biblical Tradition* (London: SPCK, 1981). For an introduction to African theology see John S. Pobee, *Toward an African Theology* (Nashville: Abingdon Press, 1979).

2. Ignatius was one of the early Christian writers (see Appendix 3). One of the disputes in the contemporary church is about the emergence of structures of authority like the ones found in the writings of Ignatius. Were those the only possibilities, or were they established precisely to squelch dissent? This question has been raised from a feminist perspective by Elaine Pagels in *The Gnostic Gospels* (New York: Random House, 1979).

3. Some episcopal churches—Methodists, for example—allow for the possibility that a woman could be a bishop (Methodists consecrated their first female bishop, Marjorie Matthews, in 1980), but the kinds of episcopal structures under consideration here—Roman Catholic, Eastern Orthodox, and Anglican—do not allow women to be ordained priests and therefore would not have women bishops. The Episcopal church (the American branch of the Anglican church) does allow for the ordination of women, but the thought of a female bishop in that church is, at this point, remote. Can women be ordained to the priesthood? Were there women apostles? The argument on these issues is heated and complicated. For a feminist reading of New Testament texts on offices and authority see Elisabeth Schüssler-Fiorenza, "'You Are Not to Be Called Father,' Early Christian History in a Feminist Perspective," in *Cross Currents* 29 (1979), pp. 301–23.

4. In England, where the Anglican church is established (supported by the state), there is a relationship between church and state that has been both troublesome and advantageous for both throughout history. Since the king or queen of England is the head of the church, appointment of new bishops is a matter of state. Congregationalists hoped to get away from this combination of protection and interference. The English government's interest in episcopal appointments is *not* an oddity of ancient history. As recently as the early 1980s, Prime Minister Thatcher announced that she would veto certain episcopal candidates. Why? Because those candidates had not been as supportive as she thought they should have been during the Falkland/Malvinas Islands war (see articles in passing in the London papers June–August 1982).

5. See Chapter 9 for a discussion of Koinonia Partners.

6. For an interesting look at one contemporary practitioner see Vincent J. Donovan, *Christianity Rediscovered*, 2nd ed. (Maryknoll, N.Y.: Orbis Books, 1982). Donovan, a Catholic missionary, has taken a radical approach to his missionary task. Instead of moving into a village as a colonizer (building schools, setting up organizations, and so on), he moves from village to village preaching the essentials of Christianity (the fundamental message about Jesus) and then leaves them to nurture their own church.

SUGGESTIONS FOR FURTHER READING

1. For a general theological analysis of various church models, see Avery Dulles, *Models of the Church* (Garden City, N.Y.: Doubleday, 1974).

2. For a scholarly analysis of the background issues raised in this chapter, see Hans von Campenhausen, *Ecclesiastical Authority and Spiritual Power in the Church of the First Three Centuries* (Stanford, Calif.: Stanford University Press, 1969). As you can imagine,

there are no simple books on this issue; each church can defend its own choices and, in the spirit of ecumenism, many are coming to appreciate differences.

3. For a more readable analysis of church models in the New Testament itself and in history, see Hans Küng, *The Church* (London: Sheed & Ward, 1967).

4. For a lucid and engaging statement of the problem of authority for Roman Catholics, especially before and after the Second Vatican Council, see John L. McKenzie, *Authority in the Church* (New York: Sheed & Ward, 1966). McKenzie is a Scripture scholar and therefore gives much time to the biblical background of some of the arguments, then brings them fully up to date in a clear and challenging style.

Christian Worship

C hristians differ in their historical experience and perceptions about the church and the gospel, but they share basic understandings about the Christian life. The core of Christian experience has always been repentance and conversion and then nurture in new life with celebrations of renewal and revitalization. Throughout history, Christians have worshipped in a community context that involves one or more of the following: sacraments (or ordinances), prayer, preaching, and congregational singing. We have already seen that a community provides the believer with a religious identity; the community also provides the locus of initiation, celebration, and interaction. In worship, believers relate to God and to each other as members of the body of Christ. Worship takes believers beyond doctrine into the feelings and expressions of the heart as the community remembers and interprets God's actions in their lives. Differences exist in contemporary Christian understandings of baptism and the Lord's Supper, and in approaches to worship in general; but one should see the similarities of intention underneath the differences. We try to do that in this chapter.

SACRED TIME AND SPACE

Before we examine this diversity and unity, let us look for a moment at the notion of sacred *time* and sacred *space*. Scholars have shown us that most religious groups, from the primitive to the modern ones, have held such notions.[1] Primitive groups believed that there were especially holy times and places (when and where the gods were more accessible or more likely to hear their prayers). That consciousness is not so firm today as it may have been then, but neither has it fully disappeared. Many Christians consider their place of worship to be sacred, and some would not use a church unless it had been blessed or consecrated (a recognition of its holiness of purpose). Other Christians prefer to see the gathered community and its actions as holy but not the building itself. Christians are similarly divided in terms of sacred time—some divide their days and their years into units based on sacred events while others do not.

Monastic communities divide their *days* according to ancient patterns of prayer. One of their purposes as a community is to recite the Divine Office, a set of prayers and readings based on the Psalms and the Bible. Historically, the hours of prayer were fixed in monastic rules (in the West, in the Benedictine Rule, for example) and followed by members of monastic orders (both men and women). In strict monastic communities the hours are still followed according to ancient custom, but most communities today have modified the ancient rules so that they conform more with modern work schedules. The Office begins with *matins,* a vigil in anticipation of the next day traditionally said at two in the morning. The next moment of prayer is *lauds,* an ancient form of Christian morning prayer said after dawn. During the day there are four times for prayer—the so-called little hours—*prime, terce, sext,* and *none,* meant to correspond to the first, third, sixth, and ninth hours of the day as reckoned in the ancient system. In the evening, before dark, one says *vespers* and before bed, *compline.* During all these hours, specific prayers are recited in an established order. The liturgy of the hours has a rhythm of time and words: each hour usually includes psalms, readings from Scripture, prayers, hymns, and canticles. The order, and most of the prayers, is ancient.

The Anglican Book of Common Prayer contains morning prayer and evening prayer comprised of a combination of matins and lauds (for morning) and compline (for evening). Efforts have been made in recent years to introduce daily prayer based on the liturgy of the hours into the devotional lives of ordinary (nonmonastic) Christians. Accordingly, new translations and simplified prayerbooks have been introduced.[2]

Many Christians—Roman Catholics, Anglicans, Lutherans, Orthodox Christians, Methodists, Presbyterians, and others—divide their *years* according to events in the life of Jesus. The liturgical year begins not on January first, but in Advent, the weeks before Christmas. Eastern Orthodox Christians do not observe Advent, but many Western Christians take the four weeks before Christmas as a time of special preparation for the coming of the Lord.[3] Accordingly, Advent is a time for fasting (in anticipation of the feast), sorrow for sinfulness, and general readiness; the coming of the Lord celebrated on Christmas is also an anticipation of the Second Coming of Christ. After Advent, Christians celebrate the Christmas season, which lasts from Christmas to the feast of the Three Kings (the Epiphany) in early January. The next major *season* of the Christian year is Lent, which begins on Ash Wednesday, forty days before Easter (the feast of the Resurrection). In many churches Ash Wednesday begins a long time of prayer, fasting, and almsgiving; Christians are reminded of their sinfulness and mortality—"Remember that you are dust and to dust you will return" (Gen. 3:19)—so that they will change their ways and renew their relationship with the Lord. The last week of Lent, Holy Week, contains the feasts of Holy Thursday (on which Jesus celebrated the Last Supper or gave Christians the Eucharist), Good Friday (on which Jesus died), and Easter Sunday (on which Jesus rose from the dead). The Easter *season* lasts for several weeks— during which time prayers are punctuated with the word *alleluia*—and ends with the feast of Pentecost (the day the Holy Spirit was sent to the young Christian church).

Differences exist between East and West about the date of Easter and the kinds of fasting to be practiced, and differences exist between Christians who follow the liturgical year and those who do not. Roman Catholics, for example, tend to use the word *alleluia* only during the Easter season, whereas Pentecostal Christians punctuate all their prayers and services with it. Both see it as a special word, full of joy, but one group concludes that it should be restricted to a specific season while the other believes it should be used all the time. Whatever differences exist on the question of liturgical time, most Christians seek to be mindful of the life, death, and resurrection of Jesus and the presence of the Holy Spirit in their communities.

SACRAMENTS (OR ORDINANCES)

Earliest Christian practice included the sacraments of baptism and the Lord's Supper—initiation into and celebration of the life, death, and resurrection of Jesus within a community context. The word *sacrament* comes from the Latin *sacramentum*, which in turn comes from the Greek word for mystery. Christians have argued heatedly and at great length about the definition of the word and about the function of sacraments in the life of the church. On the basis of their definitions, they have argued about the proper number of sacraments, their meaning, and the proper ways to celebrate them. Some Christians reject the word altogether and prefer to talk about *ordinances;* others have baptism and Communion but do not use either word, *sacrament* or *ordinance;* they just baptize and have Communion. Most Christians agree that the observance of sacraments/ordinances is essential.

A working definition of *sacrament* might be: an outward or visible sign instituted by Christ in the church to draw the participant into a relationship with Him within the context of the community of believers. Sacraments are not invisible; they use things that can be seen, touched, or consumed. Yet they are more than objects; they are signs and symbols of God's power through Christ and they recall believers to the graciousness of God. Christians argue about the relationship between sacraments and divine grace: Roman Catholics believe that sacraments "give grace" to those who receive them with the right intention; others hold that they are channels of grace—the means by which God can give grace to a person—but do not necessarily give grace themselves; still others argue that they symbolize God's grace without transmitting it.

A sacrament is a ritual action—celebrated in a special way with specific words and gestures—done because Jesus instructed people to do it and promised them they would be nearer to him, to one another, and to the kingdom of God if they did. All Christians, except those who reject all sacraments—Quakers and the Salvation Army—believe that Jesus instituted *two* sacraments/ordinances: baptism and the Lord's Supper (or Communion or Eucharist). Christians disagree about how, where, and when to perform these sacraments, but most of them agree that they do them because Jesus said to do them and that something happens when they are done.

Baptism

Baptism is a ritual of initiation into Christian faith and/or church membership. Those who accept sacraments/ordinances agree that Christians must be baptized, but they disagree about when to do it (to babies or adults), where to do it (at a font or in a river), how to do it (sprinkling, pouring, immersion), and what it does (removes sin, makes one a member of the church). Jesus was baptized in the Jordan River by John the Baptist. He commanded his disciples to baptize and (according to John 3:5) said that people had to be baptized with water and the Holy Spirit in order to enter the kingdom of Heaven. Baptism has always been bound up with repentance and conversion. Paul, interpreting baptism for Christians in the Epistle to the Romans (chapter 6), said that Christians are united with Christ in baptism. Baptism brings new life: those who were dead (in their sins) are given new life through baptism; they are purified and become members of the body of Christ. The disciples were "baptized with the Holy Spirit" on Pentecost, and manifested that Spirit by *glossolalia* (Acts 2:4).

Christian groups focus on one or more of these points in developing their doctrine of baptism. For some it is crucial to be immersed, and for others the manner is not important. For Pentecostal Christians two distinct baptisms are necessary for church membership—one must be baptized with water for the remission of sins, and with the Spirit for sanctification and full church participation—but for others, baptism with water includes the gifts of the Spirit. For most Christians baptism is the means whereby they are incorporated into the body of Christ. Baptism is an ancient Christian ritual of initiation, and amid the differences in interpretation and practice, Christians agree about its importance both as a means of participating in the life of the community and as a way to share in divine life, a possibility laid open by the death and resurrection of Jesus.

The Eucharist

Eucharist comes from the Greek word for thanksgiving. In Orthodox churches, the celebration of the Eucharist is called the Divine Liturgy. In Protestant churches this sacrament/ordinance is often called Holy Communion or the Lord's Supper. In the Orthodox tradition, the eucharistic meal is bound up with the doctrine of the Resurrection: as the Last Supper was celebrated in anticipation of the kingdom, so the Eucharist is a celebration of the kingdom already begun in the midst of the church. The mood of the Liturgy in Orthodox churches, therefore, is joyful and celebratory.

Christians believe that Jesus ate a last supper with his apostles on the night before he died. In 1 Corinthians, Chapter 11, Paul explains that on that night Jesus took bread, blessed it, broke it, and gave it to his disciples, saying, "This is my body which is for you;" and then took a cup of wine, blessed it, and said, "This cup is the new covenant in my blood."[4] Jesus commanded his followers to "do this in remembrance of me." Christians are supposed to break bread and drink wine, remembering Jesus's life, death, and resurrection, and anticipating his return; but what does that mean? Are the bread and wine literally the body and blood of Christ made present to the believers through liturgical action? Or are the bread and wine symbols of his body and blood, but still bread and wine? Or in breaking bread and drinking wine in memory of Jesus, do Christians primarily celebrate their unity as Christ's body?

According to the New Testament, early Christians cared how the meal was eaten: people were not to be greedy; they were to wait until everyone had arrived (1 Cor. 11:33f.); those who had a grudge against a brother or sister and didn't settle it before coming to the table received the meal unworthily (Matt. 5:23). In the New Testament one can find concrete, fleshy images of the Eucharist where Jesus tells people that they must chew his flesh and drink his blood (John 6:41–60). Elsewhere in the New Testament one finds symbolic descriptions that emphasize recognizing the Lord's presence in the breaking of the bread more than eating his flesh and drinking his blood (Luke 24:30–33). Both of these interpretive traditions were passed down from the early community, with some people emphasizing a more symbolic understanding and others a more realistic one. As time went on, however, the realistic interpretation predominated and became the official interpretation of the church.[5]

The Eucharist is celebrated—according to the New Testament—as a memorial of the passion and resurrection of Jesus. In the East, it was associated predominantly with the Resurrection, but in the West, the focus was on the passion and death of Jesus, especially as that was expressed in the idea of sacrifice. Medieval theologians explained the Eucharist as the reenactment of the sacrifice of the Cross; every gesture had some allegorical relationship to some moment in Christ's passion. Theologians also attempted to explain how, exactly, the bread and wine became the body and blood of Christ, and forged their explanation from Aristotelian logic.[6] The Eucharist began to take on, in the minds of some believers, a magical aspect, exacerbated by Roman Catholic developments of reserving the wine for the priest only and giving only bread to the people, restricting the number of times people could receive the Eucharist, and generally making eucharistic celebration inaccessible to common understanding.

The reformers, hoping to restore what they took to be the New Testament understanding of the Eucharist, rejected the explanations of the medieval theologians, reduced the sacrificial interpretations, and hoped to urge people to celebrate the Lord's Supper every Sunday. Variations in Protestant belief and practice followed from specific understandings of sacraments in general and of the Lord's Supper in particular. Some groups, following the Johannine (from the Gospel of John) scenario of the Last Supper entirely, bound the practice to footwashing and the "holy kiss" of peace. They celebrated it rarely, sometimes only once or twice each year. Others rejected any sacramental explanations and interpreted the Lord's Supper as a symbol of Christ's death and Christian unity. Roman Catholics restressed the sacrificial interpretation during the Reformation and did not accept the concept of the Eucharist as essentially a *meal* until the changes introduced into their liturgy by the Second Vatican Council.

In churches with a highly developed sacramental liturgy, the Eucharist is celebrated within the context of ancient prayers and gestures. Catholics and Orthodox Christians have been celebrating the Eucharist in essentially the same way for centuries, using the same prayers and gestures. Catholics have introduced some new prayers since Vatican II, but Orthodox Christians have not changed their practice since the ninth century. In nonsacramental churches, the Lord's Supper may be celebrated in different ways but usually includes some reading of the account of the Last Supper and sharing of the bread and cup; some groups use grape juice rather than wine (a legacy of the evangelical position against intoxicating liquors).

Other Sacraments

Beneath the differences of eucharistic interpretation and practice lies a common understanding of the need for fellowship and nurture within the Christian church. Protestants have traditionally accepted the mandate for fellowship and nurture in a nonsacramental context, but Catholics and Orthodox Christians have chosen to pursue the Christian life in a sacramental context that includes not only baptism and the Eucharist, but other sacraments as well.

Roman Catholics and Orthodox Christians observe *seven* sacraments, not just two. Part of the reason for the difference lies in the longer historical tradition of these churches and their association with the medieval desire to make religion all-embracing by making lists and speculating about the ways God relates to the world. For example, people had always prayed for the sick and the dying—one can find precedent for it in the Epistle of James in the New Testament—and certain prayers and rituals of anointing with oil came to be associated with it. Catholics accepted this as a sacrament, not just as a pious practice. Roman Catholics and Orthodox Christians agreed in the Middle Ages that there were seven sacraments: baptism, confirmation, penance (or reconciliation), the Eucharist, Holy Orders (whereby a man is ordained to the priesthood), matrimony (which consecrates marriage), and the anointing of the sick.

The acceptance of seven sacraments by Roman Catholics was considered to be a conservative step at the time; some medieval theologians argued that there were more than thirty of them. By the twelfth century, however, Catholics agreed on seven sacraments. At the Council of Florence (1439) and again at the Council of Trent (1545–63)—against Protestant insistence that there were only two sacraments, or none at all—Catholics declared the doctrine of seven sacraments. Catholics also, following the logic of Scholastic theology, specified the necessary elements of a sacrament: it had to have the right *matter* (water in the case of baptism), the right *form* (the words, "I baptize you in the name of the Father, and of the Son, and of the Holy Spirit"), and the right *intention* on the part of the minister (to do what the church did in that sacrament: to forgive all sins and to admit the person into church membership). The person receiving the sacrament had to be rightly *disposed* (must have faith and, in the case of baptism, repentance: Catholics baptize babies on the theory that the faith and repentance of the church can be extended to them through their godparents until they have faith and repentance of their own).

Protestants, intending to reduce the power of the priesthood by breaking its connection with the sacraments and hoping to reinstate sacraments on a more biblical (less Scholastic)[7] basis, rejected those sacraments not clearly instituted by Jesus; that is, all except baptism and the Lord's Supper. In redefining the sacraments, Protestants introduced interpretations that sometimes stressed their divergence from traditional Roman Catholic teaching. Zwingli, for example, argued that the Lord's Supper was only a memorial meal and not in any way a partaking of the real body and blood of Christ. Other Protestants took a position somewhere between Roman Catholic belief (the Eucharist *is* the body and blood of Christ) and the position of Zwingli (Communion is a fellowship meal) and thought of the Lord's Supper as a *symbol* of the real body and blood. These differences about the nature of the sacraments, especially the Lord's Supper, continue within the Christian church: those who accept some understanding of real presence of the body and blood of Christ in the Eucharist are usually groups with a sacramental tradition and relatively high liturgical consciousness.

Sacraments reflect a particular interpretation of the Christian belief in Jesus as the word of God made flesh; they suggest that God acts in the world through ordinary things and that the extraordinary or the divine can be made manifest in the ordinary things of life: in water, bread, and wine. Sacraments also reflect an understanding of the church as a community bound together in the life of Christ. Sacraments bind individual believers to God through Christ, but they also link individuals to one another in one body of Christ. For some Christians the body of Christ is the church here and now, the community one can see; for others it extends through time and space to embrace those now living and those who have died in the Lord. In Orthodox and Roman Catholic belief sharp distinctions between natural and supernatural are somewhat softened by sacramental understandings of the world; sacramental extensions of divine life are not limited to baptism and Eucharist, but can be found in many other dimensions of one's life.

PRAYER

Prayer can be defined as opening or lifting up the mind and heart to God. People pray in different ways and for a number of reasons: to adore God as Creator and Lord; to express sorrow for sins and failings; to thank God for salvation, the blessings of this life, or the beauties of the world; and to ask God's continued blessing or help. Christians believe that God is the transcendent Lord of the universe; but God is also a personal being interested in people and wanting relationship with them. Some Christians see prayer as conversation with God in order to foster relationship. One seventeenth-century poet said prayer was "the soul in paraphrase, heart in pilgrimage."[8]

Prayer is practiced both privately and publicly. The New Testament tells us that Jesus participated in public prayer by going to the synagogue; often, however, he prayed in private in lonely places or in the desert. He prayed for strength and guidance—for the power to raise Lazarus from the dead, or to endure the agony of his death—and taught his friends how to pray.

Private Prayer

People sometimes pray privately and silently. The Christian tradition has a rich vein of mystical prayer, contemplation, and meditation. The most unusual of these is *mysticism*, in which a person has a direct ecstatic encounter with God. Mystics are rare and their writings testify that they are *called* into a special, intimate relationship with God; one does not, in other words, set out to be a mystic. Christians can meditate or attempt contemplative prayer, however, and they have the writings of those well versed in the techniques to help them. Some Christians have turned to the principles and techniques of Eastern religious meditation—especially Zen—to help them with their own meditation or contemplation. *Meditation* is thinking about an image or aspect of God—about some aspect of the passion or a particular gospel story, for example—to the exclusion of everything else. The mind is cleared of all distracting images—sometimes by breathing deeply, or by being especially quiet—and one concentrates on a particular image and lets it fill up the whole consciousness. *Contemplation* does not use images, but simply stills the mind and heart to open them to direct communication with God, a kind of communion that does not need words. In Orthodox Christianity one can find the Jesus Prayer, "Lord Jesus Christ have mercy on me," or a variation thereof. This is an ancient prayer that has been used as a meditative or contemplative device as one uses a mantra: the prayer is repeated over and over again—sometimes more than ten thousand times each day—in order to clear the mind of anything else and to fill it with this thought.[9] Under ideal conditions one coordinates the prayer with one's breathing and heartbeat so that it becomes an integral part of the self. This use of the Jesus Prayer was inspired, in part, by the New Testament injunction to "pray without ceasing" (1 Thess. 5:17).

Private prayer can also be done vocally or formally. Personal devotions that include prayers or meditations, Bible reading, or devotional practices based on the Bible, are all forms of private prayer. Some people say special prayers in the morning or evening or before meals. These prayers may be set: the person repeats a prayer written by someone else or suggested by the tradition; they can also be spontaneous: the person speaks whatever words come to mind. Some Christians remember Jesus's warning against "vain repetitions" and believe that prayer must be spontaneous in order to be approved by God, just as others believe that set prayers capture the wisdom and beauty of Christian tradition. The prayer life of Christians includes both kinds of prayer.

Public Prayer

Prayer done in community is public prayer. Most often Christians engage in public prayer in the context of worship services. Sometimes this prayer is formalized and sometimes it is spontaneous. Whatever its source or style, it may be prayer of intercession, adoration, praise, thanksgiving, or contrition. In churches with sacramental worship the prayers are often set and placed in a given order. Roman Catholics, Orthodox Christians, and Anglicans have a set pattern to their worship that involves formalized prayers at specific times. In churches with nonsacramental worship, prayers are sometimes provided by the church organization but often they are written by the pastor or delivered spontaneously by a minister or by someone designated by the minister.

Several different kinds of prayer occur in most worship services. The *pastoral* prayer is the prayer said by the pastor for the needs of the whole church and for the specific needs of members of the congregation. This prayer can be stylized and set within the context of sacramental liturgy, or it can be spontaneous; sometimes it is shared by members of the congregation who pray for certain things, and sometimes it is said by the minister after a period in which people share their concerns and request intercession for themselves or others. *Congregational* prayer is the prayer of the congregation for its members or for other concerns; it is often introduced with the words "Let us pray." In some churches these words begin a period of silent reflection and prayer; the minister may articulate general concerns at the end of the silence and commend the congregation to God's care and mercy. In other congregations—such as Pentecostal churches where people "pray in the Spirit"—the words "Let us pray" begin a period of audible prayer in which people speak simultaneously, using different words, sometimes quietly, sometimes in loud voices, often accompanied by tears or raised hands. To the uninitiated, prayer "in the Spirit" looks unstructured, but it is an ancient form of congregational prayer. In still other churches "Let us pray" is an invitation to the congregation to say a specific prayer—like the Lord's Prayer—together aloud or silently. *Benedictions* are prayers calling down God's blessing and protection on people. They may follow biblical patterns like the blessing of Aaron:

> *"The Lord bless you and keep you:*
> *The Lord make his face to shine upon you and be gracious to you:*
> *The Lord lift up his countenance upon you and give you peace"*
> *(Num. 6:24–6).*

Or benedictions may be written by a pastor for a specific event. Some believers say a blessing over their food, and some people ask special blessings on their homes. In some parts of the world, the priest is asked to bless the fishing fleet. Blessings invoke God's protection on someone or something.

Some churches have special prayers—for the sick or the dying, for example—which are used in specific settings rather than in formal worship. All events that inspire prayer—birth, death, marriage, sickness, disaster, good fortune—can be responded to with formal prayers or with spontaneous ones depending on the tradition of the person praying and the availability of occasional prayers. People often gather in groups to pray together. Sometimes they come together for a specific purpose—to pray for peace, for instance; they may unite in common prayers or support each other in pursuing private prayers; they may gather in a prayer group to share individual concerns, to pray about them for each other and for fellowship together. Sometimes small groups that meet regularly for Bible study or some other kind of church fellowship also have a time of group prayer in which people pray spontaneously—quietly or out loud—with one another. Prayer sometimes has an important place in rehabilitation programs: some church-related drug abuse programs have a strong relationship to prayer, for example.

All these kinds of public prayer can be found in most Christian churches and vary according to the theology, form, intentions, and preoccupations of the congregation.

PREACHING

Preaching means different things to different people. In the early church, preachers proclaimed the gospel to those who were not Christians, witnessing to the emerging beliefs about the significance of Jesus, announcing the coming of the kingdom and salvation through his life, death, and resurrection. The New Testament records sermons of this type delivered by believers to unbelievers in the hopes of drawing them to faith. Preaching, therefore, was tied to conversion and repentance.

Early in the life of the Christian church, preaching also became part of Christian worship. Collected sermons of ancient teachers and thinkers show that much preaching was exegesis and commentary on Scripture readings. Some of the great early theologians were preachers; Augustine preached sometimes several times each day, working through a scriptural text, dealing with exegetical problems. Preaching also came to be tied to teaching and exposition.

With some variations and some historical compromises, the central argument about preaching revolves around its intention: whether it is meant to bring people to repentance and conversion or to instruct them. Preachers who preach for conversion usually follow their sermon with an invitation to come to the altar, repent of sins, and receive the forgiveness of the Lord; those who tie preaching to an invitation or altar call may refer to other, nonaltar-call preachers simply as speakers, not preachers.

Developments in preaching followed the vicissitudes of history. During the Dark Ages, for example, there was very little preaching in Christian churches or monasteries. With the reforms of Charlemagne in the ninth century, bishops were instructed to preach in the language of the people, and preaching became important again, but its quality declined. Twelfth-century preaching was done in universities (where it was expository) and by famous preachers like Bernard of Clairvaux (whose focus was mystical), but by the beginning of the thirteenth century the sad conclusion of church officials—at Lateran Council IV (1215)—was that most parish priests were illiterate and that preaching was dismal. The failure in preaching led to lay preaching movements like the Waldensians, who were later condemned by the church, and to the beginning of new religious orders of friars—Dominicans and Franciscans—whose work led to a rebirth of interest in preaching.

By the Reformation one could find several types of preaching: mystical sermons that reflected the preoccupations with religious experience, revivalist/ apocalyptic sermons urging repentance, and reform sermons used by various groups and individuals to call individuals and the church as a whole to moral reformation. Historians dispute the connection between these various types of sermons and the preaching of the gospel; medieval preaching manuals suggest that sermons dealt with practices of the time more than with the gospel.

The reformers were interested in restoring the primacy of the word of God in church life and particularly in preaching. The church for them was not the institution founded by Christ and presided over by the pope, but the place where the gospel was preached correctly and the sacraments were properly administered. The primary function of the minister, they said, was preaching;

even groups who did not have ministers as such—some Anabaptist groups—believed preaching important. Justification comes through the word, the reformers said, as contained in the Bible and proclaimed from it in the church.

Protestant preaching changed as it encountered specific historical challenges. One can find a number of different types of preaching, many of which respond to certain cultural challenges. Some preaching is fundamentalist (see Chapter 7 for the context for many of these types), and some presents treatises on Christian orthodoxy. In response to Pietism, preaching focused on individual salvation, an emphasis maintained by revivalist preachers. In response to the tenets of the Enlightenment, preaching became centered on ethical reflection and the nature of human interaction. During the nineteenth century, preachers used their pulpits to explain the findings of the new biblical critics or to urge their listeners to become more involved in social questions. Evangelical Christians have consistently emphasized a literal understanding of the Bible as a basis for preaching God's word. The return to orthodoxy signaled by Karl Barth early in the twentieth century was also a return to the centrality of God's word—more than social or historical questions—as contained in Christ, in the Bible, and in preaching.

Certain Christian groups have unusual approaches to preaching. Christian Science preachers get their sermons from the "mother church" in Boston and are not permitted to interject their own views or interpretations. Quakers do not structure their worship to include preaching at all; a preacher may be present but preaching is not a necessary part of a meeting (except in programmed meetings). The Salvation Army uses brass bands to attract people to their street corner preaching. Christians also describe preaching in different ways: some call what a preacher does *giving a sermon* while others refer to it as *bringing a message;* still others call it a *teaching* or a *homily.* All these words indicate various groups' understandings of the function of preaching.

Roman Catholics, recognizing the challenge leveled by the reformers, worked in the sixteenth century to strengthen preaching in their church. The Council of Trent instructed all priests in charge of parishes to preach each Sunday (many priests had never preached), suggested that preachers prepare special sermons for Advent and Lent (to tie the preaching in with the liturgical season), and provided for more seminaries with better-trained staffs so that priests could be better prepared to preach. Still, Roman Catholic preachers tended to focus on doctrine, morals, and explanations about the faith, not on Scripture. The Second Vatican Council stressed the link between preaching and the proclamation of the word of God as found in the Bible.

An issue related to preaching is the selection of Scripture texts for the worship service. Many groups use the Lectionary (a book of specified readings that follow the liturgical year), which gives an Old Testament reading, a Psalm response, a New Testament epistle reading, and a gospel reading for each Sunday of the year. Roman Catholics, Lutherans, Anglicans, Methodists, Presbyterians, and Disciples of Christ all use the lectionary and therefore on a given Sunday usually read the same Scripture passages. Some of these groups do not deviate from using the Lectionary; others feel free on occasion to abandon the plan in favor of other texts. Other Christian churches select the Scripture readings in different ways. Some groups have a worship committee that selects the texts, and in some churches the minister chooses the texts as the inspiration moves him or her in preparation of the sermon. In all Christian churches, however, a close relationship generally exists between the preaching and the Scripture texts chosen. The style may vary—some groups use more exegesis, some use the passages to exhort people to certain behavior—but the connection between preaching and Scripture texts generally is accepted by all Christians.

When one begins to evaluate preaching in various churches, one should ask how it is connected with the gospel, what the intentions of the preacher are, and what people are supposed to do on the basis of the sermon. The answers to those questions will disclose some of the ideas that group has about preaching.

CONGREGATIONAL SINGING

Early Christians sang psalms and used singing in other parts of their worship, but congregational singing did not survive through the Middle Ages in Western Christianity. It was reintroduced in Protestant worship by the reformers, and in Roman Catholic worship after Vatican II. Eastern Orthodox Christianity, partly because instrumental music was forbidden in their liturgy, developed a strong tradition of hymnody and choral singing. At the same time, the music that developed in Orthodox churches became increasingly complex and difficult and music was often relegated to a choir and to priests and deacons trained to perform it. Nevertheless, the notion that people—not horns and harps and organs—should be living instruments of praise is a strong part of the Orthodox tradition. With its roots in ancient Greece and its contemporary associations with the Western world, Orthodox hymnody is varied: one can find choral singing, plainsong, folk melodies, and ancient chant in the Orthodox church.

Western Christianity celebrated the liturgy in Latin and restricted music to trained choirs; congregational singing and participation was not encouraged in churches until the reformers gave it a central place in worship and made it a distinctive part of the service. Luther wrote many German hymns to encourage people to sing and participate in worship. In writing hymns in the vernacular, Luther followed the precedent of others before him; the Czech Brethren, inspired in part by John Hus a century earlier, published a Czech hymnal as early as 1501. Hymns and congregational singing have always been an important part of Protestant Christianity. In fact, one of the ways some people distinguished Protestants from Catholics before Vatican II was precisely on the issue of singing. After the council, when congregational participation and singing were emphasized in the Catholic church, many Catholics thought they were being asked to adopt a particularly Protestant practice.

Congregational singing binds people together and expresses community solidarity; it also provides a way for people to pray in unison. Most hymnals include songs of praise and petition, songs about life in Christ and his Second Coming, songs of the seasons, gospel hymns, some about the church and its mission, and songs about personal religious experience. All the attitudes people seek to express in prayer—adoration, thanksgiving, contrition, petition, fellowship—can also be articulated in song, and most hymnals reflect a broad range of hymns and theological preoccupations. Many Christians derive much of their theological understanding from hymns they sing over and over again; there they learn about the nature of God and the church, they feel encouraged to express their needs and to perceive God as merciful and kind, and they find the sustenance they need for Christian life.

Roman Catholics are relative newcomers to congregational singing. Since the mid-1960s Catholics have experimented with new forms of singing, translations of older hymns, and new music altogether. Many of the new hymns being used by other Christian groups have been written by Catholic hymnists in search of their own particular music.

Some Christians do not sing at all—Quakers do not sing at meeting—and others make a point of forbidding instrumental music during worship, relying on vocal harmonies they have developed over the years. The Amish have a distinct way of singing that apparently dates back to eighteenth-century German hymn-singing. Mennonites and members of the Church of Christ have a strong tradition of four-part harmony. Some churches use "special music" in worship, a hymn or religious classical piece sung or played by an individual or group for the congregation. These performances are meant to be special moments of praise or inspiration for the congregation.

CONCLUSION

Christians have emphasized the need for corporate worship from the very earliest times; they have observed a special Lord's Day on which members meet to recognize their unity as part of the body of Christ and be nurtured in their Christian life with fellowship and communion. Christians disagree on some points, but one can also find deeply shared understandings about the sacraments/ordinances of baptism and the Lord's Supper; with few exceptions Christians agree that these sacraments/ordinances are central in the life of the church.

In the baptism of Jesus, early Christians recognized his sonship and the inauguration of a new kind of discipleship, a new community, a new historical reality. The descent of the Spirit on Jesus at the time of his baptism underscores the importance of the Spirit in the life of the baptized Christian; the Pentecost experience describes a strong link between the gifts of the Spirit and the community. Accordingly, all Christians have some understanding of baptism as adoption by God and admission into the community. Baptism, in all the churches that practice it, is linked with faith and repentance and with the gifts of the Spirit in the life of the one baptized. Whatever their differences, Christians are joined in their understanding of the importance of baptism as the mark of new life in Christ. The Lord's Supper, too, is practiced differently and with varying understandings and theological perspectives. Nevertheless, Christians agree that they need to celebrate it as a memorial of their salvation through the life, death, and resurrection of Jesus. The breaking of the bread and the sharing of the cup—whether in a highly sacramental context or in a nonsacramental one—are rituals performed by all Christians, and believed to be a crucial part of life and nurture within the community.

The importance of conversion—including faith and repentance—and life in the community of believers has led Christians to underscore several things. Besides sacraments/ordinances one can find substantial agreement within Christianity about prayer, preaching, congregational singing, and mutual support. Virtually all Christians agree that prayer is a necessary dimension of their lives. An extraordinarily rich tradition of prayer has developed within Christianity, some of which is beginning to be recovered by Christians. During the Reformation some groups discouraged the use of set, formal prayers because they were suspicious of formalism; they thought it stifled the Holy Spirit and prevented "real" prayer. According to their interpretation, Jesus condemned formalism within Judaism, and the early church prayed in a spontaneous fashion. Protestants have a tradition of spontaneous prayer that is being discovered and appreciated by Catholics. On the other hand, the rich history of Christian prayer— poetry, song, meditative reflections, prayers for specific moments—that developed within Catholic Christianity is being rediscovered by Protestants. Interdenominational worship and conversation has led to broader areas of agreement between Catholics and Protestants on prayer.

All Christians who include preaching as part of their worship service now agree that the link between preaching and Scripture is fundamental. One can no longer fairly make glib distinctions between Catholic and Protestant on the basis of their preaching; they are united in a desire to preach the gospel during their worship services. Some Christians, as we have seen, prefer to preach for repentance and conversion and others preach in order to instruct by exposing the deeper implications of a particular text. Whatever their differences, however, they agree that preaching is an important dimension of worship and of community life and that it is necessarily linked with Scripture. Most Christians agree too that the congregation ought to participate in worship through singing. Worship is an act of community. One way of assuring congregational participation is through singing.

Finally, Christians agree that the community expresses its life with support for one another. In some churches this support takes the form of testimony;

people share their personal testimonies and receive support and encouragement for their progress in faith. Some groups, based on the conviction that Scripture is the ultimate key to Christian life, have Bible study either during the week or on the Lord's Day as part of the worship service. Sunday school or Bible study supports the community by providing a way for people to read and reflect on Scripture together. And Christians recognize the need for periodic revitalization. Some Christian churches sponsor annual revivals, which feature a special revivalist preacher; other churches make the rare celebration of the Lord's Supper a chance to renew their understandings of the Christian life. Many Christians have a retreat concept; retreats provide occasions for people to get away for a weekend or a few days to reflect on the state of their souls.

We have seen in the course of this book that Christians have extraordinarily diverse understandings of the Christian life: their histories, attitudes, and self-understandings differ considerably. At some moments in their history Christians have been highly antagonistic toward one another about almost everything. Yet beneath their profound differences they agree that Christianity is a matter of new life in Christ, nurtured within a community of believers, and celebrated in worship.

CHAPTER 11 NOTES

1. Books by Mircea Eliade are good introductions to these concepts. See especially *Cosmos and History* (New York: Harper Torchbooks, 1959).

2. This effort is most visible in the Roman Catholic tradition. See, for example, William G. Storey et al., editors, *Morning Praise and Evensong* (Notre Dame, Ind.: Fides Press, 1973).

3. Recall those Christians following William Miller in the early to mid-nineteenth century (see Chapter 7) and waiting for the return of the Lord; they called themselves Adventists. *Advent* means coming.

4. Jesus's actions and words at the Last Supper are rooted in the Jewish tradition, especially in the prayers used at Jewish ritual meals. One book on this subject, not easy to read but surely worth looking at, is Louis Bouyer, *The Eucharist* (Notre Dame, Ind.: University of Notre Dame Press, 1968), especially pp. 1–119. Bouyer gives an excellent summary of the different ways Christians interpret the command to "do this in memory of me," as well as an analysis of "new covenant."

5. The history and debate on this issue is long and complex and occurred, for the most part, during the medieval period. It might be helpful to recall that no issues in Christian belief and practice have ever been one-sided: from the beginning there has been debate about texts (whether to interpret them literally or symbolically/allegorically), about the person, nature, and work of Jesus (see Appendix 4), and many other things.

6. See Chapter 4, note 11, to review the doctrine of transubstantiation. Today most Christians do not feel constrained to attempt an explanation, and many are not sure what they think. Most are content to say that Jesus is "present somehow" when the community shares bread and wine.

7. Scholastic philosophy was perhaps the strongest school of philosophy at the time of the Reformation. Its roots go back to the ninth century and at the time of the Reformation it had been highly influenced by Aristotelian philosophy, which was *not* scriptural and therefore was vulnerable to the criticisms of the reformers.

8. Here is the whole poem:

Prayer

Prayer the Churches banquet, Angels age,
   God's breath in man returning to his birth,
   The soul in paraphrase, heart in pilgrimage,
The Christian plummet sounding heav'n and earth;
Engine against th' Almightie, sinners towre,
   Reversed thunder, Christ-side-piercing spear,
   The six-daies world transposing in an houre,
A kind of tune, which all things heare and fear;
Softnesse and peace, and joy, and love, and blisse,
   Exalted Manna, gladnesse of the best,
   Heaven in ordinarie, man well drest,
The milkie way, the bird of Paradise,
   Church-bels beyond the starres heard, the souls bloud,
   The land of spices; something understood.

George Herbert (1593–1633)

Found in Helen Gardner, editor, *The Metaphysical Poets,* rev. ed. (London: Penguin Books, 1972), p. 124.

9. For an easy and fascinating introduction to this phenomenon, see R. M. French, *The Way of the Pilgrim* (New York: Seabury Press, 1965). This is the story of a Russian peasant who wants to know what it means to "pray without ceasing" (see 1 Thess. 5:17) and is advised to say the Jesus Prayer twelve thousand times each day. The book tells you what he did and what effects it had on him. In J. D. Salinger's novel *Franny and Zooey* (New York: Little, Brown, 1961), Franny drops out of school and stays in her room reading *The Way of the Pilgrim* and trying to follow its advice.

SUGGESTIONS FOR FURTHER READING

1. For a classic (complex but worthwhile) exposition of the ways people *experience* the divine in all religions, see William James, *The Varieties of Religious Experience* (New York: New American Library, 1958; originally published in 1901).

2. Since practices change and since there is increasing dialogue and exchange among the churches, the best way to get some appreciation for what other groups do at worship is to go experience it for yourself. Books in this area are sometimes helpful, but often not reflective of subtle shifts and local practices. For some indication of the development of early Christian liturgy see Dom Gregory Dix, *The Shape of the Liturgy* (London: Dacre Press, 1945). This book is hard to read, but very good to look through just to get some sense of the territory.

3. For contemporary and ecumenical ideas about spirituality and prayer see Matthew Fox, editor, *Western Spirituality: Historical Roots, Ecumenical Routes* (Sante Fe: Bear

& Company, 1981), and W. Paul Jones, *The Province Beyond the River: The Diary of a Protestant at a Trappist Monastery* (New York: Paulist Press, 1981).

4. For some easily accessible ideas about Christianity and its relation to Eastern religions, especially Buddhism, see Frederick Franck, *Pilgrimage to Now/Here* (Maryknoll, N.Y.: Orbis Books, 1974).

5. For an introduction to the importance of liturgical time, see Marion J. Hatchett, *Sanctifying Life, Time and Space: An Introduction to Liturgical Study* (New York: Seabury Press, 1982), and H. Boone Porter, *Keeping the Church Year* (New York: Seabury Press, 1977). For an ecumenical look at the Divine Office, see Joint Liturgical Group, Ronald Claud Dudley Jasper, editor, *The Daily Office Revised: With Other Prayers and Services* (London: SPCK, 1978). This last book is the fruit of a dialogue among representatives from many different Christian churches, including Anglicans, Baptists, Methodists, Roman Catholics, Presbyterians, and members of United Reformed Churches and Churches of Christ.

APPENDIX 1
THE ORDER OF THE BOOKS
IN THE OLD TESTAMENT

The Christian Old Testament is a reordering of the books in the Hebrew Bible. The Hebrew Bible is divided into three parts: the Law (Torah), the Prophets, and the Writings. The Christian Old Testament eliminates the distinction between the Prophets and the Writings and puts the Prophets at the end, to serve as an introduction to the New Testament. Notice that the order of the books changes the tone and emphasis. Because of the differences in intention and theological signification, it is not correct to say that the Old Testament is the same thing as the Hebrew Bible.

Roman Catholics formerly used an Old Testament that contained books found in neither the Hebrew Bible nor the Protestant Old Testament. Why? Because Roman Catholics based their Old Testament on the Greek translation while Protestants used the Hebrew version. In the Douay (Roman Catholic) Version of the Old Testament, which most Roman Catholics no longer use, one can find books that appear in the Apocrypha of the Revised Standard Edition (Tobias, Judith, Wisdom, Ecclesiasticus, Baruch, and 1 and 2 Machabees).

HEBREW BIBLE		PROTESTANT OLD TESTAMENT	ROMAN CATHOLIC OLD TESTAMENT (DOUAY VERSION)
Genesis	⎫	Genesis	Genesis
Exodus		Exodus	Exodus
Leviticus	the Law	Leviticus	Leviticus
Numbers		Numbers	Numbers
Deuteronomy	⎭	Deuteronomy	Deuteronomy
		Joshua	Josue
Joshua	⎫	Judges	Judges
Judges		Ruth	Ruth
Samuel		Samuel	Kings
Kings		Kings	Paralipomenon
Isaiah		Chronicles	Esdras
Jeremiah		Ezra	Nehemias
Ezekiel		Nehemiah	*Tobias
Hosea		Esther	*Judith
Joel	the	Job	Esther
Amos	Prophets	Psalms	Job
Obadiah		Proverbs	Psalms
Jonah		Ecclesiastes	Proverbs
Micah		Song of Solomon	Ecclesiastes
Nahum		Isaiah	Canticle of Canticles
Habakkuk		Jeremiah	*Wisdom
Zephaniah		Lamentations	*Ecclesiasticus
Haggai		Ezekiel	Isaias
Zechariah		Daniel	Jeremias
Malachi	⎭	Hosea	Lamentations
		Joel	*Baruch
Psalms	⎫	Amos	Ezechiel
Proverbs		Obadiah	Daniel
Job		Jonah	Osee
Ruth		Micah	Joel
Song of Songs		Nahum	Amos
Lamentations	the	Habakkuk	Abdias
Ecclesiastes	Writings	Zephaniah	Jonas
Esther		Haggai	Micheas
Daniel		Zechariah	Nahum
Ezra		Malachi	Habacuc
Nehemiah			Sophonias
Chronicles	⎭		Aggeus
			Zacharias
			Malachias
			*Machabees

*Books not found in the Hebrew Bible or in the Protestant Old Testament.

APPENDIX 2
SYNOPSIS OF THE BOOKS
OF THE OLD AND NEW TESTAMENTS

This list is a synopsis of the *content* of the books of the Old and New Testaments, Revised Standard Version, and is for handy reference. New Testament writings have been dated along the lines suggested by Norman Perrin in his *The New Testament, An Introduction*. In some ways there are too many opinions about the origins of New Testament books; in Pauline scholarship, especially, one can find endless argumentation about authenticity and dating. Students who want more precise information should refer to a wide variety of reference works and recent scholarship and should, in any case, be advised that the system adopted here is a starting point, not a final word.

THE OLD TESTAMENT

GENESIS ("origins"): The first of the Five Books of Moses, recounting the beginnings of the world and the creation of humanity, the story of Noah and of the Patriarchs—Abraham, Isaac, and Jacob—ending with the death of Joseph.

EXODUS ("a way out"): The second of the Five Books of Moses, recounting the oppression of the Jews in Egypt, their deliverance by Moses, the covenant at Sinai, and the establishment of the Tabernacle, the movable community shrine.

LEVITICUS (Levites=assistants to the priests): The third of the Five Books of Moses, containing the legislation dictated to Moses by God after the establishment of the Tabernacle, dealing primarily with ritual purity.

NUMBERS: The fourth of the Five Books of Moses, relating the history of the Jews in the desert from the second to the fortieth year of their wanderings.

DEUTERONOMY ("repetition of the Law"): The last of the Five Books of Moses, containing Moses's review of the events since Sinai, a repetition of the Ten Commandments, and Moses's final admonitions to Israel.

JOSHUA: An account of the history of the Israelites in their conquest and division of Canaan from the death of Moses to the death of Joshua, his successor (ca. 1220 B.C.E.).

JUDGES: Describes the acts of ancient heroes and heroines of Israel from the death of Joshua until the time of Samuel (ca. 1050 B.C.E.); it includes the stories of Samson, Deborah, and Gideon.

RUTH: Story of a non-Israelite woman, Ruth, married to a Hebrew. After his death she returns to Judah with her mother-in-law to live with the Israelites. Through her marriage to Boaz, Ruth becomes great grandmother of King David.

1 AND 2 SAMUEL: Relate the history of the Jews from the end of the period of Judges to the last days of King David (972 B.C.E.), focusing on the biographies of Samuel, Saul, and David. These books depict the Davidic monarchy as a divine institution, established to represent God's rule on earth.

1 AND 2 KINGS: Contain the history of the Jews from the reign of Solomon (ca. 970 B.C.E.) to the fall of Jerusalem (587 B.C.E.), and can be seen as a continuation of the Books of Samuel. Kings recount a period of Israel's glory, division, decline, and fall.

1 AND 2 CHRONICLES: Contain geneaological lists of Israelite tribes, a history of David's rule, and an account of Solomon's rule, emphasizing the building of the temple and ending with the destruction of the temple and the exile to Babylon. Chronicles picture the events in Israel's history as divine judgments.

EZRA: Relates the events after the return from the Babylonian exile (538 B.C.E.) including the beginning of the rebuilding of the temple.

NEHEMIAH: A continuation of the Book of Ezra, recounting the reconstruction of Jerusalem.

ESTHER: A story of the deliverance of the Jews of Persia through the influence of Esther on the King of Persia, who is her husband.

JOB: Relates the story of a righteous man who suffers as a result of God's testing his faith. It points to the mystery of human suffering and the inadequacy of human knowledge in things pertaining to the purposes of God.

PSALMS ("poems sung to stringed instruments"): A collection of Hebrew poetry (150 psalms) that contains deep religious feeling and conviction. Many of the psalms are attributed to King David. This book contains some of the most beautiful poetry in the Bible.

PROVERBS: A collection of maxims on how an individual can survive and prosper.

ECCLESIASTES ("members of the assembly"): A somewhat pessimistic book that concludes that "all is vanity," and that one should resign oneself to suffering and injustice. It claims that there is no correlation between righteousness and happiness.

SONG OF SOLOMON: Contains love poems written in dialogue form that have been read as describing love between persons, love between God and Israel, or love between Jesus and the church.

ISAIAH: First of the major prophets, who protested strongly against moral laxity. Isaiah emphasizes that God will punish but not exterminate Israel for its sins and that there will come times of redemption and comfort.

JEREMIAH: Second of the major prophets, containing bitter prophecies addressed to foreign nations and some biographical material on the prophet himself. Jeremiah's ministry began ca. 627 B.C.E. and ended sometime around 580 B.C.E.

LAMENTATIONS: Contains elegies and mournings over the destruction of Jerusalem and the temple by the Babylonians.

EZEKIEL: Third of the major prophets who prophesied at the time of the destruction of the temple (587 B.C.E.). Ezekiel contains rebukes spoken before the destruction of Jerusalem and prophecies of disasters, consolation, and the coming of the new kingdom.

DANIEL: Contains two parts, the first of which recounts the miraculous experiences that occur to Daniel and his pious friends during the Babylonian exile, the second containing apocalyptic visions.

HOSEA: First of the minor prophets (so called because of the brevity of the books compared to Isaiah, Jeremiah, and Ezekiel), containing comments on the relationship between God and Israel and oracles rebuking Israel, followed by promises of salvation.

JOEL: Second of the minor prophets; describes a locust plague and the "Day of the Lord," when Israel will be restored to God.

AMOS: Third of the minor prophets, focusing on social morality as the determining factor in the history of Israel.

OBADIAH: Fourth of the minor prophets, consisting of one chapter condemning Edom (a country in Southeast Palestine) for refusing to help Jerusalem in its hour of need.

JONAH: Fifth of the minor prophets, relating episodes in Jonah's life illustrating the power of repentance and divine mercy for all creatures.

MICAH: Sixth of the minor prophets, containing prophecies against the oppression by the ruling classes and speaking of a future king of Israel who will bring peace.

NAHUM: Seventh of the minor prophets, containing a masterful foretelling of the fall of Nineveh, the capital of Assyria.

HABAKKUK: Eighth of the minor prophets, consisting of an outcry against the evil in the world, God's reply, a prayer, and a description of the "Day of the Lord."

ZEPHANIAH: Ninth of the minor prophets, containing mainly prophecies dealing with the last days, declaring the coming of the "Day of the Lord" when the wicked will disappear and the poor will inherit the land.

HAGGAI: Tenth of the minor prophets, calling for a rebuilding of the temple.

ZECHARIAH: A contemporary of Haggai, Zechariah shares his zeal for the rebuilding of the temple.

MALACHI ("my messenger"): Twelfth and last of the minor prophets, rebuking Israel for its sinfulness, complaining of mixed and broken marriages, and envisioning the "Day of the Lord" to be preceded by Elijah's coming.

THE NEW TESTAMENT

GOSPEL OF MATTHEW (written between 70 and 90 C.E.): A synoptic gospel, regarding Jesus as the new Moses, emphasizing Jesus as the fulfillment of the Hebrew Bible and as the bringer of the new law or covenant.

GOSPEL OF MARK (written between 70 and 90 C.E.): Likely the earliest synoptic gospel, viewing Jesus as the Son of God who must suffer and die. Mark emphasizes Jesus as a man of action and focuses very little attention on Jesus's teachings.

GOSPEL OF LUKE (written between 70 and 90 C.E.): Synoptic gospel emphasizing the universality of Jesus's work and message. Here Jesus is the merciful one who forgives all humanity.

GOSPEL OF JOHN (written between 80 and 100 C.E.): John emphasizes the mystery and divinity of Jesus more than the synoptics do. God's love for humanity is a central theme of this gospel.

THE ACTS OF THE APOSTLES (written between 70 and 90 C.E.): The first history of the movement of Christianity, recording outstanding events in the spread of the Gospels from Jerusalem to Rome. It pictures the apostles as guided and empowered by the Holy Spirit.

THE EPISTLE TO THE ROMANS: Written by Paul ca. 57 C.E. and considered the first work of Christian theology. The intention of this letter is to announce Paul's coming to Rome and to prepare the Christians there for his arrival. In Romans more than in any other letter, Paul discusses the meaning of Christian salvation, the powerlessness of people, and the fullness of God's redeeming work.

THE FIRST EPISTLE TO THE CORINTHIANS: Also written by Paul ca. 55 C.E. to the church at Corinth, dealing with the Eucharist, love (*agape*) as the highest of spiritual gifts, and the meaning of the Resurrection.

THE SECOND EPISTLE TO THE CORINTHIANS (written ca. 56 C.E.): Dealing principally with Paul's personal position as an apostle in relation to the activities of the church at Corinth.

THE EPISTLE TO THE GALATIANS: Written by Paul ca. 54 C.E., emphasizing the futility of trying to live by the Jewish Law and reestablishing the importance of justification by faith.

THE EPISTLE TO THE EPHESIANS: Attributed to Paul, emphasizes the universality of salvation for Jews and Gentiles alike; probably written between 70 and 90 C.E.

THE EPISTLE TO THE PHILIPPIANS: Written by Paul while in prison (ca. 52–5 C.E.), thanking the Philippians for their assistance during his imprisonment and asking them to continue to follow Christ's example of charity and humility.

THE EPISTLE TO THE COLOSSIANS: Attributed to Paul (70–90 C.E.), stressing faith in Christ as all-sufficient redeemer. The author warns against the doctrines of the Gnostics and reestablishes the church's position on God, creation, and the church.

THE FIRST EPISTLE TO THE THESSALONIANS: One of the earliest letters written by Paul (ca. 51 C.E.), assuring the Thessalonians that both the living and the dead will partake in the glory of the Second Coming of Christ.

THE SECOND EPISTLE TO THE THESSALONIANS: Not written by Paul but later (70–90 C.E.), warning the Thessalonians not to neglect their everyday duties while they await the Second Coming.

THE FIRST EPISTLE TO TIMOTHY: The first of the pastoral Epistles, discussing the practices of false teachers and methods of combating these practices; probably written between 90 and 140 C.E.

THE SECOND EPISTLE TO TIMOTHY: The second of the pastoral Epistles, again concerning false teachers, and reminding Timothy of the fidelity to tradition and the patience required of all apostles; probably written between 90 and 140 C.E.

THE EPISTLE OF TITUS: The third and last of the pastoral Epistles, discussing the duties of apostles and the need to struggle against false teachings; probably written between 90 and 140 C.E.

THE EPISTLE TO PHILEMON: Written by Paul, asking Philemon to forgive a runaway slave who has been received by Paul as a Christian, and who is to be seen as a brother in Christ.

THE EPISTLE TO THE HEBREWS: Written before 96 C.E., it focuses on the idea that Christianity is the final and absolute religion because Jesus is the true high priest and the final mediation between God and humanity. Hebrews reestablishes the ineffectuality of the law.

THE EPISTLE OF JAMES: Written between 90 and 140 C.E., this is the first of the general Epistles (not written to a specific church or person, but to Christians in general) and deals with the superiority of deeds over theory, just treatment of the poor, the danger of evil speech, and the value of humility and sincerity.

THE FIRST EPISTLE OF PETER: The second of the general Epistles, written between 90 and 140 C.E., emphasizing a life of hope in Christ, which entails faith in the redemptive work of Christ and submitting to the will of God.

THE SECOND EPISTLE OF PETER: The third general Epistle (written between 90 and 140 C.E.) warning Christians against false teachings, exhorting them to hold fast to their faith, and assuring them of salvation.

THE EPISTLES OF JOHN: The fourth general Epistle (actually contains three very short letters written between 80 and 100 C.E.), emphasizing that "God is love," that morality, fellowship, and charity are extremely important in the Christian life, and that all false teachings are to be avoided.

THE EPISTLE OF JUDE: The fifth and last of the general Epistles (written between 90 and 140 C.E.), reminding Christians that God's forgiveness of sins is not an excuse for immoral actions, that God does punish disobedience, and that Christians have duties of prayer, faith, and love for God.

REVELATION or THE APOCALYPSE: The last book of the New Testament (written between 90 and 100 C.E.), it describes the final struggle between good and evil and the eventual triumph of Christ and the church; it is written in highly symbolic language.

APPENDIX 3
EARLY CHRISTIAN WRITERS

Bishops and theologians in the early Christian community whose opinions on matters of doctrine and practice carried great weight are often referred to as "the Fathers." Because this designation makes it appear as if women made no contributions to the development of tradition in the early church, a point disputed by feminist theologians, we use the terminology *early Christian writers* here instead.[1] Little by little there came to be an appeal to tradition, especially to these early writers, for a consensus on disputed questions within Christianity. When the New Testament did not provide enough of an answer on an issue, people consulted the opinions that had been developing in the church in the works of these great theologians. According to a commonly accepted notion, these respected writers were those characterized by orthodoxy in doctrine, holiness in life, and approval of the ancient church. This last point is important: their authority is ancient. There are several geographical groupings of early Christian writers, the most important of which are Greek, Latin, and Syrian.

The tasks of these writers varied according to the place and time in which they were working. In the early church, they functioned mostly as apologists: as those who *explained* Christianity to a hostile world or to an emperor who was considering persecution of the Christians. As the church grew in numbers and power and in problems, they wrote

[1] It is not easy to find church "Mothers" as it is not easy to find women in any historical period. Nevertheless, one can name a few: Egeria, Perpetua, Proba, and Eudokia. For translations of their works, critical commentary, and an introduction to the issue of early Christian literature by women, see Patricia Wilson-Kastner et al., *A Lost Tradition: Women Writers of the Early Church*. Washington, D.C.: University Press of America, 1981.

on various disciplinary matters—marriage, divorce, paying of taxes, fighting in wars—and on theological questions—the divinity of Christ, the place of Mary in the Christian church, and so on. When the church became the dominant institution in the Western and Eastern worlds, they devised elaborate systems of theology—the doctrine of the Trinity, for example.

One can read them for an understanding of a particular period, or for some introduction to the customs and beliefs of a particular region at a particular time. One can also find in them rich sources of spiritual writing and prayer. They provide the Christian church with much of its ancient history on several levels: cultural, religious, political, and moral.

The following brief outline gives you a glimpse of this and mentions some of the important names and issues. An outline as sketchy as this is not meant to teach so much as to entice. Some people think that the only Christian writing from the ancient world is the New Testament. I hope that this list of topics and writers will show you that there was extraordinarily energetic argument, speculation, and writing going on in the early church.

A SELECTIVE OUTLINE OF THE LITERATURE

I. *Primitive Ecclesiastical Literature*
   A. Creeds developed in the period after the death of the apostles, the most famous of which is the *Apostle's Creed*.
   B. Teachings about discipline and behavior, the most famous of which is the *Didache*.
   C. Early writings associated with particular people that stressed the Christian philosophy of martyrdom, attitude towards marriage, sin, penance, and so on. Some of the most famous writers were *Clement of Rome, Ignatius of Antioch,* and *Polycarp of Smyrna;* the most famous document was a work on penance and the forgiveness of sins called *The Shepherd of Hermas.*

II. *Apologetic Literature of the Second Century*
   A. There were works that were written to an emperor precisely to show that Christians were not dangerous to the state and should therefore not be persecuted. Some of the most important literature of this type was written by *Aristedes of Athens, Justin Martyr, Tatian, Athenagoras of Athens, Minucius Felix,* and *Theophilus of Antioch,* all of whom wrote toward the end of the second century.
   B. There were works that explained Christianity in philosophical terms and tried to make a case for Christianity that was philosophically respectable: good examples of this type of literature can be found in *Justin* and *Athenagoras.*
   C. Some apologetic literature was cast in the form of a dialogue. The most famous dialogues were written by *Justin* (a Greek) and *Minicius Felix* (a Roman).

III. *Heretical and Antiheretical Literature of the Second Century*
   Various types of what was later judged to be heretical literature were written during the second century.

A. There were philosophical or religious works dealing with particular interpretations of Christianity. The most famous literature of this kind is *Gnostic literature*.

B. There were stories about Jesus and his life that were not judged to be apostolic and therefore were not included in the canon of the New Testament. These are called *Apocryphal Gospels*.

C. And there were works dealing with the final age, the end of the world: *Apocalyptic literature*.

The Christian church, as a whole, opposed much of this writing. The theologian remembered especially for his writings against Gnosticism is *Irenaeus of Lyons*.

IV. *The Beginnings of Christian Theology*

A much more elaborate Christian theology developed during the second and third centuries. The church moved into various philsophical cultures and interacted with them, writers were exposed to different ideas (especially to Stoicism and Neoplatonism), and there were problems raised not only by heretics but by the faithful, problems about Jesus, the way to live a Christian life, immortality, and so on. Early theologians tried to develop a theological position on something working mostly from the Bible and their own experience. There is great richness in this writing, a variety of opinions and solutions to problems. It is important to see that there was no single Christian answer to a problem, but a variety of creative responses.

A. Writing in Greek were the famous theologians of the Alexandrian school, *Clement of Alexandria* and *Origen*.

B. Writing in Latin were apologists and controversialists like *Tertullian,* writers on church/state politics like *Cyprian,* and writers concerned with the internal matters of the Christian church like *Hippolytus.*

V. *The Golden Age of Christian Literature*

As problems of doctrine and discipline became more difficult, the writings became more complex. When Christianity was no longer a persecuted religion, Christian writers were able to pursue their theological preoccupations more directly. Much of the writing was more overtly philosophical and specific to particular controversies or problems: the person and nature of Christ, the foundations of a theology of grace, the doctrine of Original Sin and justification, the development of a sacramental system, and so on. In the writings of this period one can find catechists (those who devised systems to teach people about Christianity), mystical writers (those who attempted to discern and articulate a theology of religious experience), preachers, theologians, and bishops all interested in specific ecclesiastical problems.

A. Writing in Greek were *Eusebius of Caesarea* (a church historian), *Cyril of Jerusalem* (a catechist), *Gregory of Nyssa* (a spiritual writer), *John Chrysostom* (a renowned preacher), *Basil* (an ecclesiastical writer), and theologians like *Athanasius, Theodore of Mopsuestia,* and *Cyril of Alexandria.*

B. Writing in Latin were those interested in political questions like *Ambrose,* and theologians like *Hilary of Poitiers* and *Augustine.* Some of the writers of the Latin church were also popes, notably *Leo* I and *Gregory* I.

APPENDIX 4
ECUMENICAL COUNCILS

A council is a formal meeting of bishops and representatives of the Christian churches convened for the purpose of regulating doctrine and discipline. There can be councils on a local or regional level (sometimes called synods), or there can be worldwide, universal councils. The great councils in the history of Christianity have been the *ecumenical* (from the Greek word meaning universal) councils, meetings that include bishops from the whole, universal church. Decrees of a council are held to possess the highest authority the Christian church can give. Roman Catholics and Eastern Orthodox Christians recognize the dogmatic decrees of ecumenical councils as truly authoritative, authentic interpretations of the gospel; for them, the dogmatic decrees of the council represent the mind of the whole church.

Some Christians do not recognize any councils; they believe Christianity to be a matter of New Testament faithfulness alone, or base their Christianity on an experience of Jesus that does not need doctrinal definitions. Thus not all Christians recognize a need for or the importance of councils. Those Christians who *do* accept ecumenical councils are divided into two groups: some Protestants and Eastern Orthodox Christians accept the first seven ecumenical councils as authoritative and have some interest in the Second Vatican Council; they reject the rest of the councils on the grounds that they were not truly ecumenical but were only local Roman synods. Roman Catholics accept twenty-one ecumenical councils and reject the Council of Pisa on the grounds that it was not authentic; many scholars accept the validity of the Council of Pisa and it has been included in this chart.

COUNCIL AND YEAR HELD	PROBLEM	WHICH MEANS	COUNCIL'S RESOLUTION
1 Nicaea I 325	Arianism	There is only one God, so Jesus is not God (creator) but a creature.	Jesus is the son of God and is God, of the same divine essence as the Father.
2 Constantinople I 381	Apollinarianism	The Logos takes the place of the human mind in Jesus; he is not, then fully human.	Jesus is divine, as Nicaea said, but also fully human. Also, Holy Spirit is divine.
3 Ephesus 431	Nestorianism	If Jesus is human and divine, then there are two persons in Christ, and Mary is mother of Jesus, not mother of God.	There are two natures (in hypostatic union) but only one person in Christ. Mary is the Mother of *God*.
4 Chalcedon 451	Monophysitism	The hypostatic union taken to an extreme so that there is only one nature (*mono physis*) in Christ.	There are *two* natures, as Ephesus said, and they are unmixed and unconfused.
5 Constantinople II 553	Three Chapters	Emperor issued a condemnation of three positions; pope refused to go along with this interference.	Council accepted the edict of the emperor, implicitly going against the pope.
6 Constantinople III 680	Monothelitism	Emperor attempts to win back the mono-physites with the theory that Christ had only one will.	There are two wills and two energies in Christ, fully coordinated, divine and human.
7 Nicaea II 787	Iconoclasm	Emperor issued edict (726) against images and icons in churches.	Iconoclasm is condemned; veneration of images is permitted.

These first seven councils accepted as authoritative by Orthodox Christians, Roman Catholics, and some Protestants.

8 Constantinople IV 870	Photian Schism	Complicated political problem involving papal authority in patriarchal appointments. Photius was the patriarch of Constantinople.	A council, actually held in Rome, deposed Photius and restored Ignatius as the patriarch of Constantinople.

Greeks do not recognize the Roman solution so held their own council in Constantinople in 880, which favored Photius as patriarch.

9	Lateran I 1123	Can an emperor choose and invest a bishop or an abbot? A political struggle for power in West between pope and emperor.	Settled by the Concordat of Worms (1122) and council called to confirm it.
10	Lateran II 1139	Arnold was an early reformer, against worldly popes and sinful priests; argued that sinful priests cannot administer sacraments.	Arnold and his views condemned.
11	Lateran III 1179	Emperor Frederick I, in political struggle with pope, had supported an antipope and caused a schism.	Schism ended; principle from now on was that the college of cardinals would always elect pope.
12	Lateran IV 1215	Church in high point of its power was plagued with questions and problems of doctrine and discipline.	Most important of Lateran councils; defined doctrine of the Eucharist and transubstantiation.
13	Lyons I 1245	Emperor in contest with the pope for supreme political power in Europe.	Council deposed emperor; a complicated chapter in history of church/state relations.
14	Lyons II 1274	Greek Orthodox church thought it politically wise to ask for reunion with Roman church.	Greeks pledged obedience to the pope, ended old schism; the peace lasted until 1289.
15	Vienne 1311–12	A twelfth-century military/religious order, highly influential and wealthy; Philip IV of France wanted their lands.	Convened during Avignon papacy; Templars condemned; Philip took their land.
16	Pisa 1409	Two men both claiming to be the legitimate pope; church had been divided on the issue from 1378.	Healed the schism (temporarily) by deposing both popes and electing new one.

Investiture

Arnold Brescia

Papal elections

Doctrine and discipline

Frederick II

Reunion with Greeks

Templars

Schism

#	Council	Topic	Description	Outcome
17	Constance 1414–18	Schism	Three men all claimed to be the rightful pope; European Christendom completely split on issue.	Ended the schism and declared that councils are superior to popes and councils ought to meet often.
18	Florence 1438–39	Reunion	Greek Orthodox church sought support of West against the Turks; also sought to discuss theological differences.	Reunion voted for but not ratified by Orthodox synods; important council for theology of the Trinity.
19	Lateran V 1512–17	Reform	Convoked by pope to invalidate the decrees of the Council of Pisa (1409), which was an antipapal power council, but not recognized by Roman Catholic church as ecumenical.	Touched on some minor areas of needed reform, but main causes of the Reformation were left untouched.
20	Trent 1545–63	Protestants	Called to respond to reformers, to define Roman Catholic doctrine, and tighten up teaching and theology.	Very important for Roman Catholics as it defined most doctrine and discipline that would hold up to twentieth century.
21	Vatican I 1870	Infallibility	Called to deal with various issues of doctrine and discipline, but also to define the limits of papal power.	Pope declared primate of the universal church and infallible in matters of faith and morals when speaking *ex cathedra*.
22	Vatican II 1962–65	Renewal	Called by John XXIII to evaluate contemporary church and to bring the Roman Catholic church up to date.	Issued documents for modernization of doctrine and practice; accepted ecumenism and principle of religious freedom.

APPENDIX 5
CREEDS AND CONFESSIONS

The word *creed* comes from the Latin word *credo,* which means "I believe." A creed summarizes the beliefs or lists the doctrines agreed upon by a particular church. For a number of reasons Christians have developed statements that outline their doctrinal positions. Some heretical groups in the early church claimed that Christians could, in good conscience, believe almost anything: some groups said that Jesus did not really rise from the dead, but just "seemed" to die and rise; others denied any link between Jesus and the God of the Bible. In response to the confusion created by heretical groups, Christians developed a systematic list of official beliefs. Creeds helped them to clarify their own positions and to oppose heretical teachings with an official statement. Early creeds were used for religious instruction and often were used in liturgical celebration as well.

One early summary of beliefs is the Apostle's Creed, so called because it contains the essential Christian doctrines as they were understood and believed in the apostolic church. The Apostle's Creed was not written by the apostles (as legend has it), but dates back to the old Roman Creed. In its present form, it probably did not exist before the middle of the seventh century, though there is evidence that it developed from the baptismal creed used in the Roman church in the second century. The Apostle's Creed is short and was apparently easy to learn; it summarizes early belief about the Father, Son, and Holy Spirit, the life and mission of Jesus, and the life of the church.

THE APOSTLE'S CREED

*I believe in God, the Father, almighty, creator of heaven
and earth.*

I believe in Jesus Christ, his only son, our Lord.

*He was conceived by the power of the Holy Spirit and born
to the Virgin Mary.*

*He suffered under Pontius Pilate, was crucified, died and
was buried.*

He descended to the dead.

On the third day he rose again.

*He ascended into heaven and is seated at the right hand of
the Father.*

He will come again to judge the living and the dead.

*I believe in the Holy Spirit, the holy catholic church,
the communion of saints, the forgiveness of sins, the
resurrection of the body, and the life everlasting.*

Creeds have been important in history as a means of further refining the basic beliefs of Christians. After the Reformation, creeds distinguished the acceptable beliefs of one group from those of another. The following list describes some of the more important creeds in the history of Christianity; they are specific to certain groups of Christians.

THE NICENE CREED (325; revised at the Council of Constantinople, 381): The official creed of Roman Catholics and Orthodox Christians, and accepted by some Protestant churches. It is often used during the liturgy as a common expression of beliefs. In the eleventh century the word *filioque* ("and the Son") was officially added to the creed by Christians in the West; this addition has long been a source of dispute between Roman Catholics and Orthodox Christians (see Chapter 4).

THE ATHANASIAN CREED (written between 381 and 428): Attributed to but probably not written by St. Athanasius, it sets forth the doctrines of the Trinity and the Incarnation and states that people who do not believe these things will be condemned to damnation. It was used until recent times only in Western Christian churches.

THE SCHLEITHEIM CONFESSION (1527): Lists points of agreement among Radical Reformation groups that fixed the direction of the Anabaptist movement. It includes insistence on adult baptism, separation from the world, refusal to swear oaths, and pacifism.

THE AUGSBURG CONFESSION (1530): The Lutheran confession of faith written, for the most part, by Philip Melanchthon. The first part lists essential Lutheran doctrines, the second part lists the abuses in the Roman church that needed to be remedied.

THE HELVETIC CONFESSIONS (1536 and 1562): Confessions of faith written in the Swiss Reformed Church. The first contained twenty-seven articles that embodied many of Zwingli's teachings yet, at the same time, sought reconciliation with Luther's positions. The second is a long discourse on the main Reformed teachings and expresses disagreement with Roman Catholicism and Lutheranism.

THE HEIDELBERG CATECHISM (1563): A Reformed confession of faith that is more concerned with Christian life than with theological formulations. It was accepted by the Reformed churches in Europe and approved by the Synod of Dort (1618–19). The catechism was designed to correspond to Paul's Epistle to the Romans: human misery in sin, redemption, and new life were key themes.

THE THIRTY-NINE ARTICLES (1563): A set of doctrinal formulas accepted by the Church of England. It is not so much a creed as it is a brief summary of acceptable doctrines. Royal supremacy over the church is clearly enunciated.

THE BOOK OF CONCORD (1580): The assembled confessions of the Lutheran church. It is a doctrinal standard that defines Lutheranism and its norms. It includes the accepted creeds (Nicene, Athanasian, and Apostle's), the Augsburg Confession, some of Luther's writings, and the Formula of Concord (drawn up in 1577 to restore unity among German Lutherans).

THE WESTMINSTER CONFESSION (1648): Profession of Presbyterian faith as set forth by the Westminster assembly. It is thoroughly Calvinist in its theology and expounds leading articles of the Christian faith from the creation to the last judgment.

THE CAMBRIDGE PLATFORM (1648): Not a doctrinal confession, but a plan for organization and practice in American Congregational churches; it includes provisions for the autonomy of local churches, covenanted membership, and the obligation to foster fellowship with other congregations.

MORMON ARTICLES OF FAITH (1842): In response to a question by a Chicago newspaper editor about Mormon beliefs, Joseph Smith listed thirteen articles of Mormon doctrine including belief in the inspiration of the Bible and the Book of Mormon, continuing revelation, and the literal gathering of Israel in the restoration of the ten tribes on the American continent.

CONFESSION OF 1967 (Presbyterian): A contemporary statement of faith designed for the union of American Presbyterian churches. The confession is biblical and is based on the themes of reconciliation, especially on issues of war, poverty, and various forms of discrimination. It represents a major doctrinal shift within Presbyterianism.

Creeds and confessions are not part of all Christian churches. Anabaptists, Quakers, and Seventh-Day Adventists have excluded creeds as rules of faith within their churches; one can be a member without accepting a particular creed. Some of these Christians may accept a statement of common beliefs to foster cooperation among themselves—some American Mennonites, for example, accept the Dordrecht Confession of Faith—but they do not impose that statement on their members. Many Baptist and Congregational churches rely only in part on general credal statements and prefer each local church to draw up its own covenant. Other churches use ancient creeds in their worship services and yet work to develop modern confessional statements; the Korean Conference Creed (1905) of the Methodist church is an example. The Disciples of Christ were founded on the phrase "No Creed but Christ."

Christianity was fragmented during the Reformation when new churches emerged and a variety of creeds were written. Major Protestant churches called their credal formulations *confessions*. The experience of fragmentation continued and, to some ways of thinking, grew worse in America. Because there were so many different creeds with contradictory statements about the nature of God or the mission of the church, some people were confused and grew suspicious of creeds in general. The rejection of all creeds played a major part in the foundation of churches whose roots were in revivalist movements. Primitivists, sometimes called Seekers, tended to move away from all organized religion in hopes of finding enlightenment elsewhere; they believed in the gifts of the

Holy Spirit and the experience of Jesus, but not in written, fixed formulations of belief. Anticredalism is opposition to any creed used as a rule of faith and is the opposite of confessionalism, the position that adherence to a creed is necessary for life within a church.

Most Christian churches have some agreed-upon principles of behavior or practice; most have some way to define the membership requirements of their church. Not all churches have creeds, however, nor do they desire to have them.

APPENDIX 6
HISTORICAL TIME LINE

Sometimes it is helpful to see when, in the context of the long line of history, certain events occurred. The following time line is general and has a greater concentration of events in earlier times than it does in modern ones. It is not meant to be all-inclusive, but to give a general sense of things, especially in less well-known periods.

Time before the Common Era (B.C.E.)

ca. 1700	God's call to Abraham
ca. 1200	Exodus from Egypt/covenant at Sinai
ca. 1013–972	David, king of Israel
587	Babylonian exile
538	Return to Palestine
470–321	Great Greek philosophers—Socrates, Plato, Aristotle—in Athens
168	Maccabean revolt and Jewish control of Palestine
63 B.C.E.–14 C.E.	Augustus, emperor of Rome
63	Romans conquer Palestine and capture Jerusalem
ca. 4	Jesus born in Palestine

Time in the Common Era (C.E.)

29–33	Preaching and crucifixion of Jesus
50s	Paul's epistles written; earliest New Testament literature
ca. 70–90	First gospel (Mark) written
64	Death of Peter (crucified in Rome)
54–68	Nero, Roman emperor

70	Temple in Jerusalem destroyed
80–150	Remaining New Testament books written
ca. 35–107	Ignatius of Antioch
120–220	Age of Apologists; first reasoned defenses of Christianity
ca. 150–215	Clement of Alexandria
ca. 160–225	Tertullian
ca. 185–254	Origen
284–305	Diocletian, emperor in Rome
ca. 251–356	Anthony ("the first hermit") living in Egyptian desert
303	The Great Persecution under Diocletian; all Christian churches ordered to be destroyed and all Scriptures burned; persecutions began with Nero in 64 and occurred periodically until 313.
313	Constantine, emperor, issues Edict of Milan; Christians no longer persecuted
318	Pachomius (ca. 290–346) founds first monastery in Egypt
ca. 260–340	Eusebius, Father of Church History and biographer of Constantine
296–373	Athanasius, theologian important at Council of Nicaea
306–37	Constantine reunites empire and moves capital to Constantinople
330–76	Bishop of Rome (pope) has no political rival in West
330–79	Basil the Great, established monastic rule for Orthodox church
325	Council of Nicaea called by Constantine to settle Christological problem
340	Monasticism moves to the West
347–407	John Chrysostom, preacher and theologian in Orthodox church; his Liturgy is in general use in Orthodox church
354–430	Augustine, preacher and theologian in Western church
382–400	Jerome (ca. 342–420) translates Bible into Latin: the Vulgate
372	Huns reach the Danube basin
395	Empire divided permanently between East and West
406	Vandals invade Gaul
410	Visigoths sack Rome
425	First Monasteries in Ireland and England
430	Vandals in Africa (Augustine's *City of God* published in 426)
440–61	Leo I, pope; meets Attila at gates of Rome in 452
476	Roman Empire in West ends
482–511	Clovis, king of the Franks; converts to Christianity in 496
496	Pope in alliance with Franks
ca. 525	Benedict founds his monastery at Monte Casino; begins Benedictine Rule
530–800	Golden Age of monastic preservation of classical manuscripts
532–37	Hagia Sophia, great Orthodox cathedral, built in Constantinople
590–604	Gregory I, pope, lays claims for papal absolutism
596	Augustine first archbishop of Canterbury sent to England as missionary
664	Synod of Whitby; English church in agreement with papacy on all issues

673–735	Venerable Bede, father of English history
723	Boniface (680–754) sent as missionary to Germanic tribes
726	Beginning of Iconoclast Controversy in Orthodox church
ca. 742–814	Charles I (Charlemagne), first emperor of Holy Roman Empire
774	Charlemagne conquers Lombards; becomes king of Franks and Lombards
800	Charlemagne crowned emperor by Pope Leo III
ca. 780–885	Carolingian renaissance; new learning, culture, schools, and so on
863–85	Cyril (826–69) and Methodius (ca. 815–85) sent from Constantinople as missionaries to Bohemia
887	Carolingian Empire ends; new invasions (Norsemen) begin
910	Monastery founded at Cluny; base for monastic reform in West
936–73	Otto the Great, emperor; revives royal authority over popes
966–72	Renaissance under patronage of Otto the Great
1027	"Truce of God" established; attempt to restrict feudal warfare
1054	Final schism between Orthodox and Roman Catholic churches
1033–1109	Anselm, theologian responsible for theory of substitutionary atonement
1073–85	Gregory VII, reforming pope; strengthens claims of papal absolutism
1077	Emperor, Henry IV, begs pope's forgiveness at Canossa
1095–99	First Crusade
1079–1142	Peter Abelard, philosopher/theologian; applies reason to mysteries of faith
1100–60	Peter Lombard, beginnings of Scholastic theology
1132–1202	Joachim of Fiore, apocalyptic preacher and reformer
1198–1216	Innocent III, pope; height of papal power
ca. 1182–1226	Francis of Assisi, founder of Franciscan friars
1202–04	Fourth Crusade; Western soldiers conquer and pillage Constantinople
1215	Magna Carta signed in England between King John and English nobles
1215	Transubstantiation defined as article of faith at a Lateran council
1216	Dominican friars founded
ca. 1217	Death of Peter Waldo, founder of "heretical" Waldensians
1225–74	Thomas Aquinas, the "angelic doctor," author of the *Summa Theologica*
1265–1321	Dante, author of *The Divine Comedy*
1265	Marco Polo visits China
1294–1303	Boniface VIII, pope; humiliated and defeated by French king, Philip IV (compare to king begging papal forgiveness in 1077)
1304	Clement V, first Avignon pope
1337	Hundred Years' War (between France and England) begins
1330–1400	English mystics: Julian of Norwich, Richard Rolle, Walter Hilton
ca. 1330–84	John Wycliffe, English reformer, associated with Lollard movement
1348–50	Black Plague decimates European population

1340–1400	Chaucer, author of *The Canterbury Tales*
ca. 1372–1415	John Hus, Czech reformer, burned at Council of Constance
1377	Avignon papacy ends
1378	Great schism begins with one pope in Avignon and another in Rome
1409	Council of Pisa called to end schism
1414–18	Council of Constance ends schism, does not reform church enough
1450	Invention of printing press
1453	Constantinople captured by Turks; overland trade route no longer safe and people begin to search for a new route to the east, which begins age of explorers: Magellan, Balboa, Columbus, and others
1453	Byzantine refugees bring priceless art and manuscript treasures to West
1454	Gutenburg Bible printed
1495–98	Leonardo da Vinci paints *The Last Supper*
1504	Michaelangelo's *David* finished
1513	Machiavelli's *The Prince* published
1517	Luther (1483–1546) posts his Ninety-five Theses on church door; mainline Protestant Reformation begins
1521	Luther condemned by the Diet of Worms
1484–1531	Ulrich Zwingli, Swiss reformer
1536	Tyndale's English Bible printed
1509–64	John Calvin, French reformer
1555	Peace of Augsburg settles religious disputes in Germany
1558–1603	Elizabeth I, queen of England
1564–1616	Shakespeare
1564–1642	Galileo
ca. 1582	Congregationalist churches established in England
1545–63	Council of Trent called to reform Roman Catholic church
1542–1621	Robert Bellarmine, Roman Catholic reformer
1540	Jesuits founded to defend Roman Catholicism and pope
1513–72	John Knox, Scottish reformer
1552–1610	Matteo Ricci, Jesuit missionary to China
1559	First Index of Forbidden Books established by Roman Catholic church
1618–48	Thirty Years' War
1620	Pilgrims land in America
1624–91	George Fox, founder of the Quakers
1685–1750	Johann Sebastian Bach
1674–1748	Isaac Watts, one of the foremost English hymn writers
1612	First Baptist church formed in England
1642–1727	Isaac Newton, physicist and scientist
1703–58	Jonathan Edwards
1703–91	John Wesley
1700–60	Count Zinzendorf, patron of the Moravians
1720–72	John Woolman, Quaker reformer

1756–91	Wolfgang Amadeus Mozart
1740s	Great Awakening
1774	Mother Ann Lee (1736–84) leads a group of Shakers to America
1776	Declaration of Independence signed
1789	French Revolution
1801	First camp meeting in America, at Cane Ridge, Kentucky
1776–91	Dawn of religious freedom for American Catholicism
1782–1849	William Miller, founder of Adventist movement
1788–1866	Alexander Campbell, founder of Disciples of Christ
1821–1910	Mary Baker Eddy, founder of Christian Science
1805–44	Joseph Smith, founder of Mormon church
1824	First performance of Beethoven's *Ninth Symphony*
1848	Karl Marx publishes the *Communist Manifesto*
1844	Y.M.C.A. founded
1833–45	Oxford movement in Anglican church
1852–84	Three Baltimore councils define program of American Catholicism
1842	Launching of American Protestant Association against Catholic church
1865	Salvation Army founded
1869–70	First Vatican Council declares papal infallibility
1914–18	First World War
1861–1918	Walter Rauschenbusch, pioneer of Social Gospel movement
1856–1939	Sigmund Freud, beginnings of psychoanalysis
1886–1968	Karl Barth, neoorthodoxy in Protestant theology
1892–1971	Reinhold Neibuhr, American neoorthodoxy
1925	Scopes Trial in Dayton, Tennessee; extreme Fundamentalism
1948	World Council of Churches established in Amsterdam
1939–45	Second World War
1962–65	Second Vatican Council called to modernize Roman Catholic church

GLOSSARY

ABRAHAM: Father of the Jewish people; first of the three patriarchs, Abraham, Isaac, and Jacob. See Genesis 17.5. Abraham=father of many.

ALEXANDER THE GREAT (356–23 B.C.E.): King of Macedon, one of the greatest leaders and conquerors of all times.

ALTAR CALL: Invitation by a preacher for members of the congregation to come up to the altar. People respond for a number of reasons: to repent and be saved, to help others accept Jesus, to pray for themselves, to confess their sins, or to ask for special prayers from the minister and others.

ANGELS (Gk=messenger): Found in Bible and New Testament, usually as God's messengers. Three angels are named: Michael, Gabriel, and Raphael.

ANSELM (1033–1109): Archbishop of Canterbury, teacher, and theologian; first to develop theory of substitutionary atonement.

ANTIOCHUS IV (d. 163 B.C.E.): Attempted to hellenize Judea and crush Judaism, a policy that instigated the Maccabean revolt.

APOCALYPTIC (Gk=uncovering): Type of Jewish and Christian literature dealing with end of world. Writing characterized by obscure symbols, visions, and vivid imagery.

APOCRYPHA (Gk=hidden things): Biblical books for which divine authorship is questioned (as opposed to canonical books). There are fifteen books or portions of books in the Apocrypha: 1 Esdras, 2 Esdras, Tobit, Judith, Additions to the Book of Esther, The Wisdom of Solomon, Ecclesiasticus (also called the Book of Sirach), Baruch, The Letter of Jeremiah; The Prayer of Azariah and the Song of the Three Young Men, Susanna, Bel and the Dragon (all three of these are additions to the Book of Daniel); The Prayer of Manasseh, and 1 and 2 Maccabees.

APOLOGIST/APOLOGETICS (Gk = speak in defense): Early Christian writers (ca. 120–220) known as apologists defended Christianity against hostile or misleading characterizations; they explained its doctrines and practices. Modern apologetics is a defense of Christianity on intellectual grounds; it argues for the reasonableness of religious faith in general and for Christianity in particular.

APOSTACY (Gk=revolt): Denial of one's beliefs. In Christianity, a knowing turning away from God and the Christian faith, the opposite of conversion.

APOSTLE: Envoy or "one sent." Refers to prime missionaries of Christianity and to the twelve men chosen by Jesus as his primary followers.

APOSTOLIC CONSTITUTIONS: Late fourth-century work comprised of eight books of administrative rules for Christians (clergy and laity) and directions for worship. Attributed to, but not written by, the apostles.

ARMINIANISM: Theological system inspired by Jacob Arminius (1560–1609). The emphasis is upon the freedom of a person to accept grace (versus the Calvinist notion of irresistible grace), though it also includes beliefs in universal atonement, conditional predestination, and human freedom. It has sometimes been used to describe liberal or rational tendencies in Christian religion. One needs to exercise caution, therefore, before applying the term to a person or group.

ASCETICISM (Gk=exercise): A system of practices designed to develop virtues and combat vice, used by Greek philosophers, Christians, and various Eastern religions.

ATONEMENT: Sometimes written as *at-one-ment* to indicate the reconciliation between God and people through the death and resurrection of Jesus. Christians agree that there is a need for reconciliation, but they argue about how atonement ought to be understood. There has been a long history of interpretation from the New Testament to the present. Substitutionary atonement, for example, was considered to be one of the Christian fundamentals when fundamentalists tried to define the minimum beliefs one should have to be Christian.

ATTILA (d. 453): King of Huns. Was going to invade Rome (452) but changed his mind either because of the diplomacy of Pope Leo I or because of lack of provisions.

AUGUSTINE (354–430 C.E.): Bishop of Hippo (North Africa) and one of the most important early Christian writers. His influence on later religious thinkers was enormous.

AUGUSTUS (63 B.C.E.–14 C.E.): First Roman emperor, reigning when Jesus was born.

BARTH, KARL (1886–1968): Swiss theologian associated with neoorthodoxy, the attempt in the twentieth century to lead Protestants back to the original principles and intentions of the Reformation.

BASIL THE GREAT (330–379): Greek Theologian who wrote monastic rule still used in Orthodox monasticism.

B.C.E.: Before the Common Era. A designation of time equivalent to B.C. but not centered on a theological claim as is B.C. (Before *Christ*).

BENEDICT OF NURSIA (ca. 480–550): Founder of Benedictines. Wrote first monastic rule used in the West.

BERNARD OF CLAIRVAUX (1090–1153): A monk and abbot of the monastery at Clairvaux in France who is renowned for his theological and mystical writings.

BISHOP (Gk=episcopos; Eng=episcopal): In Greek the word literally means overseer; bishops were the administrative officers of the early community. In some Christian churches they are the highest order of ministers and can be distinguished from other ministers by their power to ordain priests/ministers.

BOOK OF COMMON PRAYER: Authorized liturgical book of the Church of England. Its various editions and revisions reflect the doctrinal battles within the Tudor Reformation.

BYZANTIUM: Site of present-day Istanbul. Constantine had a new city built there in 330, and renamed it Constantinople when he moved the capital of the Roman Empire there in 333.

CALIGULA (12–41): Roman emperor who claimed to be a god and attempted to erect a statue of himself in the Jewish temple in Palestine.

CAMP MEETINGS: A form of revivalist meeting used on the American frontier. It originated as a form in Kentucky in 1800 during the Second Great Awakening. Camp meetings were designed to attract many people and were held outdoors; various ministers preached and conversions were often accompanied by emotional exercises and manifestations.

CANON: The Greek word means straight rod; it usually means a kind of measuring stick. In Christian language it means the official list of biblical books that are recognized as inspired. Canonical books must be distinguished from apocryphal books (books about which there is some question as to authenticity). Also, ecclesiastical title used to refer to nonmonastic clergy belonging to a cathedral (the chief church in a diocese). Canons participate in officially sanctioned religious life in a way that is technically different from monks, nuns, and friars.

C.E.: The Common Era. It corresponds to what Christians call A.D. (Anno Domini, meaning "the year of our Lord").

CELIBACY: Being unmarried. This condition is accepted by priests in the Roman Catholic church as necessary for ordination. In the Orthodox church men may marry before ordination, but not after; bishops must not be married.

CHARISMATIC (Gk=gift of grace): Possessing gifts of the spirit. In the New Testament various gifts are mentioned that help a Christian to advance spiritually. In 1 Cor. 12:8–11 these gifts (*charismata*) are listed as wisdom, knowledge, faith, healing, miracles, prophecy, discernment of spirits, tongues, and the interpretation of tongues. They are sometimes called the gifts of the spirit and thereby associated with Christians who have a special relationship to the Holy Spirit.

CHARLEMAGNE (ca. 742–814): Carolingian king of the Franks, crowned emperor of the West in 800 by Pope Leo III.

CLEMENT OF ALEXANDRIA (d. 215 C.E.): Greek theologian who first attempted a synthesis between Platonic and Christian thought.

COMMUNION OF SAINTS: Mentioned in the Apostle's Creed (see Appendix 5). To some Christians it means sharing together in the Eucharist and to others it is a description of Christian fellowship here on earth. Traditionally, however, it refers to the spiritual union between Christ and each believer and, by extension, describes the spiritual union that exists among all believers on earth and in heaven.

COMMUNITARIAN: Nonmonastic communities motivated by ethical or religious ideals. In the nineteenth century there were a wide variety of religious communitarian groups in America.

CONGREGATIONAL: A type of ecclesiastical government where authority flows throughout the congregation.

CONSTANTINE (d. 337 C.E.): First Christian Roman emperor. He conquered under the Christian sign of the cross and issued the Edict of Milan (313), which stated that Christianity would be tolerated in the empire and put an end to persecution.

CONSTANTINOPLE: Capital city of the Roman Empire under Constantine and his successors, formerly called Byzantium. Called also the "new Rome." Three ecumenical councils were held there.

CONVERSION (Gk=metanoia is one root, meaning radical turning of the heart and will): Several meanings: (1) turning from sin to God in faith and repentance (the controversy here is whether this turning is entirely an act of God, of the person, or a cooperation between them); (2) drawing closer to God by living a more dedicated Christian life; (3) changing from nonbelief to belief, as in conversion from atheism; (4) sometimes used by Roman Catholics to describe the experience of someone who has turned from one church to the Catholic church; thus *convert* is the word often used by Catholics to describe a Protestant now become Catholic.

COUNCIL OF TRENT: Roman Catholic council held periodically from 1545–63 to respond to Protestantism. Until the Second Vatican Council (1962–65), Trent was the most comprehensive statement of Catholic belief and practice.

COUNSELS OF PERFECTION: Traditionally the vocations to poverty, chastity, and obedience, which form the basis of nearly all monastic and religious life for Roman Catholicism, Orthodox Christianity, and Protestant religious orders.

COVENANT: An agreement entered into voluntarily by two or more parties. God established a covenant with Abraham and with the Jewish people at Sinai; Christians believe a new covenant began with Jesus.

COVENANT THEOLOGY: Used, especially by the Puritans, to explain the election and perseverance of the saints. It was an important part of the religious, political, and social understanding of both Presbyterian and Congregational Puritans.

CRANMER, THOMAS (1489–1556): Archbishop of Canterbury at the beginning of the English Reformation, chiefly responsible for the *Book of Common Prayer*.

CREED: Summary of basic doctrines of faith. See Appendix 5.

CRUSADES (from the Latin word for cross; the crusaders wore a cross on their official clothing): A series of military expeditions launched from the eleventh to the thirteenth centuries by Christians for the recovery of the Holy Land (Jerusalem) from the Muslims. The first one was called by Pope Urban II in 1095. There were nine of them altogether. The fourth crusade (1202–04) ended with the capture and pillaging of Constantinople. The word *crusade* came to be used for other expeditions—against heretics, for example—sanctioned by the pope.

DARK AGES: Usually refers to the period between the collapse of the old Roman Empire (in the fifth century) and beginning of a stable society (about 1000 C.E.). The Dark Ages is often associated with the barbarian invasions, unstable government, and minimal levels of education and progress.

DAVID (d. 972 B.C.E.): King of ancient Israelites, one of the great national heroes of Judaism. Some Jews expected the Messiah to come from the house of David.

DEACON (Gk=servant or minister): Mentioned in the New Testament and recognized in many Christian churches as an office or ministry (often attached to reading the gospel, visiting the sick, and so on). The role and nature of the deacon varies according to polity.

DEIFICATION: In Eastern Orthodox mysticism and theology, usually means divinization: becoming divine by way of a profound union with God.

DENOMINATIONALISM: A denomination is a specific church group united in polity and belief. *Denominationalism* has several meanings: (1) refers to the variety and independence of various churches; (2) refers to the notion that there are and ought to be many differing church bodies; (3) refers to the movement to unite local churches into one larger body. In this third sense denominationalism has been opposed by those who clearly favor congregational polities or who value their own distinctness. Antidenominationalism is resistance to any centrally organized church body.

DIDACHE: An early collection of moral precepts and directions for the celebration of the Eucharist and administration of baptism. Written somewhere between 50 and 150 C.E. in Greek. Also contains directions for bishops and deacons.

DOCTRINE: A system of beliefs or dogmas; teaching of a particular group.

DUALISM: Any philosophical system that tries to explain things in terms of two distinct and irreducible principles; in religion, good and evil or light and darkness, both of which are equally powerful.

ECUMENICAL COUNCIL (Gk=universal): Universal meeting of bishops, whose authority was accepted as official. See Appendix 4.

ECUMENISM: From the Greek word for universal or worldwide, ecumenism is an attempt to realize greater Christian unity by interchurch cooperation.

EDICT OF MILAN: Passed by Constantine (313) granting religious toleration to Christians.

ELDER (Gk=presbyter): An office in the presbyterian structure that is divided into teaching elders (ordained ministers) and ruling elders (elected from the congregation). Some Christians translate the word *presbyter* as priest rather than elder.

ENGLISH CIVIL WAR: Conflict between King Charles I of England and a significant group of his subjects. It lasted from 1642–48 and was focused on Charles's monarchical views versus the demands of the Parliamentarians. Many of the king's opponents were Puritans.

ENLIGHTENMENT: A term applied to scientific and philosophical thought in the eighteenth century characterized by belief in natural law and order, confidence in human reason, and a rational approach to religious questions.

EPISCOPAL: A type of ecclesiastical government where authority rests with bishops and flows down from them through priests to members of the congregation.

ERASMUS, DESIDERIUS (ca. 1469–1536): Usually referred to as Erasmus of Rotterdam. Renowned humanist scholar and priest; famous during the Reformation for his Latin translation of the New Testament (from Greek) and for his debates with Martin Luther on the freedom of the will.

ESCHATOLOGY (Gk=last discourse or last things): The doctrine of the last things or end of the world; eschatology is concerned with the end of the individual soul, all other people, the church, and the world. It is treated in the Old Testament and New Testament, but is mostly thoroughly treated in apocryphal books.

ESSENES: Small Jewish ascetic sect at the time of Jesus. Essenes lived pious, communal lives in the desert where they purified themselves in preparation for the Messiah. Community of goods, celibacy, and purification through baptism were some of their practices.

ESTABLISHED CHURCHES: Those churches whose practice and doctrines are supported by the state in some way. The Church of England is "established": the church is supported by and to some extent controlled by the state.

EUCHARIST (Gk=thanksgiving): Christian practice that repeats the action of Jesus at the Last Supper. Christians partake of the bread and wine in memory of Jesus. Some Christians believe the bread and wine is truly the body and blood of Christ, others believe it is a symbol of the body and blood, still others believe it is a memorial fellowship meal.

EUSEBIUS (ca. 260–340): Bishop of Caesaria and so-called Father of church history. Wrote official biography of Constantine.

EXCOMMUNICATION: An ecclesiastical punishment whereby a person is excluded from communion with the church; that is, the excommunicated person may not partake of the sacraments or, in some cases, speak to anyone in the community.

EXEGESIS (Gk=to narrate or explain): The process of explaining a text, usually a biblical one, by way of translation, paraphrase, or commentary. An exegete applies interpretive skills to a text in order to understand it more deeply. Exegesis has been done from ancient times—commentaries on Scripture predate Christianity, and Christianity, itself, has a long and varied history of exegesis—but changes as exegetical skills (linguistic, archeological, historical, spiritual) develop over time.

EXILE (the Babylonian captivity): In the history of Israel, the period from the fall of Jerusalem (587 B.C.E.) to the reconstruction in Palestine of a new Jewish state (538 B.C.E.).

EXODUS: Second book of the Jewish Bible (or Old Testament). In Jewish history, the Exodus was the flight from Egypt led by Moses (including the miraculous crossing of the Red Sea and God's victory over the Egyptians).

FAITH: For some Christians an attitude of trust in God's mercy; people may be saved through Christ by faith. For other Christians *faith* refers to a body of beliefs and is more like a creed or set of doctrines believed by people. For still others, intellectual assent to a body of beliefs.

FALL: The moment when Adam and Eve disobeyed God's command not to eat of the tree of knowledge, thus forfeiting the original blessedness that they had enjoyed. Theologically, a fall from a state of harmony to one of discord with the will of God. See Genesis 3.

FILIOQUE (Lat=and the Son): Words added to the Nicene Creed by Western Christians. Long a source of friction between Roman Catholics and Orthodox Christians.

FLAGELLANTS: Groups of people who, in medieval times, scourged themselves in public procession or in town squares in order to lead people to repentance and to do penance themselves for their own sins and the sins of the world.

FORTY-TWO ARTICLES: Collection of Anglican doctrines issued in 1553 but never enforced (due to the restoration of Roman Catholicism under Queen Mary I). They form the basis of the present-day Anglican doctrinal formulation, the Thirty-nine Articles.

FRANCISCANS: The order of friars founded by Francis of Assisi (1182–1226), distinguished by complete poverty.

FRIARS: Religious beggars living an officially-sanctioned, vowed religious life. Friars were called *fraters* (brothers); they were usually distinguished by the color of their cloaks (Gray Friars, Black Friars, and so on).

GENTILE (Hb=the nations): A term applied to non-Jews.

GENTILE MISSION: Refers to St. Paul's spreading the gospel message not just to Jews, but to Gentiles; to anyone who would believe in Jesus as the Christ.

GLOSSOLALIA (Gk=tongue talking): The ability or gift of speaking "in tongues," which may mean speaking in a real language unknown to the speaker (one might, for instance, speak Chinese under the influence of the Spirit), or in an unknown language (which then may or may not be interpreted to the congregation). In Pentecostal churches, speaking in tongues is considered a sign of baptism of the Spirit.

GNOSTICS (Gk=knowledge): The term is used to describe a variety of early

Christian heretics whose interpretation of the Gospels and the Christian life was based on secret knowledge; in order to be saved, they said, one had to know the secret signs and words. Recent research on the manuscripts found at Nag Hammadi (in Egypt) have given us a more thorough understanding of the Gnostics, who were heretofore known mostly through the condemnations of their opponents. Many of the apocryphal gospels were written by Gnostics.

GOSPELS ("good tidings"): Any of the first four books of the New Testament preaching the "good news," namely, that there is salvation through the birth, life, passion, death, and resurrection of Jesus. The four Gospels in the New Testament are Matthew, Mark, Luke, and John.

GRACE: In Christian theology it means God's favor or supernatural assistance. People receive grace so that they may be sanctified. Christians admit the need for some kind of divine help in their lives, but there has been much disagreement about what exactly this help is, how it comes to people, how people accept it, whether it is there all the time or only for specific acts.

HEBREWS: See *Jews*.

HELENA (ca. 255–330): Mother of Constantine. According to a later tradition, she found the true cross in Jerusalem.

HELLENISM: The culture, ideals, and pattern of life of ancient Greece. As a system it competed with Christianity and challenged it to develop a philosophical language.

HERESY: Formal denial of a defined doctrine.

HERMIT (Gk=desert): Individual who, for religious motives, retires from the general society and goes out to a lonely place in order to focus on an intense relationship with God. In the early church these people went into the deserts of Egypt and Syria.

HEROD: Dynasty reigning in Palestine at time of Jesus. Herod the Great (d. 4 B.C.E.) gave the family its name, and was king of Judea. His son Herod Antipas (d. 39 C.E.) executed John the Baptist and was reigning at the time of Jesus's death.

HOLY SPIRIT (HOLY GHOST): Theologically, the third person of the Trinity; biblically, a manifestation of God's power in this world. The Holy Spirit was promised by Jesus, and Christians believe it is present in the church in some way.

HUMANISM: A philosophical and literary movement that extolled human capabilities. In its Renaissance form it signaled a return to classical antiquity. It inspired some of the scriptural research that led to the Reformation.

HUSSITES: Followers of John Hus, they were Czech nationalists who resisted armed attempts to squelch their religious protests. One of their main tenets was the reception of the Eucharist under both species; that is, they believed that people should receive both the bread and the wine. A Czech flag still used today has Eucharistic symbols on it.

ICONOCLAST CONTROVERSY (Gk iconoclasm=image breaking): Opposition to religious use of images, from the fourth to the ninth centuries a raging battle in Orthodox Christianity. In the Reformation some Protestants (especially Puritans) considered the use of religious images idolatrous.

ICONOSTASIS: Screen in Orthodox churches that separates the sanctuary from the rest of the church.

ICONS (Gk=image, picture): Flat pictures of God and saints venerated in Orthodox churches.

IGNATIUS OF ANTIOCH (ca. 35–ca. 107): Bishop of Antioch and martyr. In an age of doctrinal questioning, he argued that the best way to safeguard true beliefs was through the teaching and ruling authority of the bishop.

IMMANENCE (Lat. *in manere*=to dwell in): God's dwelling in and being active in the world. The doctrine of immanence sees the world as, in some sense, containing God within it (see *transcendence*).

INCARNATION: Christian doctrine that the eternal Son of God took flesh; Jesus Christ as both fully divine and fully human.

INDEX: Officially, *Index Librorum Prohibitorum* (Index of Forbidden Books). A list of books considered to be dangerous to the faith and morals of Catholics, drawn up by a censoring agency established by the church in the sixteenth century. The Index was abolished in 1966.

INDULGENCES: Remission by the church of punishment due for sin. Based on the merits of Christ and the saints, the medieval Catholic church reasoned that it could grant indulgences drawn from a treasury of merits available to help sinners on earth.

INFALLIBILITY: The ability to speak on religious matters without making a mistake. There have been arguments about biblical infallibility; that is, to what extent the Bible is infallible. Roman Catholics believe that the pope is infallible when speaking *ex cathedra* (from the chair): when the pope is speaking to the whole church, on matters of faith and morals. The issue of papal infallibility is a matter of continued debate within Roman Catholic Christianity; some argue that the calling of Vatican II indicates that infallibility is not entirely vested in the pope, but in the church as it meets in ecumenical council.

INQUISITION: The official persecution of heresy by designated ecclesiastical courts; established in the thirteenth century. Called the Holy Office from 1908 to 1965, when it became the Congregation for the Doctrine of the Faith with the function of promoting faith and morals, not just safeguarding them.

INSPIRATION (Gk=breath, Spirit): Doctrine that Scripture was written under influence of Holy Spirit. How it works is a matter of some dispute and speculation among Christians.

ISRAELITES: See *Jews*.

JESUS: Theologically, the son of God and second person of the Trinity; biblically, the savior who died and rose from the dead; historically, a carpenter from Nazareth born in the reign of Caesar Augustus.

JEWS: Three terms must be distinguished here. *Hebrew* refers to the Semitic people not yet formed into the nation Israel. *Israelites* refers to those Hebrews who were part of the nation Israel formed under the leadership of Moses and Joshua circa 1200 B.C.E. Jews, as a term, derives from the last surviving Israelite tribe, Judah, and is a term applied to these people after the exile (587 B.C.E.). In chronological order, then, one speaks of the Hebrews up to the Exodus, of the Israelites from the Exodus to the exile, and of the Jews after the exile. In a more embracing sense, however, Judaism traces itself back to the days of Abraham, Isaac, and Jacob, and Jews are descendants of Abraham and Sarah.

JOHN THE BAPTIST: Cousin of Jesus who after retiring into the desert emerged to preach repentance and to baptize in preparation for the Messiah. He baptized Jesus.

JOHN XXIII: Name taken by two popes: (1) Baldassare Cossa (d. 1419), who was elected pope by the Council of Pisa (1409) and was an antipope (that is, was pope in contest with two other men who also claimed to be the rightful pope); he called the Council of Constance; (2) Angelo Roncalli (pope from 1958–63), who called the Second Vatican Council, which reformed and modernized the Roman Catholic church.

JUSTIFICATION (Lat=make just; Gk=pronounce just): A person's passage from sinfulness to righteousness (or justice). Also, that act whereby God makes a person just (conveys grace to a person's soul); or the act whereby God, because of the sacrifice of Christ, treats a person mercifully—as though that person were just or righteous. Christians share the belief that justification is bound up with rebirth or regeneration, but they disagree about what that rebirth means, how it is accomplished and how, exactly, it affects the person.

JUSTIN MARTYR (100–65 C.E.): Christian apologist who tried to convert people to Christianity by way of philosophical argument.

LITURGY (Gk=work of the people): Used to describe worship in general and the Eucharist especially.

LOLLARDS: Followers of John Wycliffe in England. There is no sure derivation for the word.

MACCABEES: Jewish family of second and first centuries B.C.E. that brought about restoration of Jewish political and religious life.

MANTRA (Sanskrit=instrument of thought): A sacred text or word used as a prayer or incantation. One uses a mantra to clear the mind of other thought and to bring the divine into focus. Mantras arose in Hindu and Buddhist forms of Tantrism.

MARTYR (Gk=witness): During persecution, used exclusively for those who suffered for their religious beliefs; finally restricted to those who died for them. Martyrs are honored as saints by the church.

MARY (Hb=Miriam): Mother of Jesus. She occupies a place of honor—principal saint—in Roman Catholic and Orthodox churches. Theological statements about her acknowledge her virginity and title Mother of God. During the Reformation, Protestants reacted against what they interpreted as excessive devotion to Mary. Her place in the devotional life of the church is a serious issue between Roman Catholics and Protestants.

MASS: A name—along with Lord's Supper and Holy Communion—for the celebration of the Eucharist. It is usually used by Roman Catholics, but has also been used by Anglicans.

MESSIAH (Hb=annointed one): In Judaism, a man sent by God to restore Israel and reign righteously for all people. Christians consider Jesus to be the Messiah and interpret the Messiah as a suffering savior (see Isaiah 52–55).

MILLENNIALISM: (Gk=thousand) Based on Revelation 20:1–10, the belief that Christ promised faithful believers a thousand years of bliss, and will return to establish it.

MOSES (Thirteenth century B.C.E.): Leader and law-giver of the Jewish people. Called by God to take the Jews to Mt. Sinai, where God made a covenant with them.

MYSTERY (Lat=sacramentum) RELIGIONS: In Greek and Roman religion, secret cults that required elaborate initiations, purification rites, and accepting occult ideas.

MYSTICISM: A form of religious experience that emphasizes the possibility and desirability of a direct and intuitive apprehension of divinity. A mystic is one who strives for this direct personal union with God.

NEOPLATONISM: Ancient mystical philosophy based on doctrines of Plato. Had a lasting effect on the development of Christian mysticism.

NEW TESTAMENT: The Christian portion of the Bible: twenty-seven books.

NICENE CREED: Official statement of beliefs from the Council of Nicaea (see Appendix 4).

OLD CATHOLICS: Catholics who split off from Roman Catholicism in the nineteenth century as a protest against papal infallibility. Old Catholics are a coalition of small national churches whose liturgy and edifices appear to be Roman Catholic, but whose beliefs deny many Roman Catholic doctrines (especially those about Mary).

OLD TESTAMENT: The Christian name for the Hebrew Bible, as rearranged by Christians.

ORDINANCES: Nonliturgical churches—for example, Baptists and Mennonites—rejected the word *sacrament* and adopted the word *ordinance* because they thought *sacrament* had medieval connotations of magic.

ORIGEN (ca. 185–254 C.E.): Christian philosopher and scholar, one of the first theological geniuses of the Christian church. Attempted to synthesize Neoplatonism and Stoicism with Christian creed so as to provide a Christian view of the universe.

ORIGINAL SIN: In Christian theology, the sin of Adam and Eve. The effect of it is the fundamentally graceless nature of human beings; that is, all people are regarded as having a sinful nature.

ORTHODOXY: Right belief (as contrasted with heresy). The word is used for the ancient Greek Christian church (Orthodox Christianity: Greek Orthodox, Russian Orthodox, and so on). It can also refer to adherence to traditional or established belief (as opposed to liberalism or innovation).

OTTO I (The Great) (912–73): Holy Roman emperor from 962, reviving the Carolingian claims.

PARLIAMENTARIANS: Group opposed to King Charles I in the English Civil War; many of them were Puritans, and the English Civil War is sometimes referred to as the Puritan Revolution.

PASSOVER: A Jewish feast of highest importance. In the Bible it is an act of deliverance from the Egyptians, where an angel of death passed over the Hebrews in the last of the great plagues (Exodus 12).

PATRIARCH: One of the progenitors of the Jewish people, especially Abraham, Isaac, and Jacob. In the Christian church, a title of certain exalted bishops. In the early church there were five great patriarchates—Rome, Constantinople, Alexandria, Antioch, and Jerusalem.

PAUL (d. 64 or 67 C.E.): Apostle to the Gentiles. Born and reared a Jew, he converted to Christianity after an "experience of the risen Lord." Author of major epistles in the New Testament, great missionary, and early theologian.

PEACE OF AUGSBURG (1555): Settled the religious battles in Germany with the formula *cuius regio eius religio:* the people in a given region must follow the religion of the ruler of that region (those who opposed their ruler's religion should move to a more congenial place).

PEACE OF WESTPHALIA (1648): The general settlement ending the Thirty Years' War.

PEASANTS' REVOLT: An uprising of German peasants in 1524–26. Although their grievances were economic, the peasants were urged on by some religious reformers and others who were impatient for change. Their list of demands included some religious reforms, but their methods were variations of mob violence. Luther called for their extermination.

PENANCE: In Orthodox and Roman Catholic churches, a sacrament of the forgiveness of sins. It can also mean a punishment of some sort (as in one "doing penance" for sins).

PENTECOST (Gk=fiftieth): In Judaism, a spring feast fifty days after Passover, commemorating the Sinai covenant. In Christianity, the feast celebrating the coming of the Holy Spirit to the apostles and into the church.

PERSECUTIONS: Sporadic but systematic attempts on the part of Roman authorities to destroy Christianity. Began with Nero (64 C.E.) and ended with the Edict of Milan (313).

PETER (d. 64 C.E.): Most prominent of the twelve apostles of Jesus. Traditionally, the first bishop of Rome.

PETER THE GREAT (1672–1725): Czar of Russia.

PHARISEES: One of two great political parties (with Sadducees) in Jerusalem at time of Jesus. They were extreme in their attempt to keep all that was Jewish away from what was non-Jewish; they were liberal in accepting both written law (Torah) and oral law (tradition).

PIUS V (1504–72; pope from 1566): Recognized as a saint in the Roman Catholic church, he was an austere and zealous reformer, instrumental in promoting the reforms of the Council of Trent. In 1570 he excommunicated Elizabeth I, queen of England, and greatly aggravated the position of Catholics there.

PLAGUES OF EGYPT: In the Bible, the troubles visited on Egyptians by God so that the pharoah would let the Jewish people go out of Egypt. There were ten plagues. See Exodus 7:19–12:36.

PLATO: (427–347 B.C.E.) Greek philosopher. One of the most important and influential thinkers in the history of the world.

PLURALISM: The belief that no single theory can explain the universe which, according to pluralists, is composed of many principles. In religion it is the coexistence of a variety of religious forms and beliefs.

POLITY: Church structure or government.

POMPEY (106–48 B.C.E.): Rival of Julius Caesar. Conquered Jerusalem for Rome in 63 B.C.E.

PONTIUS PILATE: Roman procurator of Judea when Jesus was crucified. According to the New Testament, he evaded responsibility for Jesus's death because he feared Jewish high priests' power.

POPE/PAPACY (Lat=father): Title restricted to the bishop of Rome since the fourth century.

PREDESTINATION: The idea that God decrees beforehand for all eternity the fate of individual souls. Some Christians believe that God predestines people to both heaven and hell; others say that God predestines to heaven but reprobates to hell. Predestination is deduced on the basis of divine foreknowledge.

PRESBYTERIAN: A type of ecclesiastical government where authority rests with a group of elected elders.

PRIEST (Gk=presbyter): As a special ministry (apart from elder) priesthood does not appear in the New Testament, but by the second century the office of the priest had developed to include a share in the powers of the bishop, specifically powers to celebrate the Eucharist and to forgive sins.

PROPHETS (Hb=called by God): Prophets were those called in the Old Testament to speak God's word to the people (usually to call them back to the terms of the covenant). Sometimes prophets predicted future events, but their main function was to speak for God, not to be seers.

PROVIDENCE: The doctrine that the world is divinely administered; that God, in some way, rules the world; and that the events that occur in the world are understood and controlled (or allowed) by God. The doctrine of providence need not destroy free will.

RATIONALISM: Theory that reason alone (unaided by experience) can arrive at some basic truths about the world. In religion it is often opposed to revelation: it holds that religion can be understood on the basis of reason alone and that revelation is unnecessary.

REFORMATION: A complex series of changes occurring in Christianity from the fourteenth to the seventeenth centuries.

RELICS: Material remains of a saint, or sacred objects that touched the body.

RENAISSANCE: From the word for rebirth, it was a development of Western civilization from the fourteenth to the sixteenth centuries that marked the passage from medieval to modern times. In it there was a new importance given to individual expression, culture, and worldly experience.

RESURRECTION (Lat=rising again): Rising from death to life. In Christianity, the resurrection of Jesus is the central fact of Christian experience. Christians believe that all believers will rise from the dead at the end of the world.

REVIVALISM: A form of evangelical preaching that is highly emotional in style, characterized by its focus on sin and salvation, and designed to bring listeners to a conversion experience.

SABBATARIANS: Those who observe Saturday as the Sabbath, or those who observe the Sunday Sabbath rigorously, by abstaining from all work and recreation on Sundays.

SABBATH (Hb=repose): Last day of the week in Judaism, first day of the week in Christianity. Observed on Saturday as a day of rest for Jews. Observed on Sunday as a celebration of the Resurrection for Christians.

SACRAMENT (Gk=mystery): An outward sign instituted by Christ to draw people into relationship with God. Historically there have been arguments about how many sacraments there are, whether or not they give grace, and what they mean. Some Christians prefer the term *ordinances,* and others may "have communion" but never use the words *sacrament* or *ordinance.* Most Christians—except Quakers and the Salvation Army, who have no sacraments—accept baptism and the Lord's Supper (Eucharist or Communion) as sacraments and some accept the forgiveness of sins. Roman Catholics and Orthodox Christians accept seven sacraments: baptism, confirmation, reconciliation, the Eucharist, ordination, matrimony, and the annointing of the sick.

SADDUCEES: Jewish sect or party made up of the priestly aristocracy (the Jewish establishment); political collaborationists with the Romans who accepted only written law (Torah).

SAMARITANS: Descendants of non-Jewish colonists who settled in Samaria in the eighth century B.C.E. They accepted only the first five books of the Bible and were considered by the Jews to be heretics.

SANCTIFICATION: Once a sinner has been turned to God through conversion and justification, there remains the possibility and task of drawing closer to God or to Christian perfection. Sanctification is a "second step" or second blessing.

SANCTUARY: That part of the church that contains the altar. In some churches the altar is called a table and the sanctuary contains the table, the Bible, and a pulpit (for preaching). In Roman Catholic, Orthodox, and many Anglican churches the sanctuary contains a tabernacle: a locked, enclosed space built into the high altar where the consecrated bread (called the Blessed Sacrament) is kept. In Orthodox churches the tabernacle and sanctuary are behind the iconastasis. In all churches where the Blessed Sacrament is kept one can find a sanctuary light or candle always lighted to indicate that the Blessed Sacrament is present there.

SANHEDRIN: Ancient Jewish legal and religious institution that operated as a court of law for Jews.

SATAN (Hb=adversary): A devil or demon, the great adversary of people and enemy of God.

SCHISM (Gk=to tear): A rift in the unity of the church.

SCHOLASTICISM (SCHOLASTIC THEOLOGY): The educational system of the medieval schools, which consisted in methods of disputation and philosophical and theological speculation. It was stimulated by the discoveries of Aristotelian logic in the eleventh century and led to logical speculation and systematization of Christian faith on every conceivable level.

SIN: In religion, an unethical act, disobedience to a personal God. There is disagreement about what constitutes a sin, but agreement that it is a rebellion against God.

SOCIAL DARWINISM: The application of the teachings of Charles Darwin (1809–82) about organic evolution to society so that poverty, crime, and disease can be explained in relation to survival of the fittest.

STOREFRONT CHURCHES: Some evangelical churches have an outreach to inner city areas by means of churches set up in abandoned stores; some religious individuals with a mission of their own to preach about Jesus also are sometimes drawn to downtrodden, urban settings. The churches set up in abandoned stores are called storefront churches; they do not form a denomination and often have little in common in terms of preaching, doctrine, and practice.

SYNOD: A formal meeting of religious leaders, usually of a particular region. To be distinguished from an ecumenical council, which involves the leaders of the church from all regions of the world.

SYNOPTICS (Gk=to see together): The books of Matthew, Mark, and Luke in the New Testament are considered synoptic Gospels: they bear greater similarities to each other than any of them do to the Book of John.

TALMUD (Aramaic from Hb=learning): The vast body of Hebrew oral tradition containing the elucidations, elaborations, and commentaries of the rabbis. Accepted as authoritative by orthodox Jews.

TEMPERANCE MOVEMENT: An effort to get people to abstain from drinking alcohol (totally or partially), which grew particularly strong in nineteenth century America with help of the WCTU (Women's Christian Temperance Union) and the Anti-Saloon League. Their efforts (and others) led to the Eighteenth Amendment, prohibiting the sale and consumption of alcohol (Prohibition).

TESTIMONY: An account of the power of Jesus in one's life shared with fellow believers. It is distinguished by some Christians from witness, which is an account shared with nonbelievers. Testimony is meant to support the faith of one's fellow believers.

THEOPHANY: An appearance of God in some visible form, temporary and not necessarily material.

THEOPHILUS (late second century): Bishop of Antioch and apologist.

THIRTY-NINE ARTICLES: The doctrinal positions of the Anglican church (see Appendix 5).

TIBERIUS (42 B.C.E.–37 C.E.): Second Roman emperor (14–37 C.E.), in power when Jesus was killed.

TORAH (Hb=teaching): Hebrew name for the first five books of the Bible: Genesis, Exodus, Leviticus, Numbers, and Deuteronomy. Believed to have been handed down to Moses on Sinai, it contains laws of moral and physical conduct and love of Jewish people.

TRANSCENDENCE (Lat trans=across; scandare=to climb): The transcendence of God is existence prior to and above the world. God is different from the world. See *immanence*.

TRANSCENDENTALISM: A literary, philosophical, and religious movement that flourished in New England from about 1836 to 1860. It originated with a small group of intellectuals who were against the teachings of Calvin and against the option offered by the Unitarians. They developed their own doctrine, which featured the divinity of human beings.

TRANSUBSTANTIATION: One explanation—along with transignification and consubstantiation—of how the bread and wine used in the celebration of the Eucharist are transformed into the body and blood of Christ. It was adopted as the official teaching of the Roman Catholic church in the thirteenth century, but arguments about it continue within Catholicism and Christianity in general.

TYPOLOGY (Gr=example): A method of scriptural interpretation used by some early writers to show how Jesus could be understood by way of Old Testament figures.

UNAM SANCTAM: The papal bull (or letter) issued by Pope Boniface VIII in 1302 during his quarrel with Philip IV of France. In it the pope defined the four marks of the church as being one, holy, Catholic, and apostolic, and argued that "outside the church there is no salvation."

UNIATE CHURCHES: Churches of Eastern Christendom that are in communion with Rome, yet retain their own languages, church laws, and rites.

VATICAN: Modern papal residence in Rome. By the Italian Law of Guarantees (1871) and the Lateran Accords (1929), the Vatican, the Lateran cathedral, and the papal villa at Castel Gandolfo were granted extraterritoriality (not subject to the Italian government). Vatican City—including the library—is a separate city-state within Italy.

VATICAN II (1962–65): Council called by the Roman Catholic church in order to respond to liturgical and pastoral needs of Catholics in the twentieth century. Some significant changes were made in Catholic practice and attitude as well as in theological understanding.

VOLUNTARISM: The theory and practice whereby church membership is a matter of personal choice, not civil control or some other form of coercion.

VULGATE: Latin version of the Bible compiled and translated by St. Jerome in the fourth century to provide one authorized version of the Bible to Christians (instead of the many versions in circulation at the time). It was adopted by the Roman Catholic church as the only official version, a position opposed by the Reformers.

WALDENSIANS: Followers of Peter Waldo (d. 1217) who, like Francis of Assisi, gave his money to the poor in order to live in holy poverty according to the Gospels. When the Waldensians began to preach without permission from the local clergy, they were condemned. They continued to preach—often against abuses in the church—and were hunted down and burned as heretics.

WISDOM LITERATURE: Those biblical books that deal with what we might call profound common sense, instructions about life and conduct passed on from teacher to disciple, often dealing with moral conduct. The Wisdom books in the Old Testament include Job, Proverbs, and Ecclesiastes.

WITNESS: An account of the power of Jesus in one's life shared with nonbelievers.

It is distinguished by some Christians from testimony, which is an account shared with fellow believers. The purpose of witness is to bring people to an awareness of Jesus by virtue of one individual's faith and example.

ZEALOTS: A revolutionary party extremely concerned with national liberation of the Jews from the Romans. They expected the Messiah to be a warrior-king.

ZEN: Nickname for a Buddhist sect in Japan that makes the practice of meditation its central tenet. Many of its meditative techniques—breathing, posture, relaxation—have been adopted by Christians to enhance their own meditation.

ZEUS: In Greek religion, the supreme god, who ruled other gods and people from Mt. Olympus.

SELECTED REFERENCES

Bowden, Henry Warner. *Dictionary of American Religious Biography*. Westport, Conn.: Greenwood Press, 1977.

Brauer, Jerald C. *The Westminster Dictionary of Church History*. Philadelphia: Westminster Press, 1971.

Brown, Raymond E., Fitzmyer, Joseph A., and Murphy, Roland E. *The Jerome Biblical Commentary*. Englewood Cliffs, N.J.: Prentice-Hall, 1968.

Buttrick, George Arthur, ed. *The Interpreter's Bible*. 12 vols. New York and Nashville: Abingdon Press, 1952–57.

_____. *The Interpreter's Dictionary of the Bible*. New York: Abingdon Press, 1962.

Canney, Maurice A. *An Encyclopedia of Religions*. Detroit: Gale Research, 1970.

Cross, F. L., ed. *The Oxford Dictionary of the Christian Church*. 2nd ed. Oxford: Oxford University Press, 1978.

Douglas, J. D., ed. *The New International Dictionary of the Christian Church*. Rev. ed. Grand Rapids: Zondervan Press, 1978.

al Faruqi, Isma'il Ragi, and Soper, David E. *Historical Atlas of the Religions of the World*. New York: Macmillan, 1974.

Feiner, Johannes, and Vischer, Lukas, eds. *The Common Catechism: A Book of Christian Faith*. New York: Seabury Press, 1975.

Gehman, Henry Snyder, ed. *The New Westminster Dictionary of the Bible*. Philadelphia: Westminster Press, 1970.

Hastings, James, ed. *Encyclopedia of Religion and Ethics*. 12 vols. New York: Scribner's, 1961.

Langer, William L., ed. *An Encyclopedia of World History*. 4th ed. New York: Houghton Mifflin, 1968.

Leith, John H. *Creeds of the Churches*. Rev. ed. Richmond, Va.: John Knox Press, 1973.

Leon–Dufour, Xavier, ed. *Dictionary of Biblical Theology,* New York: Desclee, 1967.

Macquarrie, John. *Dictionary of Christian Ethics*. Philadelphia: Westminster Press, 1967.

Manschreck, Clyde L., ed. *A History of Christianity: Readings in the History of the Church from the Reformation to the Present*. Englewood Cliffs, N.J.: Prentice-Hall, 1964.

Meagher, Paul Kevil, ed. *Encyclopedic Dictionary of Religion*. 3 vols. Washington, D.C.: Corpus Publications, 1978.

Melton, J. Gordon, ed. *A Directory of Religious Bodies in the United States*. New York: Garland Publishing, 1977.

———. *The Encyclopedia of American Religions*. 2 vols. Wilmington, N.C.: McGrath Publishing, 1978.

Neill, Stephen, ed. *Concise Dictionary of the Christian World Mission*. Nashville: Abingdon Press, 1971.

New Catholic Encyclopedia. 17 vols. New York: McGraw-Hill, 1967–79.

O'Brien, T. C., ed. *Corpus Dictionary of Western Churches*. Washington, D.C.: Corpus Publications, 1970.

Palmer, R. R., ed. *Atlas of World History*. New York: Rand McNally, 1970.

Petry, Ray C., ed. *A History of Christianity: Reading in the History of the Early and Medieval Church*. Englewood Cliffs, N.J.: Prentice-Hall, 1962.

Piepkorn, Arthur Carl. *Profiles in Belief: The Religious Bodies of the United States and Canada*. 4 vols. New York: Harper & Row, 1977–9.

Schaff, Philip, ed. *The Creeds of Christendom*. 3 vols. New York: Harper Brothers, 1877.

Seeberg, Reinhold. *Textbook of the History of Doctrines*. Grand Rapids: Baker House, 1952.

Weiser, Francis X. *Handbook of Christian Feasts and Customs*. New York: Harcourt, Brace, Jovanovich, 1952.

Who's Who in Religion. 2nd ed. Chicago: Marquis Who's Who, 1977.

BIBLIOGRAPHY

Abell, Aaron I. *American Catholicism and Social Action: A Search for Social Justice 1865–1950*. Notre Dame, Ind.: University of Notre Dame Press, 1963.

Acton, John Emerich Dalberg. *Essays on Church and State*. Edited by Douglas Woodruff. London: Hollis & Carter, 1952.

Ahlstrom, Sydney E. *A Religious History of the American People*. New Haven: Yale University Press, 1972.

Albright, Raymond W. *A History of the Protestant Episcopal Church*. New York: Macmillan, 1964.

Anderson, Bernhard W. *Understanding the Old Testament*. 3rd ed. Englewood Cliffs, N.J.: Prentice-Hall, 1975.

Anderson, Gerald H., and Stransky, Thomas F., eds. *Mission Trends No. 3: Third World Theologies*. New York: Paulist Press, 1976.

———. *Mission Trends No. 4: Liberation Theologies*. New York: Paulist Press, 1979.

Anderson, Hugh, ed. *Jesus*. Englewood Cliffs, N.J.: Prentice-Hall, 1967.

Anderson, Robert Mapes. *Vision of the Disinherited: The Making of American Pentecostalism*. New York: Oxford University Press, 1979.

Bainton, Roland H. *Early and Medieval Christianity*. Boston: Beacon Press, 1962.

———. *The Reformation of the Sixteenth Century*. Boston: Beacon Press, 1952.

Barkley, John M. *The Worship of the Reformed Church*. Richmond: John Knox Press, 1967.

Barraclough, Geoffrey. *The Medieval Papacy*. New York: Harcourt, Brace & World, 1972.

Barrett, Charles D. *Understanding the Christian Faith*. Englewood Cliffs, N.J.: Prentice-Hall, 1980.

Barrett, C. K. *The New Testament Background: Selected Documents*. London: SPCK., 1956.

Beach, Waldo, and Neibuhr, H. Richard., eds. *Christian Ethics*. New York: The Ronald Press, 1955.

Bede, Venerable. *A History of the English Church and Peoples*. London: Penguin, 1955.

Bedell, George C., Sandon, Leo Jr.; and Wellborn, Charles T., eds. *Religion in America*, 2nd ed. New York: Macmillan, 1982.

Bellah, Robert. "Civil Religion in America." *Daedalus* 96 (1967): 1–21.

Benko, Stephen, and O'Rourke, John J., eds. *The Catacombs and the Colosseum: The Roman Empire as the Setting of Primitive Christianity*. Valley Forge, Pa.: Judson Press, 1971.

Benz, Ernst. *The Eastern Orthodox Church—Its Thought and Life*. New York: Doubleday, 1963.

Bettenson, Henry, ed. *The Early Christian Fathers*. Oxford: Oxford University Press, 1969.

――――. *The Later Christian Fathers*. Oxford: Oxford University Press, 1970.

Blenkinsopp, Joseph. *From Adam to Abraham: Introduction to Sacred History*. Glen Rock, N.J.: Paulist Press, 1965.

Boff, Leonardo. *Jesus Christ Liberator: A Critical Christology for Our Time*. Maryknoll, N.Y.: Orbis Books, 1979.

"Born Again Politics." *Newsweek* 96 (15 September 1980): 27–36.

Bornkamm, Günther. *The New Testament: A Guide to Its Writings*. Philadelphia: Fortress Press, 1973.

Bouyer, Louis. *The Eucharist*. Notre Dame, Ind.: University of Notre Dame Press, 1968.

Braithwaite, W. C. *The Beginnings of Quakerism*. Cambridge: Cambridge University Press, 1961.

Brown, Peter. *Augustine of Hippo: A Biography*. London: Faber & Faber, 1967.

――――. *Religion and Society in the Age of Saint Augustine*. London: Faber & Faber, 1972.

Brown, Raymond, et al. *Peter in the New Testament: A Collaborative Assessment by Protestant and Roman Catholic Scholars*. Minneapolis: Augsburg Press, 1973.

Burghardt, Walter. "Without Contemplation the People Perish." *America* 127 (1972): 29–32.

Burkholder, J. R., ed. *Kingdom, Cross and Community: Essays on Mennonite Themes*. Scottdale, Pa.: Herald Press, 1976.

Campenhausen, Hans von. *Ecclesiastical Authority and Spiritual Power in the Church of the First Three Centuries*. Stanford, Calif.: Stanford University Press, 1969.

――――. *Tradition and Life in the Church*. Philadelphia: Fortress Press, 1968.

Cantor, Norman F. *Medieval History: The Life and Death of a Civilization*. 2nd ed. New York: Macmillan, 1969.

Chadwick, Henry. *Early Christian Thought and the Classical Tradition: Studies in Justin, Clement, and Origen*. Oxford: Clarendon Press, 1966.

――――. *The Early Church*. London: Penguin Books, 1967.

Chadwick, Owen. *The Reformation*. London: Penguin Books, 1964.

Chamberlin, E. R. *The Bad Popes*. New York: New American Library, 1969.

Christ, Carol P., and Plaskow, Judith. *Womanspirit Rising*. New York: Harper & Row, 1979.

Clark, Kenneth. *Civilisation*. New York: Harper & Row, 1969.

Cochrane, Charles Norris. *Christianity and Classical Culture: A Study of Thought and Action from Augustus to Augustine*. Rev. ed. Oxford: Oxford University Press, 1968.

Cogley, John. *Catholic America*. New York: Doubleday, 1974.

Cohn, Norman. *The Pursuit of the Millennium*. Oxford: Oxford University Press, 1970.

Congar, Yves. *Tradition and Traditions*. London: Burns & Oates, 1966.

Conwell, Russell H. *Acres of Diamonds*. New York: Harper Brothers, 1915.

Copleston, F. C. *A History of Medieval Philosophy*. New York: Harper & Row, 1972.

Coughlan, Robert. "Konklave in Kokomo." In *The Aspirin Age: 1919–1941*, edited by Isabel Leighton. New York: Simon & Schuster, 1943, pp. 105–30.

Coutts, John. *This We Believe: A Study of the Background and Meaning of Salvation Army Doctrines*. London: Challenge Books, 1979.

Cragg, Gerald R. *The Church and the Age of Reason 1648–1789*. London: Penguin Books, 1960.

Cullman, Oscar. *The New Testament: An Introduction for the General Reader*. London: SCM Press, 1968.

————. *Peter: Disciple, Apostle and Martyr: A Historical and Theological Essay*. New York: Meridian Books, 1958.

Daly, Mary. *The Church and the Second Sex*. 2nd ed. New York: Harper & Row, 1975.

————. *Beyond God the Father*. Boston: Beacon Press, 1973.

Danielou, Jean. *The Theology of Jewish Christianity*. London: Darton, Longman & Todd, 1964.

Dante. *Purgatory*. Translated with an introduction by Dorothy L. Sayers. London: Penguin Books, 1955.

Dawson, Christopher. *Religion and the Rise of Western Culture*. New York: Doubleday, 1958.

Day, Dorothy. *The Long Loneliness*. New York: Curtis Books, 1952.

Devine, George. *American Catholicism: Where Do We Go From Here?* Englewood Cliffs, N.J.: Prentice-Hall, 1975.

Dick, Ignace. *What is the Christian Orient?* Westminster, Md.: Newman Press, 1967.

Dickens, A. G. *The Counter Reformation*. New York: Harcourt, Brace & World, 1969.

————. *Reformation and Society in Sixteenth-Century Europe*. New York: Harcourt, Brace & World, 1966.

Dillenberger, J, and Welch, C. *Protestant Christianity*. New York: Scribner, 1954.

Dix, Gregory. *The Shape of the Liturgy*. London: Dacre Press, 1945.

Dodd, Charles Harold. *Authority of the Bible*. Rev. ed. London: Collins, 1978.

Doerries, Hermann. *Constantine the Great*. New York: Harper & Row, 1972.

Dolan, Jay P. *Catholic Revivalism: The American Experience 1830–1900*. Notre Dame, Ind.: University of Notre Dame Press, 1978.

Donovan, Vincent J. *Christianity Rediscovered*. 2nd ed. Maryknoll, N.Y.: Orbis Books, 1982.

Duckett, Eleanor. *The Wandering Saints of the Early Middle Ages.* New York: W. W. Norton, 1964.

Dulles, Avery. *Models of the Church.* New York: Doubleday, 1974.

———. *Revelation Theology—A History.* New York: Herder & Herder, 1969.

Durnbaugh, Donald F. *The Believers' Church: The History and Character of Radical Protestantism.* New York: Macmillan, 1968.

Dvornik, Francis. *Byzantium and the Roman Primacy.* New York: Fordham University Press, 1966.

Eliade, Mircea. *Cosmos and History.* New York: Harper & Row, 1959.

Eller, Vernard. *The Most Revealing Book of the Bible: Making Sense out of Revelation.* Grand Rapids: Eerdmans, 1974.

Ellis, John Tracy. *American Catholicism.* Rev. ed. Chicago: University of Chicago Press, 1969.

———. *Documents of American Catholic History.* Milwaukee: Bruce Publishing, 1956.

Eusebius of Caesarea. *Vita Constantini.* Translated by A. C. McGiffert as *The Life of Constantine.* A Selected Library of Nicene and Post-Nicene Fathers of the Christian Church, Second Series, vol. 1. Grand Rapids: Eerdmans, 1952.

Everyday Life in Bible Times. Washington, D.C.: National Geographic Society, 1976.

Falwell, Jerry. *Listen, America!* New York: Doubleday, 1980.

Fawcett, Thomas. *Hebrew Myth and Christian Gospel.* London: SCM Press, 1973.

Ferm, Robert L., ed. *Issues in American Protestantism: A Documentary History From the Puritans to the Present.* New York: Doubleday, 1969.

Ferm, V., ed. *The American Church of the Protestant Heritage.* New York: Philosophical Library, 1953.

Finegan, Jack. *Let My People Go: A Journey through Exodus.* New York: Harper & Row, 1963.

Fiorenza, Elisabeth Schüssler. "Sexism and Conversion." *Network* 9 (1981): 15–22.

———. "'You are not to be called Father': Early Christian History in a Feminist Perspective." *Cross Currents* 29 (1979): 301–23.

———. *In Memory of Her: A Feminist Theological Reconstruction of Christian Origins.* New York: Crossroad/Continuum, 1983.

Fitzgerald, Francis. "A Disciplined, Charging Army." *The New Yorker* 57(18 May 1981): 53–141.

Fitzmyer, Joseph A. *Pauline Theology: A Brief Sketch.* Englewood Cliffs, N.J.: Prentice-Hall, 1967.

Flannery, Austin, ed. *Vatican Council II: The Conciliar and Post-Conciliar Documents.* New York: Costello Publishing, 1975.

Forell, George W., ed. *Christian Social Teachings: A Reader in Christian Social Ethics from the Bible to the Present.* Minneapolis: Augsburg, 1966.

Fousek, Mariana S. *The Church in a Changing World: Events and Trends from 250–600.* St. Louis: Concordia, 1971.

Fox, Matthew. *Breakthrough: Meister Eckhart's Creation Spirituality in a New Translation.* New York: Doubleday, 1980.

———, ed. *Western Spirituality: Historical Roots, Ecumenical Routes.* Santa Fe, N.M.: Bear & Company, 1981.

Franck, Frederick. *Pilgrimage to Now/Here.* Maryknoll, N.Y.: Orbis Books, 1974.

Freemantle, Anne, ed. *The Papal Encyclicals in their Historical Context*. New York: New American Library, 1963.

French, R. M. *The Way of the Pilgrim*. New York: Seabury Press, 1965.

Frend, W. H. C. *Martyrdom and Persecution in the Early Church: A Study of Conflict from the Maccabees to Donatus*. New York: Doubleday, 1967.

Freyne, Sean. *The Twelve: Disciples and Apostles: A Study in the Theology of the First Three Gospels*. London: Sheed & Ward, 1968.

Gager, John G. *Kingdom and Community*. Englewood Cliffs, N.J.: Prentice-Hall, 1975.

Gardner, Helen, ed. *The Metaphysical Poets*. Rev. ed. London: Penguin, 1972.

Gelin, Albert. *The Poor of Yahweh*. Collegeville, Minn.: Liturgical Press, 1964.

Gibellini, Rosino, ed. *Frontiers of Theology in Latin America*. Maryknoll, N.Y.: Orbis Books, 1979.

Gleason, Philip, ed. *Catholicism in America*. New York: Harper & Row, 1970.

Gottschalk, Stephen. *The Emergence of Christian Science in American Life*. Berkeley: University of California Press, 1974.

Grant, Robert M. *Augustus to Constantine: The Thrust of the Christian Movement into the Roman World*. New York: Harper & Row, 1970.

_____. *Gnosticism and Early Christianity*. New York: Harper & Row, 1966.

_____. *A Historical Introduction to the New Testament*. New York: Harper & Row, 1963.

Greeley, Andrew M. *The Catholic Experience*. New York: Doubleday, 1969.

Grollenberg, Lucas. *A Bible for Our Time*. London: SCM Press, 1979.

Gutierrez, Gustavo. *A Theology of Liberation*. Maryknoll, N.Y.: Orbis Books, 1973.

Hammell, Patrick J. *Handbook of Patrology*. New York: Alba House, 1968.

Harrell, David. *All Things Are Possible: The Healing and Charismatic Revivals in Modern America*. Bloomington: Indiana University Press, 1975.

Harrelson, Walter. *Interpreting the Old Testament*. New York: Holt, Rinehart & Winston, 1964.

Harrison, Barbara Grizzuti. *Visions of Glory: A History and a Memory of Jehovah's Witnesses*. New York: Simon & Schuster, 1978.

Hatchett, Marion J. *Sanctifying Life, Time and Space: An Introduction to Liturgical Study*. New York: Seabury Press, 1982.

Heath, R. G. "The Western Schism of the Franks and the *Filioque*." *Journal of Ecclesiastical History* 23 (1972): 97–115.

Hedgepeth, William. *The Alternative: Communal Life in the New America*. New York: Macmillan, 1970.

Heer, Friedrich. *The Medieval World 1100–1350*. New York: New American Library, 1961.

Hennecke, Edgar, and Schneemelcher, Wilhelm, eds. *New Testament Apocrypha*. 2 vols. Philadelphia: Westminster Press, 1963.

Higham, John. *Strangers in the Land—Patterns of American Nativism 1860–1925*. 2nd ed. New York: Atheneum, 1977.

Hill, Bennett D., ed. *Church and State in the Middle Ages*. New York: John Wiley & Sons, 1970.

Hillenbrand, Hans J., ed. *The Reformation: A Narrative History Related by Contemporary Observers and Participants*. Grand Rapids: Baker Book House, 1964.

Hoekema, Anthony A. *The Four Major Cults: Christian Science, Jehovah's Witnesses, Mormonism and Seventh-Day Adventists*. Grand Rapids: Eerdmans, 1965.

Hofstadter, Richard. *Social Darwinism in American Thought*. Rev. ed. Boston: Beacon Press, 1967.

Hollenweger, W. J. *The Pentecostals*. Minneapolis: Augsburg, 1972.

Holloway, Mark. *Heavens on Earth: Utopian communities in America 1680–1880*. Rev. ed. New York: Dover, 1966.

Hope, Marjorie, and Young, James, eds. *The Struggle for Humanity: Agents of Nonviolent Change in a Violent World*. Maryknoll, N.Y.: Orbis Books, 1977.

Hopkins, Charles H. *The Rise of the Social Gospel in American Protestantism 1865–1915*. New Haven: Yale University Press, 1967.

Hordern, William. *A Layman's Guide to Protestant Theology*. Rev. ed. New York: Macmillan, 1968.

Hostetler, John A. *Amish Society*. Rev. ed. Baltimore: Johns Hopkins University Press, 1963.

Hubbard, Geoffrey. *Quaker by Convincement*. London: Penguin Books, 1974.

Hudson, Winthrop S. *Religion in America: An Historical Account of the Development of American Religious Life*. 3rd ed. New York: Scribners, 1981.

Hughes, Philip. *A Popular History of the Reformation*. New York: Doubleday, 1957.

Hunt, Noreen. *Cluny under Saint Hugh 1049–1109*. Notre Dame, Ind.: University of Notre Dame Press, 1967.

James, William. *The Varieties of Religious Experience*. New York: New American Library, 1958.

Jeremias, Joachim. *Jerusalem in the Time of Jesus*. Philadephia: Fortress Press, 1969.

Jeschke, Marlin. *Discipling the Brother: Congregational Discipline According to the Gospel*. Scottdale, Pa.: Herald Press, 1972.

Joint Liturgical Group, Ronald Claud Dudley Jasper, ed. *The Daily Office Revised: With Other Prayers and Services*. London: SPCK, 1978.

Jonas, Hans. *The Gnostic Religion: The Message of the Alien God and the Beginnings of Christianity*. Boston: Beacon Press, 1963.

Jones, A. H. M. *Constantine and the Conversion of Europe*. London: Penguin, 1962.

Jones, W. Paul. *The Province Beyond the River: The Diary of a Protestant at a Trappist Monastery*. New York: Paulist Press, 1981.

Jules-Rosette, Bennetta. *African Apostles: Ritual and Conversion in the Church of Maranke*. Ithaca: Cornell University Press, 1975.

Kastner, Patricia Wilson, et al. *A Lost Tradition: Women Writers of the Early Church*. Washington, D.C.: University Press of America, 1981.

Kee, Howard C. *Jesus in History: An Approach to the Study of the Gospels*. 2nd ed. New York: Harcourt Brace Jovanovich, 1977.

Kee, Howard C.; Young, Franklin W.; and Froehlich, Karlfried. *Understanding the New Testament*. 3rd ed. Englewood Cliffs, N.J.: Prentice-Hall, 1973.

Kelly, J. N. D. *Early Christian Creeds*. London: Longmans, Green & Co., 1960.

Knowles, David. *The English Mystical Tradition*. London: Burns & Oates, 1964.

————. *The Evolution of Medieval Thought*. London: Longman Group Ltd., 1962.

Küng, Hans. *The Council, Reform and Reunion*. London: Sheed & Ward, 1961.

————. *The Church*. London: Sheed & Ward, 1967.

————. *On Being a Christian*. New York: Doubleday, 1976.

Lernoux, Penny. *Cry of the People*. New York: Doubleday, 1980.

Lesy, Michael. *Wisconsin Death Trip*. New York: Random House, 1973.

Lewis, C. S. *The Magician's Nephew*. New York: Macmillan, 1955.

Lincoln, C. Eric, and Frazier, E. Franklin. *The Black Church Since Frazier* and *The Negro Church in America*. New York: Schocken Books, 1963.

Loetscher, L. A. *A Brief History of the Presbyterians*. 3rd ed. Philadelphia: Westminster Press, 1978.

Lohfink, Gerhard. *The Bible, Now I Get It: A Form-Criticism Handbook*. New York: Doubleday, 1979.

Lohse, E., ed. *The New Testament Environment*. Nashville: Abingdon, 1976.

McAvoy, Thomas T. *A History of the Catholic Church in the United States*. Notre Dame, Ind.: University of Notre Dame Press, 1969.

McBrien, Richard P. *Catholicism*. 2 vols. Minneapolis: Winston Press, 1980.

MacEoin, Gary. *What Happened at Rome?: The Council and Its Implications for the Modern World*. New York: Doubleday, 1967.

McGiffert, Arthur Cushman. *A History of Christian Thought*. New York: Scribners, 1961.

McGinnis, James B. *Bread and Justice*. New York: Paulist Press, 1979.

McKenzie, John L. *Authority in the Church*. New York: Sheed & Ward, 1966.

McKinley, Edward H. *Marching to Glory: The History of the Salvation Army in the United States of America 1880–1980*. San Francisco: Harper & Row, 1980.

Maguire, Daniel C. *The New Subversives: Anti-Americanism of the Religious Right*. New York: Crossroad/Continuum, 1982.

Malherbe, Abraham J. *Social Aspects of Early Christianity*. Baton Rouge: Lousiana State University Press, 1977.

Manschreck, Clyde L. *A History of Christianity in the World*. Englewood Cliffs, N.J.: Prentice-Hall, 1974.

Markus, R. A. *Christianity in the Roman Empire*. London: Thames & Hudson, 1974.

Marty, Martin E. *Righteous Empire: The Protestant Experience in America*. New York: Dial Press, 1970.

Mead, Sidney. *The Lively Experiment: The Shaping of Christianity in America*. New York: Harper & Row, 1963.

Meeks, Wayne A., and Wilken, Robert. *Jews and Christians in Antioch in the First Four Centuries of the Common Era*. Missoula, Mont.: Scholar's Press, 1978.

Merton, Thomas. *The Seven Storey Mountain*. New York: New American Library, 1943.

Meyendorf, John. *Christ in Eastern Christian Thought*. Crestwood, N.Y.: St. Vladimir's Seminary Press, 1975.

————. *The Orthodox Church: Its Past and Its Role in the World Today*. 3rd rev. ed. Crestwood, N.Y.: St. Vladimir's Seminary Press, 1981.

Miller, John H., ed. *Vatican II: An Interfaith Appraisal*. Notre Dame, Ind.: University of Notre Dame Press, 1966.

Miller, William. *A Harsh and Dreadful Love*. New York: Doubleday, 1974.

————. *Dorothy Day: A Biography*. New York: Harper & Row, 1982.

Mirgeler, Albert. *Mutations of Western Christianity*. Notre Dame, Ind.: University of Notre Dame Press, 1968.

Montgomery, John. *Abodes of Love*. London: Putnam, 1962.

Moore, William T. *A Comprehensive History of the Disciples of Christ*. New York: F. H. Revell, 1909.

Morgan, Edmund S. *The Puritan Dilemma: The Story of John Winthrop*. New York: Little, Brown, 1958.

Murphy, Francis X. *Politics and the Early Christian*. New York: Desclée, 1967.

Ndiokwere, Nathaniel I. *Prophecy and Revolution: The Role of Prophets in the Independent African Churches and in Biblical Tradition*. London: SPCK, 1981.

Neill, Stephen. *A History of Christian Missions*. London: Penguin, 1964.

Nelson, E. C. *The Lutherans in North America*. Philadelphia: Fortress Press, 1975.

Niebuhr, H. Richard. *Christ and Culture*. New York: Harper & Row, 1951.

Niesel, Wilhelm. *The Gospel and the Churches*. Philadelphia: Westminster, 1962.

Nock, A. D. *Conversion: The Old and the New in Religion from Alexander the Great to Augustine of Hippo*. Reprint. Oxford: Oxford University Press, 1969.

Norwood, Fredrick A. *The Story of American Methodism*. Nashville: Abingdon Press, 1974.

O'Brien, David J. *The Renewal of American Catholicism*. Oxford: Oxford University Press, 1972.

O'Brien, William V. *The Conduct of a Just and Limited War*. New York: Praeger, 1981.

O'Dea, Thomas F. *The Mormons*. Chicago: University of Chicago Press, 1957.

Outler, Albert. *Methodist Observer at Vatican II*. Westminster, Md.: Newman Press, 1967.

Pagels, Elaine. *The Gnostic Gospels*. New York: Random House, 1979.

Payne, Daniel A. *The Semi-Centenary and the Retrospection of the A.M.E. Church*. New York: Books for Libraries Press, 1972.

Peel, Robert. *Christian Science*. New York: Holt, Rinehart and Winston, 1959.

Pelikan, Jaroslav. *The Emergence of the Catholic Tradition 100–600*. Chicago: University of Chicago Press, 1971.

———. *The Spirit of Eastern Christendom 600–1700*. Chicago: University of Chicago Press, 1974.

Perrin, Norman, and Duling, Dennis. *The New Testament, An Introduction: Proclamation and Parenesis, Myth and History*, 2nd ed. New York: Harcourt Brace Jovanovich, 1982.

Pike, Edgar R. *Jehovah's Witnesses*. New York: Philosophical Library, 1954.

Plowman, Edward E. "Is Morality All Right?" *Christianity Today* 23 (2 November 1979): 76–85.

Pobee, John S. *Toward an African Theology*. Nashville: Abingdon Press, 1979.

Porter, H. Boone. *Keeping the Church Year*. New York: Seabury Press, 1977.

Prestige, G. L. *Fathers and Heretics: Six Studies in Dogmatic Faith with Prologue and Epilogue*. London: SPCK., 1940.

Rauschenbusch, Walter. *A Theology for the Social Gospel*. Nashville: Abingdon Press, 1945.

Reynolds, Stephen. *The Christian Religious Tradition*. Encino, Calif.: Dickenson, 1977.

Rhoads, David M. *Israel in Revolution, 6–74 C.E.: A Political History Based on the Writings of Josephus*. Philadelphia: Fortress Press, 1976.

Ridderbos, Herman. *Paul: An Outline of His Theology*. London: SPCK, 1977.

Ruether, Rosemary Radford. "Male Chauvinist Theology and the Anger of Women." *Cross Currents* 21 (1971): 173–85.

_____. *New Woman New Earth: Sexist Ideologies and Human Liberation*. New York: Seabury, 1975.

Ruether, Rosemary, and Keller, Rosemary Skinner, eds. *Women and Religion in America*. New York: Harper & Row, 1981.

Russell, Jeffrey Burton. *Witchcraft in the Middle Ages*. Ithaca: Cornell University Press, 1972.

Russell, Letty M. *Human Liberation in a Feminist Perspective*. Philadelphia: Westminster Press, 1974.

Salinger, J. D. *Franny and Zooey*. New York: Little, Brown, 1961.

Sandmel, Samuel. *The Hebrew Scriptures*. New York: Alfred A. Knopf, 1963.

Sayers, Dorothy L. *The Emperor Constantine*. Grand Rapids: Eerdmans, 1976.

Schmemann, Alexander. *The Historical Road of Eastern Orthodoxy*. New York: Holt, Rinehart and Winston, 1963.

Scholem, Gershom. "Revelation and Tradition as Religious Categories in Judaism," in *The Messianic Idea in Judaism and Other Essays in Jewish Spirituality*. New York: Schocken Books, 1971, pp. 282–303.

Seeberg, Rinhold. *Textbook of the History of Doctrines*. Grand Rapids: Baker Book House, 1966.

Shipps, Jan. "Mormons: Looking Forward and Outward." *Christian Century* 95 (16–23 August, 1978), 761–6.

Sider, Ronald J. *Rich Christians in an Age of Hunger*. Downers Grove, Ill.: Inter Varsity Press, 1977.

Simon, Arthur. *Bread for the World*. New York: Paulist Press, 1975.

Simon, Marcel. *Jewish Sects at the Time of Jesus*. Philadelphia: Fortress Press, 1967.

Sobrino, Jon. *Christology at the Crossroads*. Maryknoll, N.Y.: Orbis Books, 1978.

Sojourners 6 (January, 1977) 14–31.

Southern, R. W. *The Making of the Middle Ages*. London: Hutchinson, 1967.

_____. *Western Society and the Church in the Middle Ages*. London: Penguin, 1970.

Stanton, Elizabeth Cady. *The Women's Bible*. Reprint. Seattle: Coalition Task Force on Women and Religion, 1974.

Stevenson, J., ed. *Creeds, Councils and Controversies*. London: SPCK., 1966.

_____. *A New Eusebius*. London: SPCK., 1968.

Storey, William G. *Morning Praise and Evensong*. Notre Dame, Ind.: Fides, 1973.

Sweet, William W. *The Baptists: A Collection of Source Materials*. New York: Holt, 1931; reissued New York: Cooper Square Press, 1964.

_____. *The Congregationalists: A Collection of Source Materials*. Chicago: University of Chicago Press, 1939; reissued New York: Cooper Square Press, 1964.

_____. *The Methodists: A Collection of Source Materials*. Chicago: University of Chicago Press, 1946; reissued New York: Cooper Square Press, 1964.

_____. *The Presbyterians: A Collection of Source Materials*. New York: Harper Brothers, 1936; reissued New York: Cooper Square Press, 1964.

Synan, Vinson. *The Holiness-Pentecostal Movement in the United States*. Grand Rapids: Eerdmans, 1972.

Tacitus, Cornelius. *The Annals of Tacitus, Books One To Six,* edited with a commentary by R.R.D. Goodyear. Cambridge: Cambridge University Press, 1972.

Tavard, George. *Woman in Christian Tradition*. Notre Dame, Ind.: University of Notre Dame Press, 1973.

Taylor, Richard K. *Blockade: A Guide to Nonviolent Intervention*. Maryknoll, N.Y.: Orbis Books, 1977.

Theissen, Gerd. *The Sociology of Early Palestinian Christianity*. Philadelphia: Fortress Press, 1979.

Thielicke, Helmut. *I Believe: The Christian Creed*. Philadelphia: Fortress Press, 1965.

Tierney, Brian. *The Crisis of Church and State 1050–1300*. Englewood Cliffs, N.J.: Prentice-Hall, 1964.

_____. *Foundations of the Conciliar Theory*. Cambridge: Cambridge University Press, 1955.

Time cover story on American Catholic bishops and nuclear war. 120 (29 November 1982): 68–78.

Topel, L. John. *The Way to Peace: Liberation through the Bible*. Maryknoll, N.Y.: Orbis Books, 1979.

Torres, Sergio, and Eagleson, John, eds. *The Challenge of Basic Christian Communities*. Maryknoll, N.Y.: Orbis Books, 1981.

Treece, Henry. *The Crusades*. New York: New American Library, 1962.

Trible, Phyllis. *God and the Rhetoric of Sexuality*. Philadelphia: Fortress Press, 1978.

Troeltsch, Ernst. *The Social Teachings of the Christian Church*. London: Allen and Unwin, 1931.

Trueblood, David E. *The People Called Quakers*. New York: Harper & Row, 1966.

Tyler, Alice Felt. *Freedom's Ferment: Phases of American Social History from the Colonial Period to the Outbreak of the Civil War*. New York: Harper & Row, 1944.

Waddell, Helen. *The Desert Fathers*. Ann Arbor: University of Michigan Press, 1966.

Weinstein, Donald, ed. *The Renaissance and the Reformation 1300–1600*. New York: The Free Press, 1965.

West, James King. *Introduction to the Old Testament*. New York: Macmillan, 1971.

Whalen, William J. *Minority Religions in America*. New York: Alba House, 1971.

Wilken, Robert L. *The Myth of Christian Beginnings: History's Impact on Belief*. New York: Doubleday, 1971.

Williams, Peter W. *Popular Religion in America*. Englewood Cliffs, N.J.: Prentice-Hall, 1980.

Wilmore, Gayraud S., and Cone, James H. *Black Theology: A Documentary History 1966–1979*. Maryknoll, N.Y.: Orbis Books, 1979.

Wilson, Bryan R. *Patterns of Sectarianism*. London: Heinemann Educational Books, Ltd., 1967.

Yoder, John Howard. *The Politics of Jesus*. Grand Rapids: Eerdmans, 1972.

Index